黒鷺死体宅配便
the KUROSAGI corpse delivery service

12

story
EIJI OTSUKA

art
HOUSUI YAMAZAKI

original cover design
BUNPEI YORIFUJI

translation
TOSHIFUMI YOSHIDA

editor and english adaptation
CARL GUSTAV HORN

lettering and touchup
IHL

DARK
HORSE
MANGA

W9-CPD-877

contents

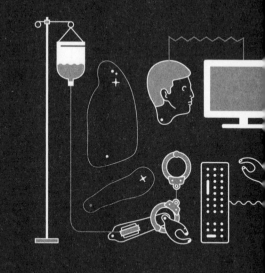

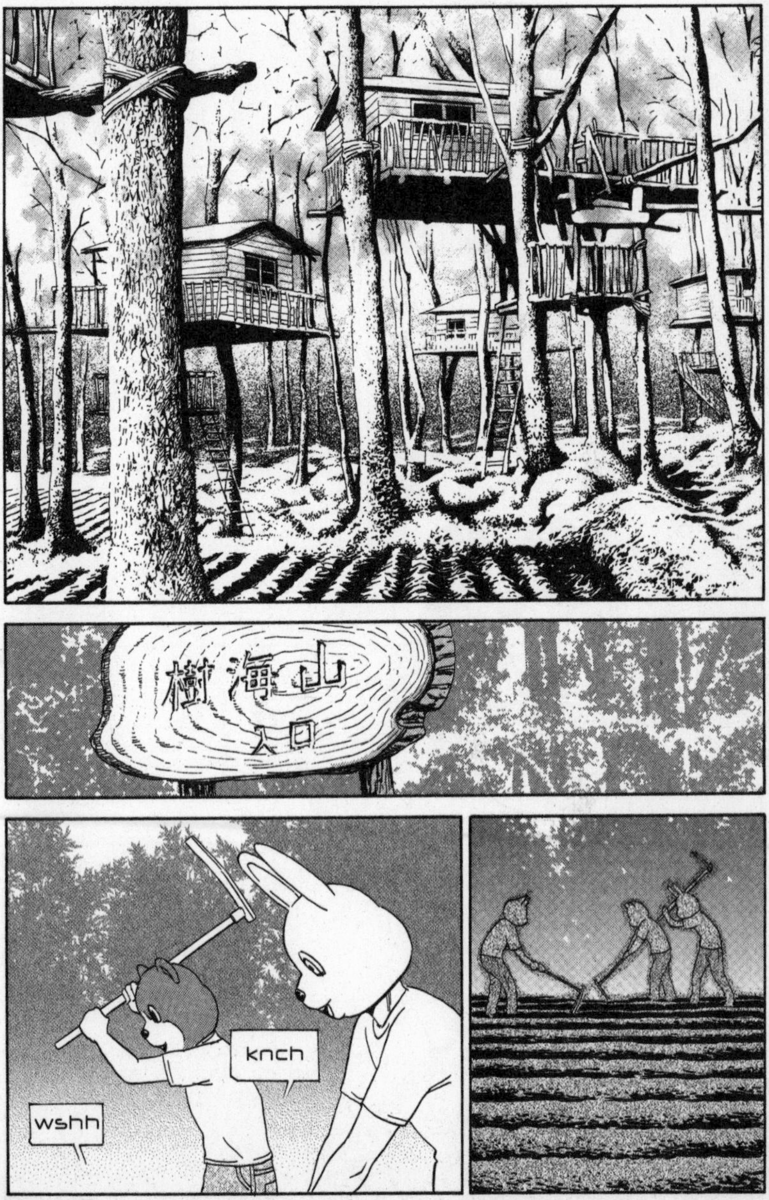
樹海山
入口
knch
wshh

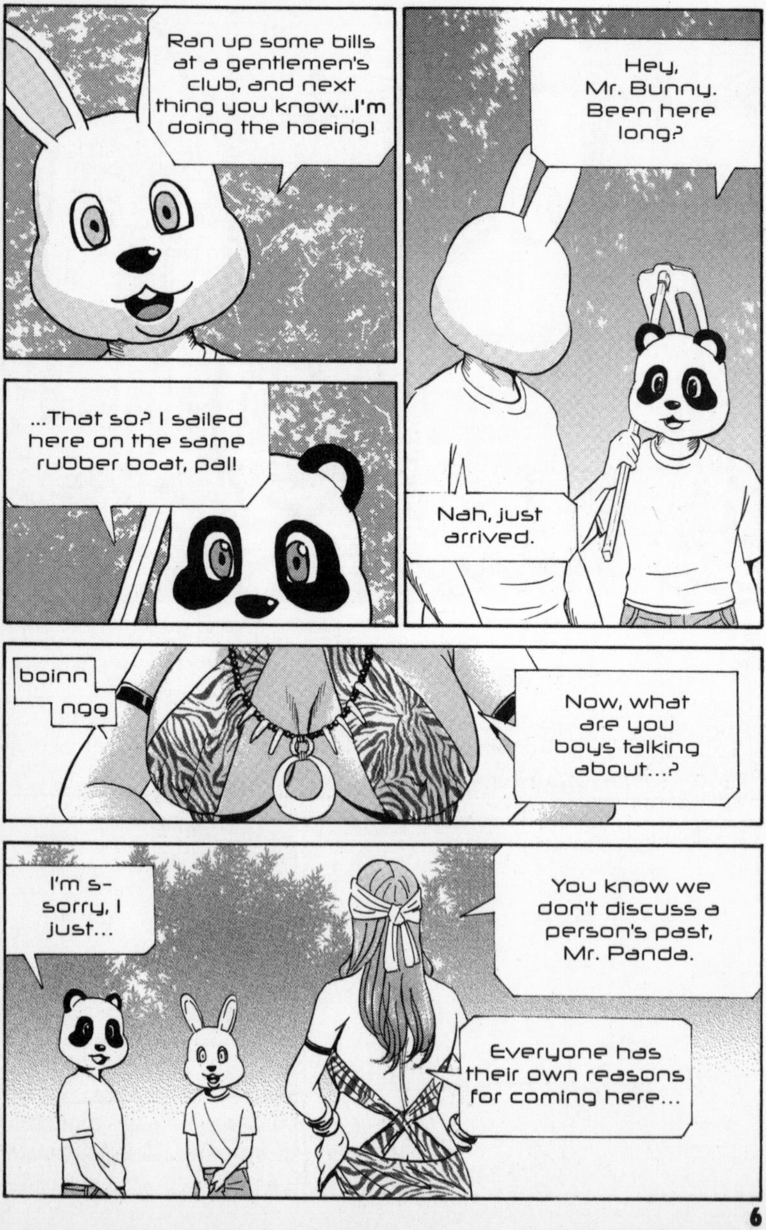
Hey, Mr. Bunny. Been here long?
Nah, just arrived.
Ran up some bills at a gentlemen's club, and next thing you know...I'm doing the hoeing!
...That so? I sailed here on the same rubber boat, pal!
Now, what are you boys talking about...?
boinn ngg
You know we don't discuss a person's past, Mr. Panda.
I'm s-sorry, I just...
Everyone has their own reasons for coming here...

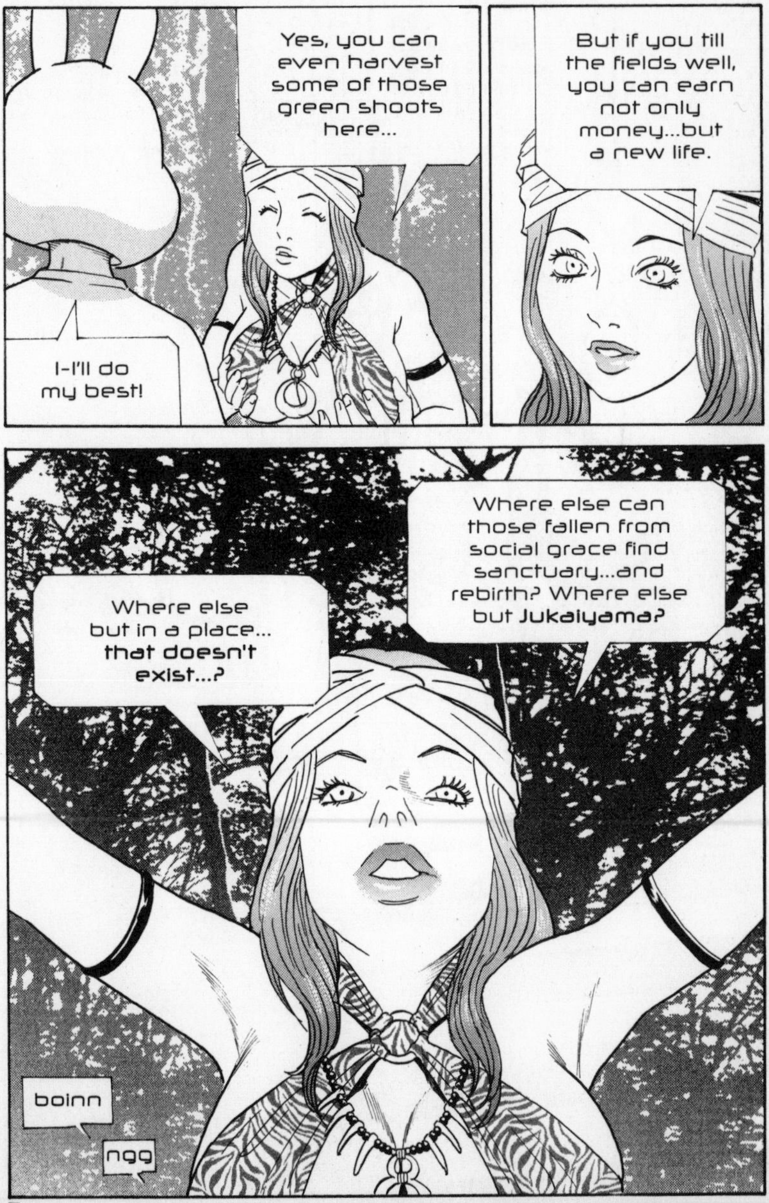
But if you till the fields well, you can earn not only money...but a new life.
Yes, you can even harvest some of those green shoots here...
I-I'll do my best!
Where else can those fallen from social grace find sanctuary...and rebirth? Where else but Jukaiyama?
Where else but in a place... that doesn't exist...?
boinn
ngg

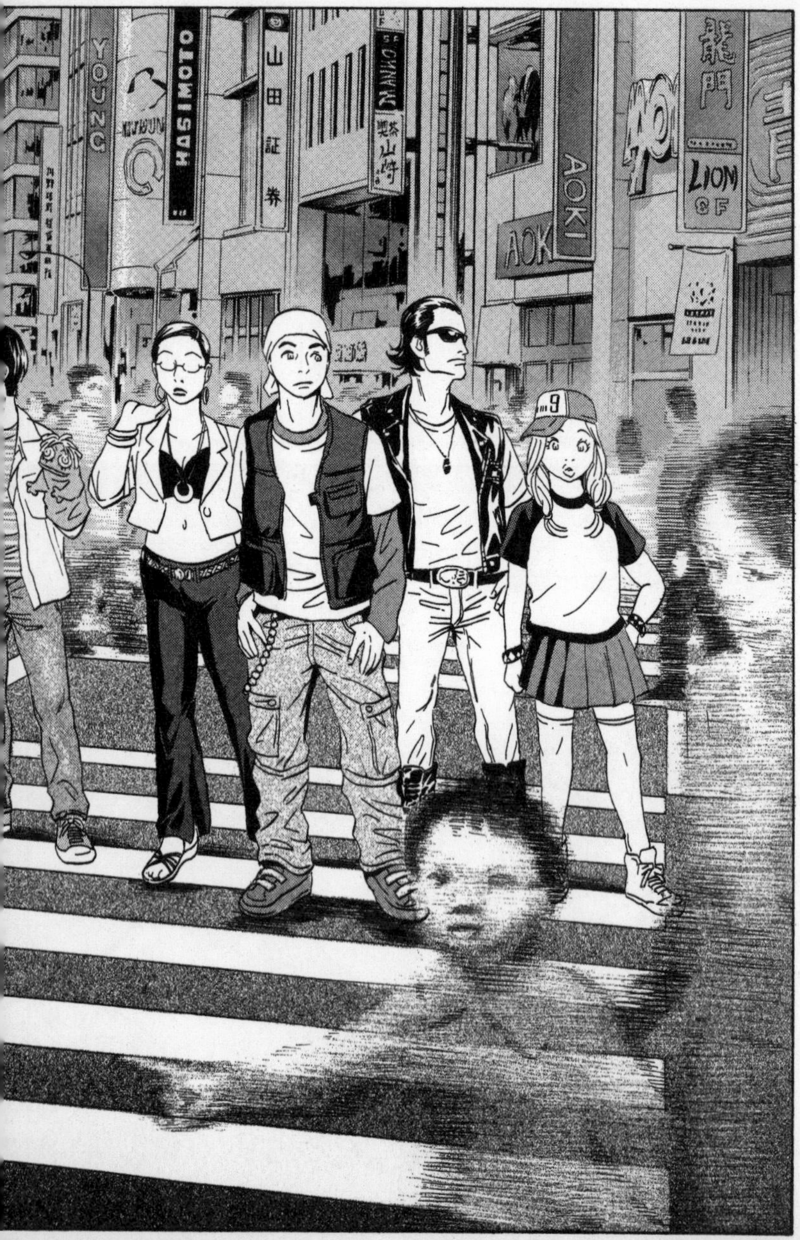
YOUNG
HASIMOTO
山田証券
喫茶山崎
AOKI
AOKI
龍門
LION

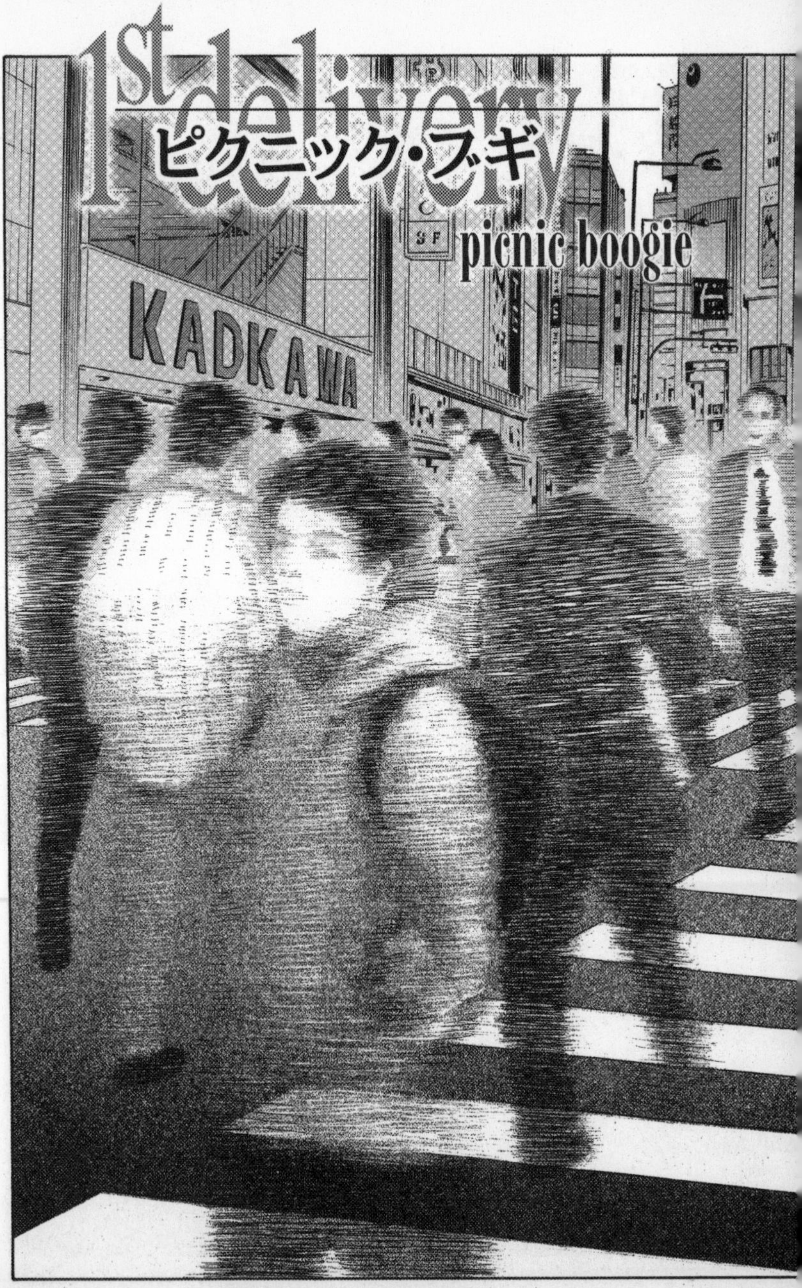
1st delivery
ピクニック・ブギ
picnic boogie
KADKAWA

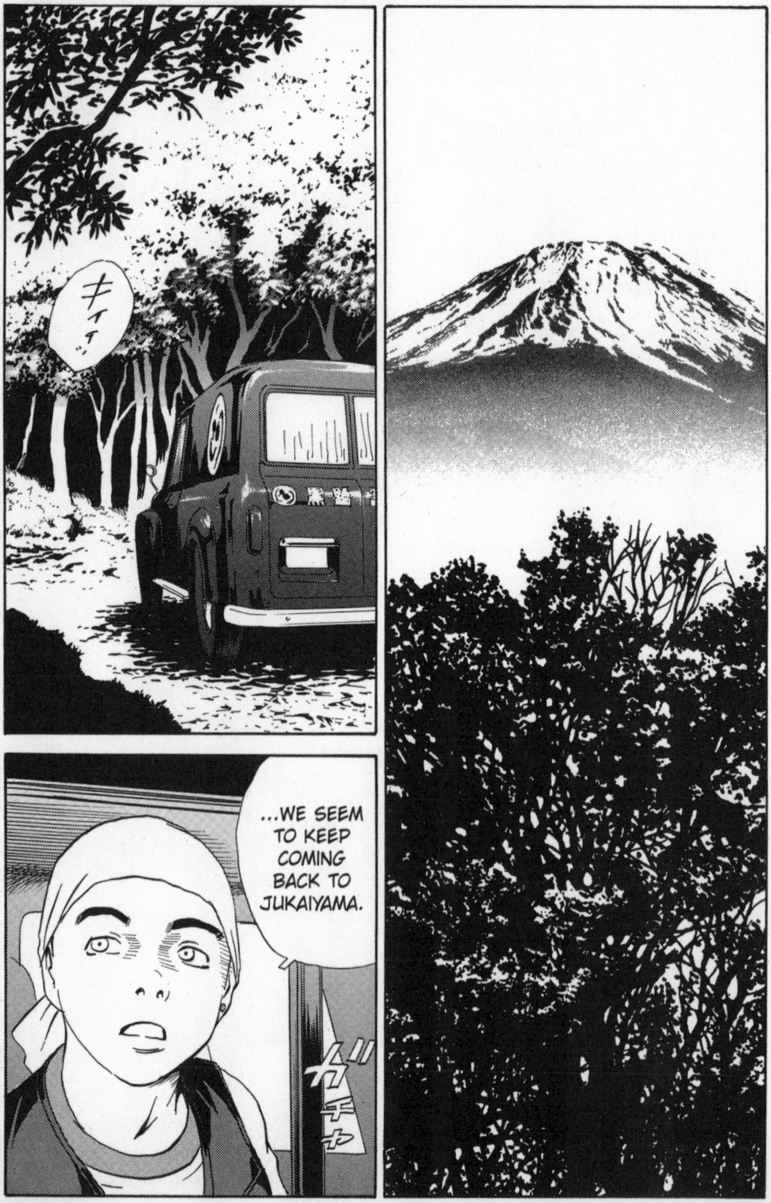
キイィッ
...WE SEEM TO KEEP COMING BACK TO JUKAIYAMA.
ガチャ

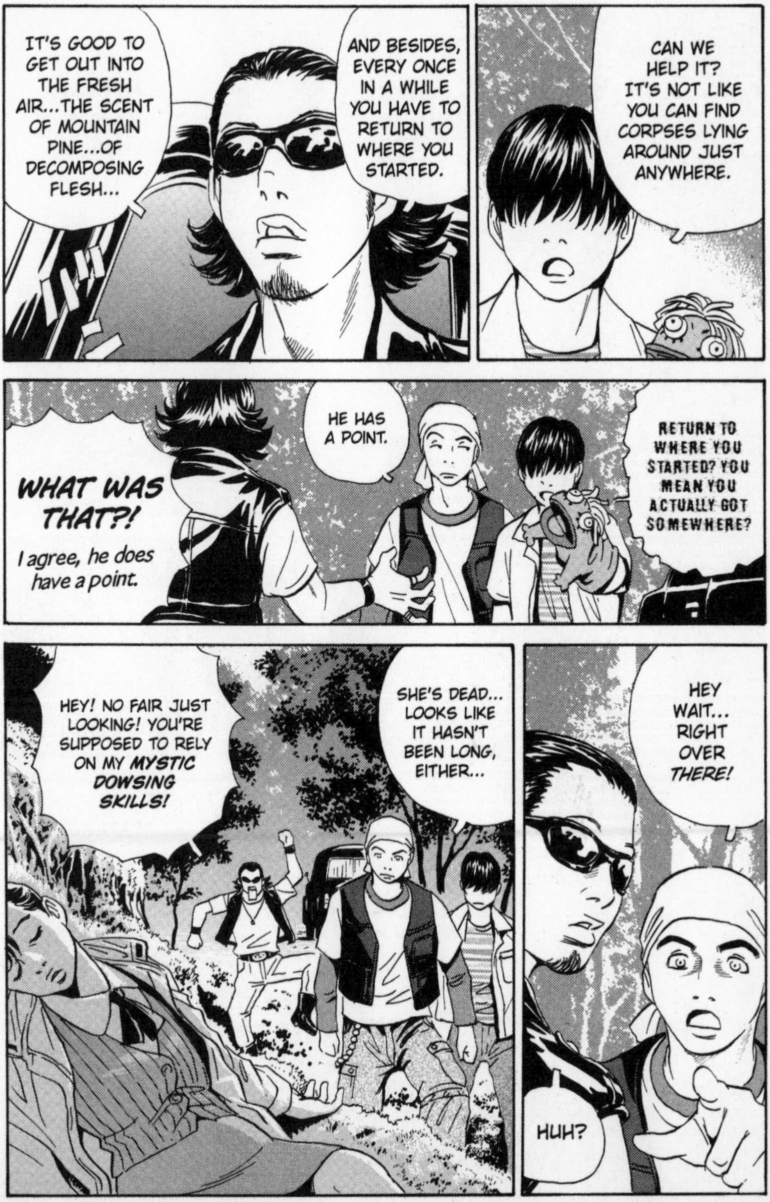
CAN WE HELP IT? IT'S NOT LIKE YOU CAN FIND CORPSES LYING AROUND JUST ANYWHERE.
IT'S GOOD TO GET OUT INTO THE FRESH AIR...THE SCENT OF MOUNTAIN PINE...OF DECOMPOSING FLESH...
AND BESIDES, EVERY ONCE IN A WHILE YOU HAVE TO RETURN TO WHERE YOU STARTED.
RETURN TO WHERE YOU STARTED? YOU MEAN YOU ACTUALLY GOT SOMEWHERE?
HE HAS A POINT.
WHAT WAS THAT?!
I agree, he does have a point.
HEY WAIT... RIGHT OVER THERE!
HUH?
SHE'S DEAD... LOOKS LIKE IT HASN'T BEEN LONG, EITHER...
HEY! NO FAIR JUST LOOKING! YOU'RE SUPPOSED TO RELY ON MY MYSTIC DOWSING SKILLS!

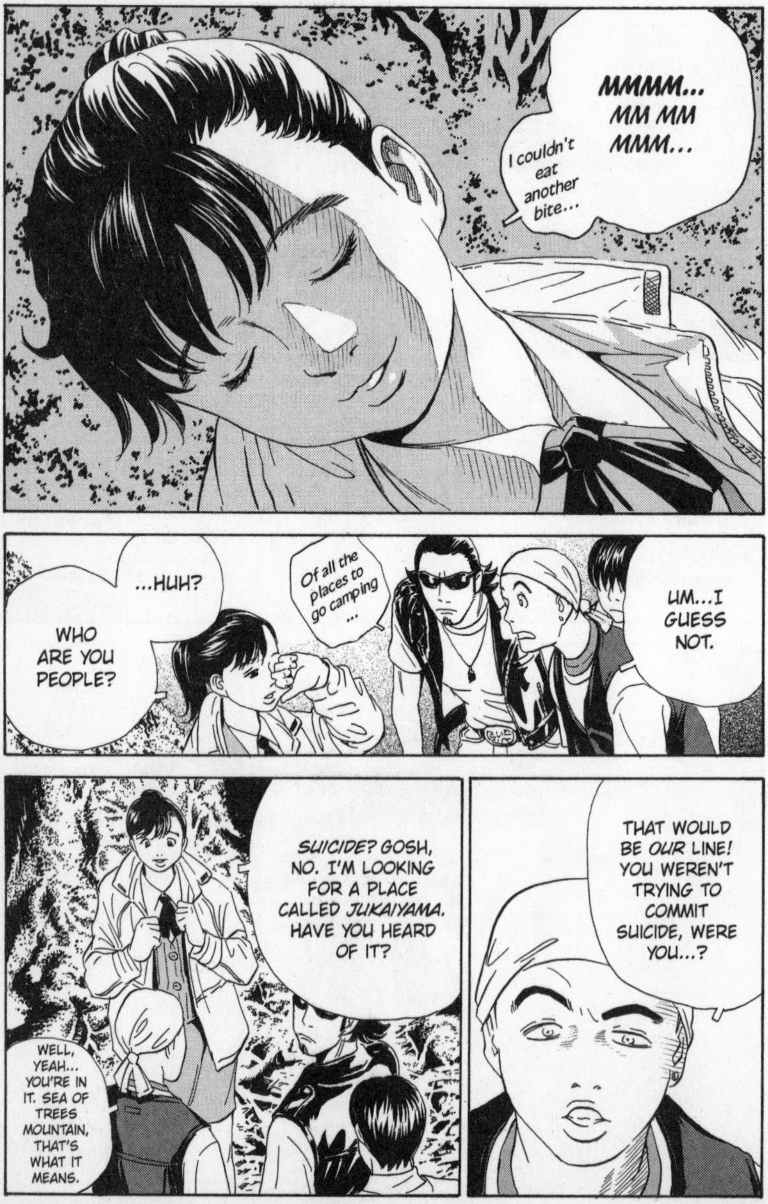
MMMM... MM MM MMM...
I couldn't eat another bite...
UM...I GUESS NOT.
Of all the places to go camping ...
...HUH?
WHO ARE YOU PEOPLE?
THAT WOULD BE *OUR* LINE! YOU WEREN'T TRYING TO COMMIT SUICIDE, WERE YOU...?
SUICIDE? GOSH, NO. I'M LOOKING FOR A PLACE CALLED *JUKAIYAMA.* HAVE YOU HEARD OF IT?
WELL, YEAH... YOU'RE IN IT. SEA OF TREES MOUNTAIN, THAT'S WHAT IT MEANS.

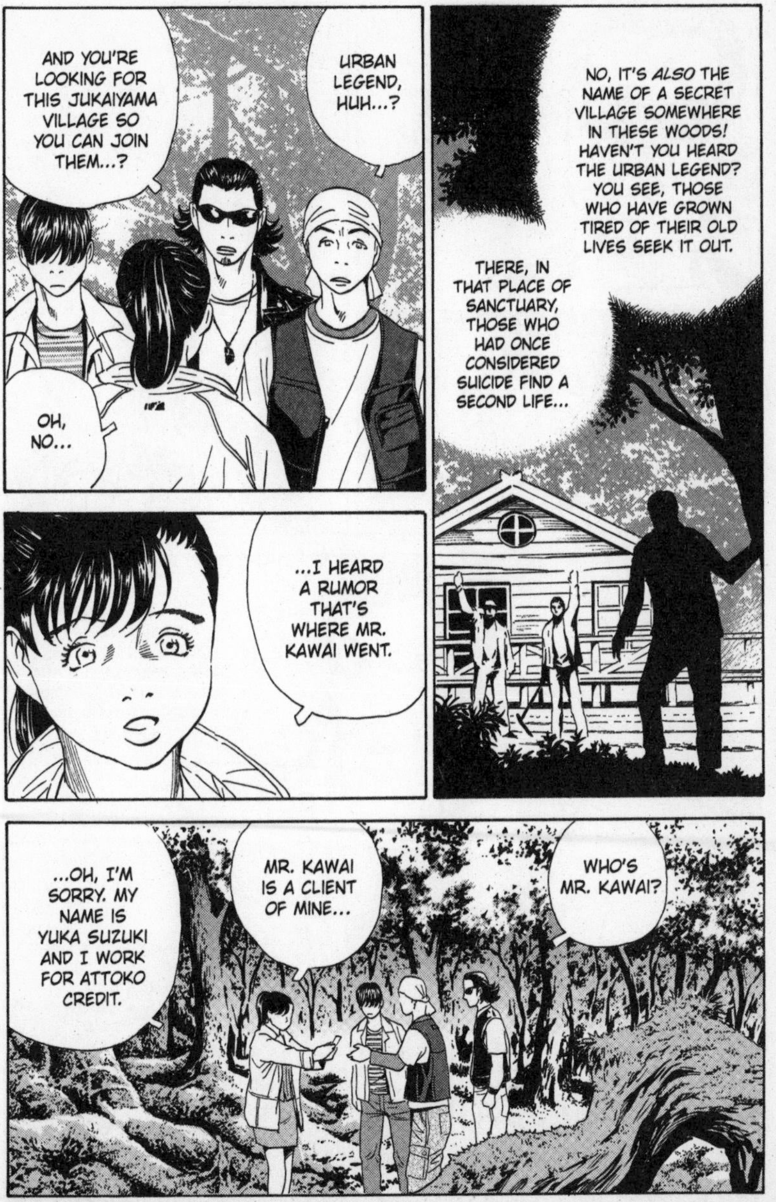
NO, IT'S *ALSO* THE NAME OF A SECRET VILLAGE SOMEWHERE IN THESE WOODS! HAVEN'T YOU HEARD THE URBAN LEGEND? YOU SEE, THOSE WHO HAVE GROWN TIRED OF THEIR OLD LIVES SEEK IT OUT.
THERE, IN THAT PLACE OF SANCTUARY, THOSE WHO HAD ONCE CONSIDERED SUICIDE FIND A SECOND LIFE...
URBAN LEGEND, HUH...?
AND YOU'RE LOOKING FOR THIS JUKAIYAMA VILLAGE SO YOU CAN JOIN THEM...?
OH, NO...
...I HEARD A RUMOR THAT'S WHERE MR. KAWAI WENT.
WHO'S MR. KAWAI?
MR. KAWAI IS A CLIENT OF MINE...
...OH, I'M SORRY. MY NAME IS YUKA SUZUKI AND I WORK FOR ATTOKO CREDIT.

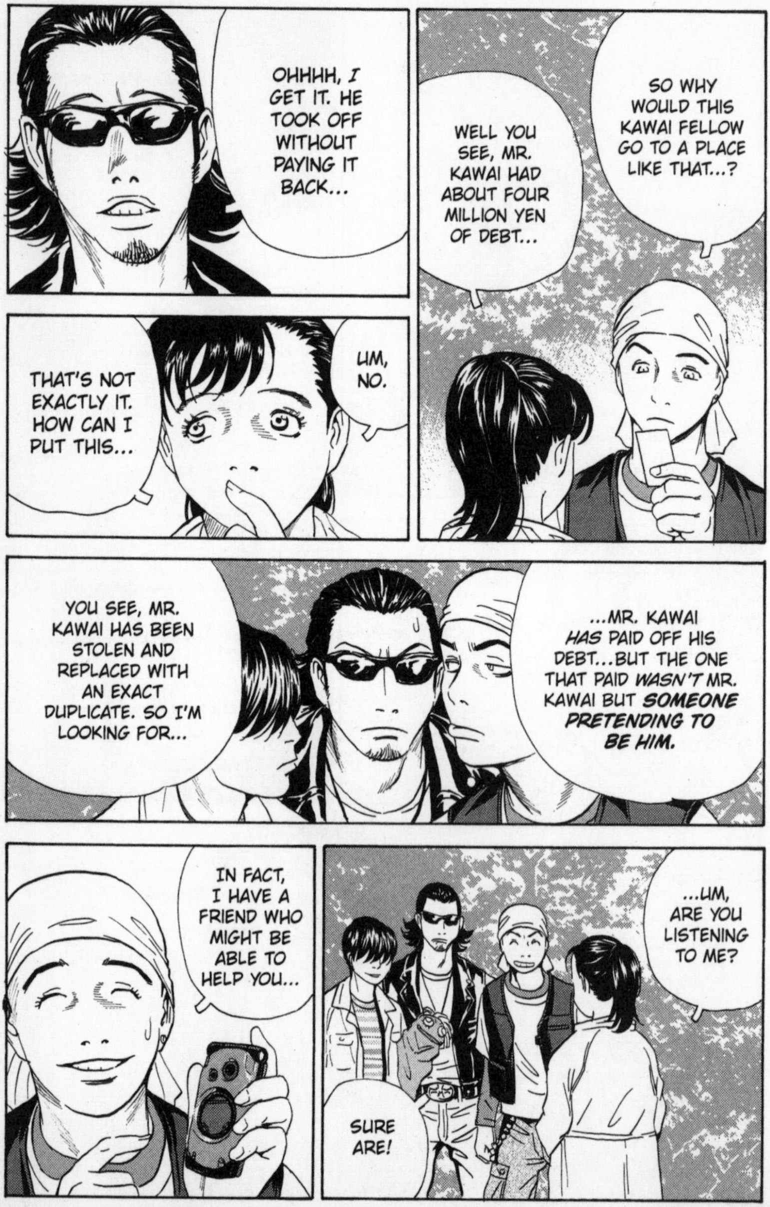
SO WHY WOULD THIS KAWAI FELLOW GO TO A PLACE LIKE THAT...?
WELL YOU SEE, MR. KAWAI HAD ABOUT FOUR MILLION YEN OF DEBT...
OHHHH, *I* GET IT. HE TOOK OFF WITHOUT PAYING IT BACK...
UM, NO.
THAT'S NOT EXACTLY IT. HOW CAN I PUT THIS...
...MR. KAWAI *HAS* PAID OFF HIS DEBT...BUT THE ONE THAT PAID *WASN'T* MR. KAWAI BUT ***SOMEONE PRETENDING TO BE HIM.***
YOU SEE, MR. KAWAI HAS BEEN STOLEN AND REPLACED WITH AN EXACT DUPLICATE. SO I'M LOOKING FOR...
...UM, ARE YOU LISTENING TO ME?
SURE ARE!
IN FACT, I HAVE A FRIEND WHO MIGHT BE ABLE TO HELP YOU...

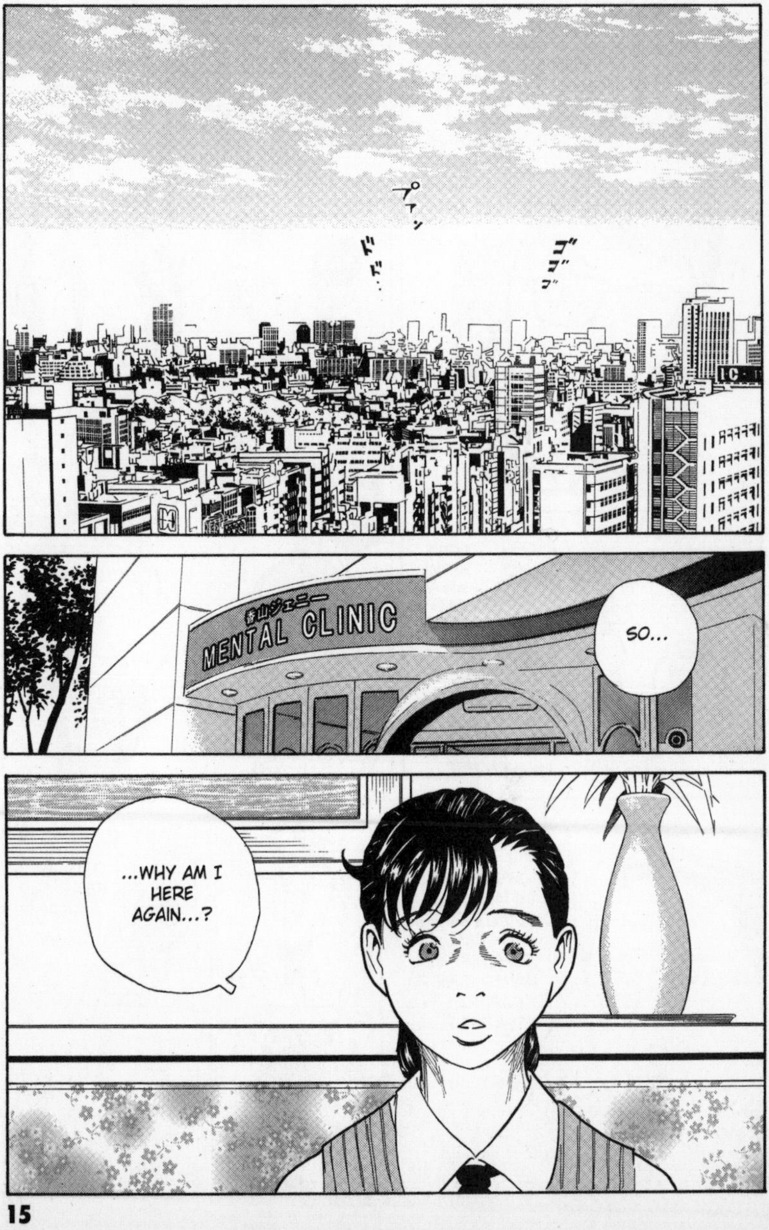
MENTAL CLINIC
SO...
...WHY AM I HERE AGAIN...?

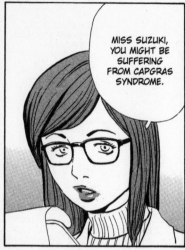

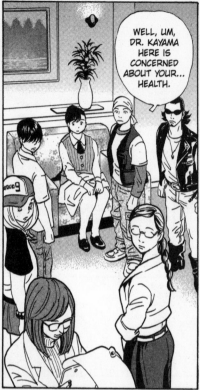

WELL, UM, DR. KAYAMA HERE IS CONCERNED ABOUT YOUR... HEALTH.
MISS SUZUKI, YOU MIGHT BE SUFFERING FROM CAPGRAS SYNDROME.
OKAY, I DON'T KNOW WHAT THAT IS EITHER.
CAPGRAS SYNDROME?
SASAKI-CHAN, BE A DEAR AND EXPLAIN?
UM...
IT'S A DELUSIONAL STATE FIRST IDENTIFIED BY A FRENCH PSYCHIATRIST NAMED JOSEPH CAPGRAS IN THE 1920s...

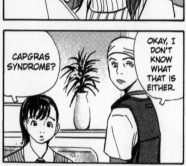

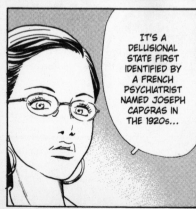

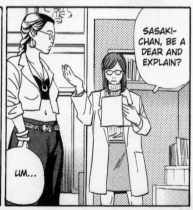

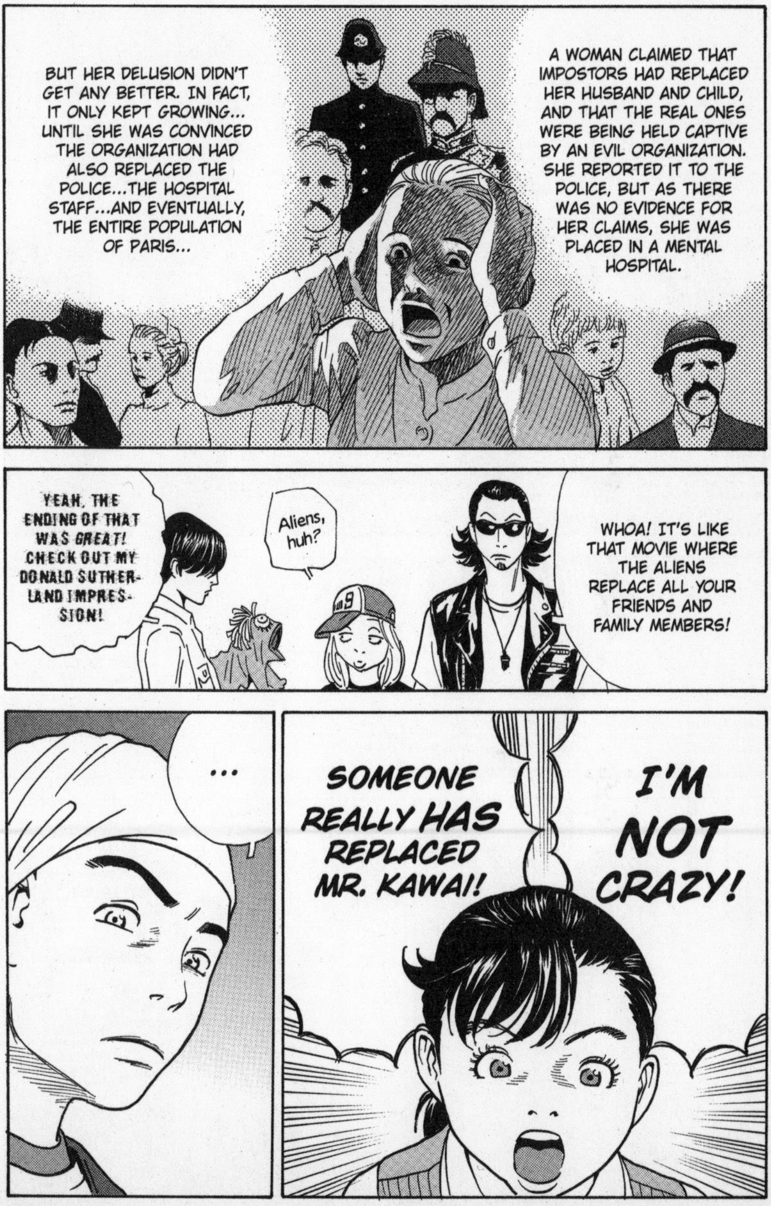
A WOMAN CLAIMED THAT IMPOSTORS HAD REPLACED HER HUSBAND AND CHILD, AND THAT THE REAL ONES WERE BEING HELD CAPTIVE BY AN EVIL ORGANIZATION. SHE REPORTED IT TO THE POLICE, BUT AS THERE WAS NO EVIDENCE FOR HER CLAIMS, SHE WAS PLACED IN A MENTAL HOSPITAL.
BUT HER DELUSION DIDN'T GET ANY BETTER. IN FACT, IT ONLY KEPT GROWING... UNTIL SHE WAS CONVINCED THE ORGANIZATION HAD ALSO REPLACED THE POLICE...THE HOSPITAL STAFF...AND EVENTUALLY, THE ENTIRE POPULATION OF PARIS...
WHOA! IT'S LIKE THAT MOVIE WHERE THE ALIENS REPLACE ALL YOUR FRIENDS AND FAMILY MEMBERS!
Aliens, huh?
YEAH, THE ENDING OF THAT WAS GREAT! CHECK OUT MY DONALD SUTHERLAND IMPRESSION!
I'M NOT CRAZY!
SOMEONE REALLY HAS REPLACED MR. KAWAI!
...

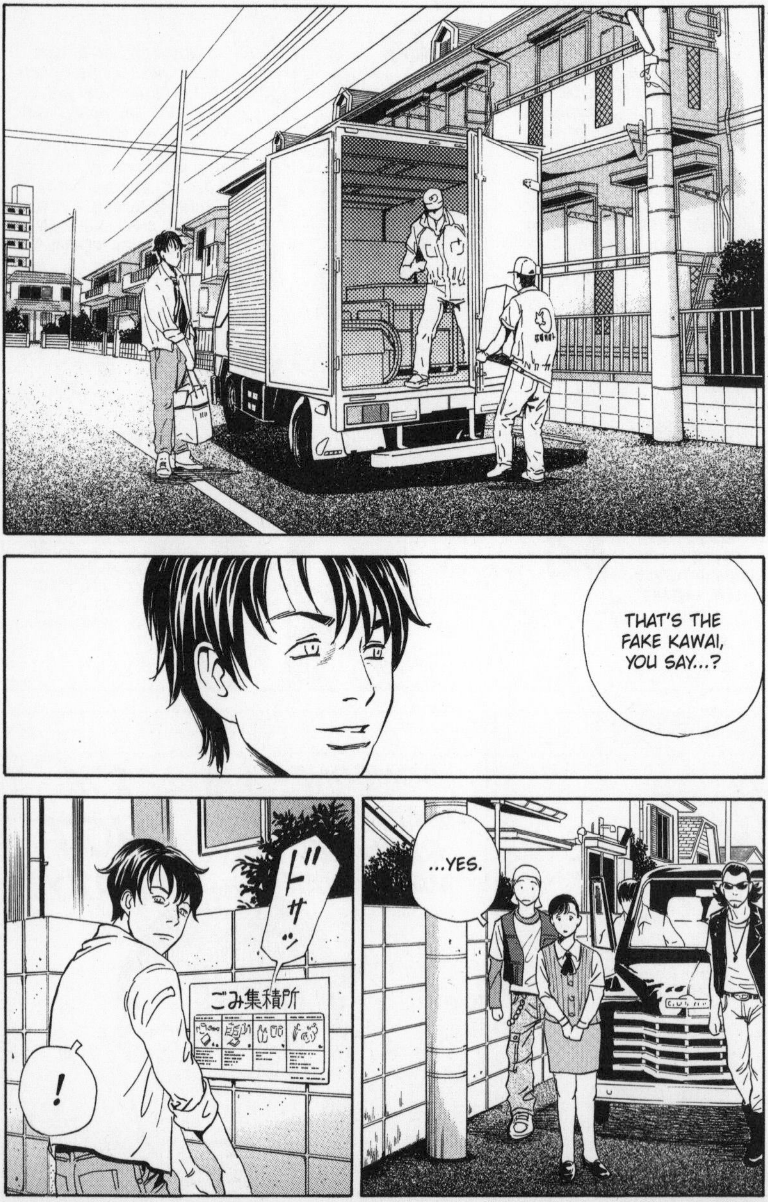
THAT'S THE FAKE KAWAI, YOU SAY...?
...YES.
ドサッ
ごみ集積所
!

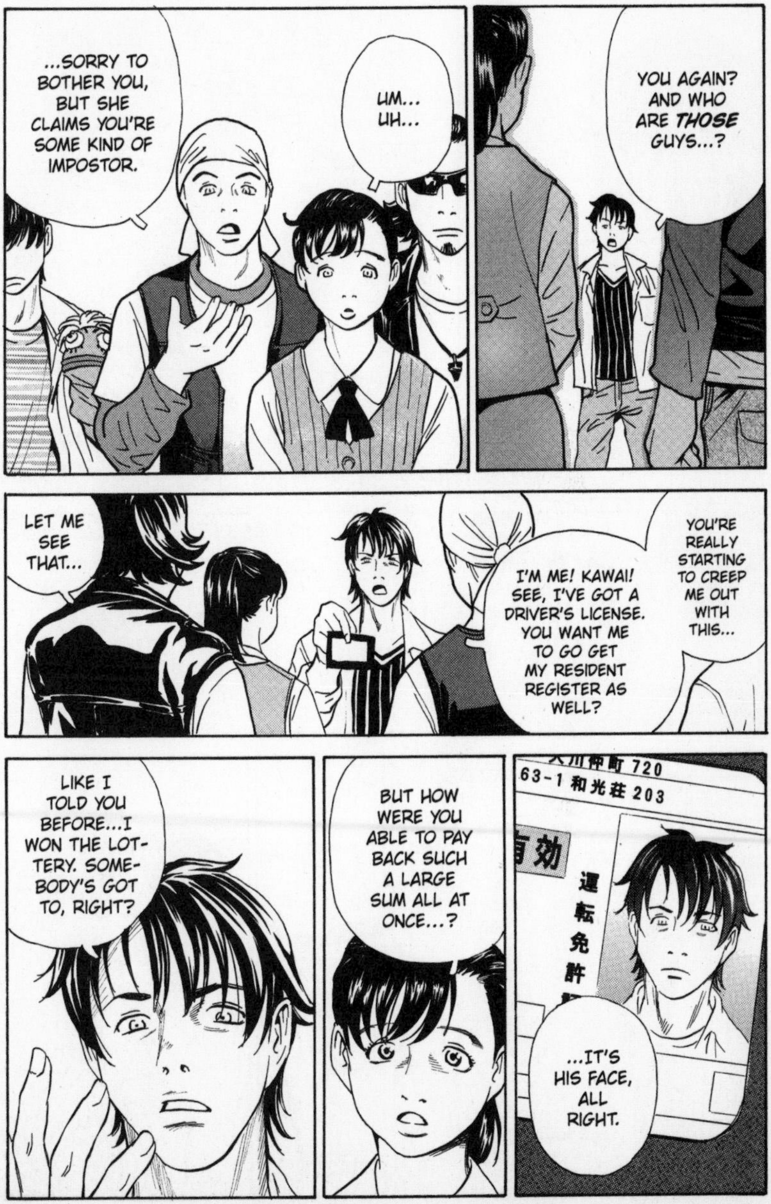
YOU AGAIN? AND WHO ARE *THOSE* GUYS...?
UM... UH...
...SORRY TO BOTHER YOU, BUT SHE CLAIMS YOU'RE SOME KIND OF IMPOSTOR.
YOU'RE REALLY STARTING TO CREEP ME OUT WITH THIS...
I'M ME! KAWAI! SEE, I'VE GOT A DRIVER'S LICENSE. YOU WANT ME TO GO GET MY RESIDENT REGISTER AS WELL?
LET ME SEE THAT...
63-1 和光荘 203
...IT'S HIS FACE, ALL RIGHT.
BUT HOW WERE YOU ABLE TO PAY BACK SUCH A LARGE SUM ALL AT ONCE...?
LIKE I TOLD YOU BEFORE...I WON THE LOTTERY. SOMEBODY'S GOT TO, RIGHT?

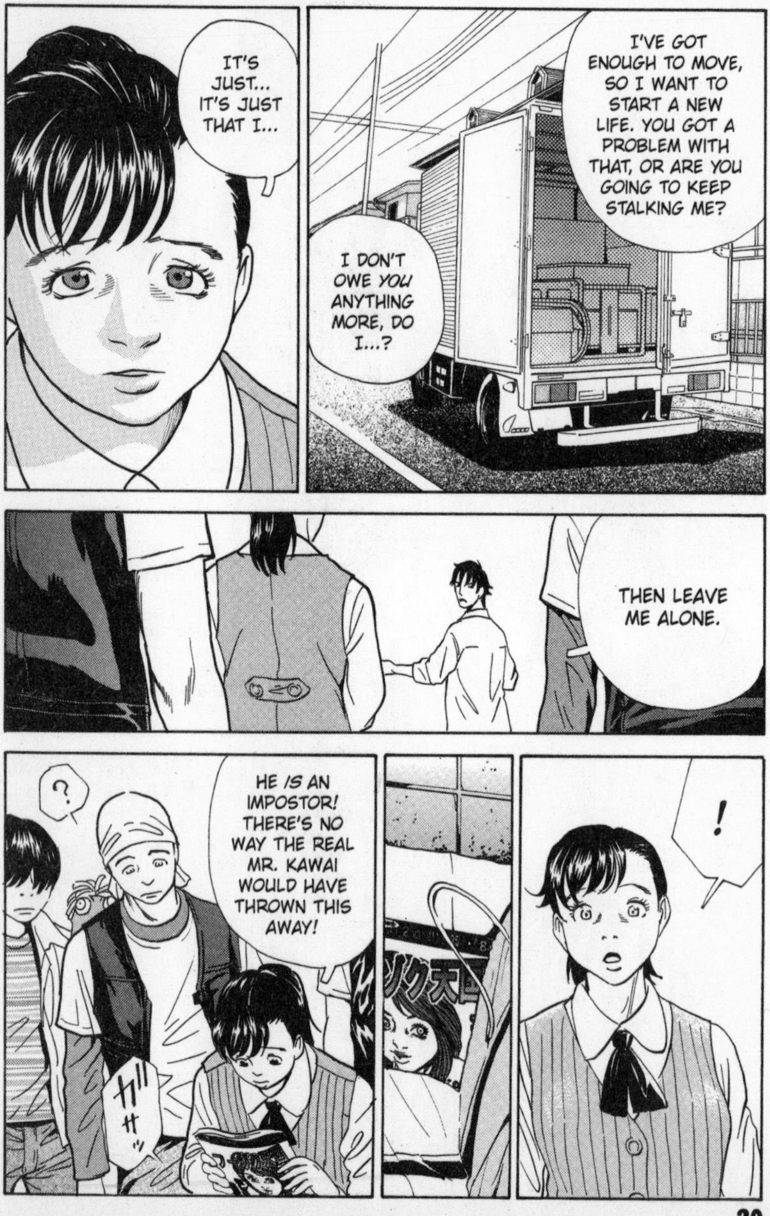
I'VE GOT ENOUGH TO MOVE, SO I WANT TO START A NEW LIFE. YOU GOT A PROBLEM WITH THAT, OR ARE YOU GOING TO KEEP STALKING ME?
I DON'T OWE *YOU* ANYTHING MORE, DO I...?
IT'S JUST... IT'S JUST THAT I...
THEN LEAVE ME ALONE.
!
HE *IS* AN IMPOSTOR! THERE'S NO WAY THE REAL MR. KAWAI WOULD HAVE THROWN THIS AWAY!
?
ガサッ

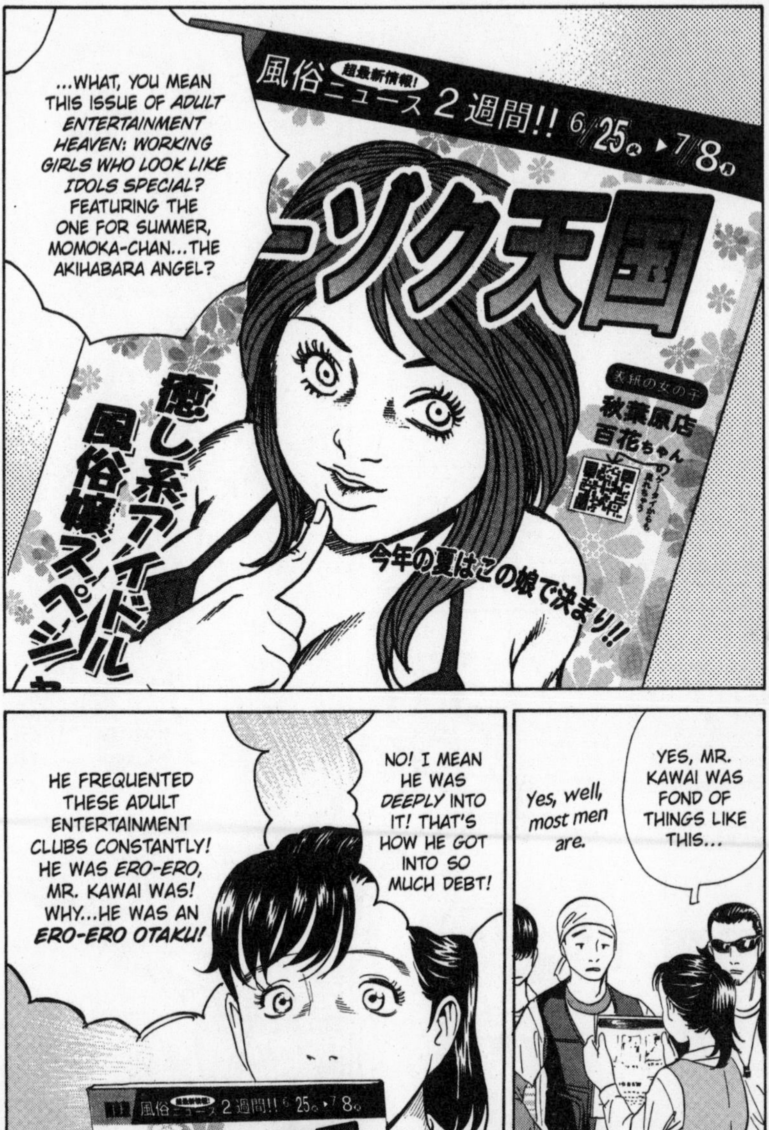

超最新情報!
風俗ニュース 2週間!! 6/25火 ▶7/8月
ーゾク天国
表紙の女の子
秋葉原店
百花ちゃん
今年の夏はこの娘で決まり!!
癒し系アイドル風俗嬢スペシャ
...WHAT, YOU MEAN THIS ISSUE OF *ADULT ENTERTAINMENT HEAVEN: WORKING GIRLS WHO LOOK LIKE IDOLS SPECIAL?* FEATURING THE ONE FOR SUMMER, MOMOKA-CHAN...THE AKIHABARA ANGEL?
YES, MR. KAWAI WAS FOND OF THINGS LIKE THIS...
Yes, well, most men are.
NO! I MEAN HE WAS *DEEPLY* INTO IT! THAT'S HOW HE GOT INTO SO MUCH DEBT!
HE FREQUENTED THESE ADULT ENTERTAINMENT CLUBS CONSTANTLY! HE WAS *ERO-ERO*, MR. KAWAI WAS! WHY...HE WAS AN *ERO-ERO OTAKU!*
風俗 超最新情報! ニュース 2週間!! 6/25 ▶7/8
ーゾク天国

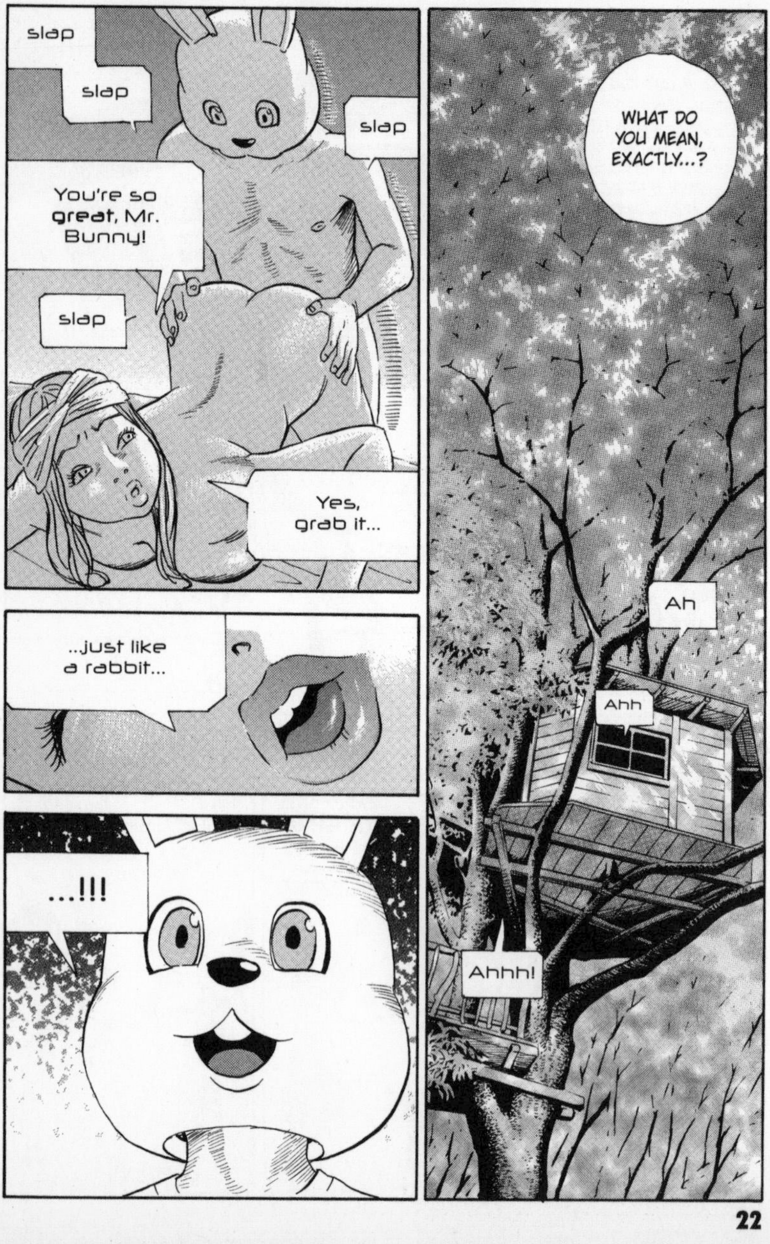

WHAT DO YOU MEAN, EXACTLY...?
Ah
Ahh
Ahhh!
slap
slap
slap
You're so great, Mr. Bunny!
slap
Yes, grab it...
...just like a rabbit...
...!!!

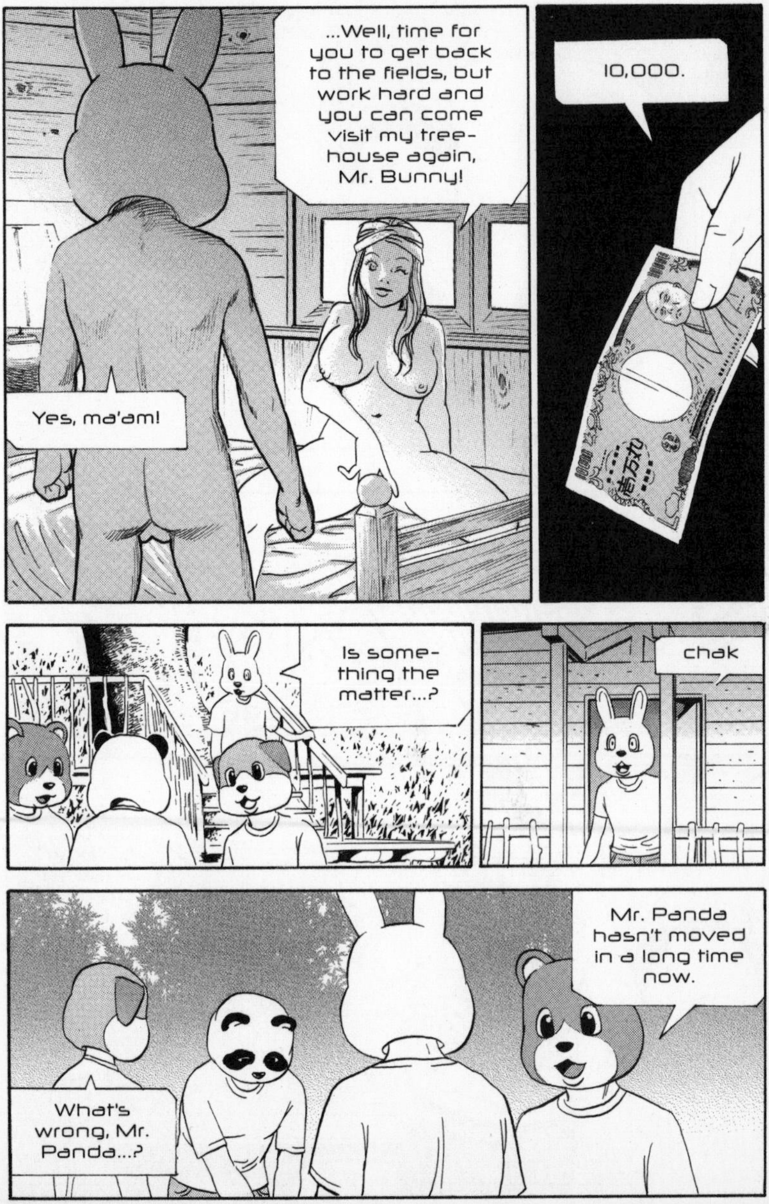
10,000.
...Well, time for you to get back to the fields, but work hard and you can come visit my tree-house again, Mr. Bunny!
Yes, ma'am!
chak
Is some-thing the matter...?
Mr. Panda hasn't moved in a long time now.
What's wrong, Mr. Panda...?

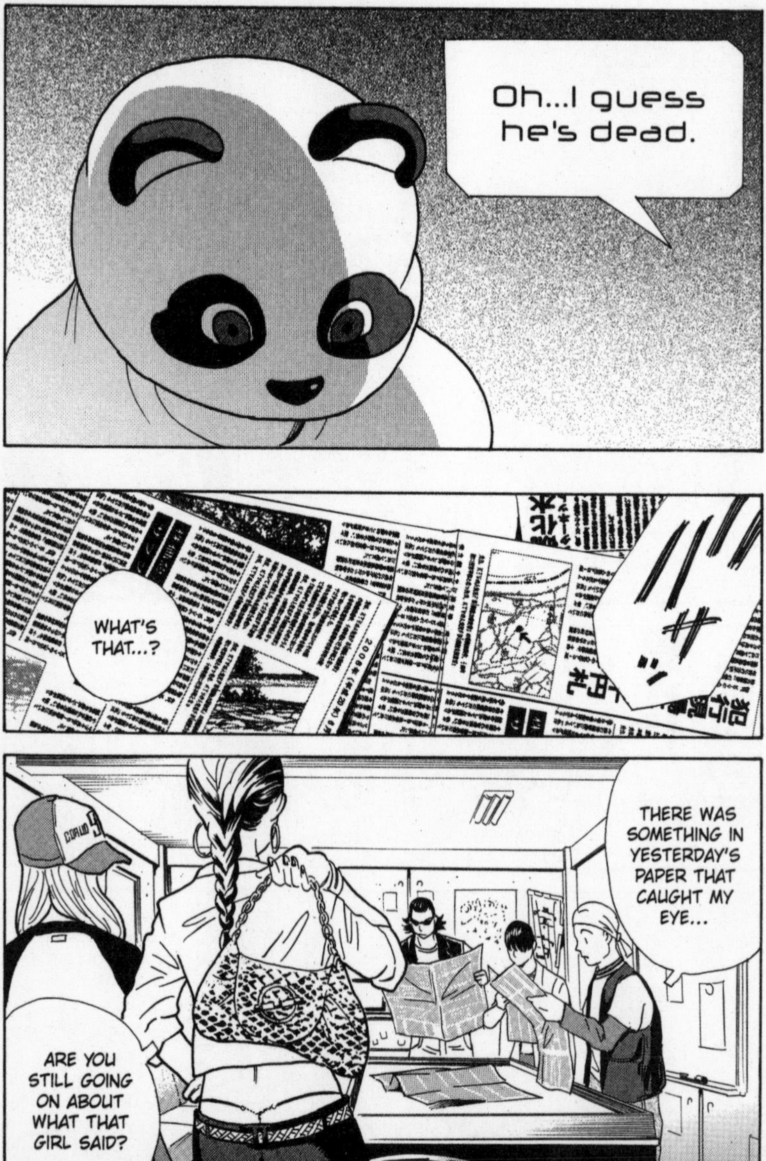
Oh...I guess he's dead.
WHAT'S THAT...?
THERE WAS SOMETHING IN YESTERDAY'S PAPER THAT CAUGHT MY EYE...
ARE YOU STILL GOING ON ABOUT WHAT THAT GIRL SAID?

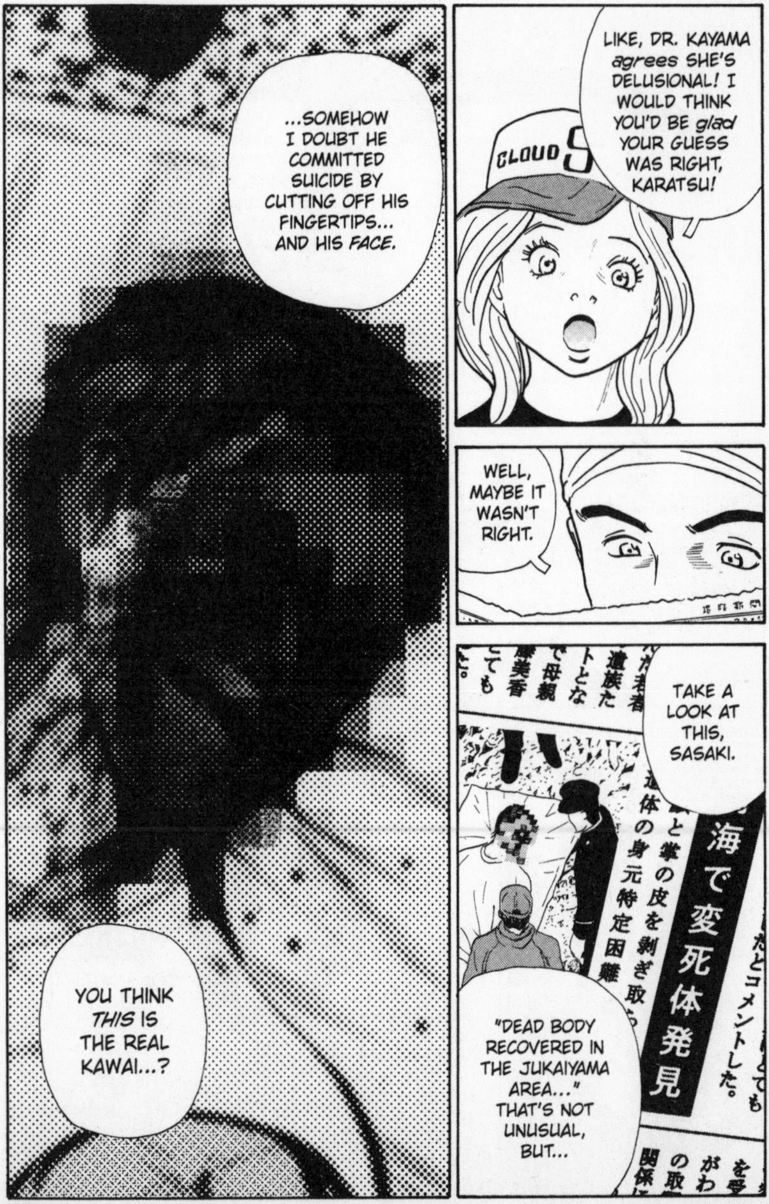
LIKE, DR. KAYAMA *agrees* SHE'S DELUSIONAL! I WOULD THINK YOU'D BE *glad* YOUR GUESS WAS RIGHT, KARATSU!
WELL, MAYBE IT WASN'T RIGHT.
TAKE A LOOK AT THIS, SASAKI.
海で変死体発見
"DEAD BODY RECOVERED IN THE JUKAIYAMA AREA..." THAT'S NOT UNUSUAL, BUT...
...SOMEHOW I DOUBT HE COMMITTED SUICIDE BY CUTTING OFF HIS FINGERTIPS... AND HIS *FACE.*
YOU THINK *THIS* IS THE REAL KAWAI...?

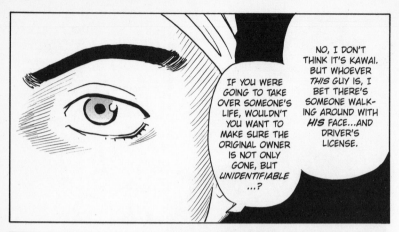

NO, I DON'T THINK IT'S KAWAI. BUT WHOEVER *THIS* GUY IS, I BET THERE'S SOMEONE WALKING AROUND WITH *HIS* FACE...AND DRIVER'S LICENSE.
IF YOU WERE GOING TO TAKE OVER SOMEONE'S LIFE, WOULDN'T YOU WANT TO MAKE SURE THE ORIGINAL OWNER IS NOT ONLY GONE, BUT *UNIDENTIFIABLE* ...?
I SUPPOSE IT'S POSSIBLE, BUT...
BUT WHAT ABOUT THE *village* SHE CLAIMED KAWAI WENT TO? THE ARTICLE DOESN'T SAY ANYTHING LIKE THAT...
MAYBE HE WAS KILLED THERE AND THEN DRAGGED AWAY...?
HAPPY END
JUST LEAVE IT
I DON'T BUY IT. WE'VE BEEN ALL UP AND DOWN THOSE WOODS. IF PEOPLE WERE ACTUALLY *LIVING* THERE, WE WOULD HAVE RUN INTO THEM BEFORE.
ジャカジャンジャラララ♪

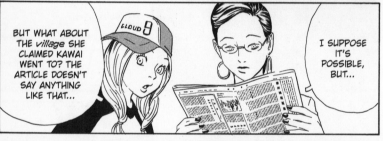

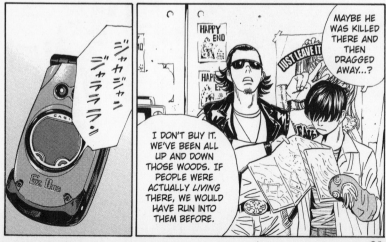

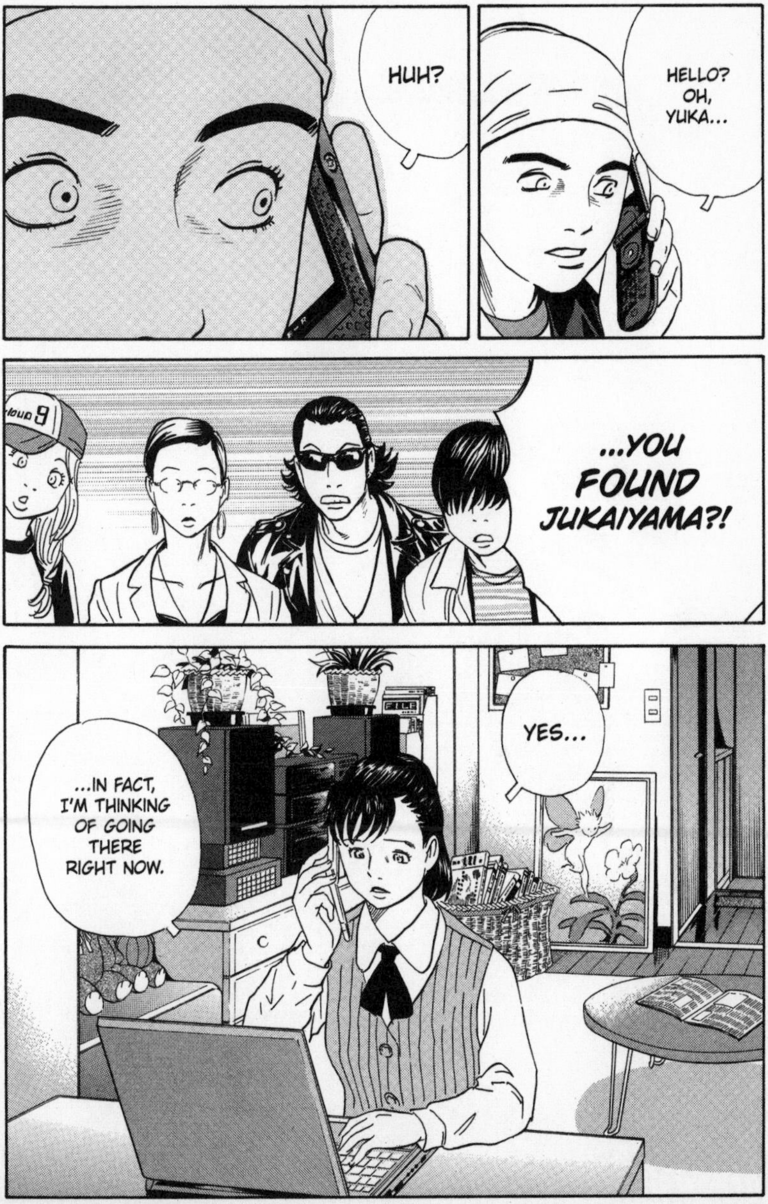
HELLO? OH, YUKA...
HUH?
...YOU FOUND JUKAIYAMA?!
YES...
...IN FACT, I'M THINKING OF GOING THERE RIGHT NOW.

1st delivery: picnic boogie—the end

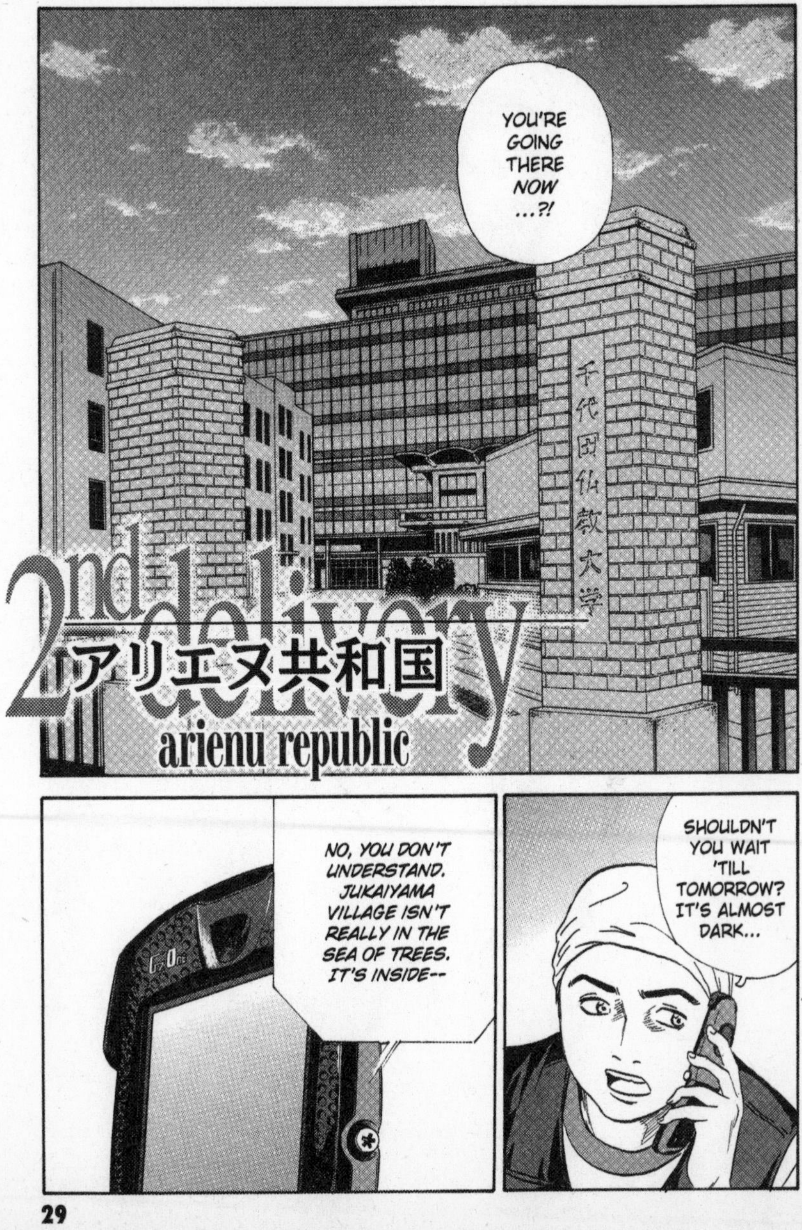
YOU'RE GOING THERE NOW ...?!
千代田仏教大学
2nd delivery
アリエヌ共和国
arienu republic
SHOULDN'T YOU WAIT 'TILL TOMORROW? IT'S ALMOST DARK...
NO, YOU DON'T UNDERSTAND. JUKAIYAMA VILLAGE ISN'T REALLY IN THE SEA OF TREES. IT'S INSIDE--

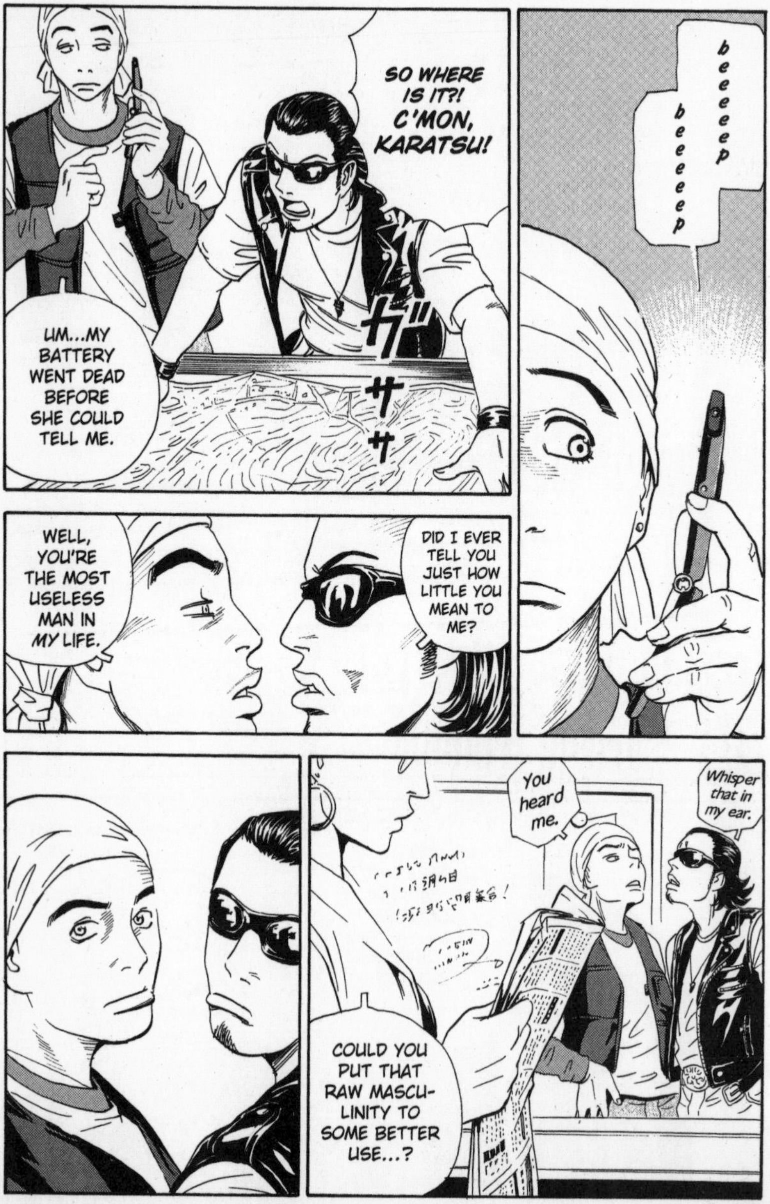
beeeeep
beeeeep
SO WHERE IS IT?! C'MON, KARATSU!
ガササ
UM...MY BATTERY WENT DEAD BEFORE SHE COULD TELL ME.
DID I EVER TELL YOU JUST HOW LITTLE YOU MEAN TO ME?
WELL, YOU'RE THE MOST USELESS MAN IN *MY* LIFE.
Whisper that in my ear.
You heard me.
COULD YOU PUT THAT RAW MASCULINITY TO SOME BETTER USE...?

...SHE MIGHT BE RUNNING INTO WHO- EVER DID *THIS.*

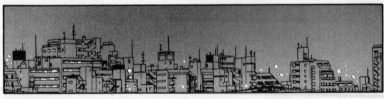

krnch

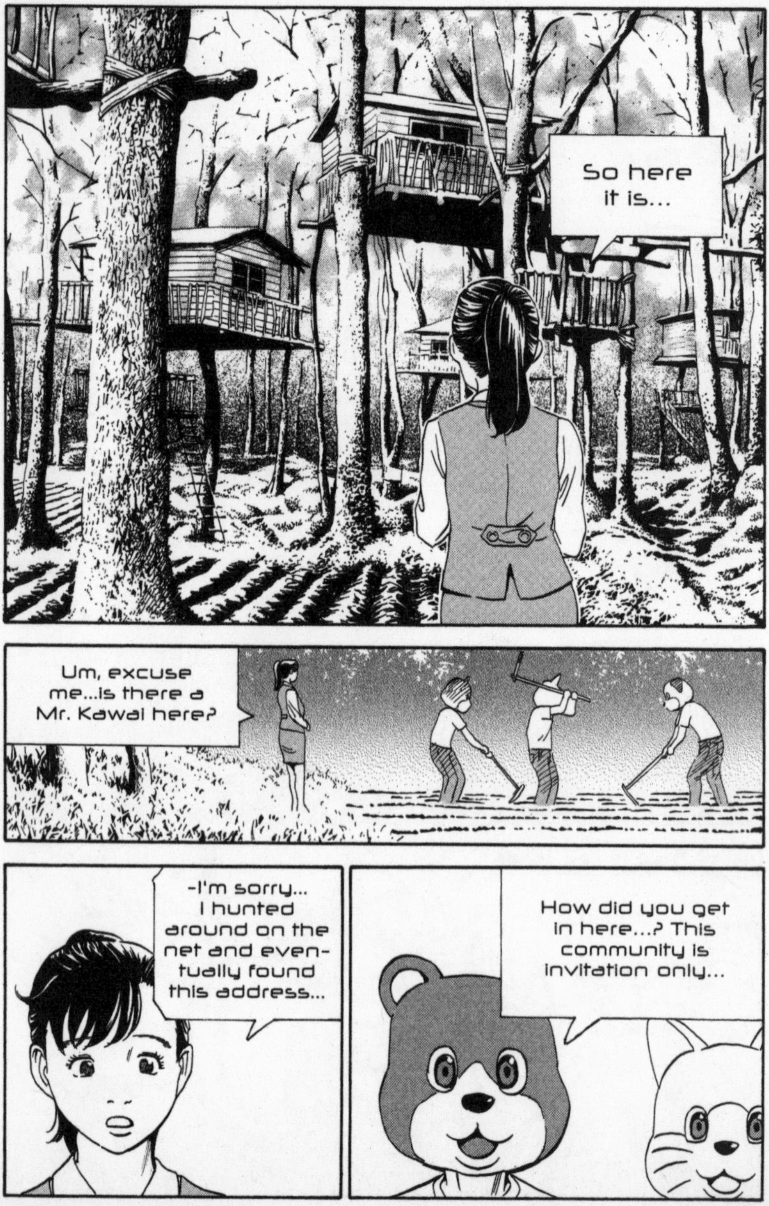
So here it is...
Um, excuse me...is there a Mr. Kawai here?
How did you get in here...? This community is invitation only...
-I'm sorry... I hunted around on the net and eventually found this address...

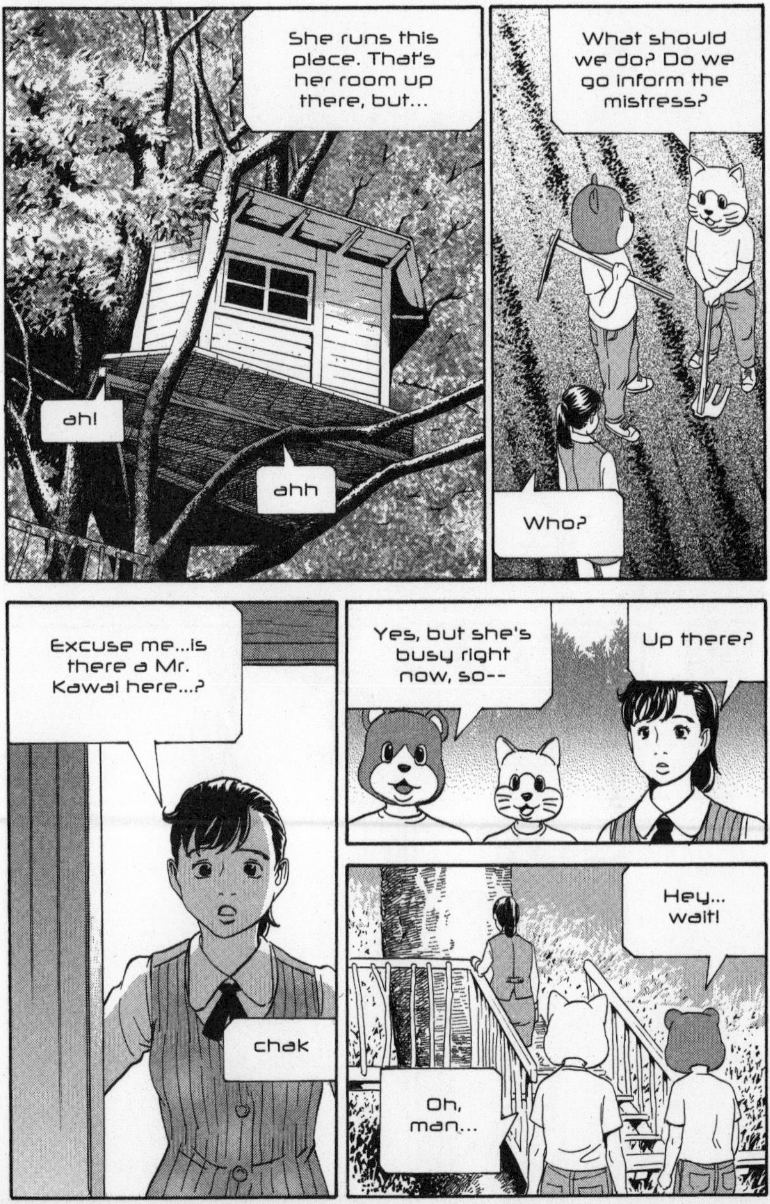

What should we do? Do we go inform the mistress?
Who?
She runs this place. That's her room up there, but...
ah!
ahh
Up there?
Yes, but she's busy right now, so--
Hey... wait!
Oh, man...
Excuse me...is there a Mr. Kawai here...?
chak

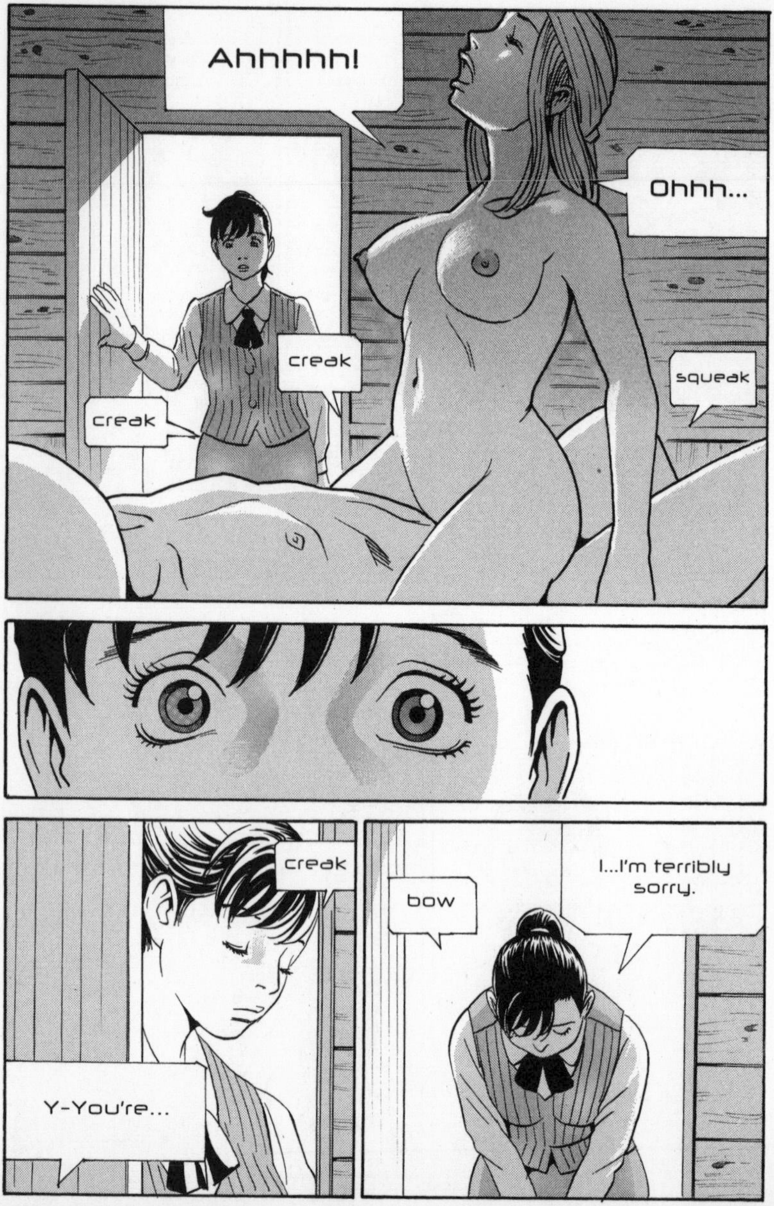

Ahhhhh!
Ohhh...
squeak
creak
creak
I...I'm terribly sorry.
bow
creak
Y-You're...

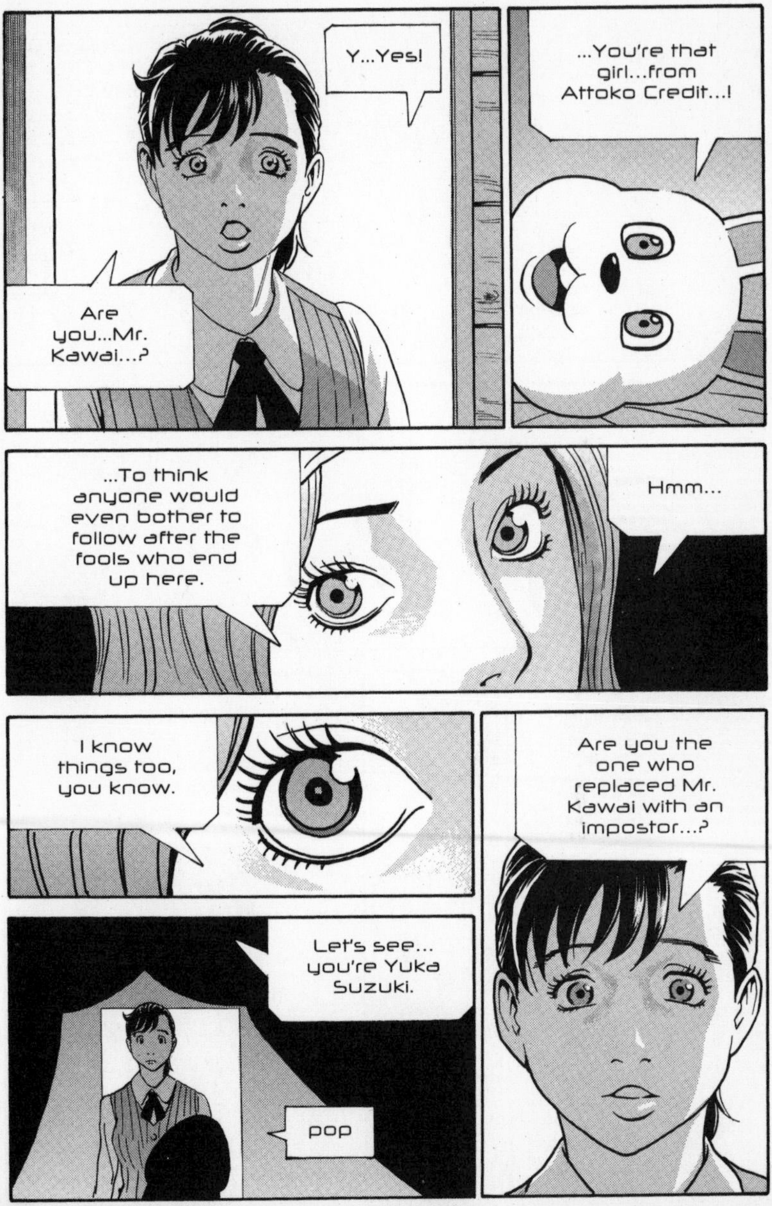

...You're that girl...from Attoko Credit...!
Y...Yes!
Are you...Mr. Kawai...?
Hmm...
...To think anyone would even bother to follow after the fools who end up here.
Are you the one who replaced Mr. Kawai with an impostor...?
I know things too, you know.
Let's see... you're Yuka Suzuki.
pop

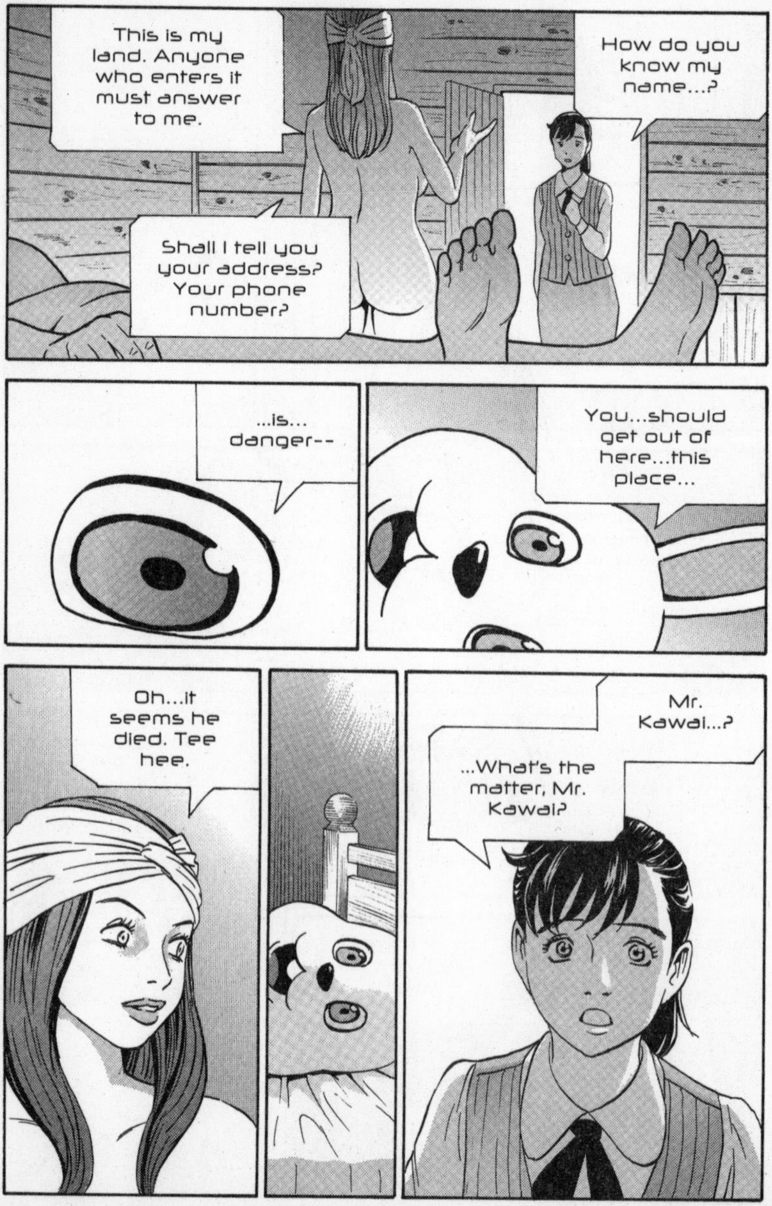
How do you know my name...?
This is my land. Anyone who enters it must answer to me.
Shall I tell you your address? Your phone number?
You...should get out of here...this place...
...is... danger--
Mr. Kawai...?
...What's the matter, Mr. Kawai?
Oh...it seems he died. Tee hee.

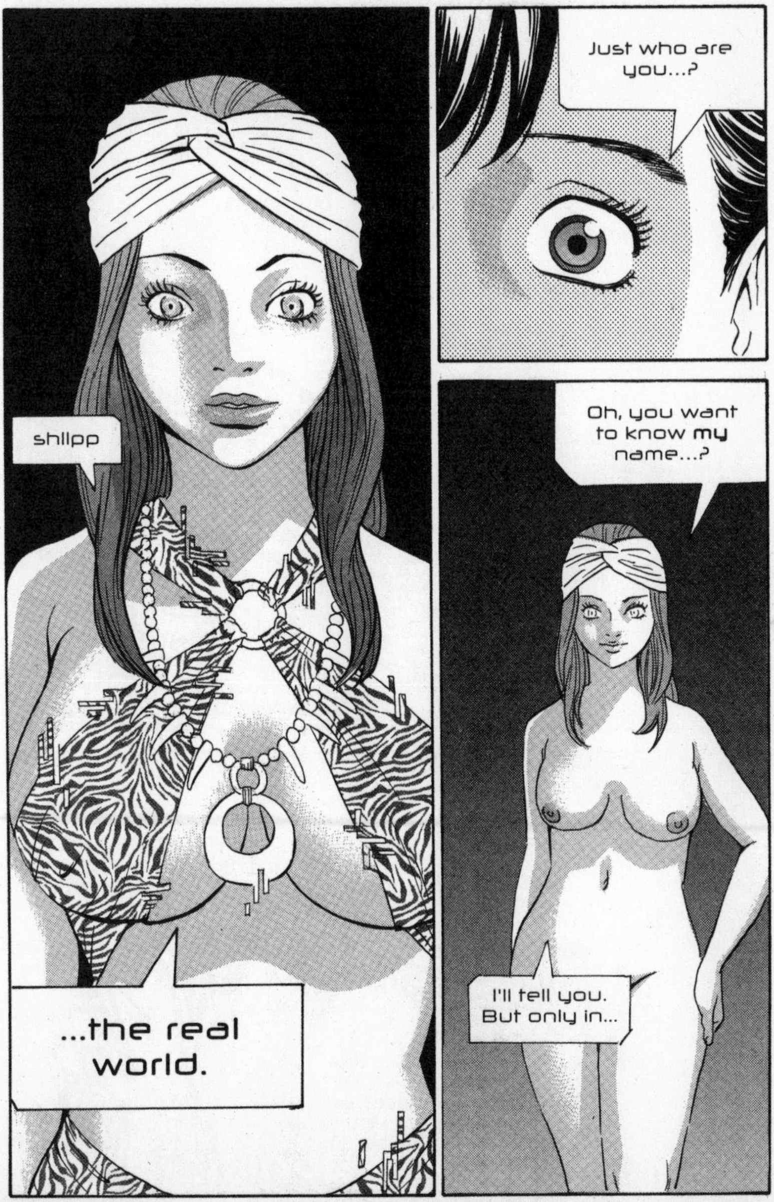
Just who are you...?
Oh, you want to know **my** name...?
I'll tell you. But only in...
shllpp
...the real world.

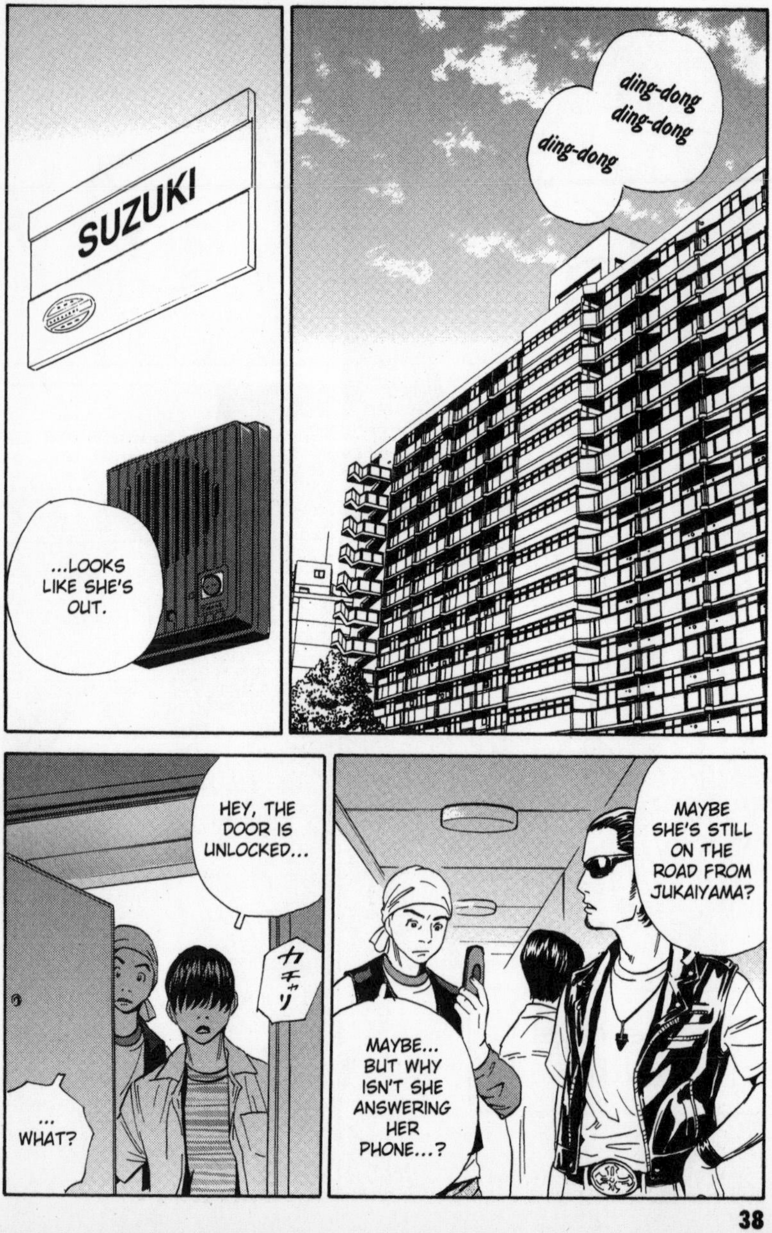
ding-dong
ding-dong
ding-dong
SUZUKI
...LOOKS LIKE SHE'S OUT.
MAYBE SHE'S STILL ON THE ROAD FROM JUKAIYAMA?
MAYBE... BUT WHY ISN'T SHE ANSWERING HER PHONE...?
HEY, THE DOOR IS UNLOCKED...
カチャリ
... WHAT?

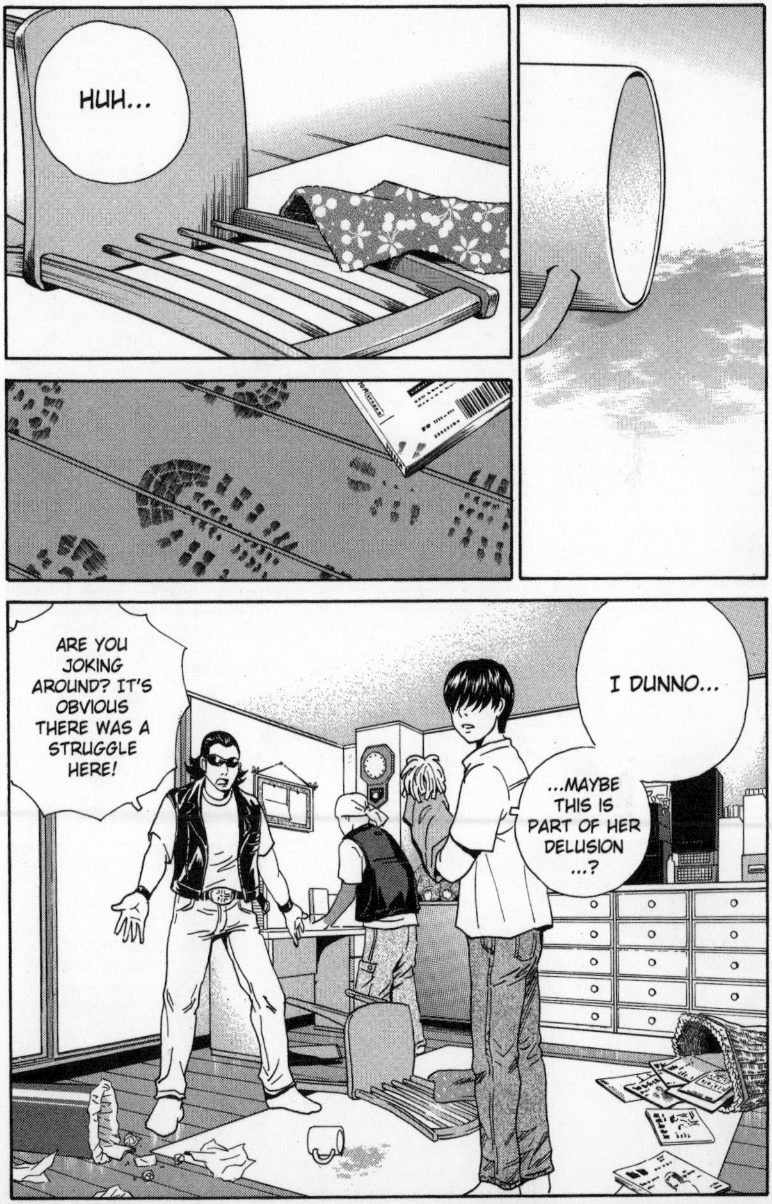
HUH...
I DUNNO...
...MAYBE THIS IS PART OF HER DELUSION ...?
ARE YOU JOKING AROUND? IT'S OBVIOUS THERE WAS A STRUGGLE HERE!

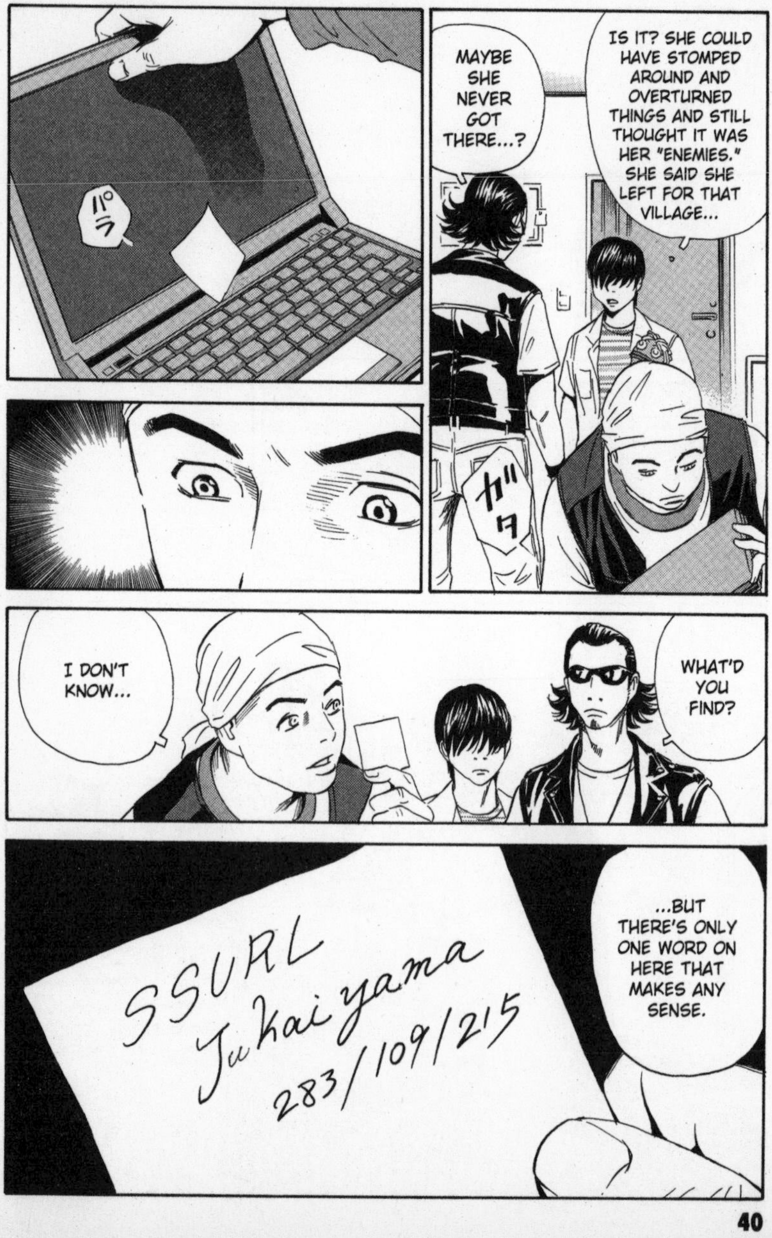
IS IT? SHE COULD HAVE STOMPED AROUND AND OVERTURNED THINGS AND STILL THOUGHT IT WAS HER "ENEMIES." SHE SAID SHE LEFT FOR THAT VILLAGE...
MAYBE SHE NEVER GOT THERE...?
ガタ
パラ
WHAT'D YOU FIND?
I DON'T KNOW...
...BUT THERE'S ONLY ONE WORD ON HERE THAT MAKES ANY SENSE.
SSURL
Jukaiyama
283/109/215

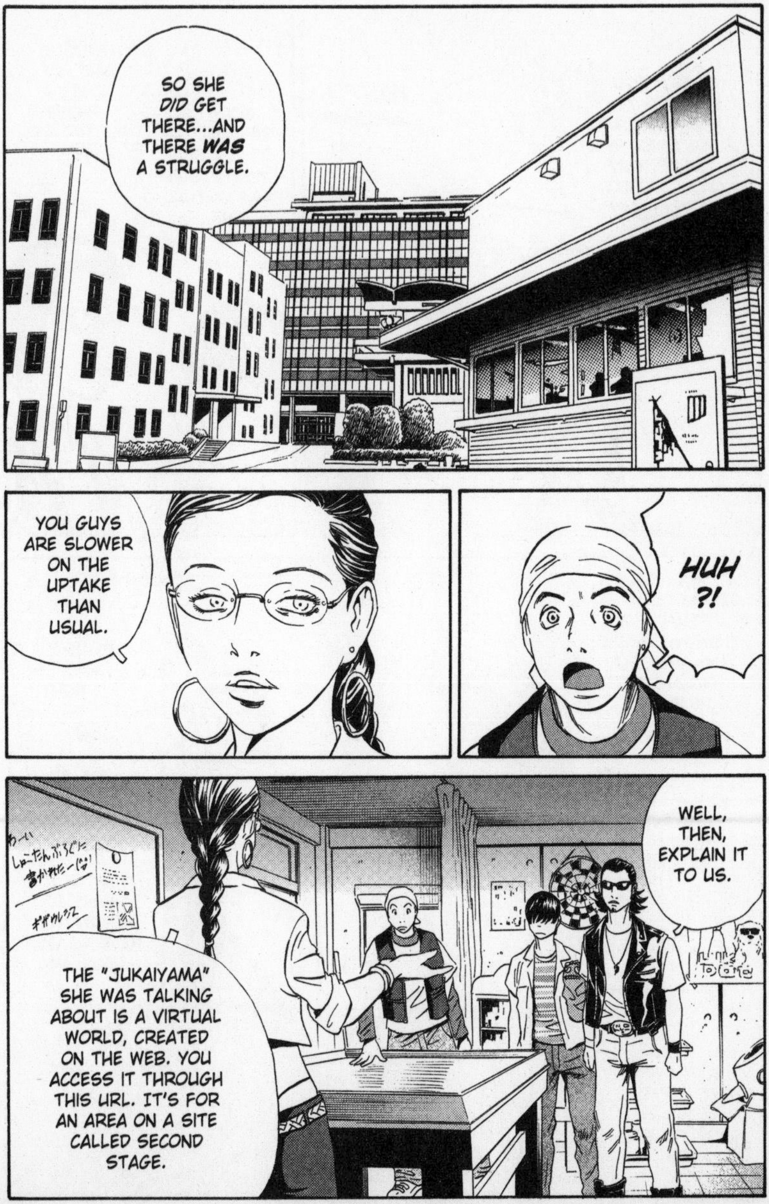
SO SHE *DID* GET THERE...AND THERE **WAS** A STRUGGLE.
HUH ?!
YOU GUYS ARE SLOWER ON THE UPTAKE THAN USUAL.
WELL, THEN, EXPLAIN IT TO US.
THE "JUKAIYAMA" SHE WAS TALKING ABOUT IS A VIRTUAL WORLD, CREATED ON THE WEB. YOU ACCESS IT THROUGH THIS URL. IT'S FOR AN AREA ON A SITE CALLED SECOND STAGE.

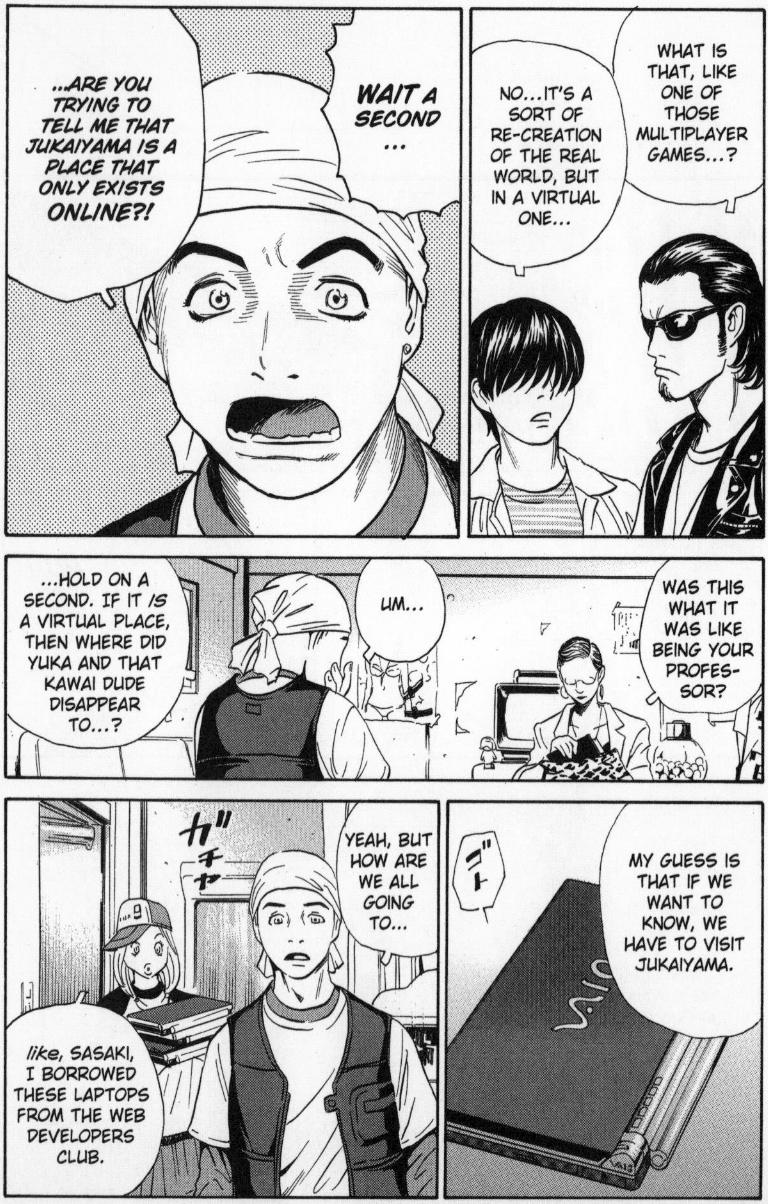
WHAT IS THAT, LIKE ONE OF THOSE MULTIPLAYER GAMES...?
NO...IT'S A SORT OF RE-CREATION OF THE REAL WORLD, BUT IN A VIRTUAL ONE...
WAIT A SECOND ...
...ARE YOU TRYING TO TELL ME THAT JUKAIYAMA IS A PLACE THAT ONLY EXISTS ONLINE?!
WAS THIS WHAT IT WAS LIKE BEING YOUR PROFES-SOR?
UM...
...HOLD ON A SECOND. IF IT IS A VIRTUAL PLACE, THEN WHERE DID YUKA AND THAT KAWAI DUDE DISAPPEAR TO...?
ゴト
MY GUESS IS THAT IF WE WANT TO KNOW, WE HAVE TO VISIT JUKAIYAMA.
ガチャ
YEAH, BUT HOW ARE WE ALL GOING TO...
like, SASAKI, I BORROWED THESE LAPTOPS FROM THE WEB DEVELOPERS CLUB.

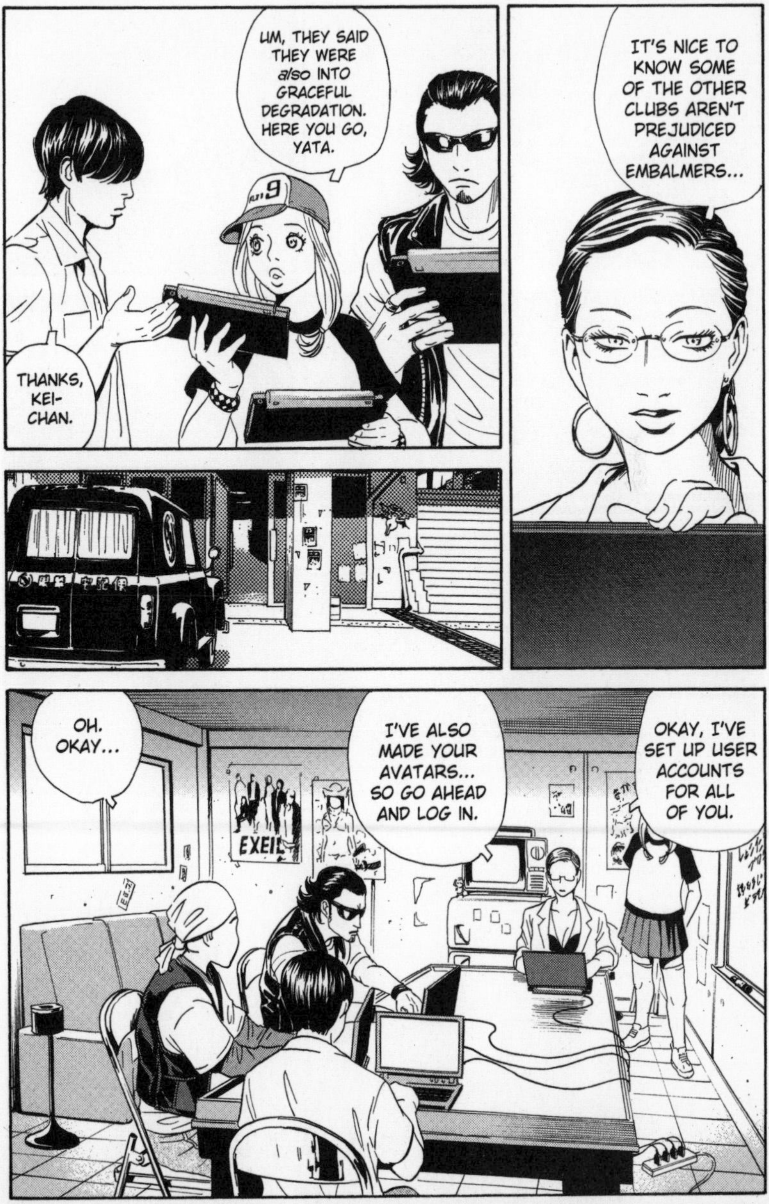
IT'S NICE TO KNOW SOME OF THE OTHER CLUBS AREN'T PREJUDICED AGAINST EMBALMERS...
UM, THEY SAID THEY WERE *also* INTO GRACEFUL DEGRADATION. HERE YOU GO, YATA.
THANKS, KEI-CHAN.
OKAY, I'VE SET UP USER ACCOUNTS FOR ALL OF YOU.
I'VE ALSO MADE YOUR AVATARS... SO GO AHEAD AND LOG IN.
OH. OKAY...
EXEIL

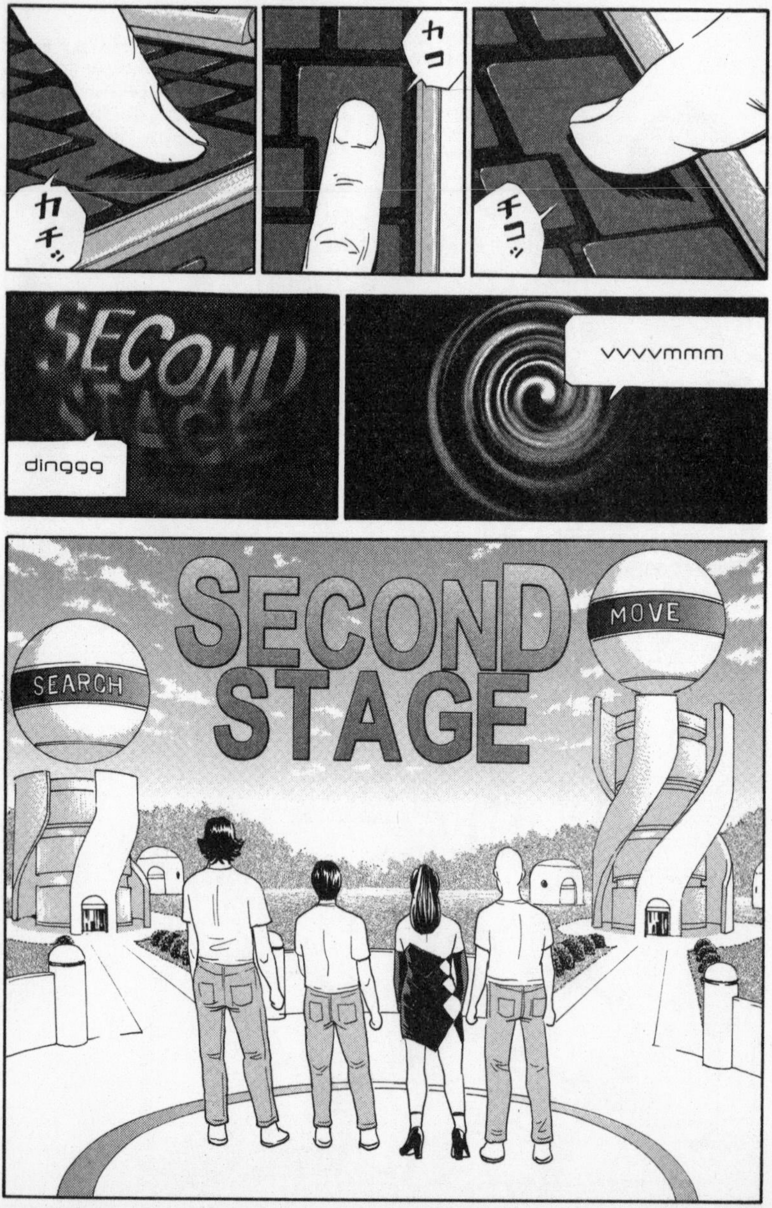
チコッ
カコ
カチッ
vvvvmmm
dinggg
SECOND STAGE
MOVE
SEARCH

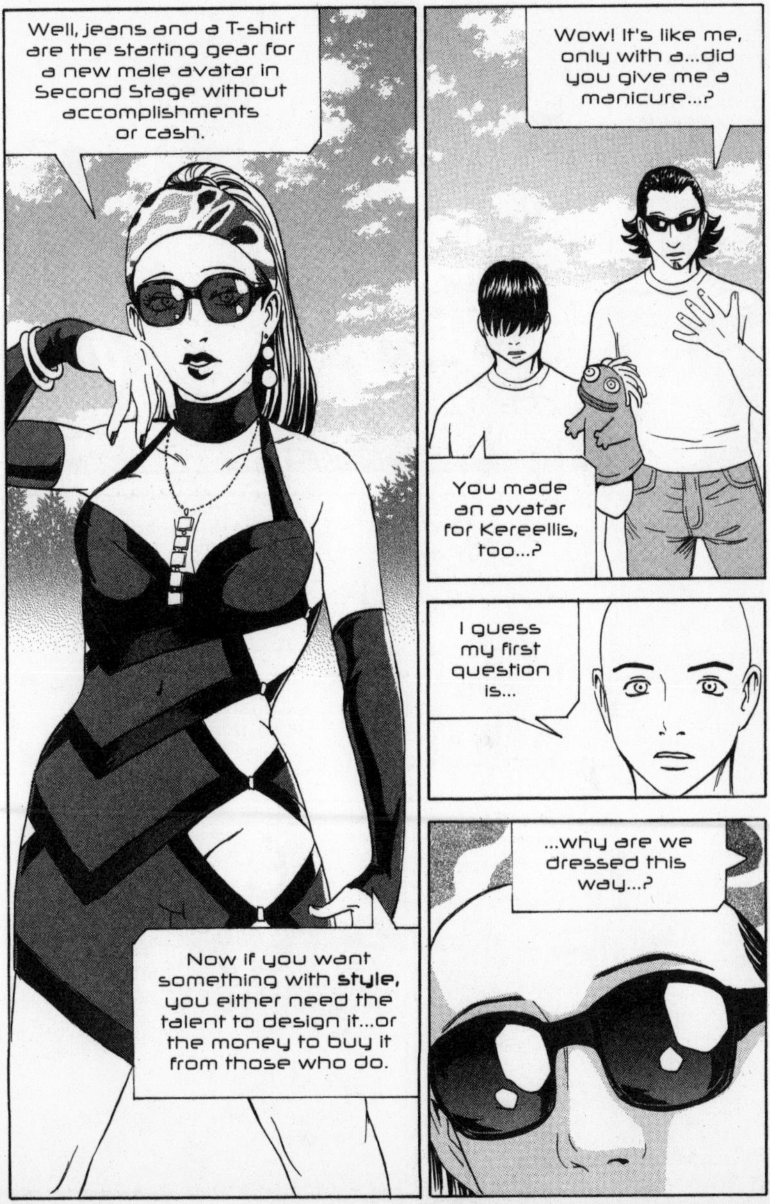
Wow! It's like me, only with a...did you give me a manicure...?
You made an avatar for Kereellis, too...?
I guess my first question is...
...why are we dressed this way...?
Well, jeans and a T-shirt are the starting gear for a new male avatar in Second Stage without accomplishments or cash.
Now if you want something with **style,** you either need the talent to design it...or the money to buy it from those who do.

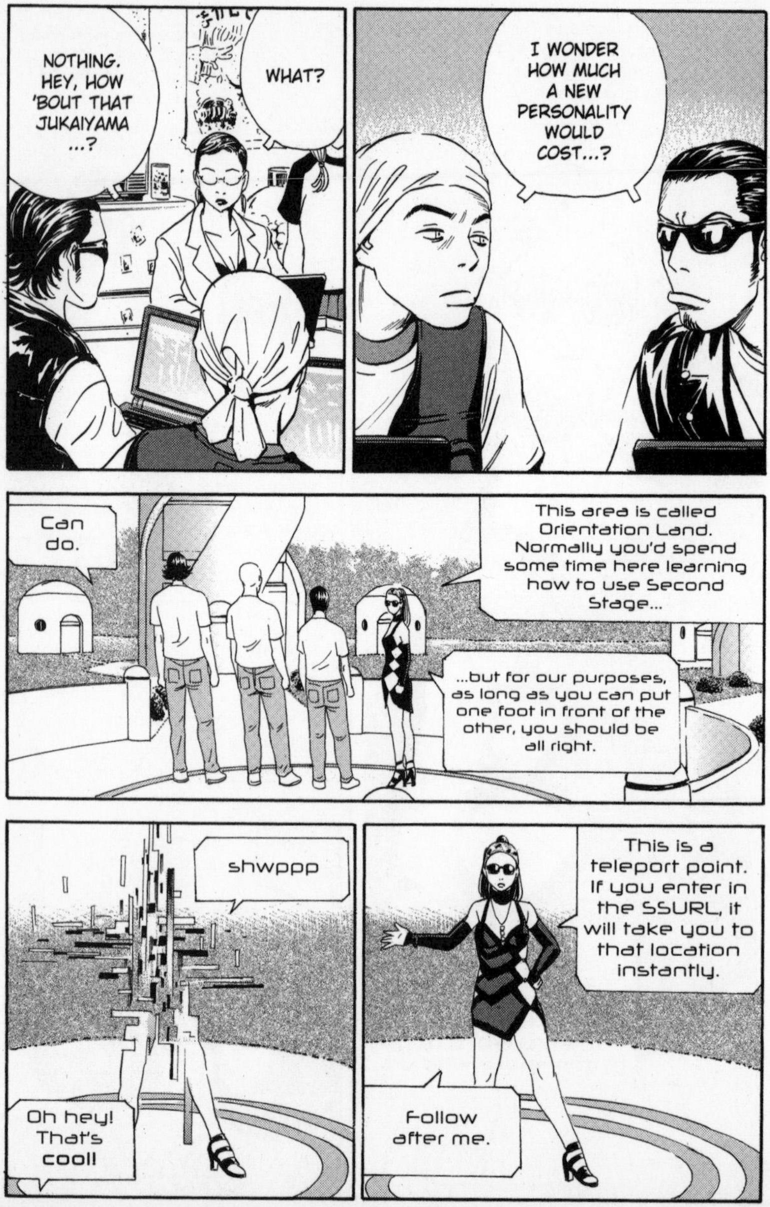
I WONDER HOW MUCH A NEW PERSONALITY WOULD COST...?
WHAT?
NOTHING. HEY, HOW 'BOUT THAT JUKAIYAMA ...?
This area is called Orientation Land. Normally you'd spend some time here learning how to use Second Stage...
...but for our purposes, as long as you can put one foot in front of the other, you should be all right.
Can do.
This is a teleport point. If you enter in the SSURL, it will take you to that location instantly.
Follow after me.
shwppp
Oh hey! That's cool!

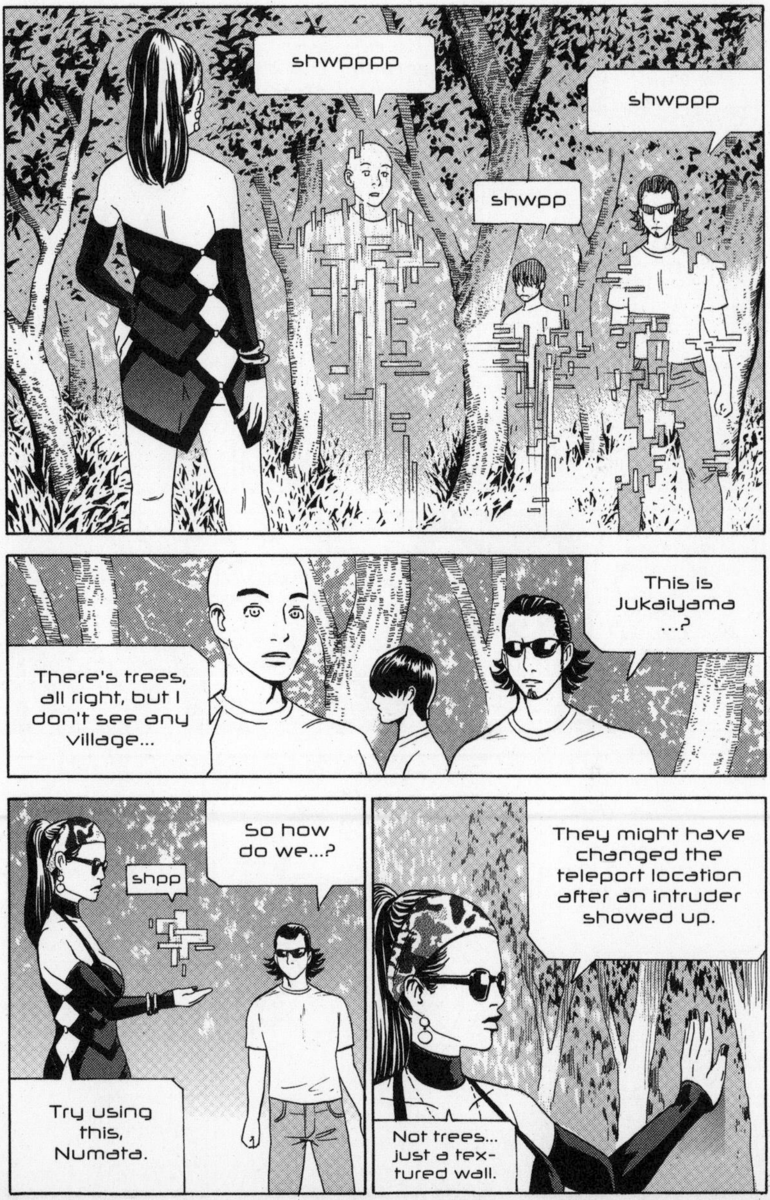
shwpppp
shwppp
shwpp
This is Jukaiyama ...?
There's trees, all right, but I don't see any village...
They might have changed the teleport location after an intruder showed up.
Not trees... just a textured wall.
So how do we...?
shpp
Try using this, Numata.

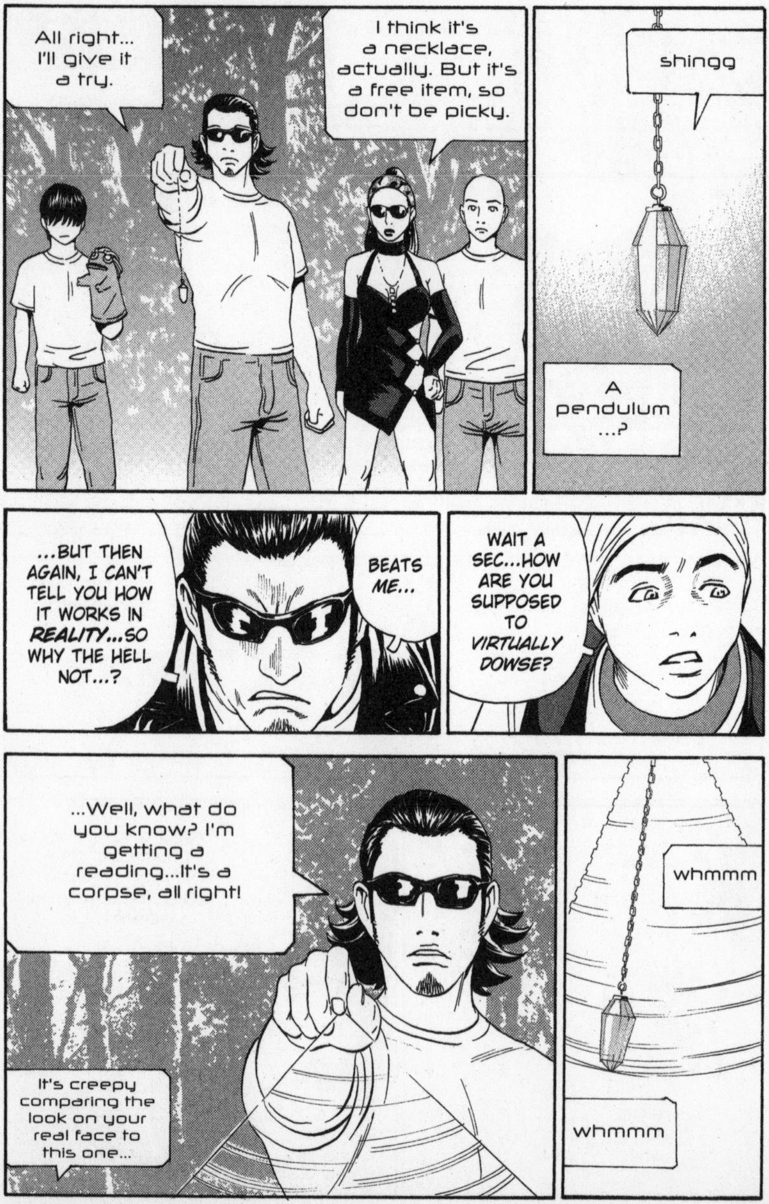
shingg
A pendulum ...?
I think it's a necklace, actually. But it's a free item, so don't be picky.
All right... I'll give it a try.
WAIT A SEC...HOW ARE YOU SUPPOSED TO *VIRTUALLY* DOWSE?
BEATS ME...
...BUT THEN AGAIN, I CAN'T TELL YOU HOW IT WORKS IN ***REALITY***...SO WHY THE HELL NOT...?
whmmm
whmmm
...Well, what do you know? I'm getting a reading...It's a corpse, all right!
It's creepy comparing the look on your real face to this one...

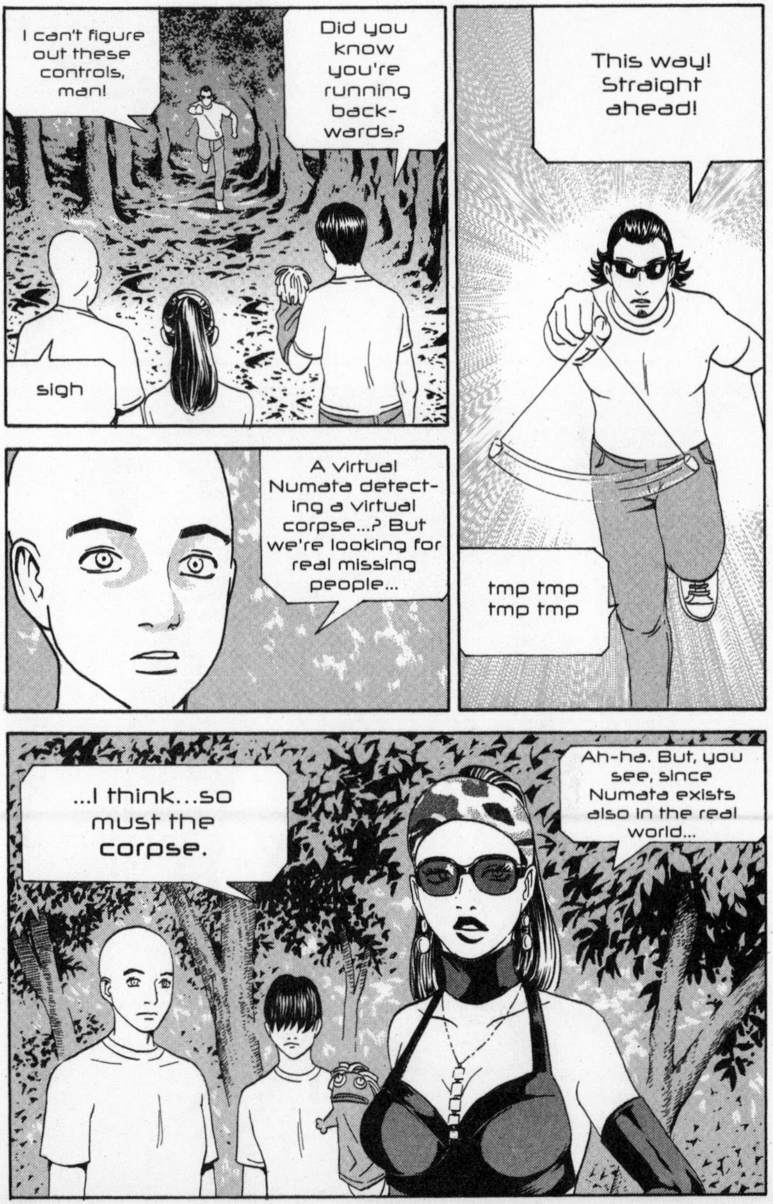
This way! Straight ahead!
tmp tmp tmp tmp
Did you know you're running back-wards?
I can't figure out these controls, man!
sigh
A virtual Numata detect-ing a virtual corpse...? But we're looking for real missing people...
Ah-ha. But, you see, since Numata exists also in the real world...
...I think...so must the corpse.

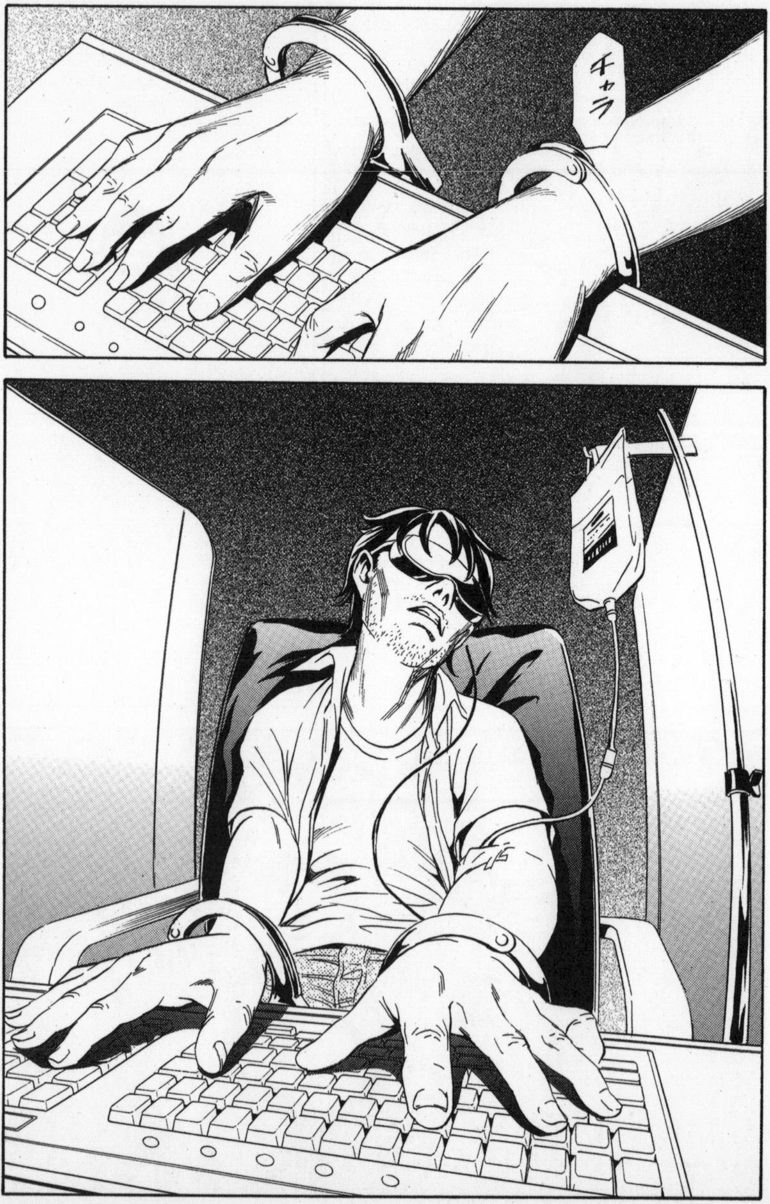
チャラ

2nd delivery: arienu republic—the end

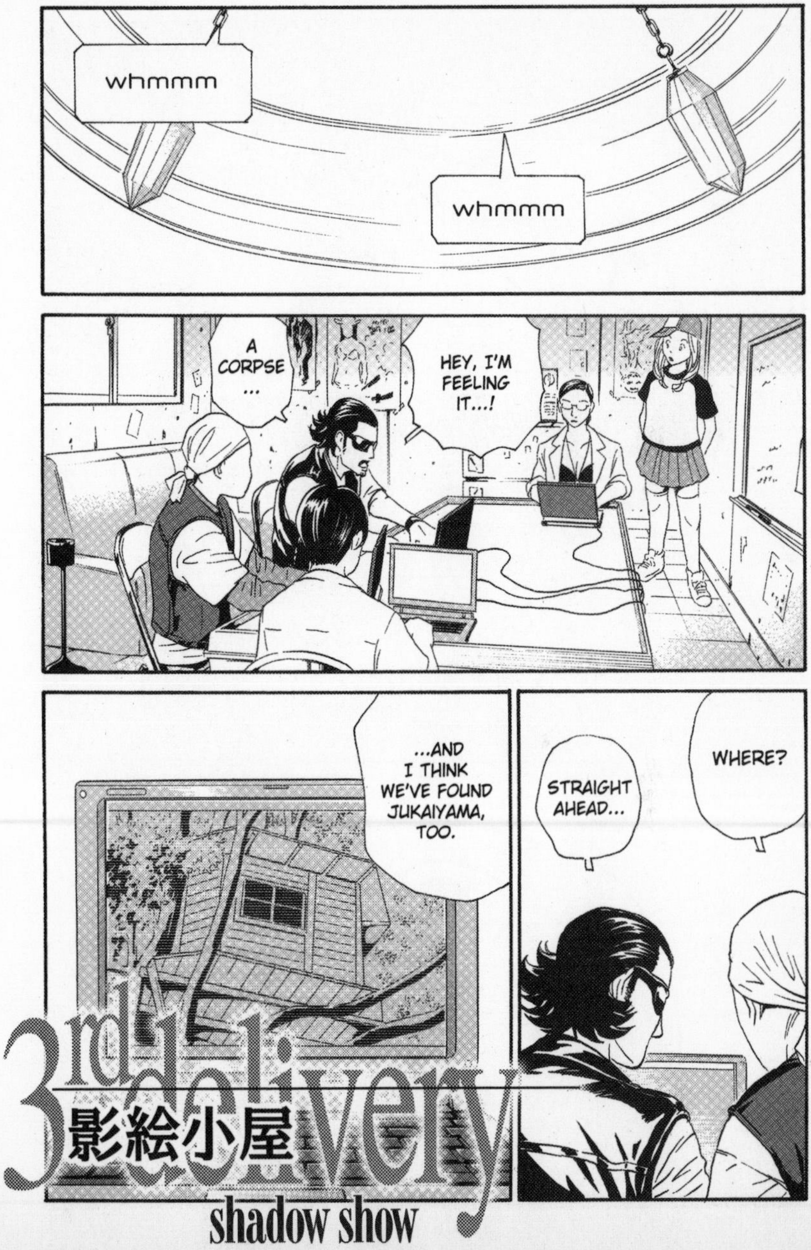
whmmm
whmmm
HEY, I'M FEELING IT...!
A CORPSE ...
WHERE?
STRAIGHT AHEAD...
...AND I THINK WE'VE FOUND JUKAIYAMA, TOO.

3rd delivery 影絵小屋

shadow show

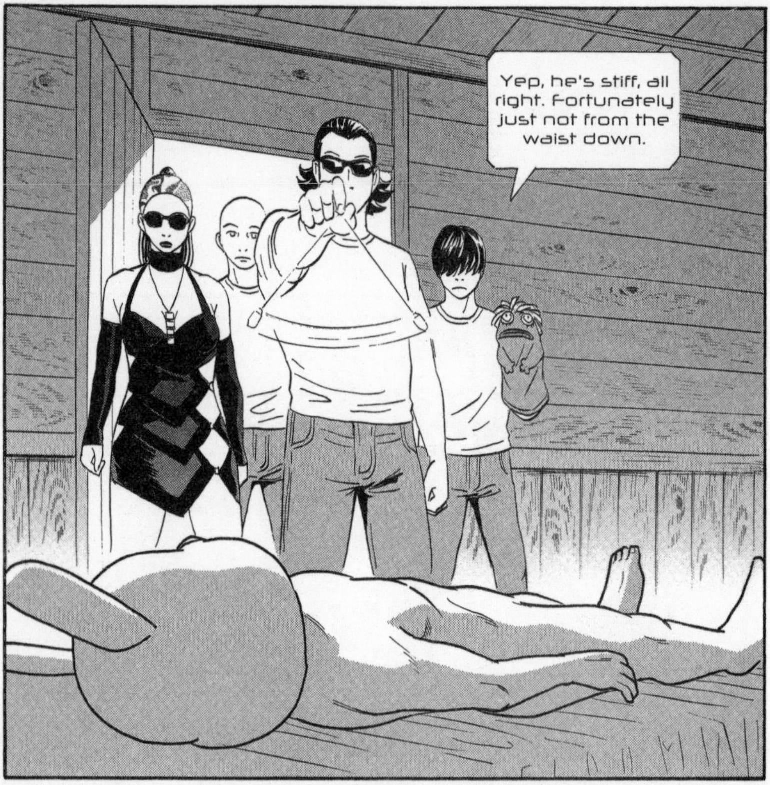
Yep, he's stiff, all right. Fortunately just not from the waist down.

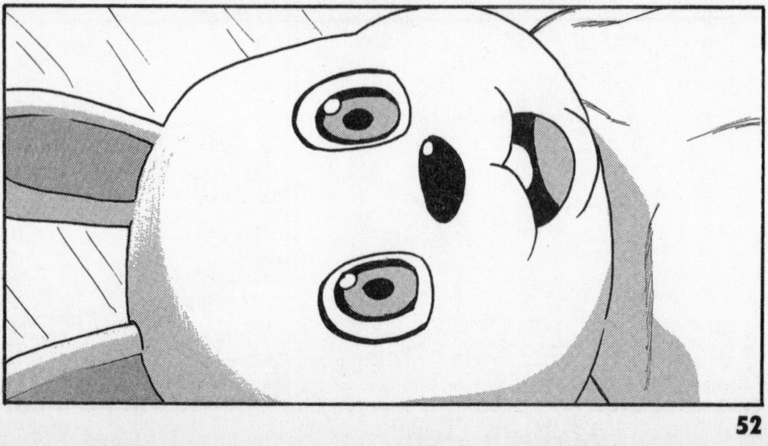

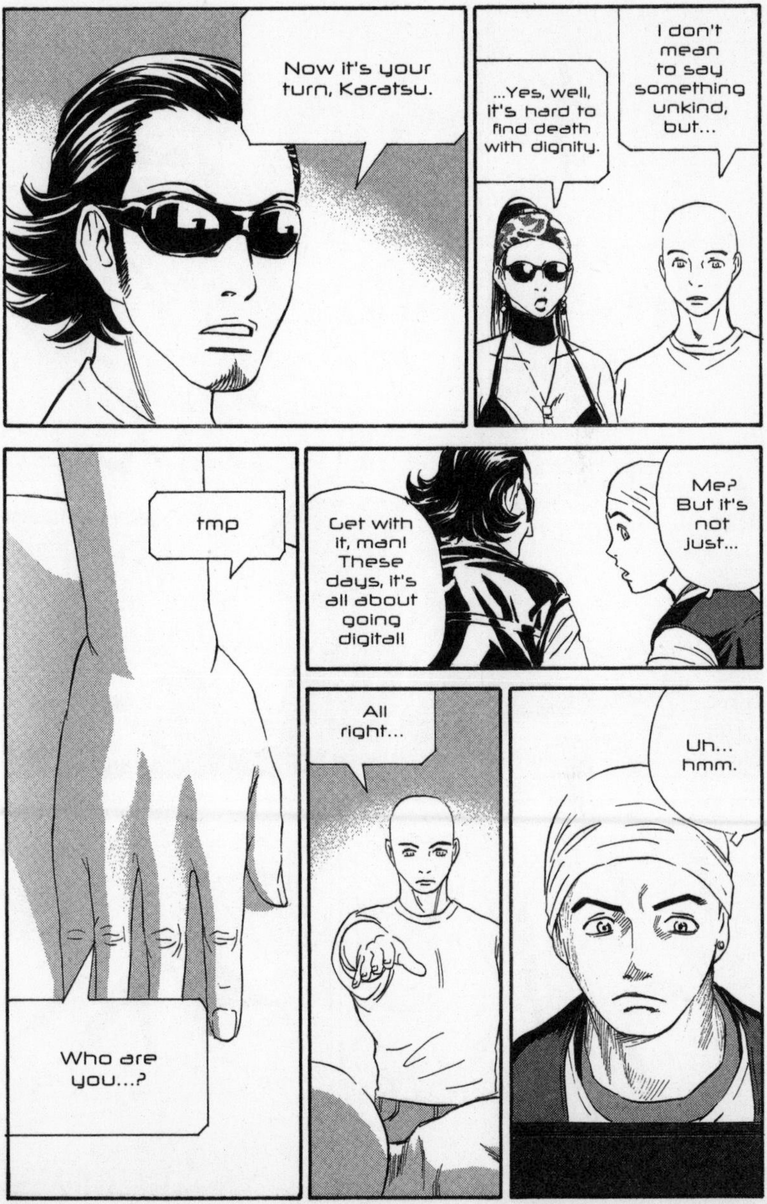
I don't mean to say something unkind, but...
...Yes, well, it's hard to find death with dignity.
Now it's your turn, Karatsu.
Me? But it's not just...
Get with it, man! These days, it's all about going digital!
Uh... hmm.
All right...
tmp
Who are you...?

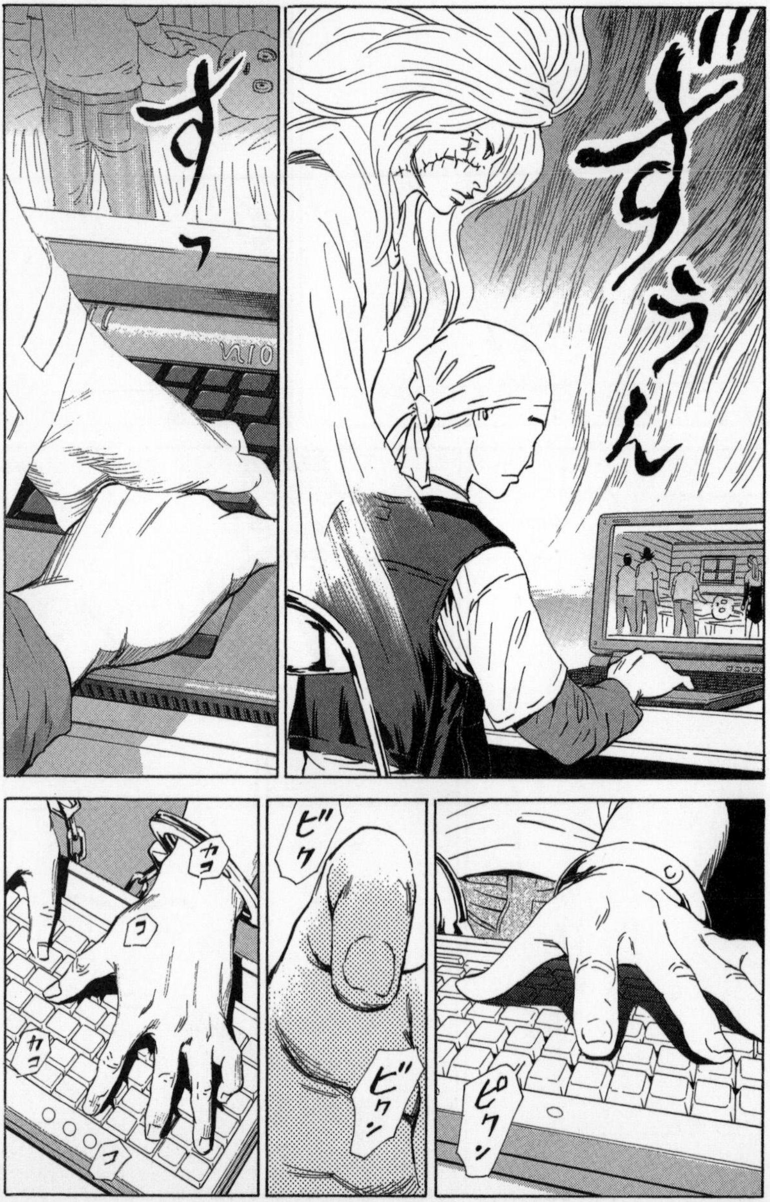
ずずうん
すぅ
ピクン
ビク
ビクン
カコ
コ
カコ
コ

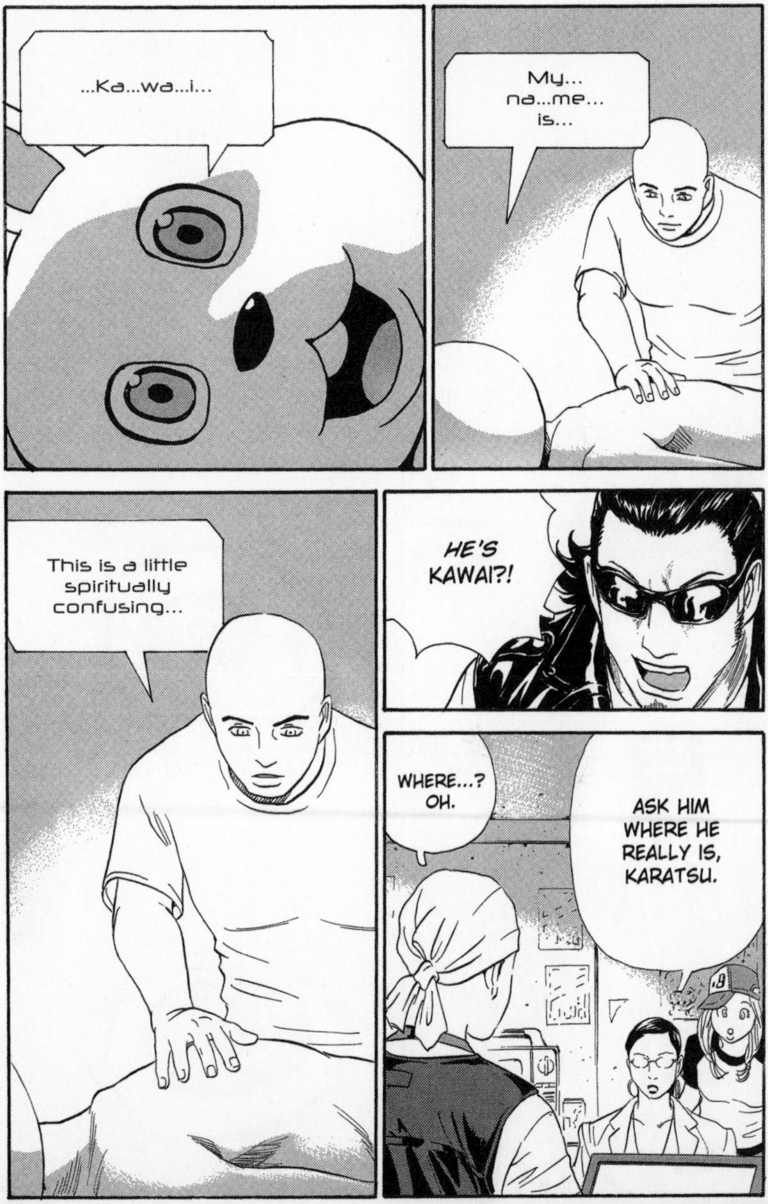
My... na...me... is...
...Ka...wa...i...
HE'S KAWAI?!
ASK HIM WHERE HE REALLY IS, KARATSU.
WHERE...? OH.
This is a little spiritually confusing...

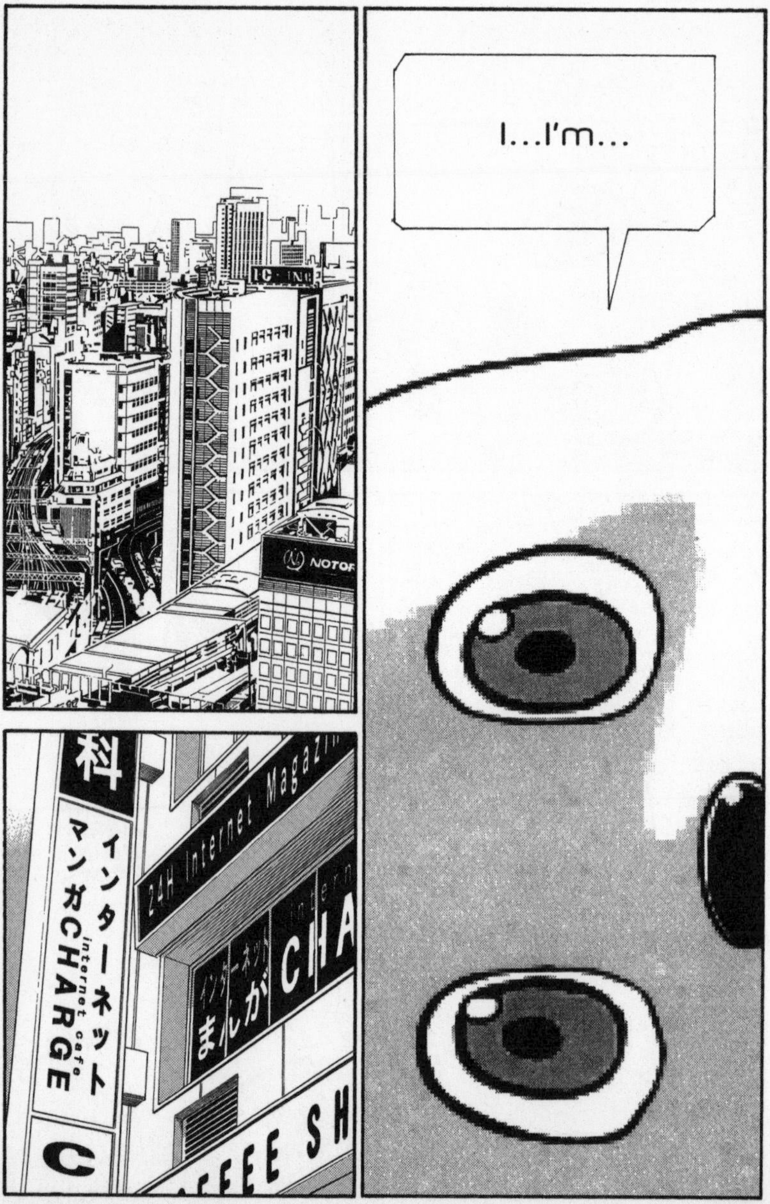
I...I'm...
IC INC
NOTOR
科
インターネット
マンガ
internet cafe
CHARGE
24H Internet Magazi
インターネット
まんが
CHA
COFFEE SH

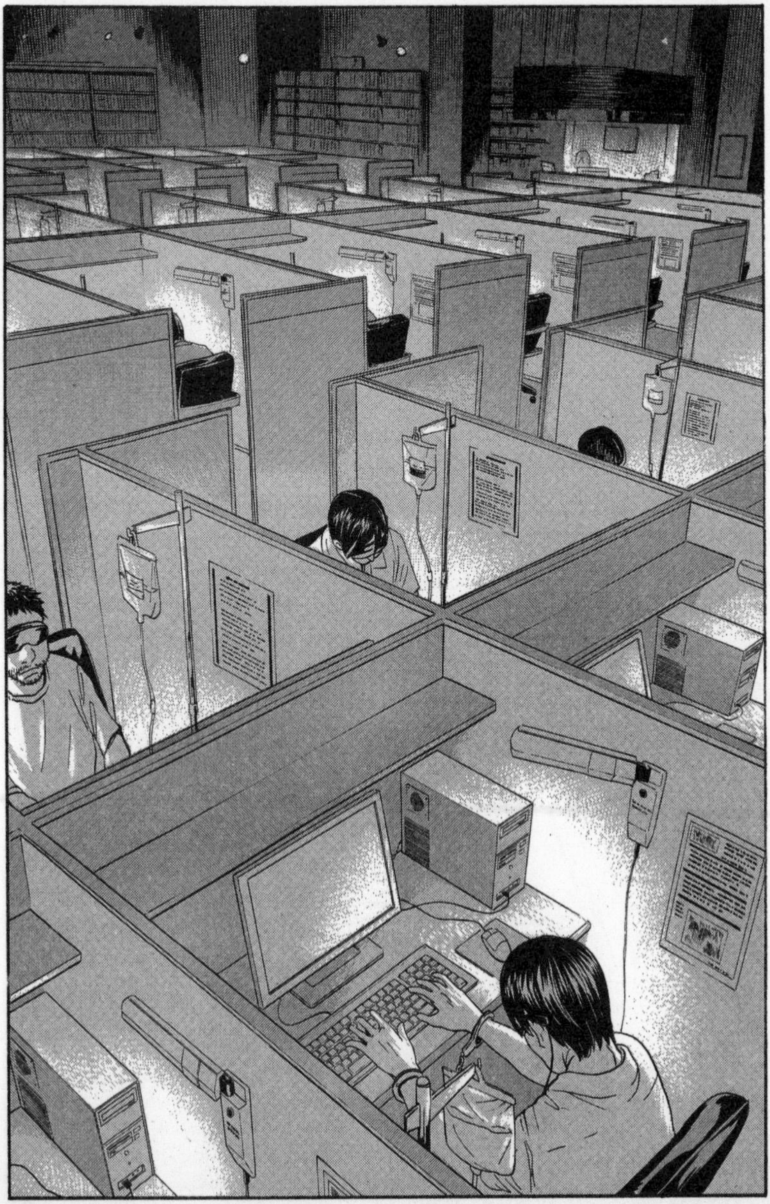

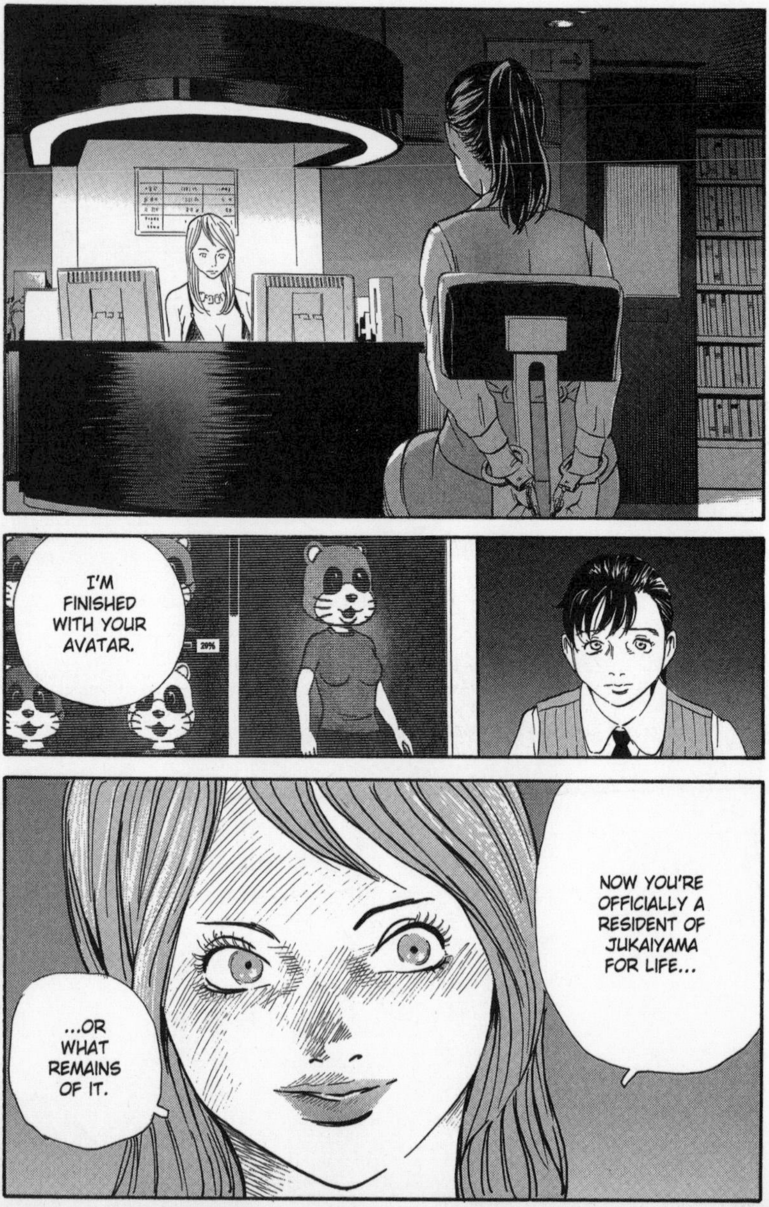
I'M FINISHED WITH YOUR AVATAR.
29%
NOW YOU'RE OFFICIALLY A RESIDENT OF JUKAIYAMA FOR LIFE...
...OR WHAT REMAINS OF IT.

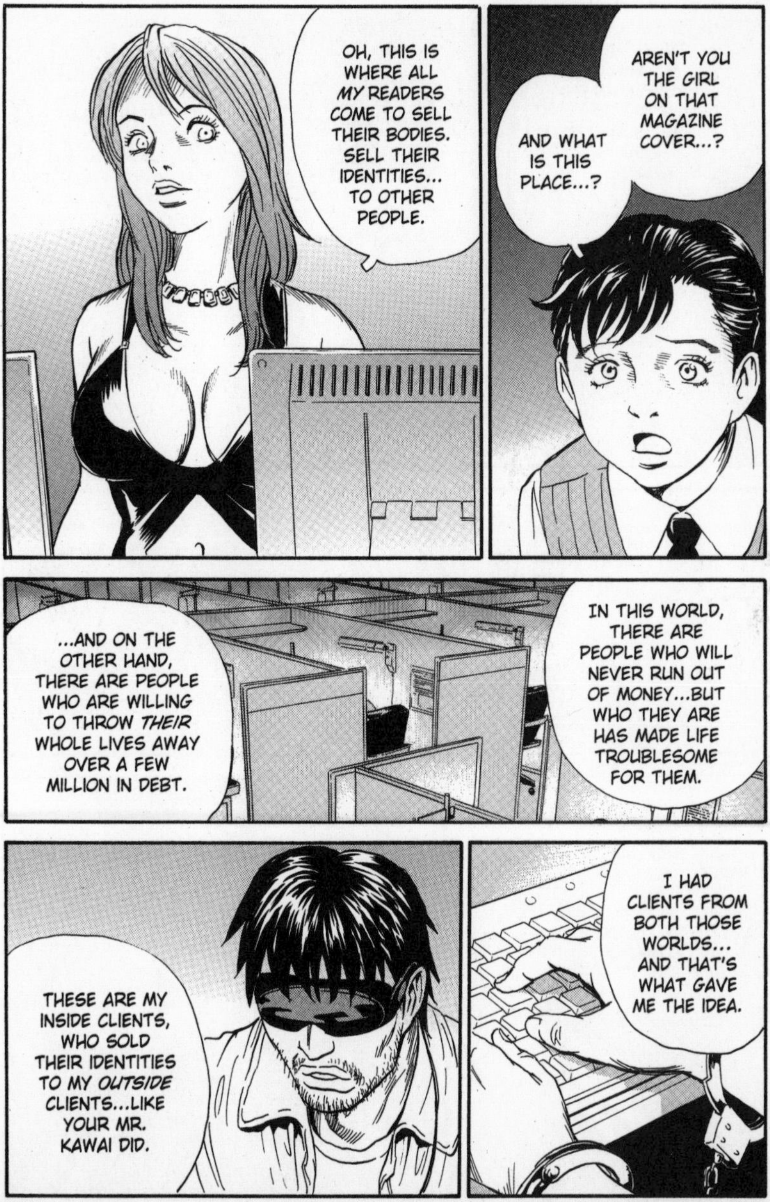
AREN'T YOU THE GIRL ON THAT MAGAZINE COVER...?
AND WHAT IS THIS PLACE...?
OH, THIS IS WHERE ALL *MY* READERS COME TO SELL THEIR BODIES. SELL THEIR IDENTITIES... TO OTHER PEOPLE.
IN THIS WORLD, THERE ARE PEOPLE WHO WILL NEVER RUN OUT OF MONEY...BUT WHO THEY ARE HAS MADE LIFE TROUBLESOME FOR THEM.
...AND ON THE OTHER HAND, THERE ARE PEOPLE WHO ARE WILLING TO THROW *THEIR* WHOLE LIVES AWAY OVER A FEW MILLION IN DEBT.
I HAD CLIENTS FROM BOTH THOSE WORLDS... AND THAT'S WHAT GAVE ME THE IDEA.
THESE ARE MY INSIDE CLIENTS, WHO SOLD THEIR IDENTITIES TO MY *OUTSIDE* CLIENTS...LIKE YOUR MR. KAWAI DID.

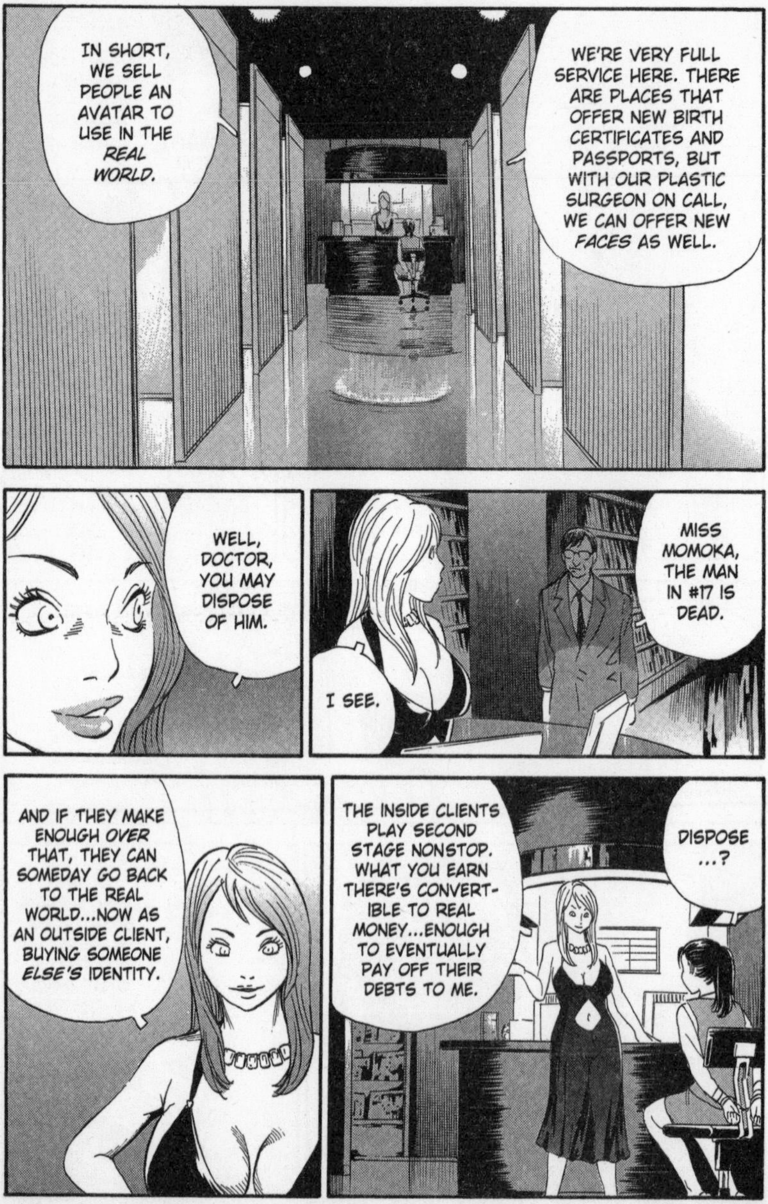
WE'RE VERY FULL SERVICE HERE. THERE ARE PLACES THAT OFFER NEW BIRTH CERTIFICATES AND PASSPORTS, BUT WITH OUR PLASTIC SURGEON ON CALL, WE CAN OFFER NEW *FACES* AS WELL.
IN SHORT, WE SELL PEOPLE AN AVATAR TO USE IN THE *REAL WORLD.*
MISS MOMOKA, THE MAN IN #17 IS DEAD.
I SEE.
WELL, DOCTOR, YOU MAY DISPOSE OF HIM.
DISPOSE ...?
THE INSIDE CLIENTS PLAY SECOND STAGE NONSTOP. WHAT YOU EARN THERE'S CONVERTIBLE TO REAL MONEY...ENOUGH TO EVENTUALLY PAY OFF THEIR DEBTS TO ME.
AND IF THEY MAKE ENOUGH *OVER* THAT, THEY CAN SOMEDAY GO BACK TO THE REAL WORLD...NOW AS AN OUTSIDE CLIENT, BUYING SOMEONE *ELSE'S* IDENTITY.

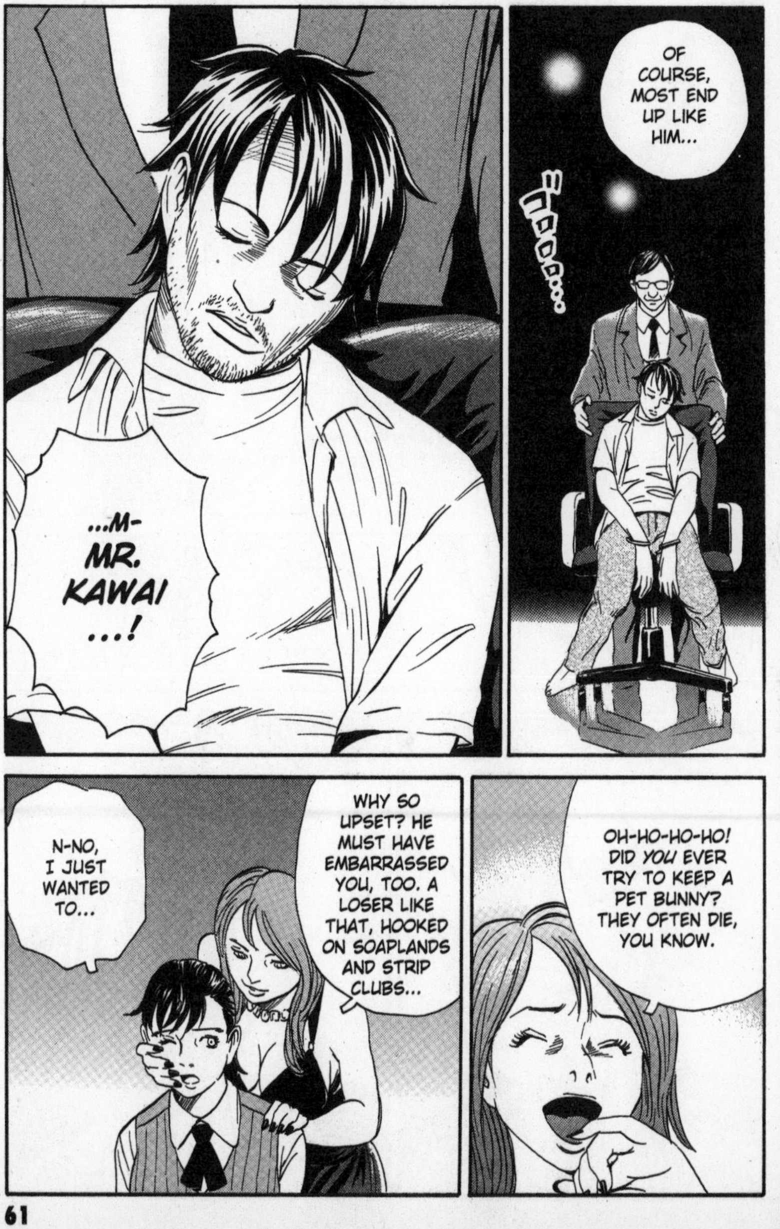
OF COURSE, MOST END UP LIKE HIM...
...M- MR. KAWAI ...!
OH-HO-HO-HO! DID *YOU* EVER TRY TO KEEP A PET BUNNY? THEY OFTEN DIE, YOU KNOW.
WHY SO UPSET? HE MUST HAVE EMBARRASSED YOU, TOO. A LOSER LIKE THAT, HOOKED ON SOAPLANDS AND STRIP CLUBS...
N-NO, I JUST WANTED TO...

YES,
MA'AM.

...NOW, ORDINARILY, HE WOULD DO THIS WITH A SCALPEL, BUT YOU'LL GET THE GENERAL IDEA.

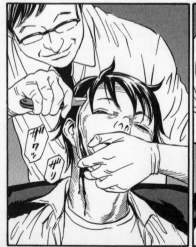

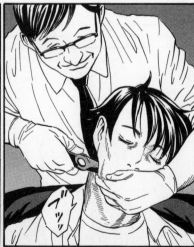

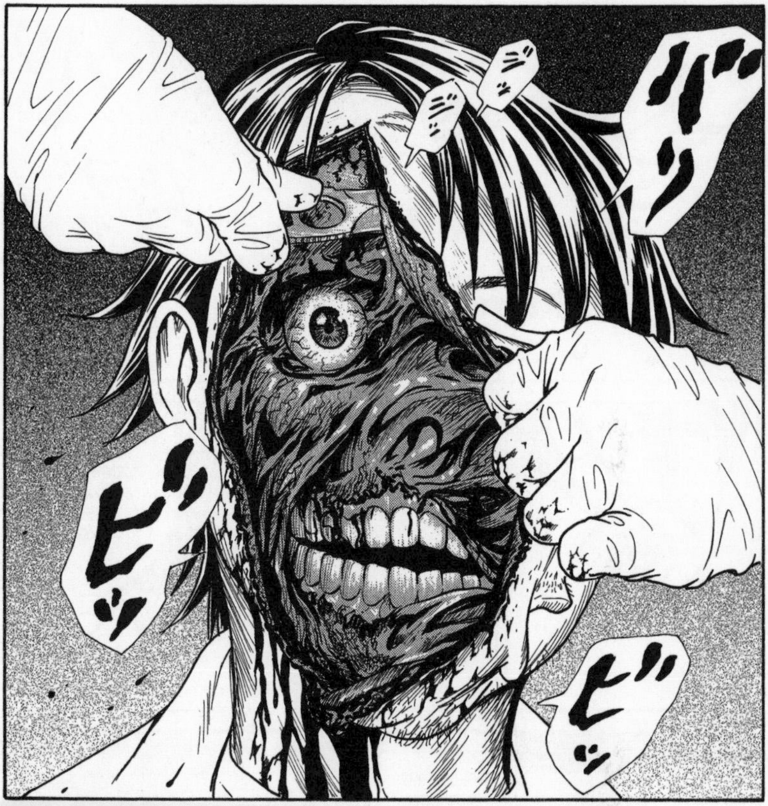
バリッ
ビッ
ビッ

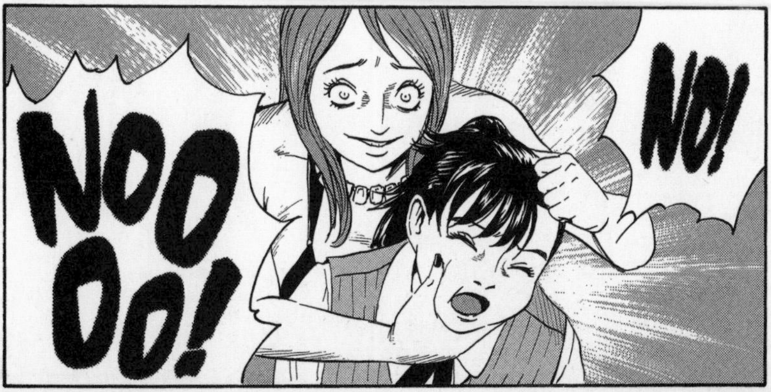
NO!
NOOOO!

THEY ALL COME OFF SO EASILY THESE DAYS...

...DON'T THEY ...?

WELL, TIME FOR YOU TO GET TO WORK.

I HAVE PROSPECTIVE WOMEN CLIENTS, TOO. THERE'S A WAITING LIST FOR *FEMALE* REAL AVATARS, YOU KNOW...

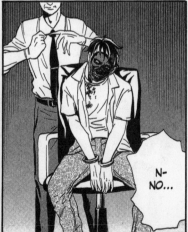

N-NO...

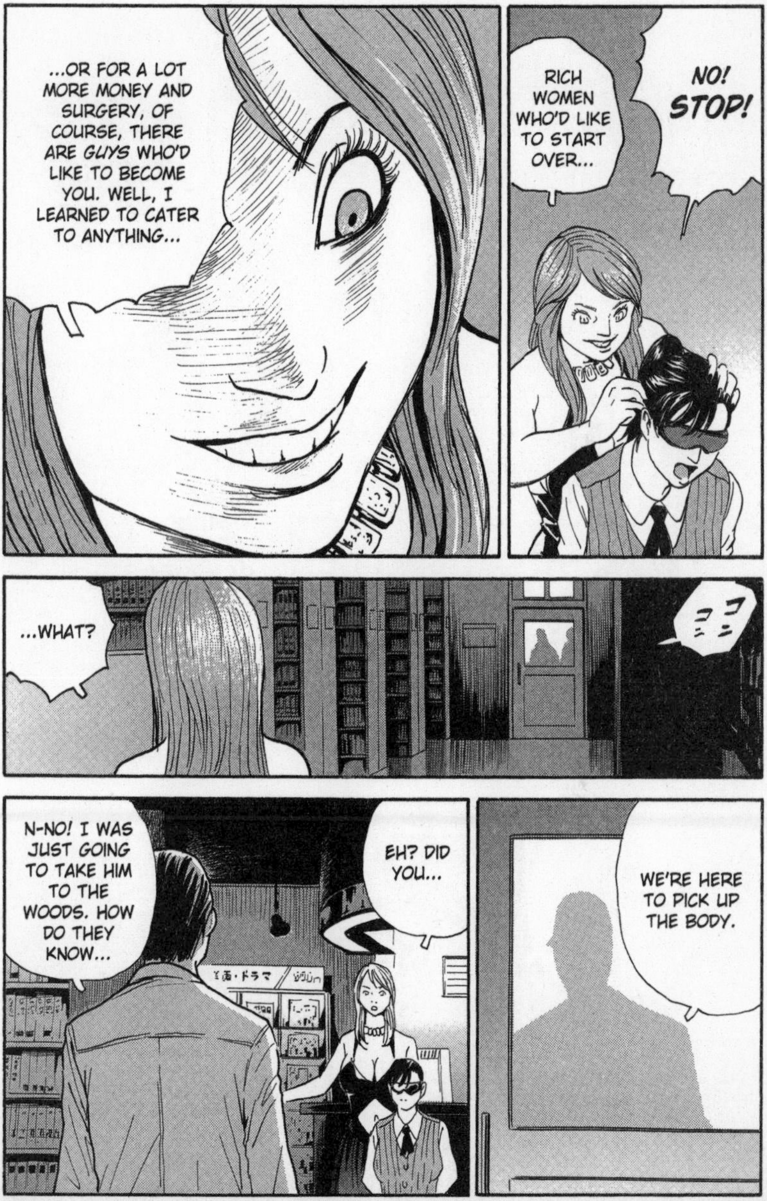
NO! STOP!
RICH WOMEN WHO'D LIKE TO START OVER...
...OR FOR A LOT MORE MONEY AND SURGERY, OF COURSE, THERE ARE *GUYS* WHO'D LIKE TO BECOME YOU. WELL, I LEARNED TO CATER TO ANYTHING...
コンコン
...WHAT?
WE'RE HERE TO PICK UP THE BODY.
EH? DID YOU...
N-NO! I WAS JUST GOING TO TAKE HIM TO THE WOODS. HOW DO THEY KNOW...

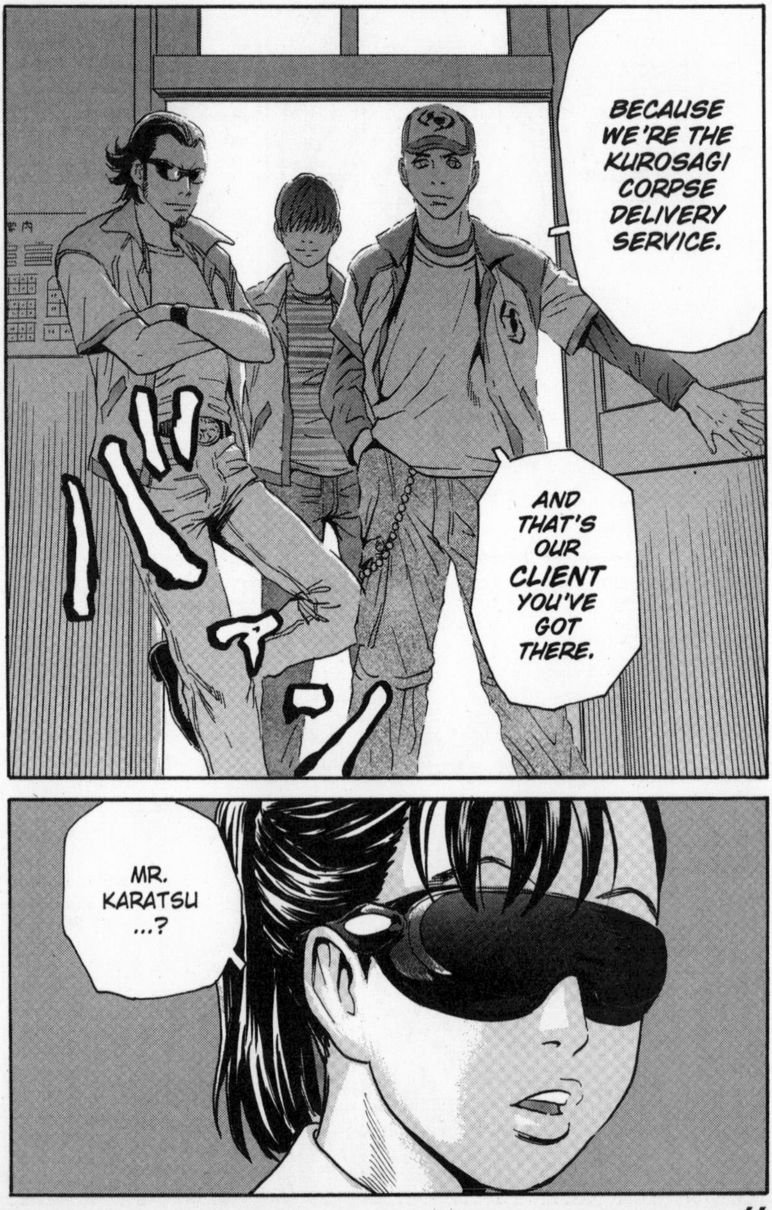
BECAUSE WE'RE THE KUROSAGI CORPSE DELIVERY SERVICE.
AND THAT'S OUR CLIENT YOU'VE GOT THERE.
MR. KARATSU ...?

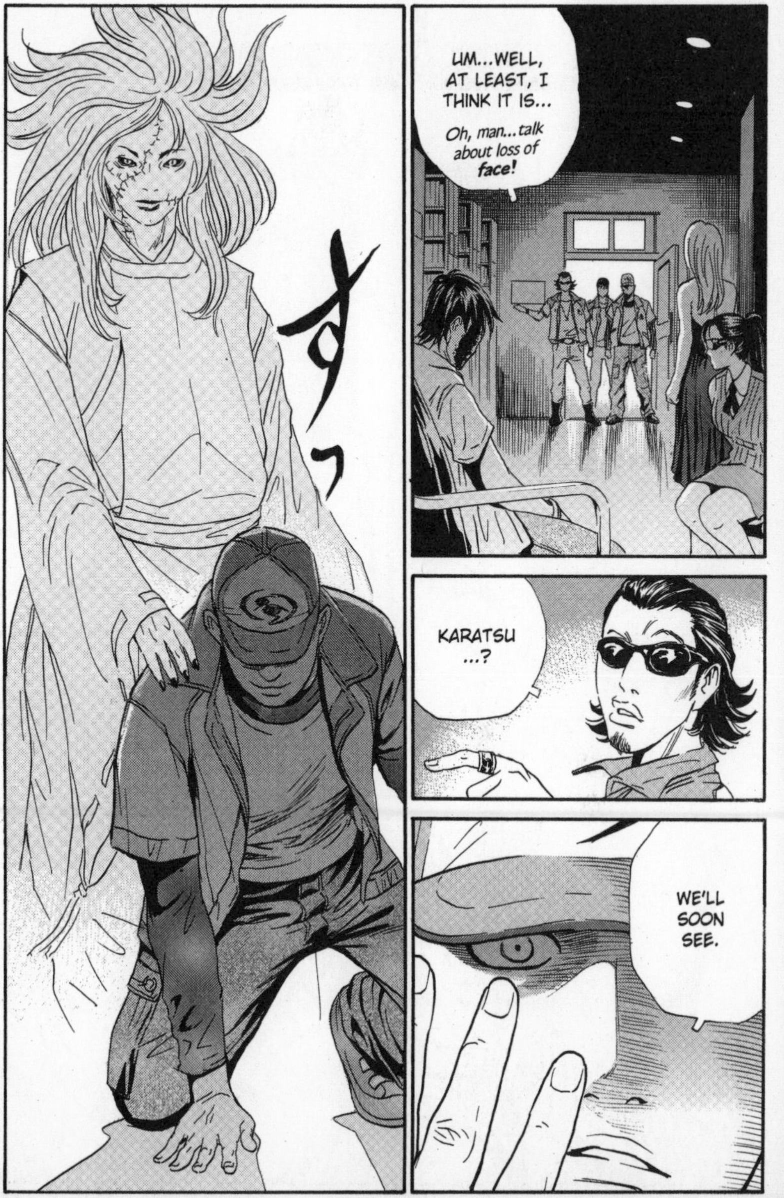
UM...WELL, AT LEAST, I THINK IT IS...
Oh, man...talk about loss of face!
KARATSU ...?
WE'LL SOON SEE.
すっ

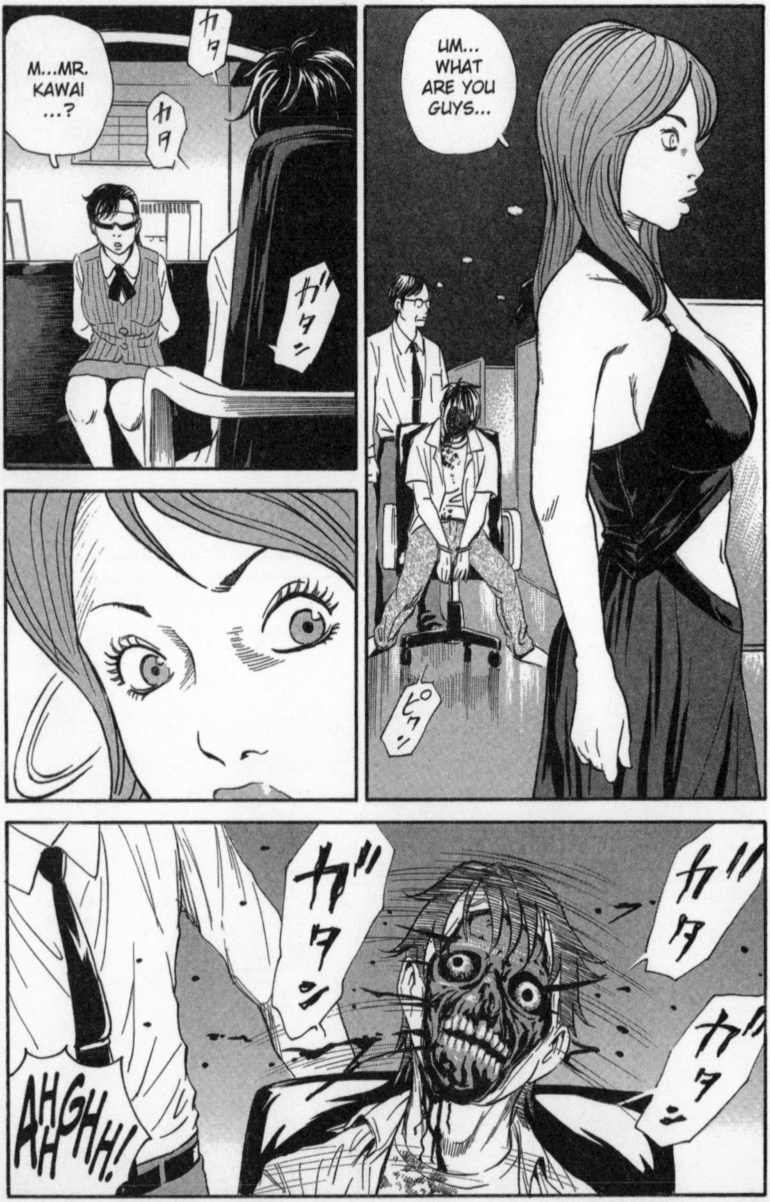
UM... WHAT ARE YOU GUYS...
ピクン
M...MR. KAWAI ...?
カタ
カタ
ガタン
ガタ
ガタン
ガタン
AHGHHH!

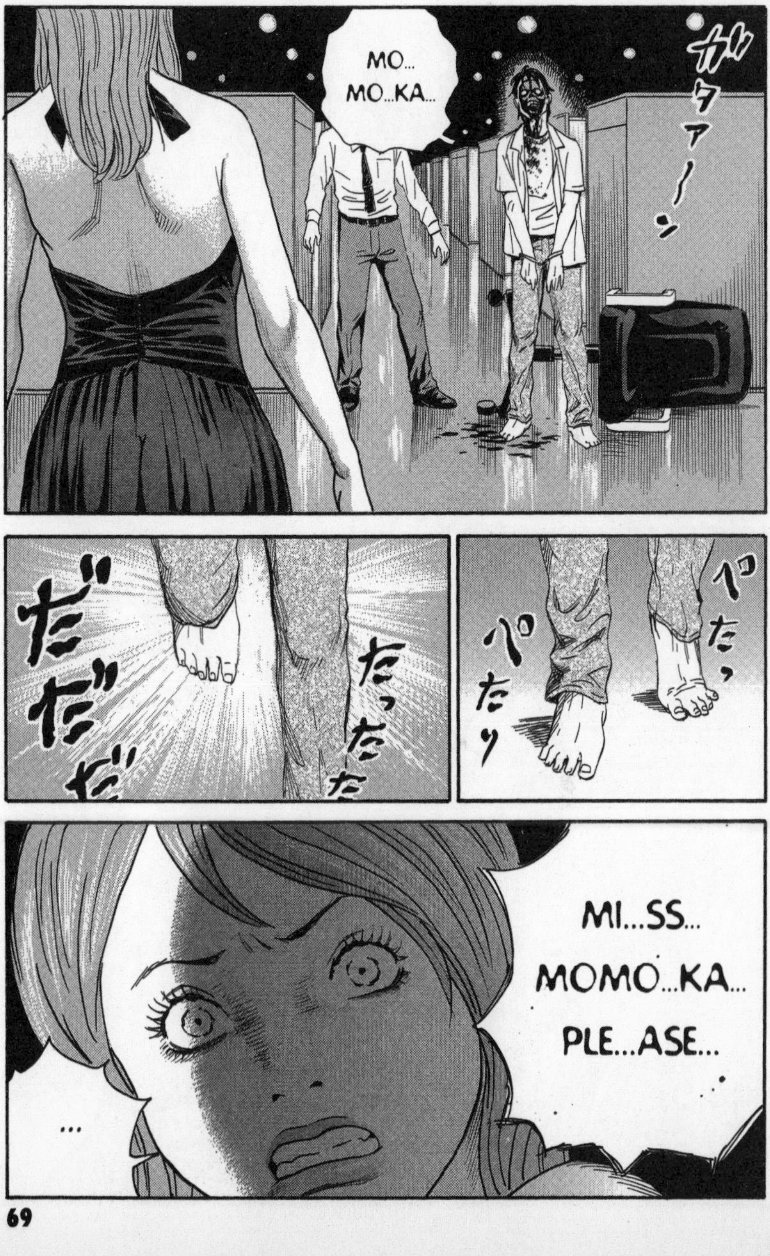
ガタァーーン
MO... MO...KA...
ぺたっ
ぺたり
だだ
たった
MI...SS... MOMO...KA... PLE...ASE...
...

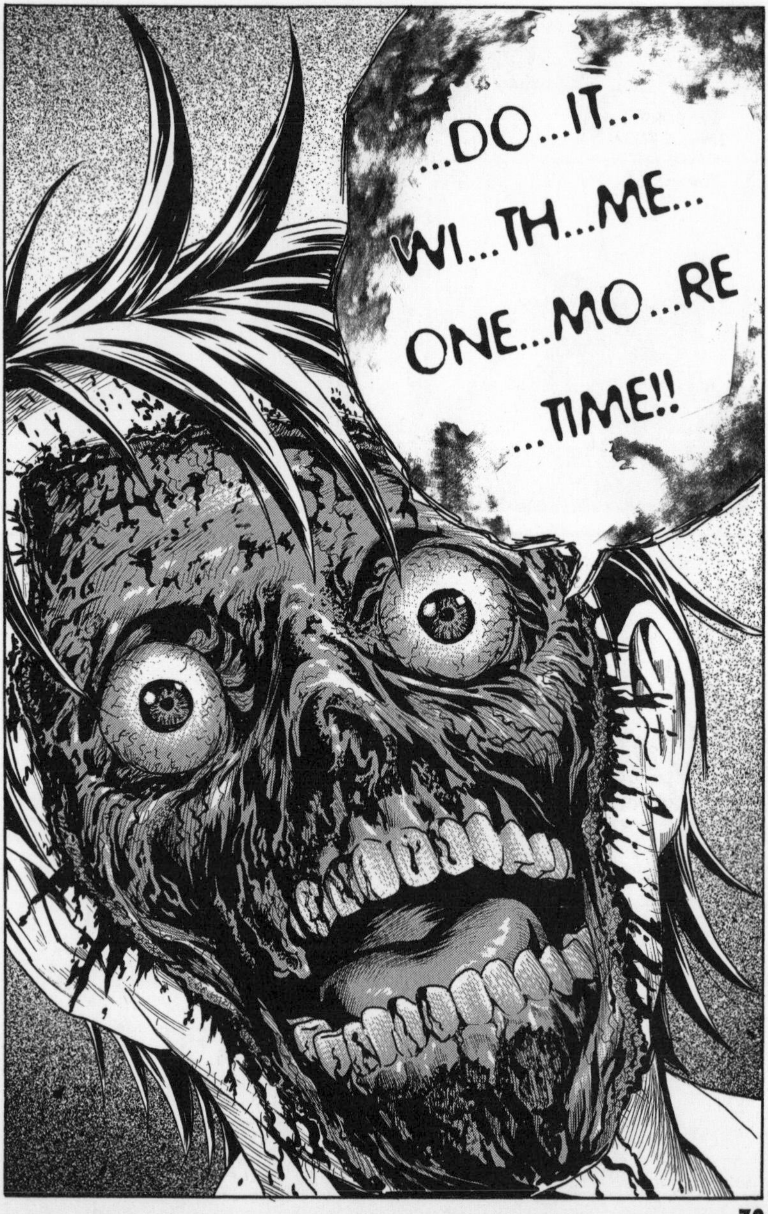
...DO...IT...
WI...TH...ME...
ONE...MO...RE
...TIME!!

WE WERE TOO LATE... I'M SORRY, YUKA...I KNOW HE WAS MORE THAN JUST A CLIENT TO YOU.

YAAAA!!

THEN...WHY DID YOU TRY SO HARD TO FIND HIM...?

HUH? NO, HE WASN'T. WHY DOES EVERYONE KEEP THINKING THAT? IT'S NOT LIKE I WANTED TO GO OUT WITH HIM.

I HAD MISCALCULATED THE INTEREST, YOU SEE. HE WAS, AS OF TODAY, STILL 13,542 YEN SHORT.

And I couldn't take it from an impostor...

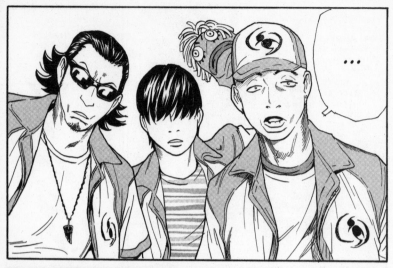

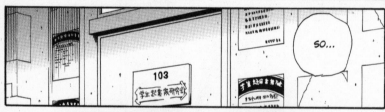

...
SO...
103
...YOU GAVE HER THE MONEY...?
...NOT EXACTLY *mack men,* ARE YOU?
SHUT UP! KARMA AIN'T SHIT COMPARED TO *OUTSTANDING DEBT!*

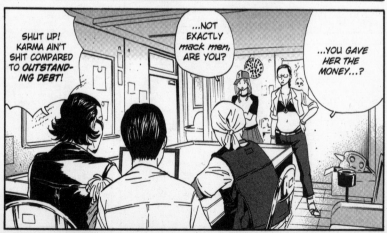

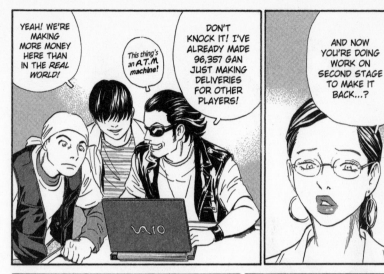

AND NOW YOU'RE DOING WORK ON SECOND STAGE TO MAKE IT BACK...?
DON'T KNOCK IT! I'VE ALREADY MADE 96,357 GAN JUST MAKING DELIVERIES FOR OTHER PLAYERS!
This thing's an A.T.M. machine!
YEAH! WE'RE MAKING MORE MONEY HERE THAN IN THE REAL WORLD!
BUT, like, GAN IS SECOND STAGE MONEY. WHAT'S THE EXCHANGE rate, SASAKI ...?
1,000 GAN TO THE YEN.
...oh.
LET'S NOT TELL THEM YET...

3rd delivery: shadow show—the end

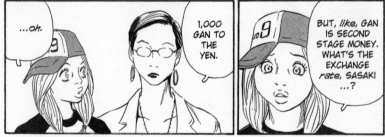

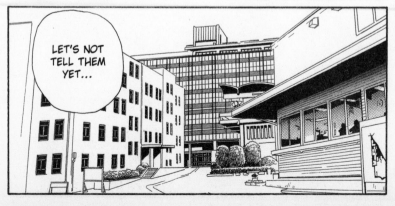

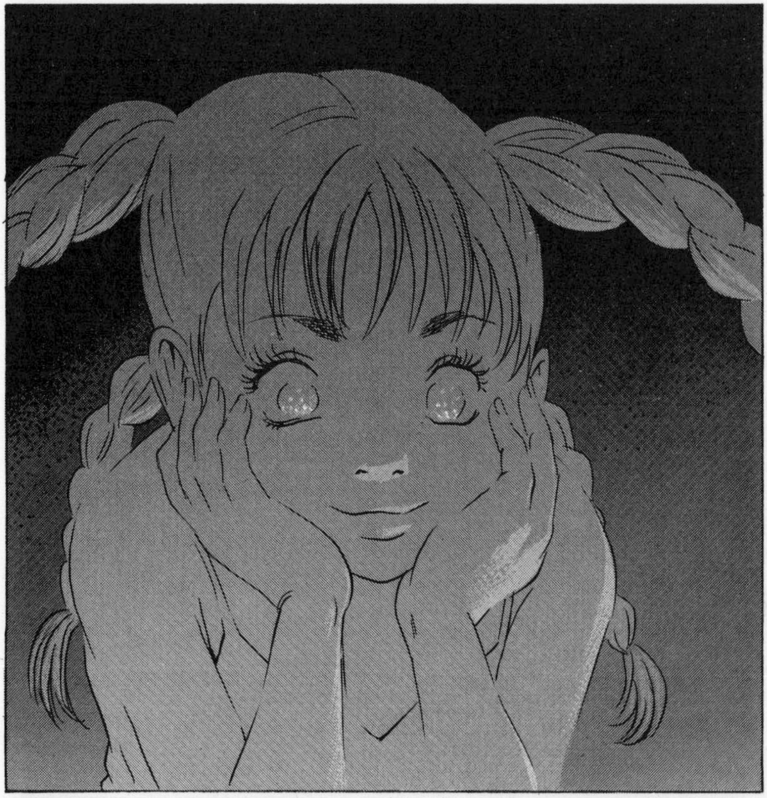

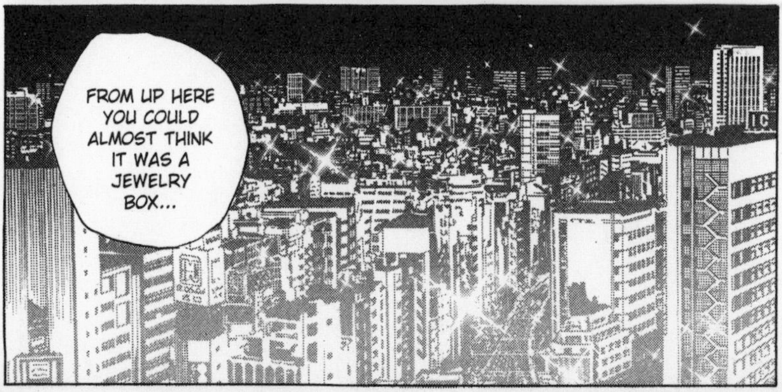
FROM UP HERE YOU COULD ALMOST THINK IT WAS A JEWELRY BOX...

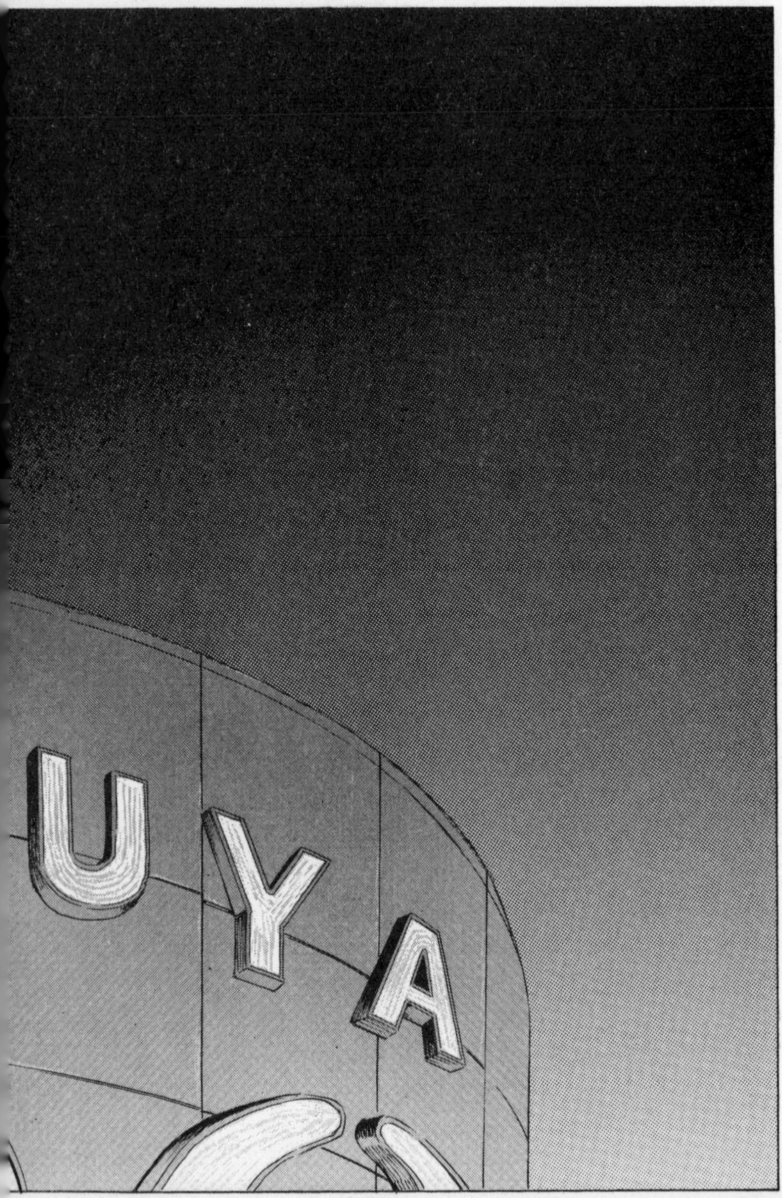
UYA

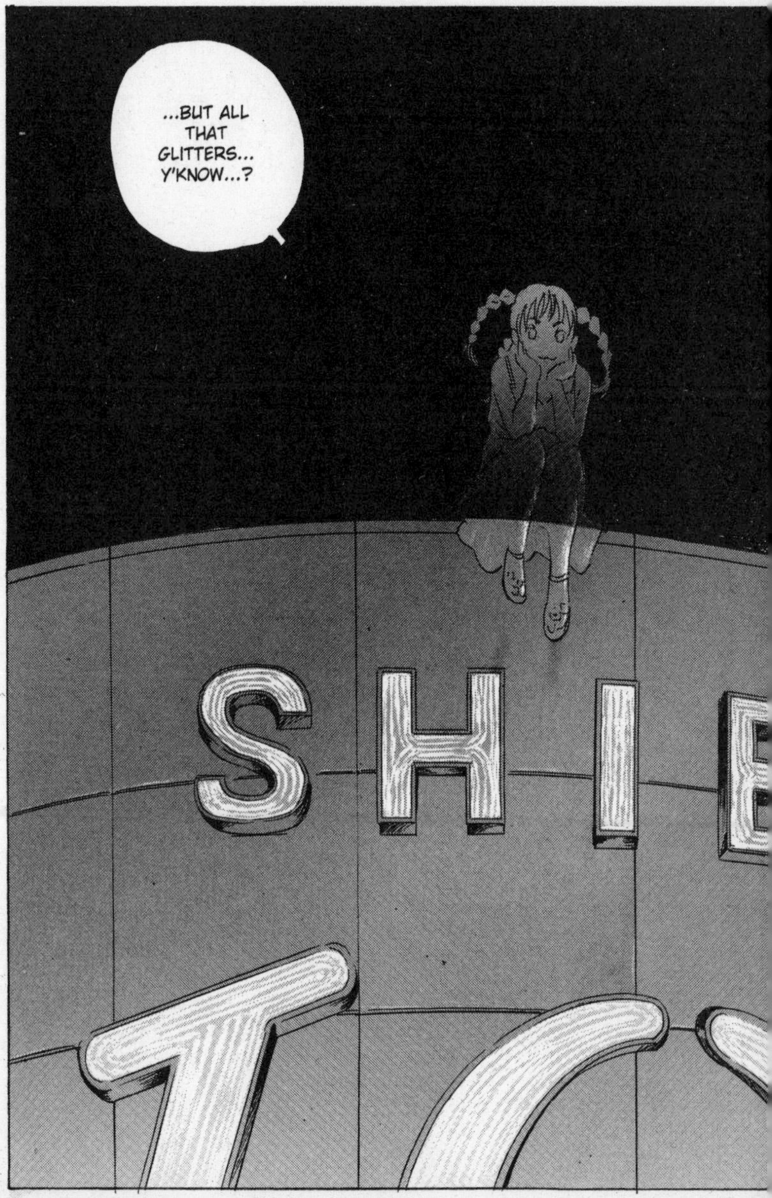
...BUT ALL THAT GLITTERS... Y'KNOW...?

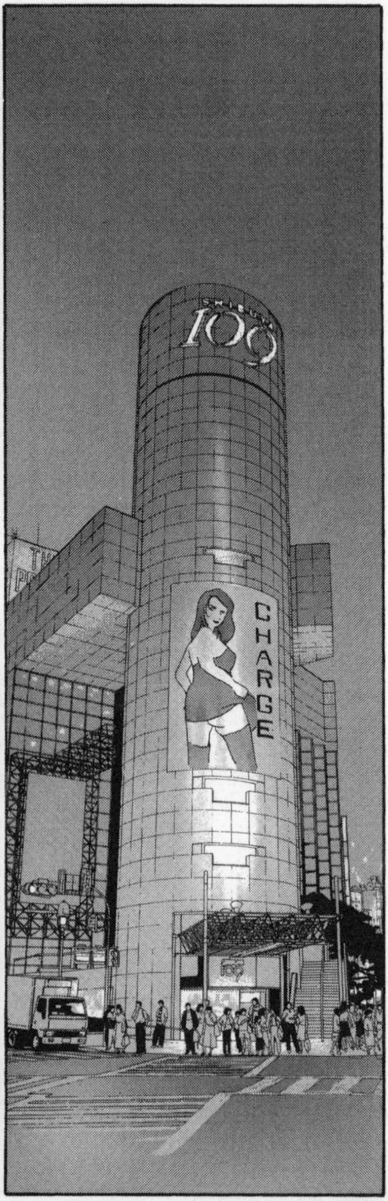
109
CHARGE

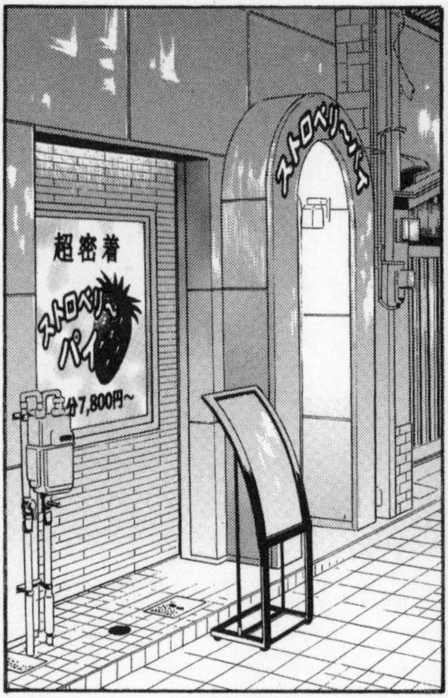
ストロベリーパイ
超密着
ストロベリー
パイ
分7,800円~

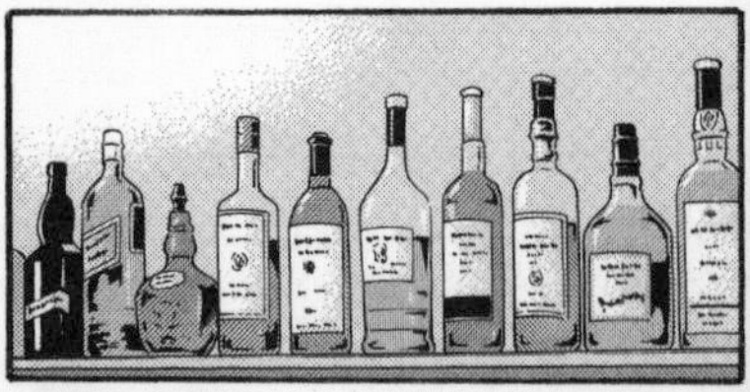

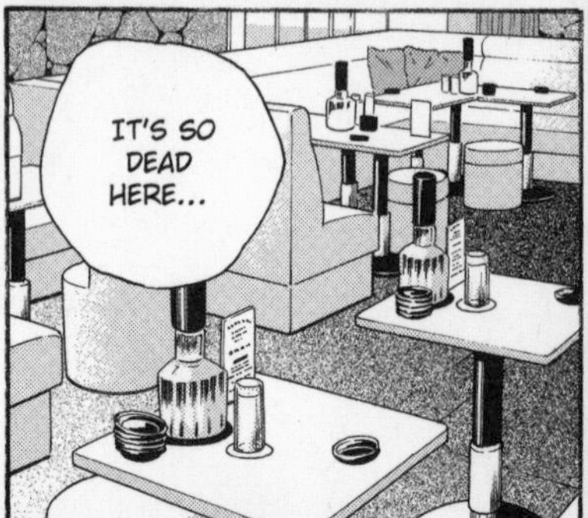
IT'S SO DEAD HERE...

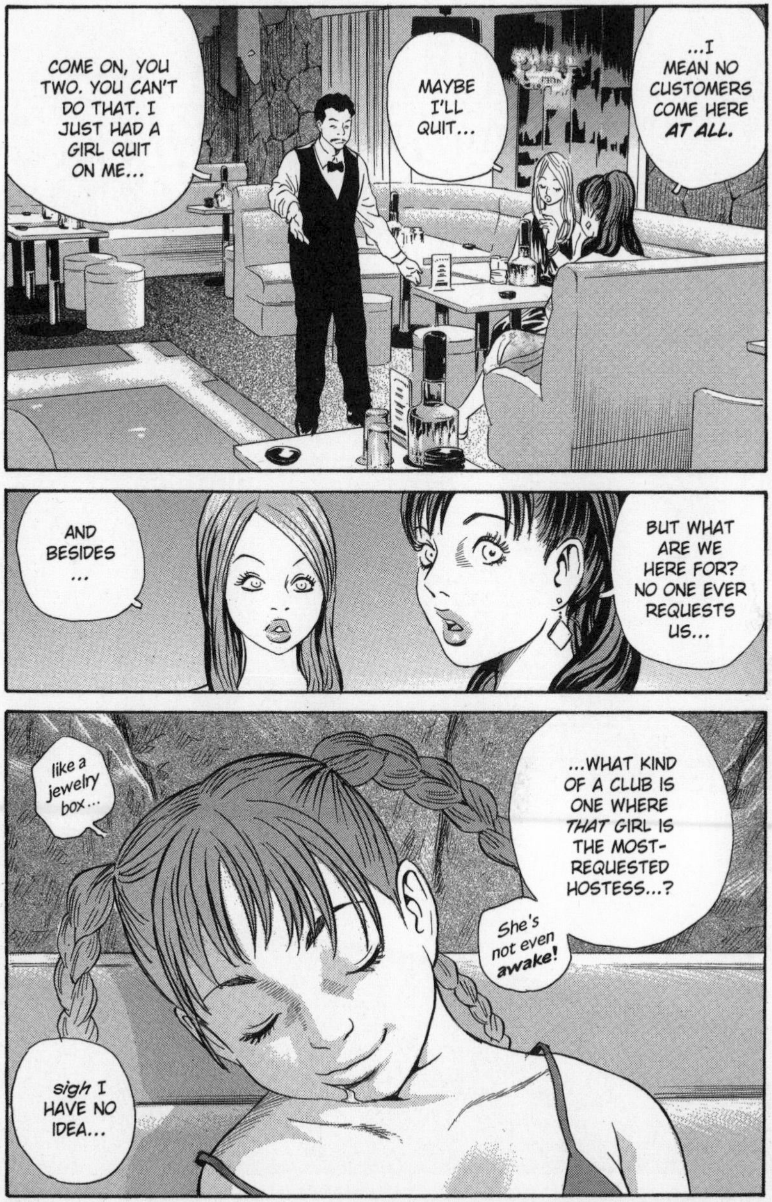
...I MEAN NO CUSTOMERS COME HERE **AT ALL.**
MAYBE I'LL QUIT...
COME ON, YOU TWO. YOU CAN'T DO THAT. I JUST HAD A GIRL QUIT ON ME...
BUT WHAT ARE WE HERE FOR? NO ONE EVER REQUESTS US...
AND BESIDES ...
...WHAT KIND OF A CLUB IS ONE WHERE *THAT* GIRL IS THE MOST-REQUESTED HOSTESS...?
like a jewelry box...
She's not even **awake!**
sigh I HAVE NO IDEA...

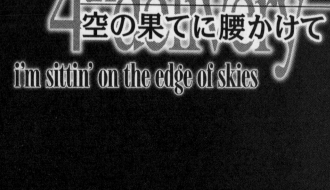

4th delivery

空の果てに腰かけて

i'm sittin' on the edge of skies

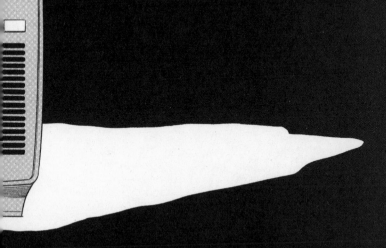

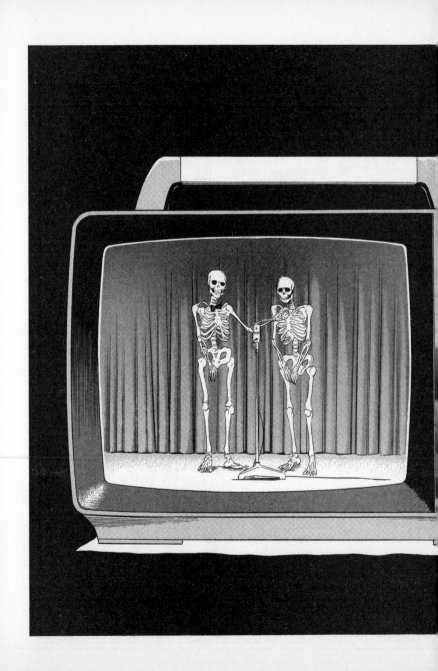

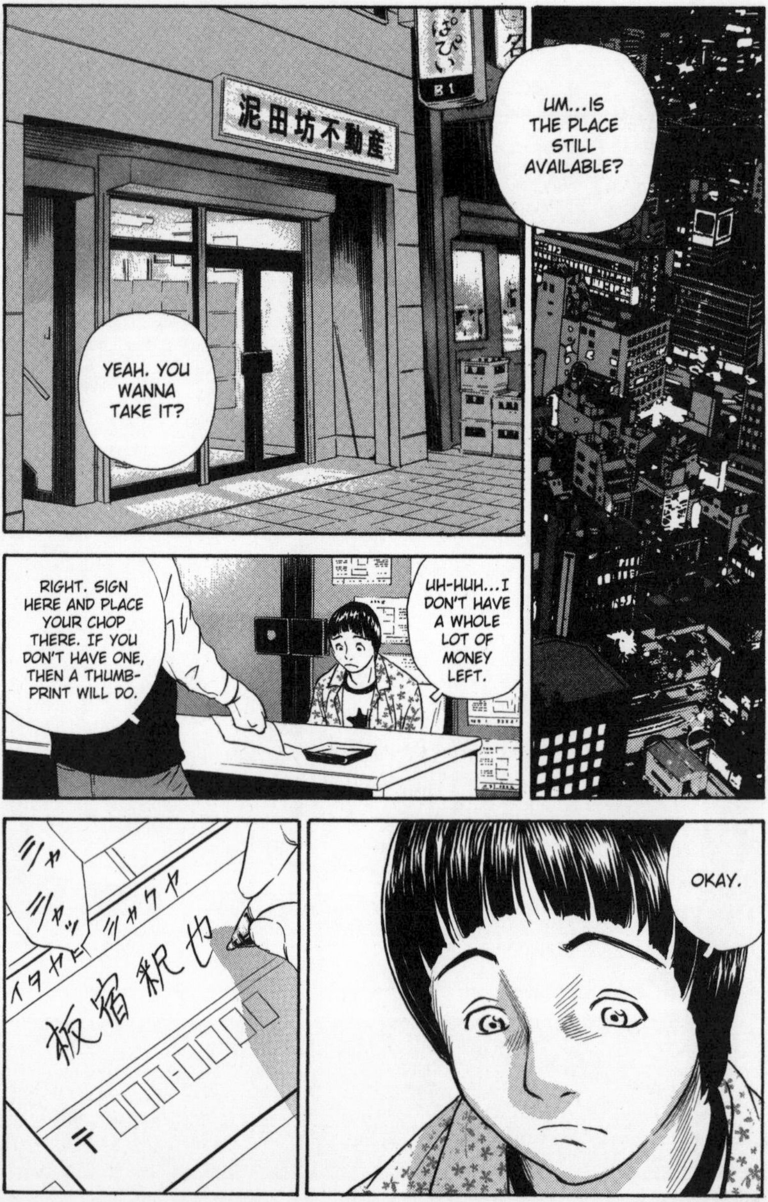
UM...IS THE PLACE STILL AVAILABLE?
泥田坊不動産
YEAH. YOU WANNA TAKE IT?
UH-HUH...I DON'T HAVE A WHOLE LOT OF MONEY LEFT.
RIGHT. SIGN HERE AND PLACE YOUR CHOP THERE. IF YOU DON'T HAVE ONE, THEN A THUMB-PRINT WILL DO.
OKAY.
シャ
シャッ
イタヤド シャクヤ
板宿釈也
〒

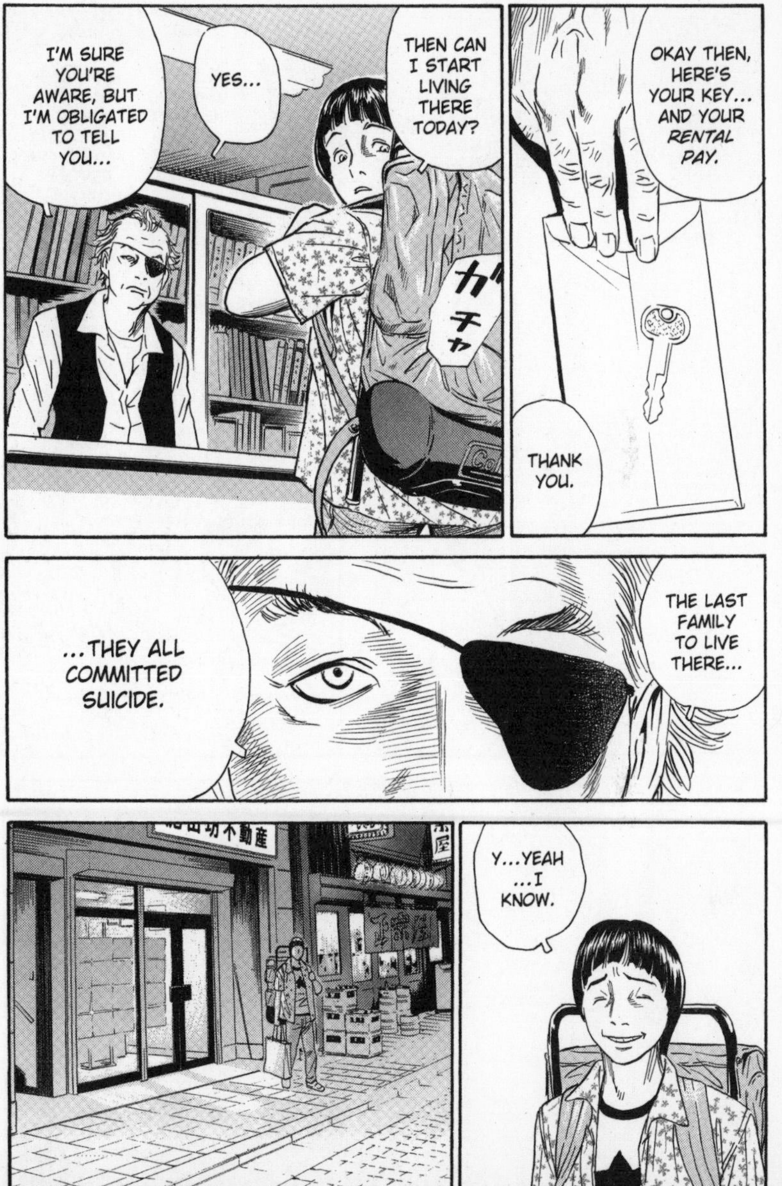
OKAY THEN, HERE'S YOUR KEY... AND YOUR *RENTAL* PAY.
THANK YOU.
THEN CAN I START LIVING THERE TODAY?
YES...
ガチャ
I'M SURE YOU'RE AWARE, BUT I'M OBLIGATED TO TELL YOU...
THE LAST FAMILY TO LIVE THERE...
...THEY ALL COMMITTED SUICIDE.
Y...YEAH ...I KNOW.

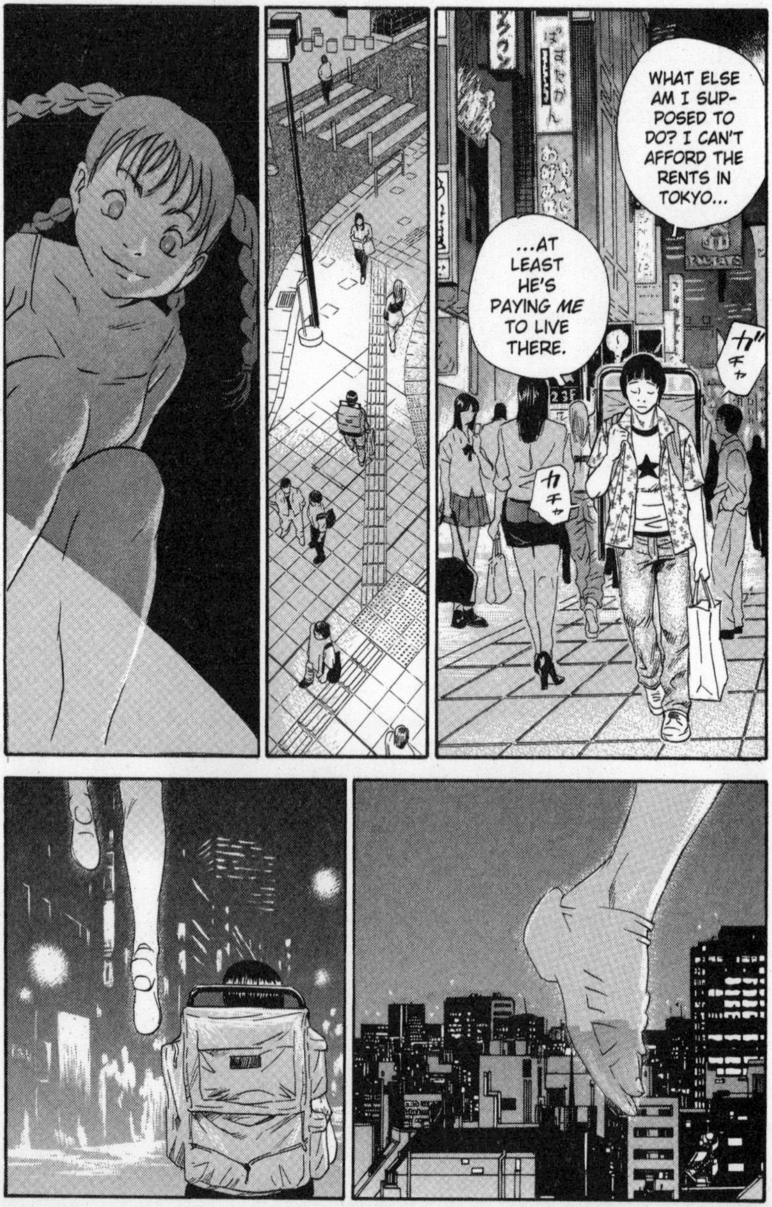
WHAT ELSE AM I SUP-POSED TO DO? I CAN'T AFFORD THE RENTS IN TOKYO...
...AT LEAST HE'S PAYING *ME* TO LIVE THERE.
ガチャ
カチャ

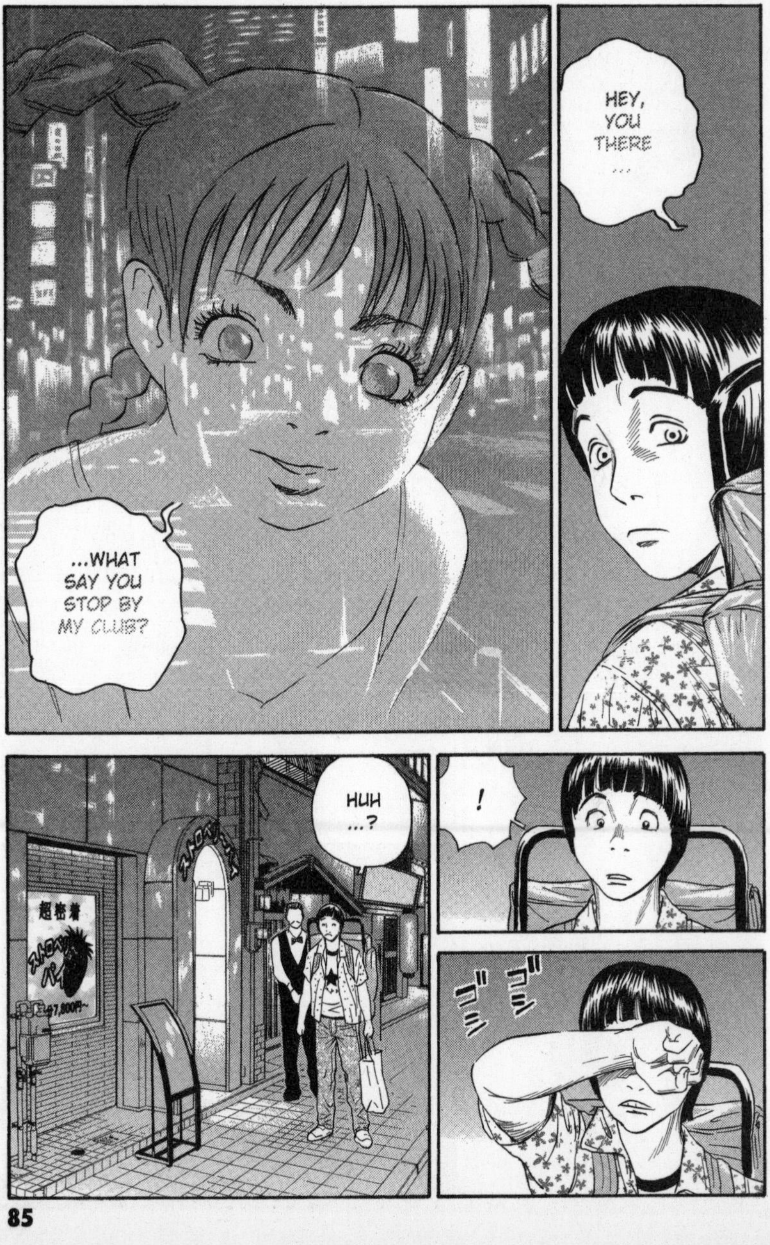
HEY, YOU THERE ...
...WHAT SAY YOU STOP BY MY CLUB?
!
ゴシゴシ
HUH ...?
超密着

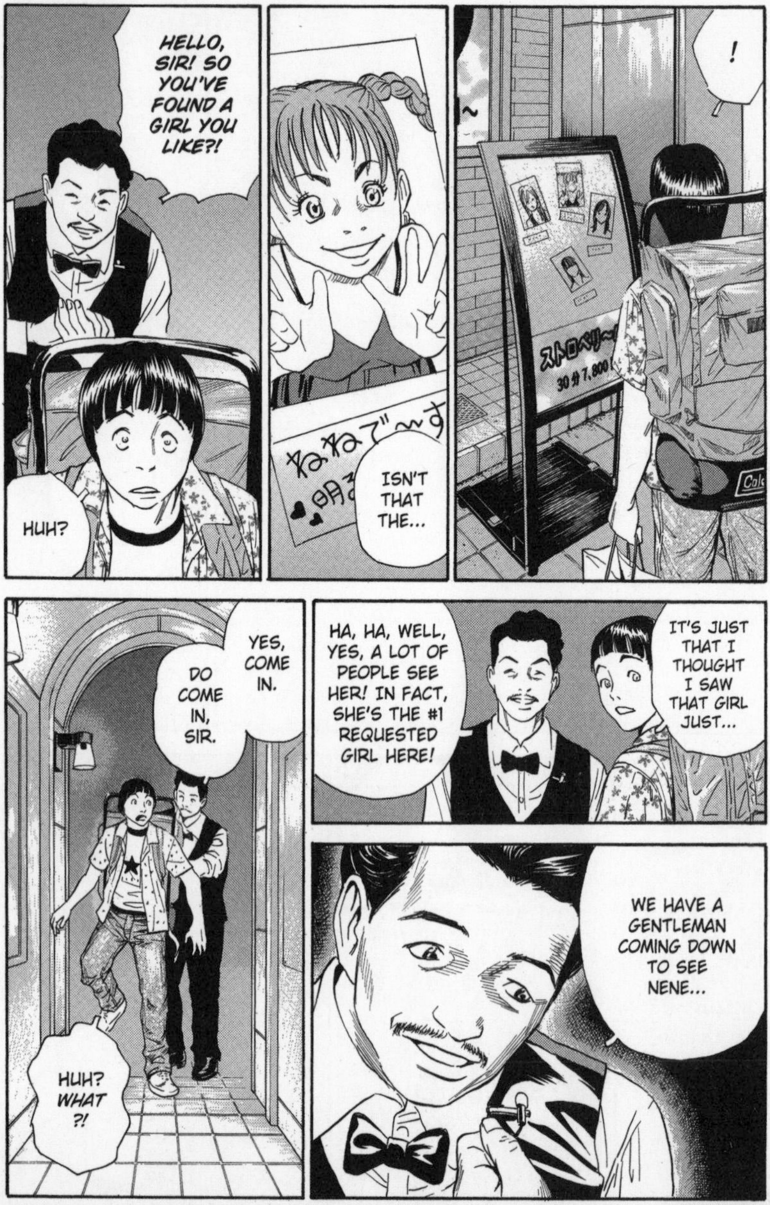
!
ISN'T THAT THE...
ねねで〜す
HELLO, SIR! SO YOU'VE FOUND A GIRL YOU LIKE?!
HUH?
IT'S JUST THAT I THOUGHT I SAW THAT GIRL JUST...
HA, HA, WELL, YES, A LOT OF PEOPLE SEE HER! IN FACT, SHE'S THE #1 REQUESTED GIRL HERE!
WE HAVE A GENTLEMAN COMING DOWN TO SEE NENE...
YES, COME IN.
DO COME IN, SIR.
HUH? WHAT ?!

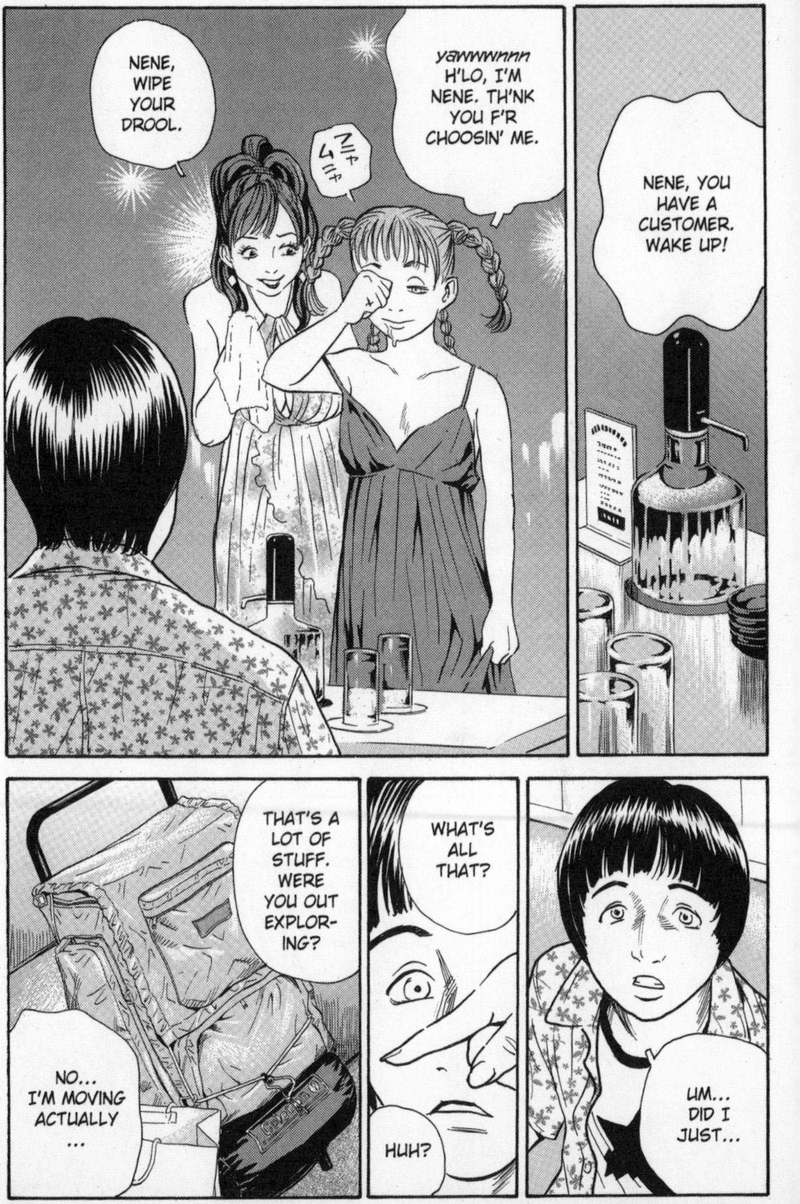
NENE, YOU HAVE A CUSTOMER. WAKE UP!
yawwwnnn H'LO, I'M NENE. TH'NK YOU F'R CHOOSIN' ME.
ムニャムニャ
NENE, WIPE YOUR DROOL.
UM... DID I JUST...
WHAT'S ALL THAT?
HUH?
THAT'S A LOT OF STUFF. WERE YOU OUT EXPLOR-ING?
NO... I'M MOVING ACTUALLY ...

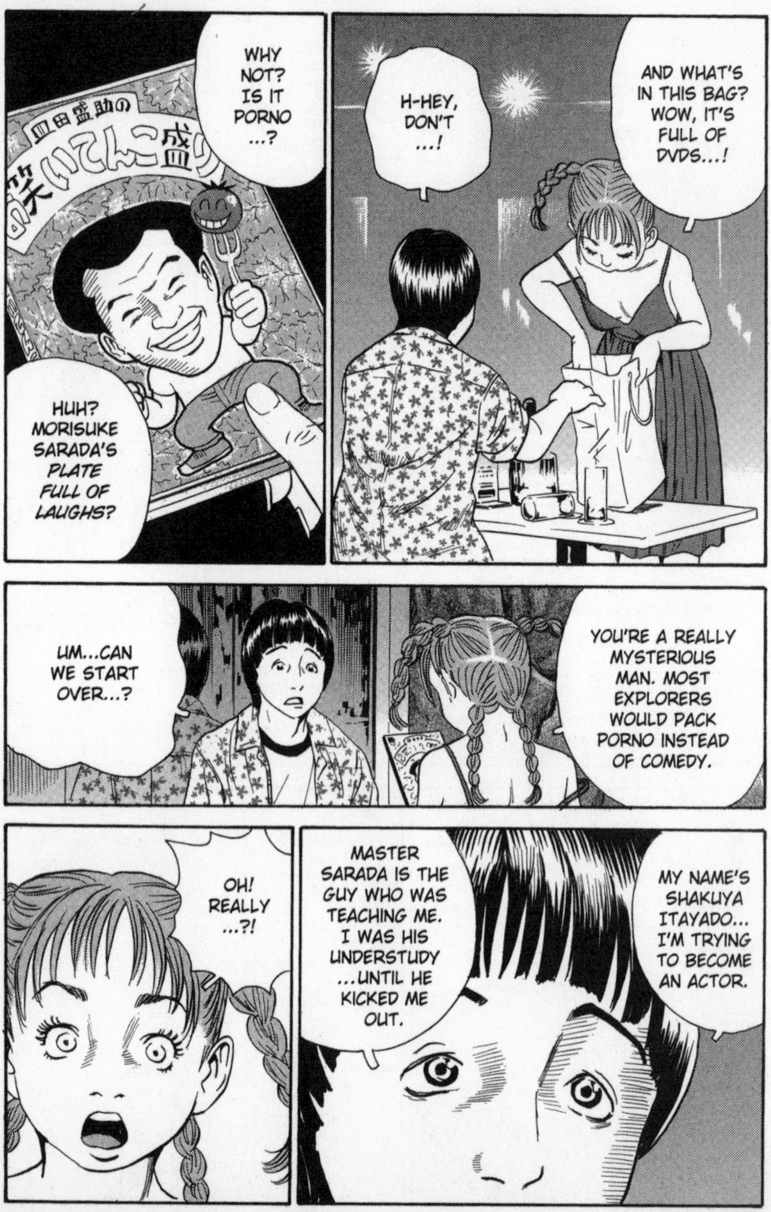
AND WHAT'S IN THIS BAG? WOW, IT'S FULL OF DVDS...!
H-HEY, DON'T ...!
WHY NOT? IS IT PORNO ...?
皿田盛助の
笑いてんこ盛り
HUH? MORISUKE SARADA'S *PLATE FULL OF LAUGHS?*
YOU'RE A REALLY MYSTERIOUS MAN. MOST EXPLORERS WOULD PACK PORNO INSTEAD OF COMEDY.
UM...CAN WE START OVER...?
MY NAME'S SHAKUYA ITAYADO... I'M TRYING TO BECOME AN ACTOR.
MASTER SARADA IS THE GUY WHO WAS TEACHING ME. I WAS HIS UNDERSTUDY ...UNTIL HE KICKED ME OUT.
OH! REALLY ...?!

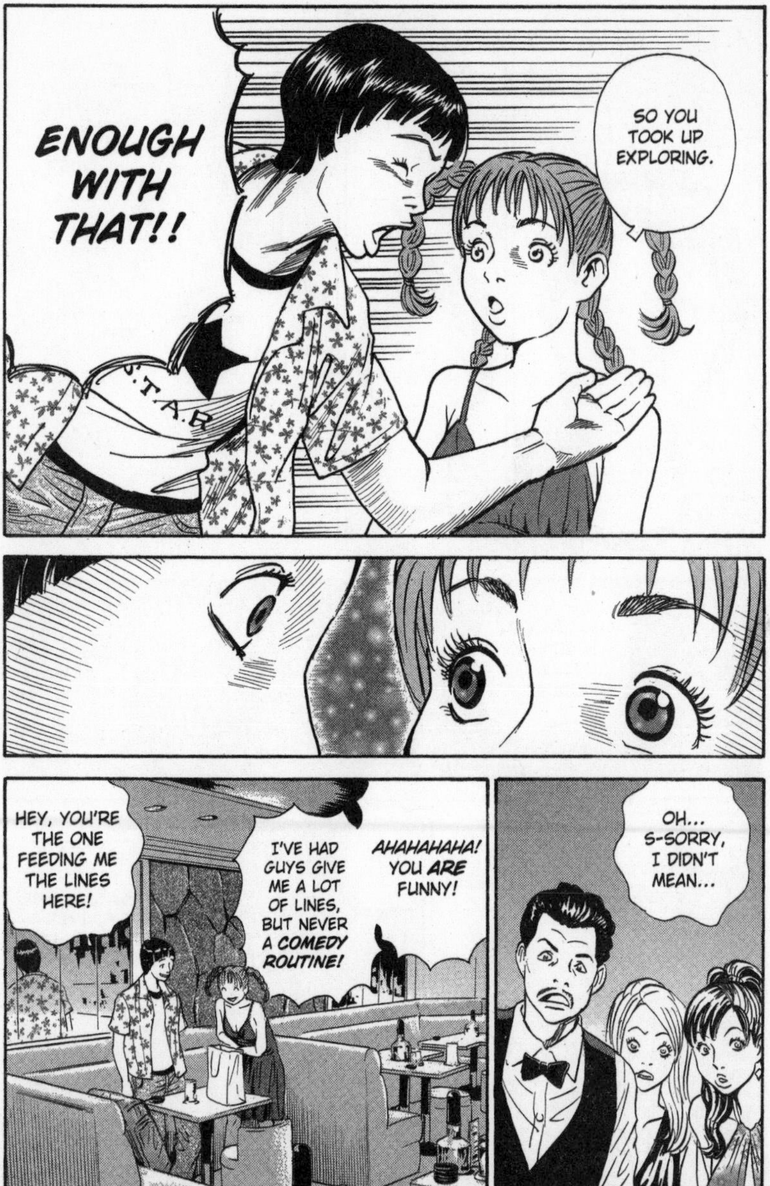
SO YOU TOOK UP EXPLORING.
ENOUGH WITH THAT!!
S.T.A.R
OH... S-SORRY, I DIDN'T MEAN...
AHAHAHAHA! YOU ARE FUNNY!
I'VE HAD GUYS GIVE ME A LOT OF LINES, BUT NEVER A COMEDY ROUTINE!
HEY, YOU'RE THE ONE FEEDING ME THE LINES HERE!

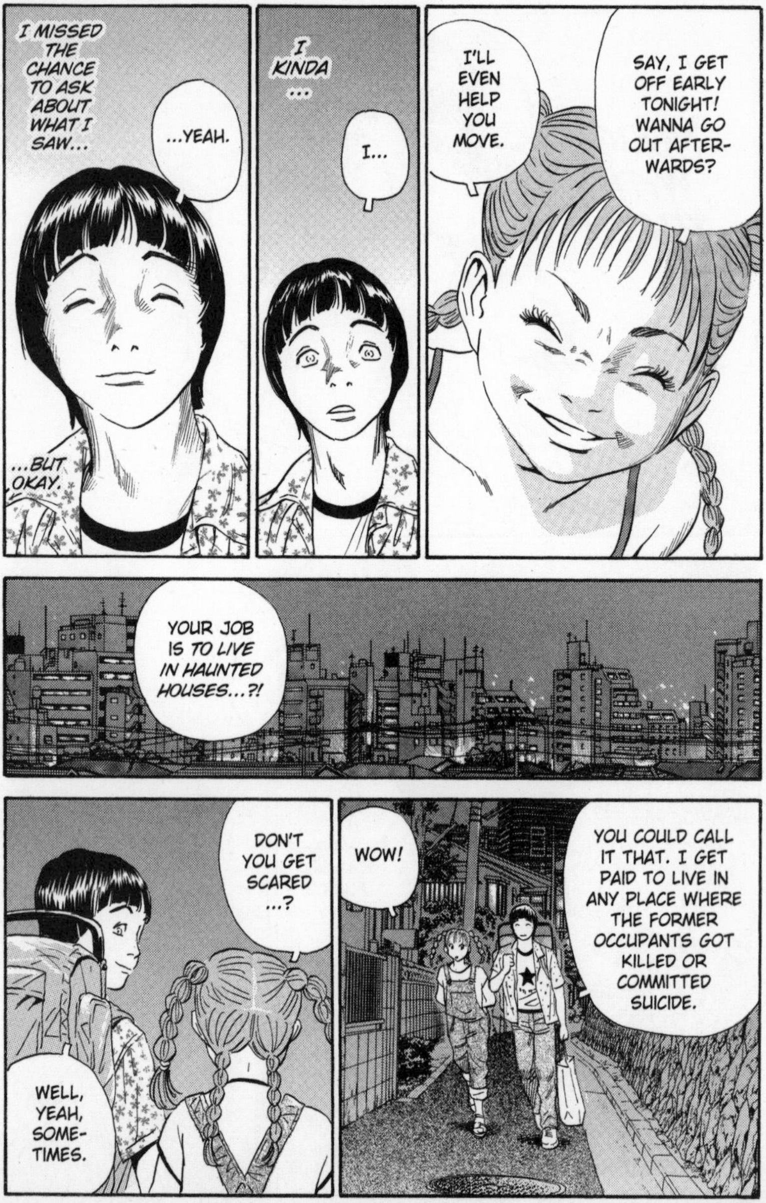
SAY, I GET OFF EARLY TONIGHT! WANNA GO OUT AFTER-WARDS?
I'LL EVEN HELP YOU MOVE.
I KINDA...
I...
...YEAH.
I MISSED THE CHANCE TO ASK ABOUT WHAT I SAW...
...BUT OKAY.
YOUR JOB IS TO LIVE IN HAUNTED HOUSES...?!
YOU COULD CALL IT THAT. I GET PAID TO LIVE IN ANY PLACE WHERE THE FORMER OCCUPANTS GOT KILLED OR COMMITTED SUICIDE.
WOW!
DON'T YOU GET SCARED...?
WELL, YEAH, SOME-TIMES.

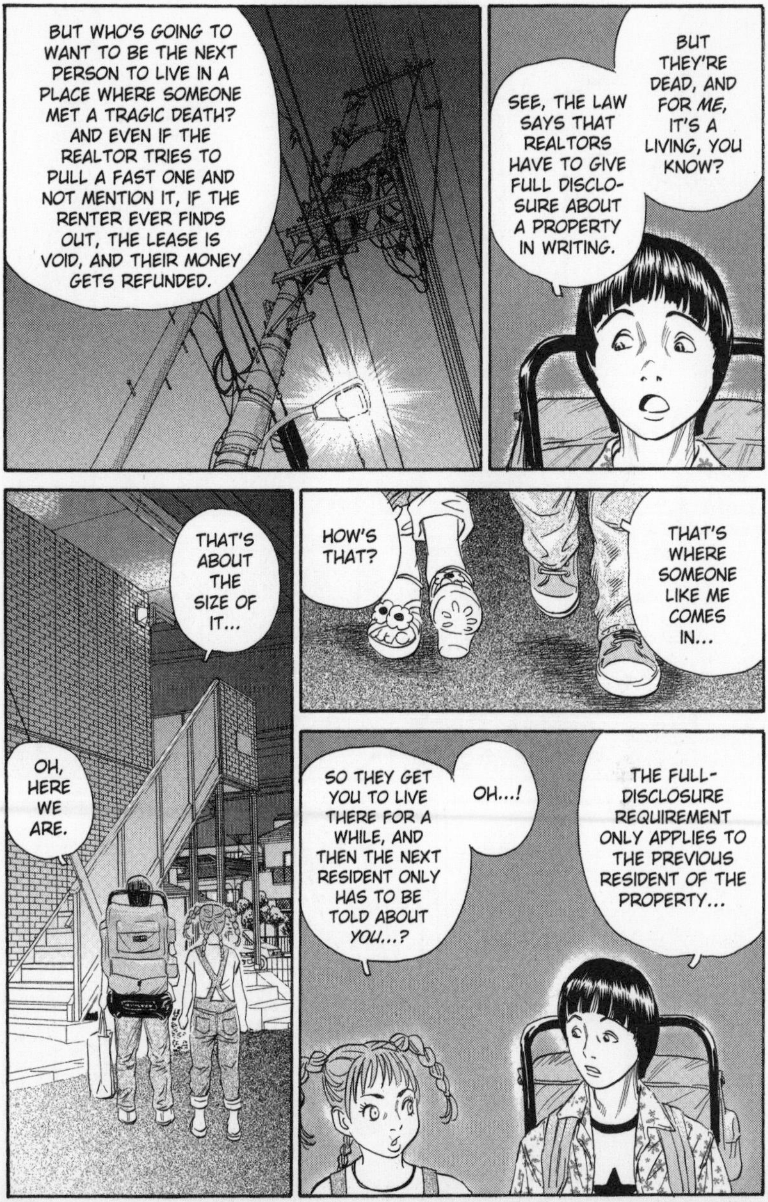
BUT THEY'RE DEAD, AND FOR *ME*, IT'S A LIVING, YOU KNOW?
SEE, THE LAW SAYS THAT REALTORS HAVE TO GIVE FULL DISCLOSURE ABOUT A PROPERTY IN WRITING.
BUT WHO'S GOING TO WANT TO BE THE NEXT PERSON TO LIVE IN A PLACE WHERE SOMEONE MET A TRAGIC DEATH? AND EVEN IF THE REALTOR TRIES TO PULL A FAST ONE AND NOT MENTION IT, IF THE RENTER EVER FINDS OUT, THE LEASE IS VOID, AND THEIR MONEY GETS REFUNDED.
THAT'S WHERE SOMEONE LIKE ME COMES IN...
HOW'S THAT?
THE FULL-DISCLOSURE REQUIREMENT ONLY APPLIES TO THE PREVIOUS RESIDENT OF THE PROPERTY...
OH...!
SO THEY GET YOU TO LIVE THERE FOR A WHILE, AND THEN THE NEXT RESIDENT ONLY HAS TO BE TOLD ABOUT *YOU*...?
THAT'S ABOUT THE SIZE OF IT...
OH, HERE WE ARE.

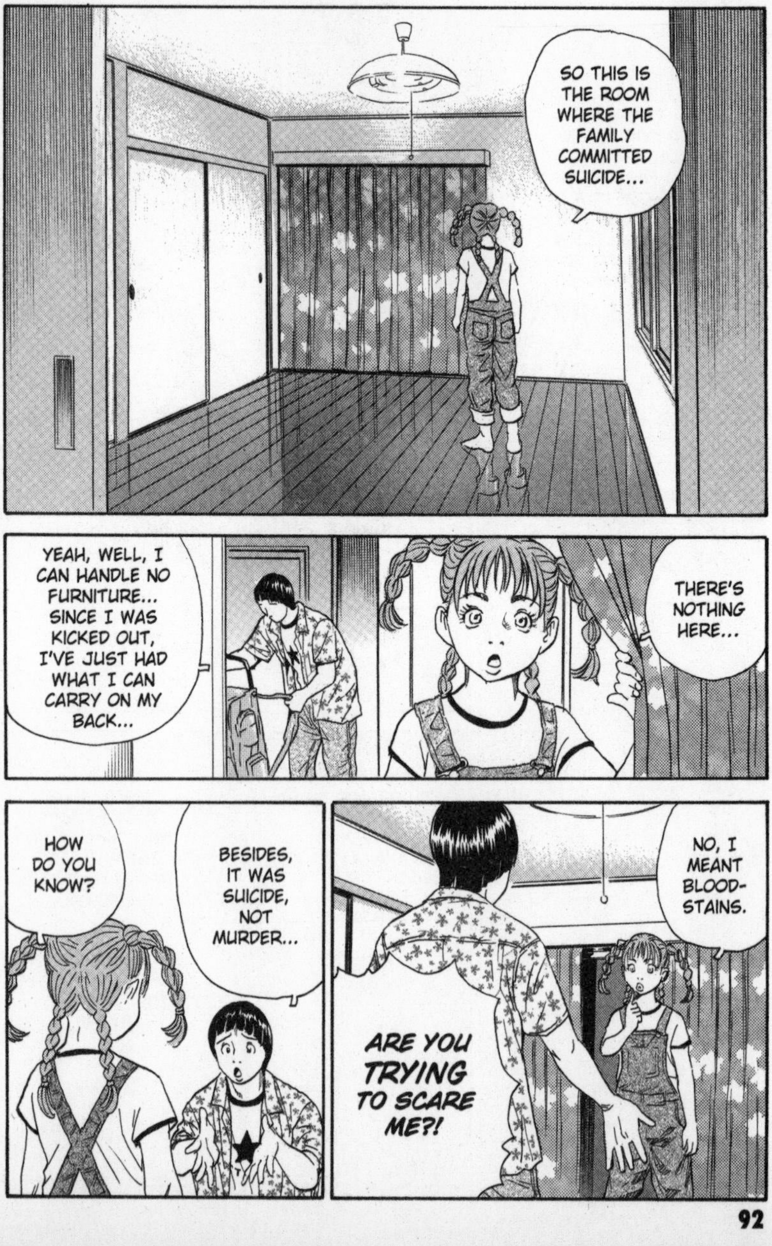
SO THIS IS THE ROOM WHERE THE FAMILY COMMITTED SUICIDE...
THERE'S NOTHING HERE...
YEAH, WELL, I CAN HANDLE NO FURNITURE... SINCE I WAS KICKED OUT, I'VE JUST HAD WHAT I CAN CARRY ON MY BACK...
NO, I MEANT BLOOD-STAINS.
ARE YOU TRYING TO SCARE ME?!
BESIDES, IT WAS SUICIDE, NOT MURDER...
HOW DO YOU KNOW?

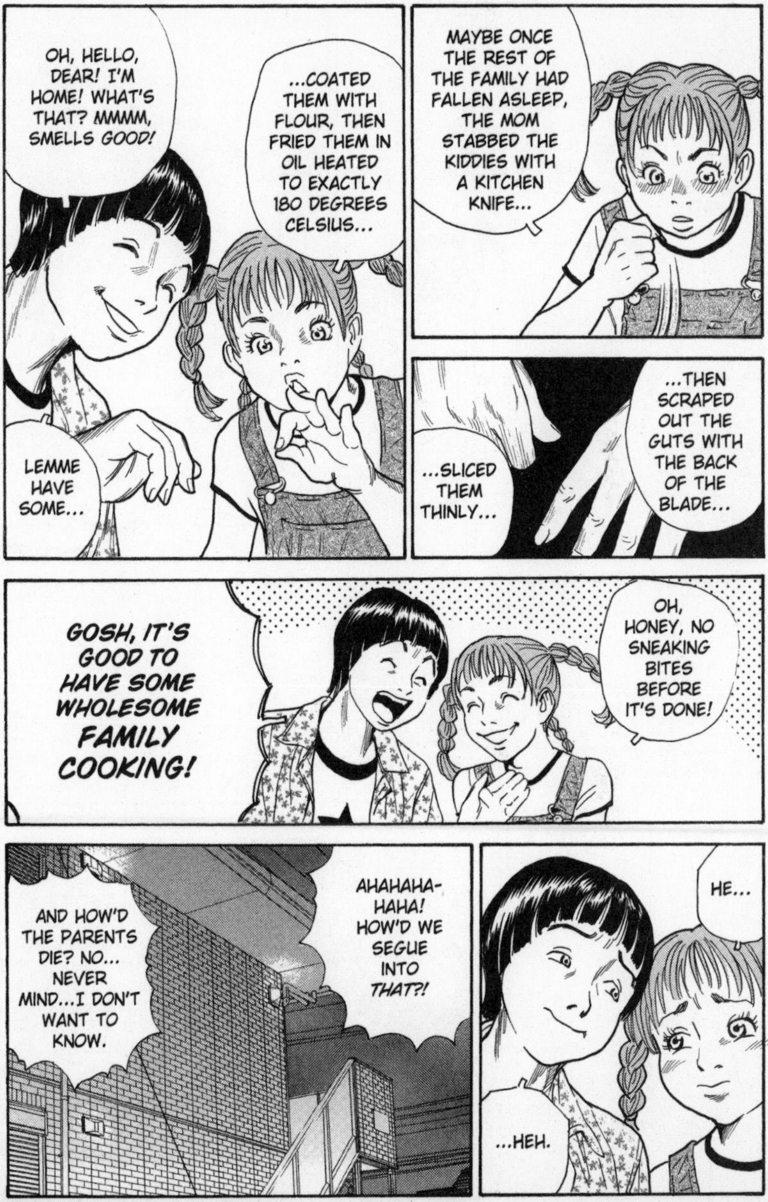
MAYBE ONCE THE REST OF THE FAMILY HAD FALLEN ASLEEP, THE MOM STABBED THE KIDDIES WITH A KITCHEN KNIFE...
...THEN SCRAPED OUT THE GUTS WITH THE BACK OF THE BLADE...
...SLICED THEM THINLY...
...COATED THEM WITH FLOUR, THEN FRIED THEM IN OIL HEATED TO EXACTLY 180 DEGREES CELSIUS...
OH, HELLO, DEAR! I'M HOME! WHAT'S THAT? MMMM, SMELLS *GOOD!*
LEMME HAVE SOME...
OH, HONEY, NO SNEAKING BITES BEFORE IT'S DONE!
GOSH, IT'S GOOD TO HAVE SOME WHOLESOME FAMILY COOKING!
HE...
...HEH.
AHAHAHA-HAHA! HOW'D WE SEGUE INTO *THAT?!*
AND HOW'D THE PARENTS DIE? NO... NEVER MIND...I DON'T WANT TO KNOW.

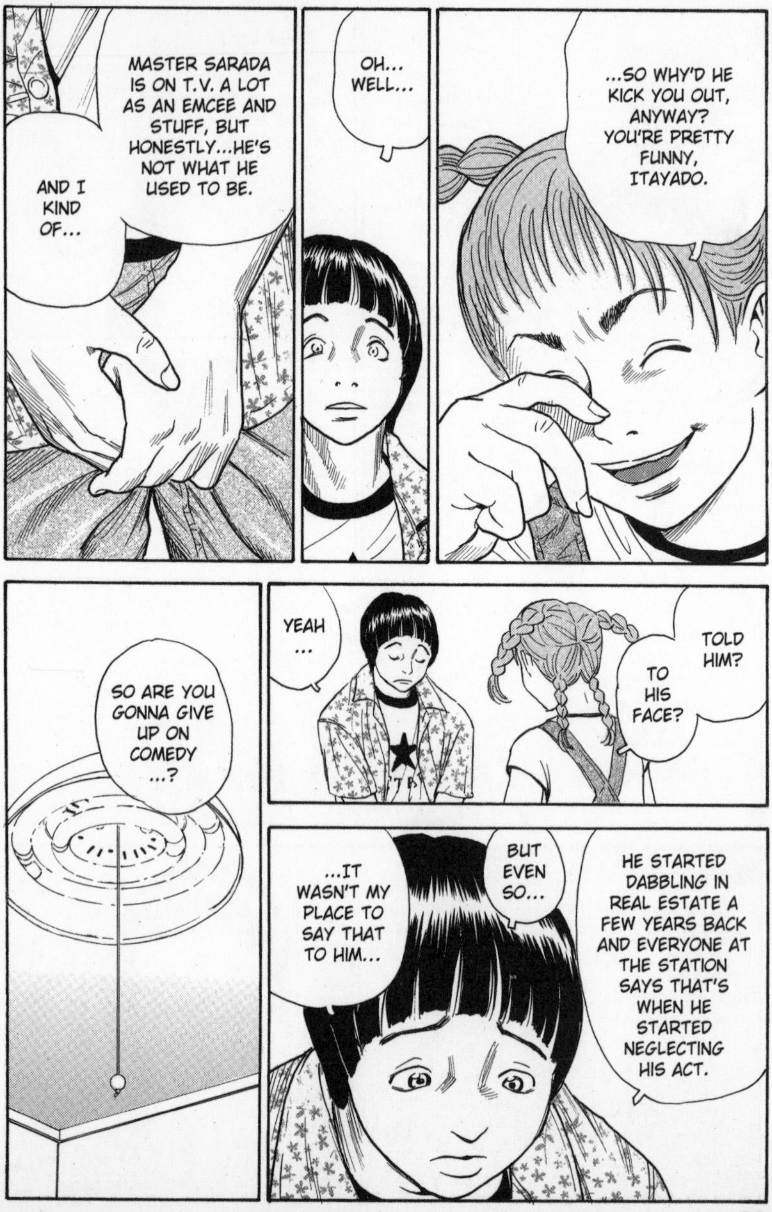
...SO WHY'D HE KICK YOU OUT, ANYWAY? YOU'RE PRETTY FUNNY, ITAYADO.
OH... WELL...
MASTER SARADA IS ON T.V. A LOT AS AN EMCEE AND STUFF, BUT HONESTLY...HE'S NOT WHAT HE USED TO BE.
AND I KIND OF...
TOLD HIM? TO HIS FACE?
YEAH ...
HE STARTED DABBLING IN REAL ESTATE A FEW YEARS BACK AND EVERYONE AT THE STATION SAYS THAT'S WHEN HE STARTED NEGLECTING HIS ACT.
BUT EVEN SO...
...IT WASN'T MY PLACE TO SAY THAT TO HIM...
SO ARE YOU GONNA GIVE UP ON COMEDY ...?

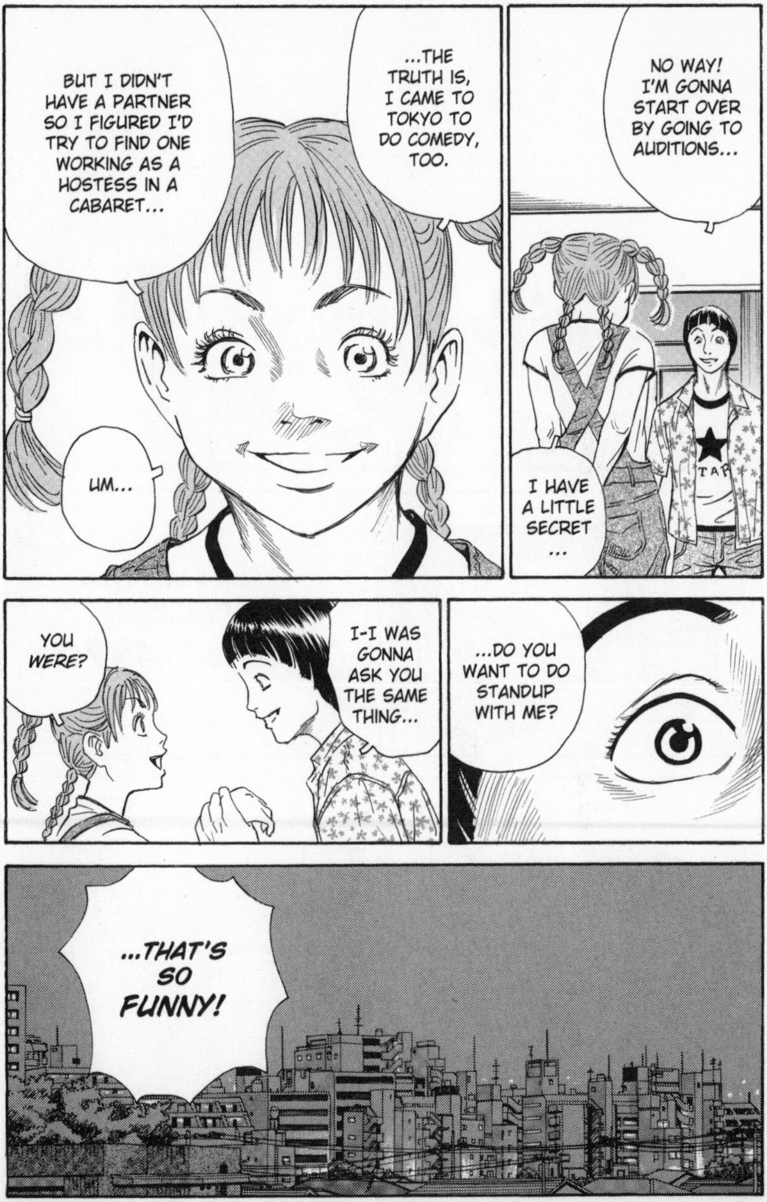
NO WAY! I'M GONNA START OVER BY GOING TO AUDITIONS...
I HAVE A LITTLE SECRET ...
...THE TRUTH IS, I CAME TO TOKYO TO DO COMEDY, TOO.
BUT I DIDN'T HAVE A PARTNER SO I FIGURED I'D TRY TO FIND ONE WORKING AS A HOSTESS IN A CABARET...
UM...
...DO YOU WANT TO DO STANDUP WITH ME?
I-I WAS GONNA ASK YOU THE SAME THING...
YOU WERE?
...THAT'S SO FUNNY!

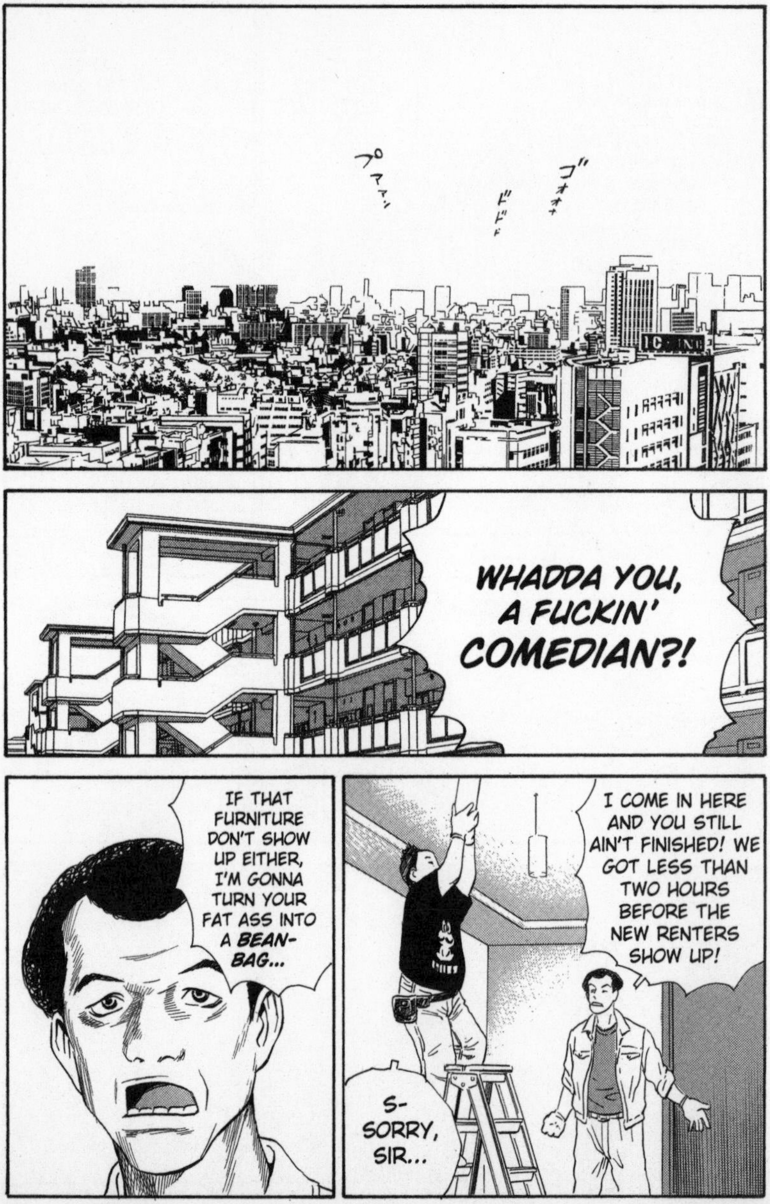
ゴオオォ
ドドド
プァァン
WHADDA YOU, A FUCKIN' COMEDIAN?!
I COME IN HERE AND YOU STILL AIN'T FINISHED! WE GOT LESS THAN TWO HOURS BEFORE THE NEW RENTERS SHOW UP!
S- SORRY, SIR...
IF THAT FURNITURE DON'T SHOW UP EITHER, I'M GONNA TURN YOUR FAT ASS INTO A BEAN-BAG...

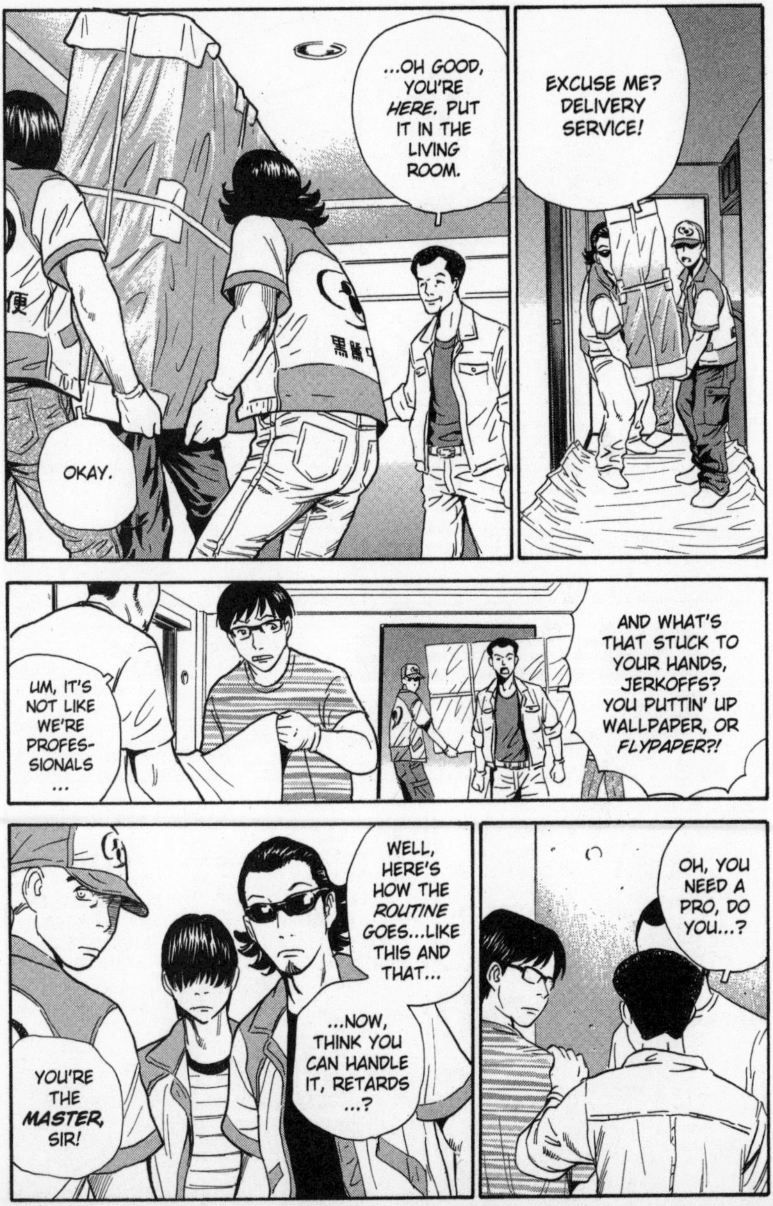
EXCUSE ME? DELIVERY SERVICE!
...OH GOOD, YOU'RE *HERE*. PUT IT IN THE LIVING ROOM.
OKAY.
AND WHAT'S THAT STUCK TO YOUR HANDS, JERKOFFS? YOU PUTTIN' UP WALLPAPER, OR *FLYPAPER*?!
UM, IT'S NOT LIKE WE'RE PROFES-SIONALS ...
OH, YOU NEED A PRO, DO YOU...?
WELL, HERE'S HOW THE *ROUTINE* GOES...LIKE THIS AND THAT...
...NOW, THINK YOU CAN HANDLE IT, RETARDS ...?
YOU'RE THE ***MASTER***, SIR!

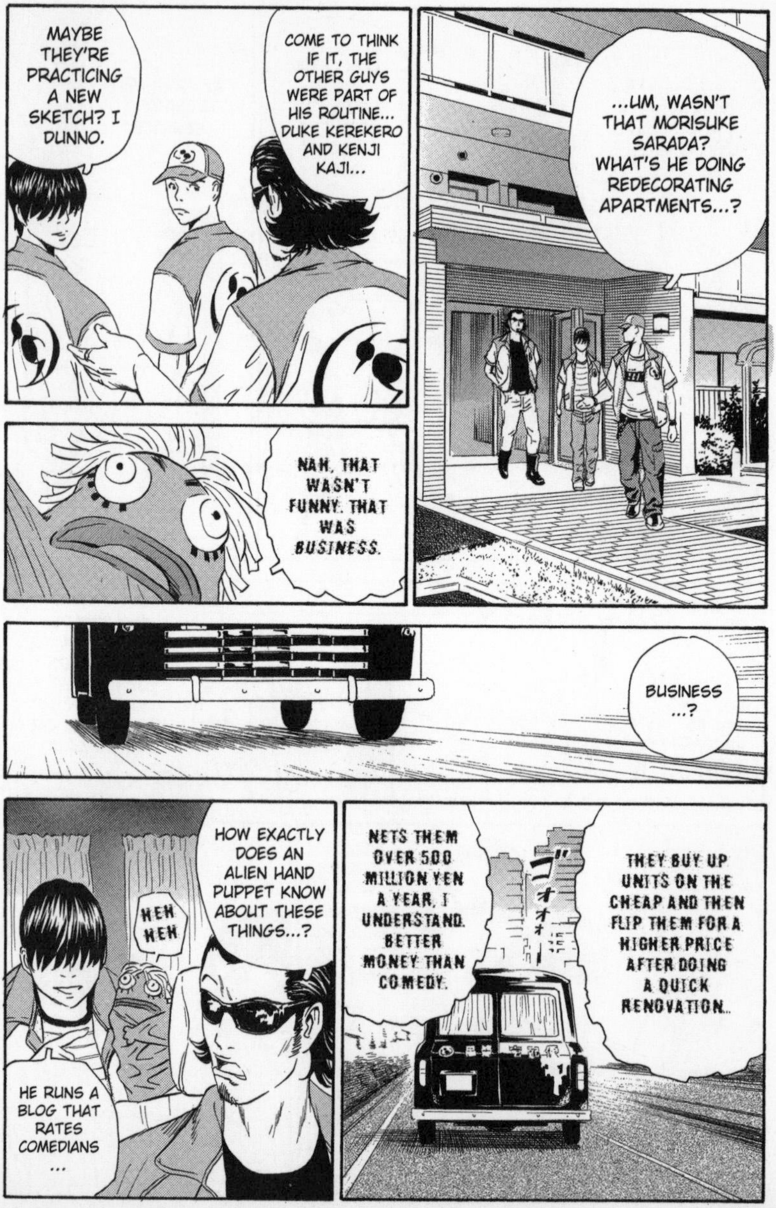
...UM, WASN'T THAT MORISUKE SARADA? WHAT'S HE DOING REDECORATING APARTMENTS...?
COME TO THINK IF IT, THE OTHER GUYS WERE PART OF HIS ROUTINE... DUKE KEREKERO AND KENJI KAJI...
MAYBE THEY'RE PRACTICING A NEW SKETCH? I DUNNO.
NAH, THAT WASN'T FUNNY. THAT WAS *BUSINESS.*
BUSINESS ...?
THEY BUY UP UNITS ON THE CHEAP AND THEN FLIP THEM FOR A HIGHER PRICE AFTER DOING A QUICK RENOVATION..
NETS THEM OVER 500 MILLION YEN A YEAR, I UNDERSTAND. BETTER MONEY THAN COMEDY.
HOW EXACTLY DOES AN ALIEN HAND PUPPET KNOW ABOUT THESE THINGS...?
HEH HEH
HE RUNS A BLOG THAT RATES COMEDIANS ...

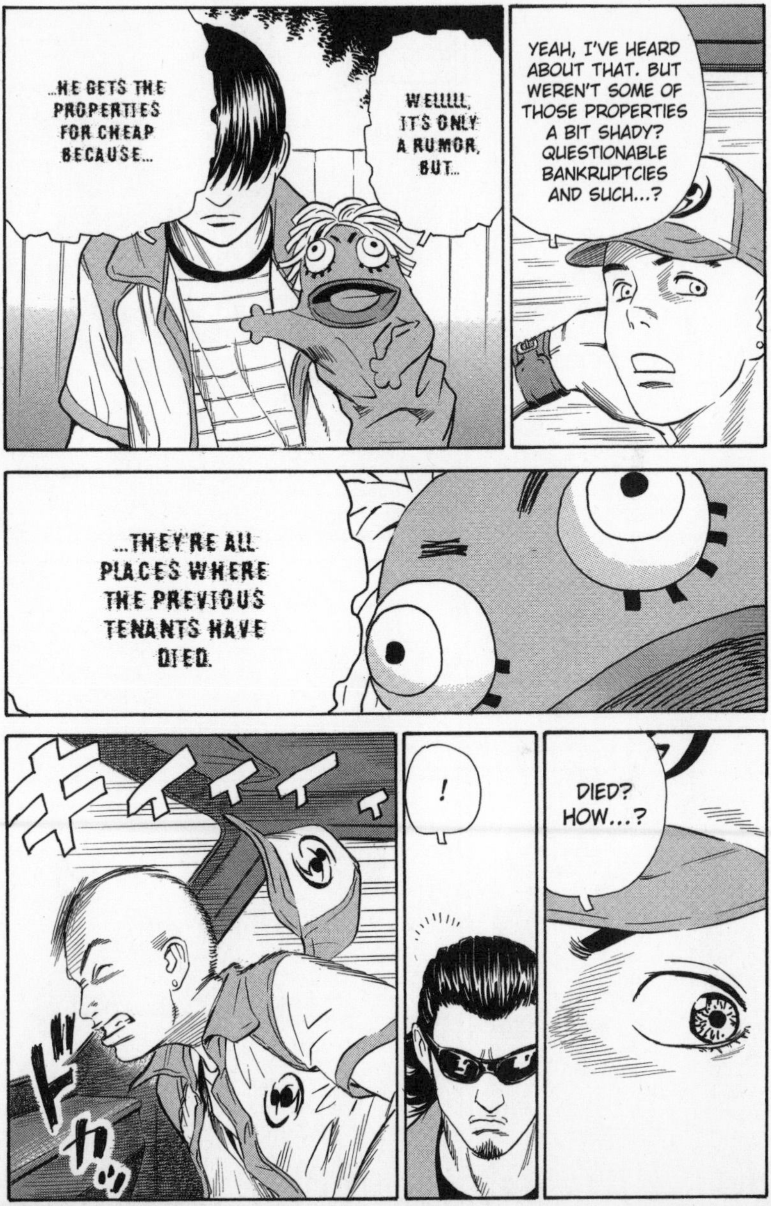
YEAH, I'VE HEARD ABOUT THAT. BUT WEREN'T SOME OF THOSE PROPERTIES A BIT SHADY? QUESTIONABLE BANKRUPTCIES AND SUCH...?
WELLLLL, IT'S ONLY A RUMOR, BUT...
...HE GETS THE PROPERTIES FOR CHEAP BECAUSE...
...THEY'RE ALL PLACES WHERE THE PREVIOUS TENANTS HAVE DIED.
DIED? HOW...?
!
キイイィ
ドカッ

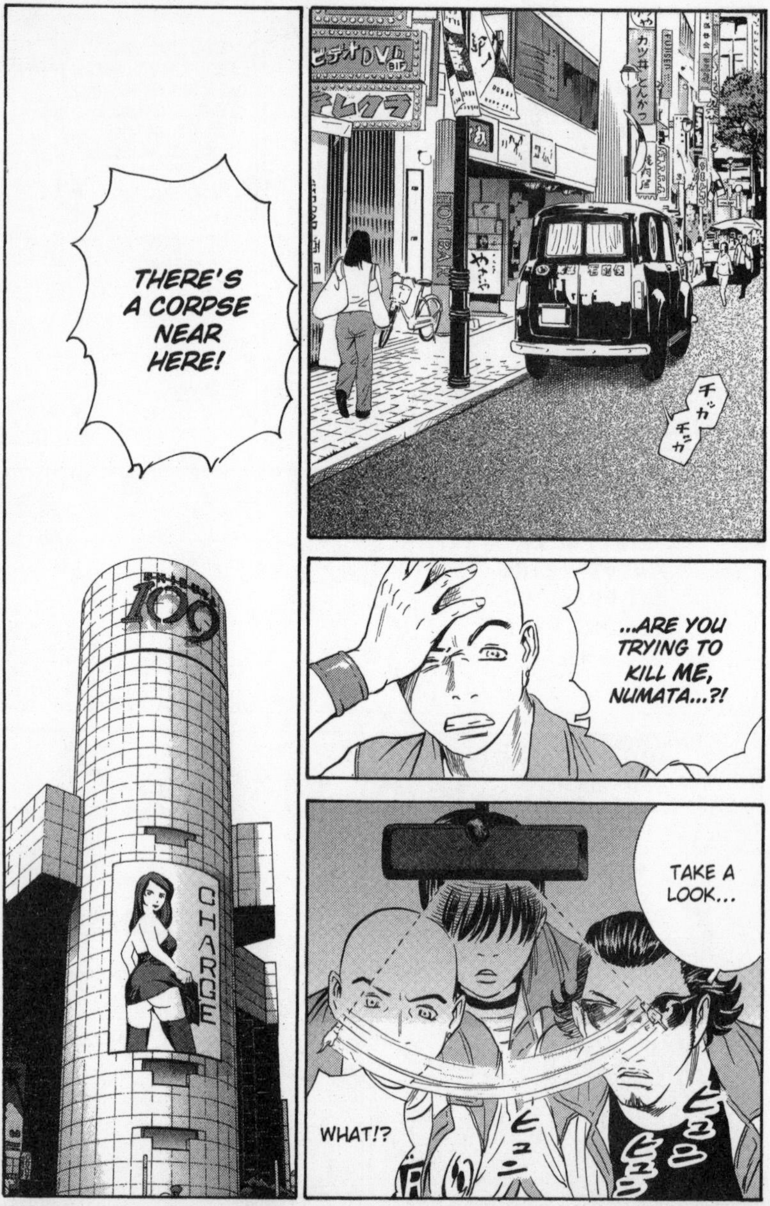
ビデオDVD
テレクラ
カツ丼 とんかつ
HOT BAR
チッカ
チッカ
...ARE YOU TRYING TO KILL ME, NUMATA...?!
TAKE A LOOK...
WHAT!?
109
CHARGE
THERE'S A CORPSE NEAR HERE!

4th delivery: i'm sittin' on the edge of skies—the end

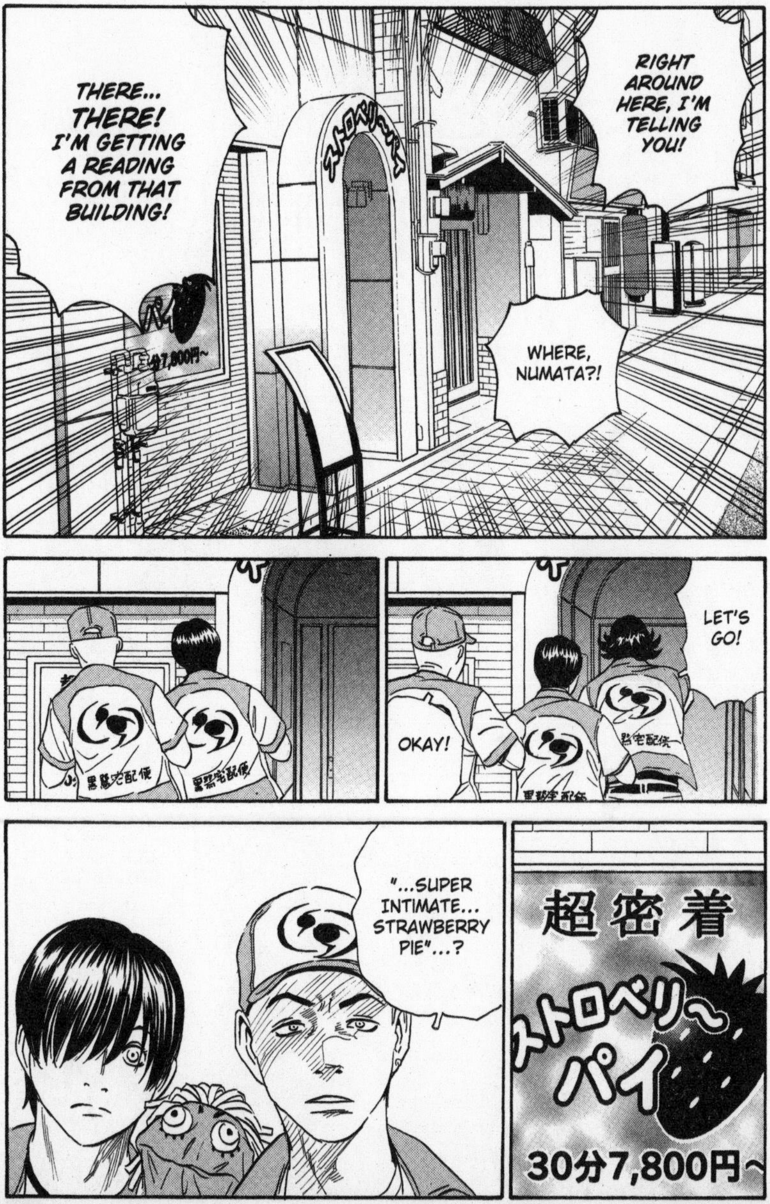
RIGHT AROUND HERE, I'M TELLING YOU!
WHERE, NUMATA?!
THERE... THERE! I'M GETTING A READING FROM THAT BUILDING!
LET'S GO!
OKAY!
超密着
ストロベリ〜
パイ
30分7,800円〜
"...SUPER INTIMATE... STRAWBERRY PIE"...?

5th delivery
堀までひとっとび
a single bound to the moat

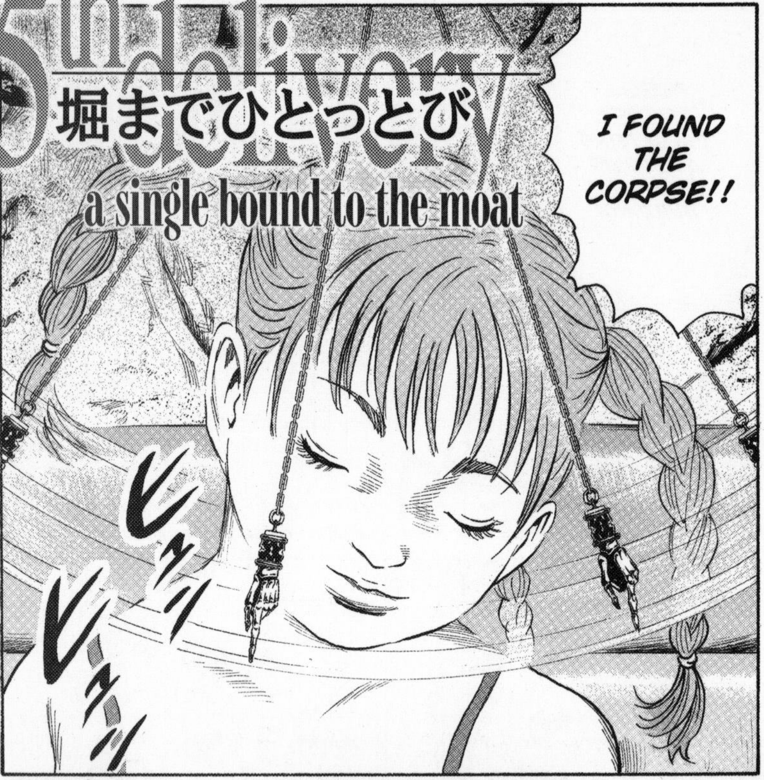
I FOUND THE CORPSE!!
ヒュン
ヒュン

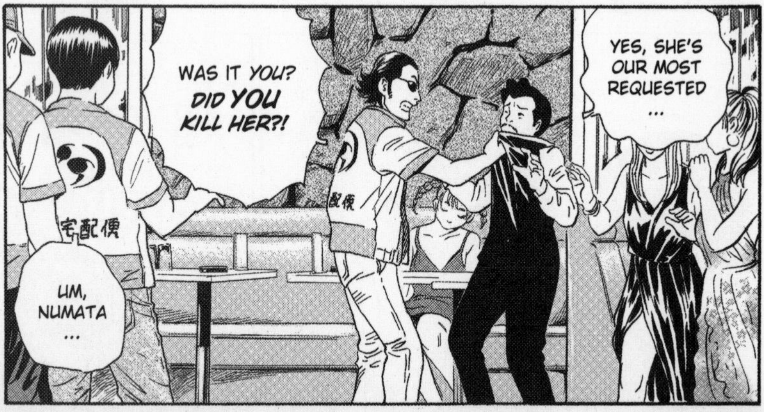
YES, SHE'S OUR MOST REQUESTED ...
WAS IT YOU? DID YOU KILL HER?!
配便
宅配便
UM, NUMATA ...

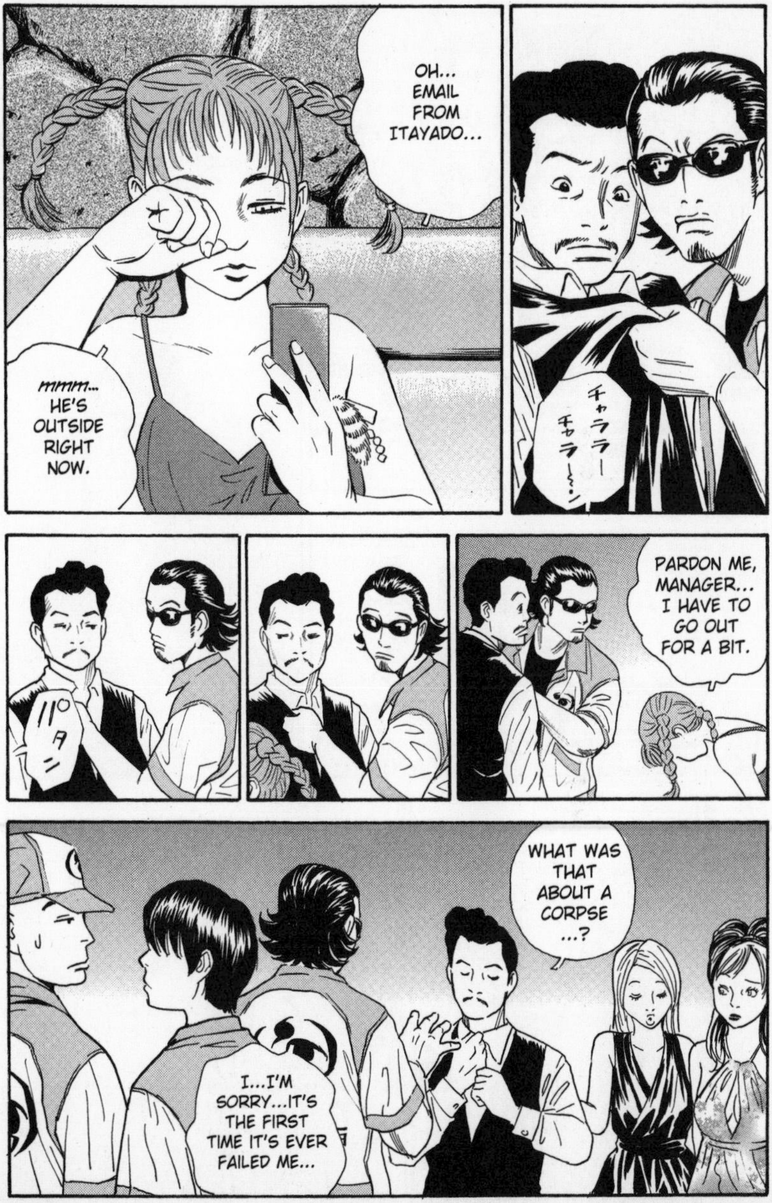
チャララー
チャラ ラー〜♪
OH... EMAIL FROM ITAYADO...
mmmm... HE'S OUTSIDE RIGHT NOW.
PARDON ME, MANAGER... I HAVE TO GO OUT FOR A BIT.
パタン
WHAT WAS THAT ABOUT A CORPSE ...?
I...I'M SORRY...IT'S THE FIRST TIME IT'S EVER FAILED ME...

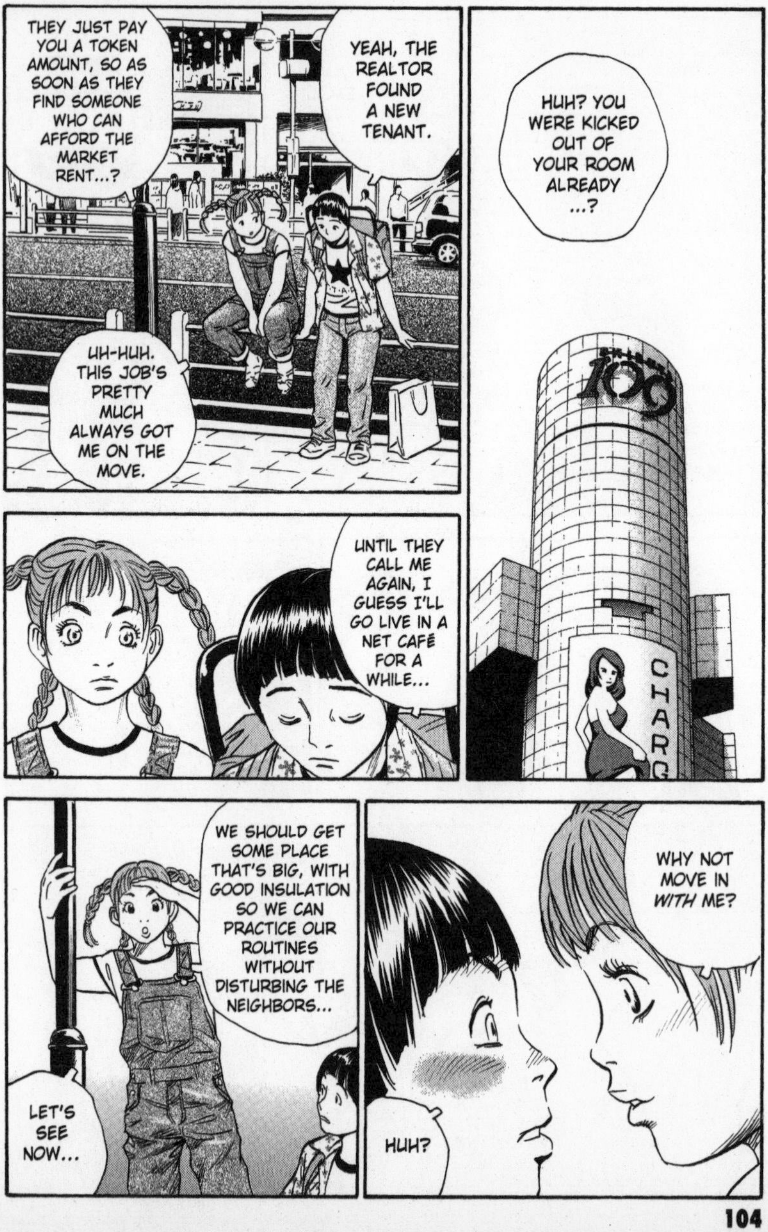

HUH? YOU WERE KICKED OUT OF YOUR ROOM ALREADY ...?
109
CHARG
YEAH, THE REALTOR FOUND A NEW TENANT.
THEY JUST PAY YOU A TOKEN AMOUNT, SO AS SOON AS THEY FIND SOMEONE WHO CAN AFFORD THE MARKET RENT...?
UH-HUH. THIS JOB'S PRETTY MUCH ALWAYS GOT ME ON THE MOVE.
UNTIL THEY CALL ME AGAIN, I GUESS I'LL GO LIVE IN A NET CAFÉ FOR A WHILE...
WHY NOT MOVE IN *WITH* ME?
HUH?
WE SHOULD GET SOME PLACE THAT'S BIG, WITH GOOD INSULATION SO WE CAN PRACTICE OUR ROUTINES WITHOUT DISTURBING THE NEIGHBORS...
LET'S SEE NOW...

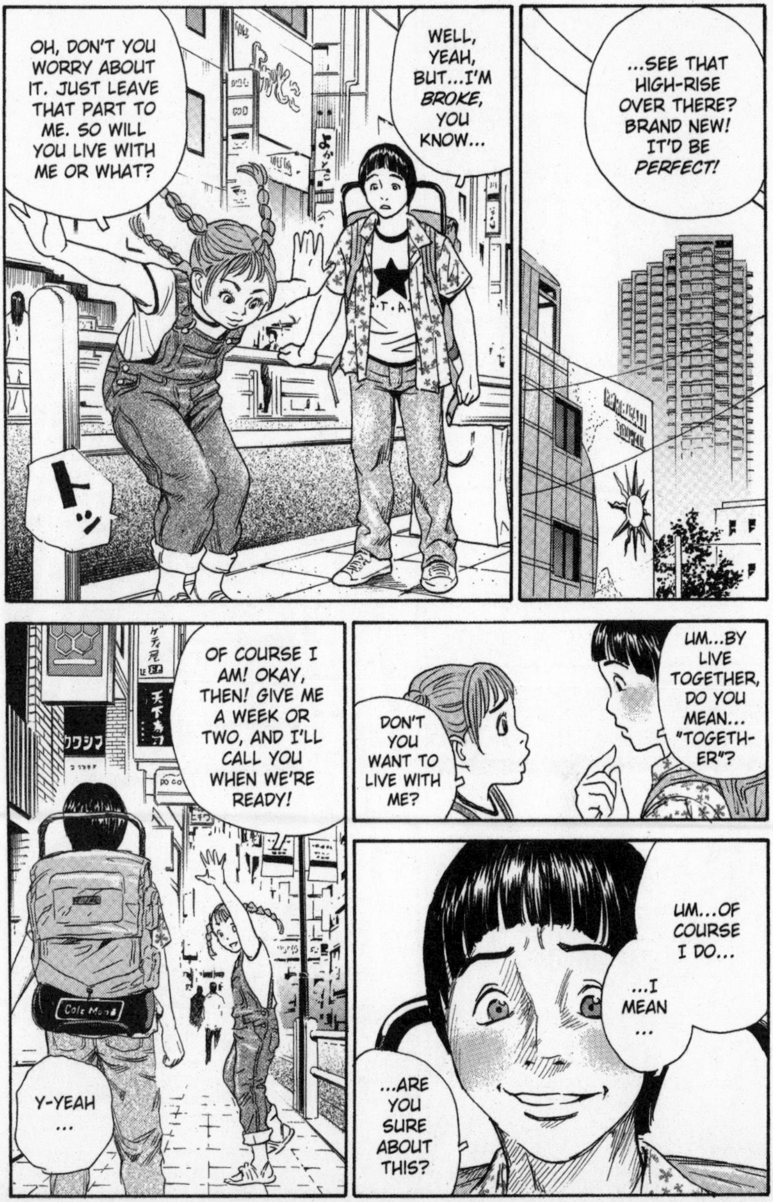
...SEE THAT HIGH-RISE OVER THERE? BRAND NEW! IT'D BE PERFECT!
WELL, YEAH, BUT...I'M BROKE, YOU KNOW...
OH, DON'T YOU WORRY ABOUT IT. JUST LEAVE THAT PART TO ME. SO WILL YOU LIVE WITH ME OR WHAT?
トッ
UM...BY LIVE TOGETHER, DO YOU MEAN... "TOGETH-ER"?
DON'T YOU WANT TO LIVE WITH ME?
UM...OF COURSE I DO...
...I MEAN...
...ARE YOU SURE ABOUT THIS?
OF COURSE I AM! OKAY, THEN! GIVE ME A WEEK OR TWO, AND I'LL CALL YOU WHEN WE'RE READY!
Y-YEAH...

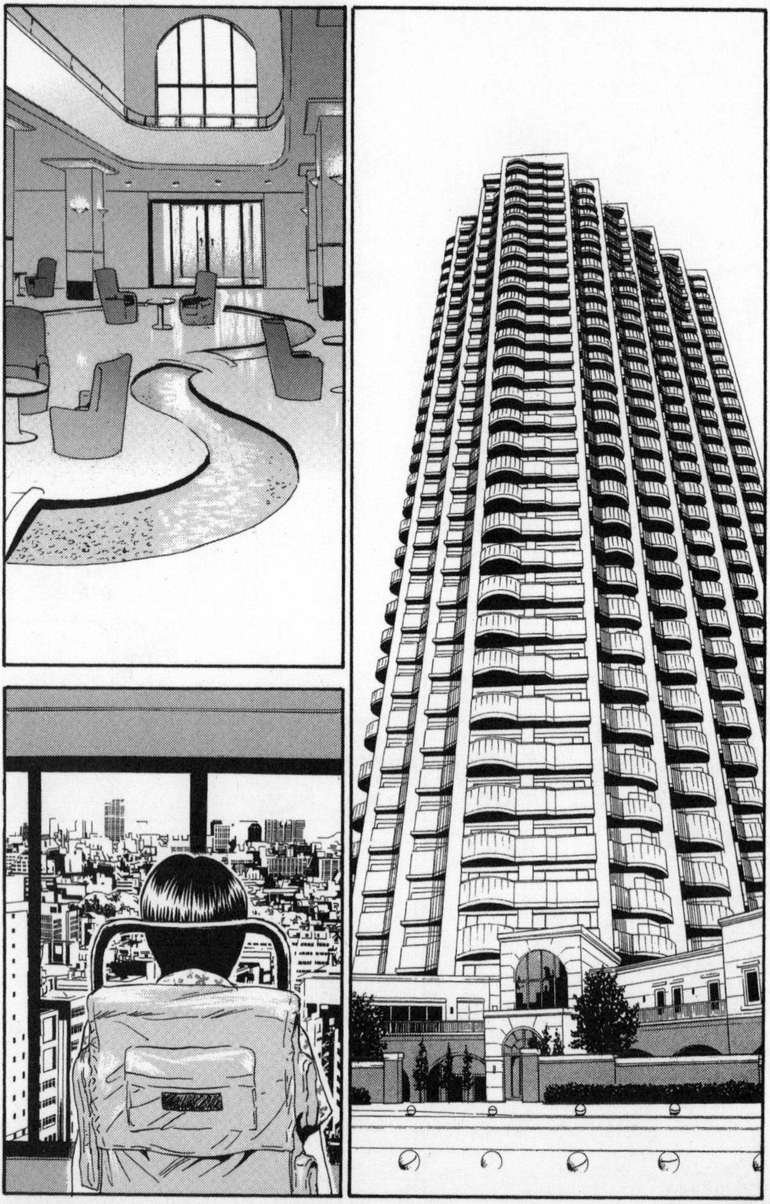

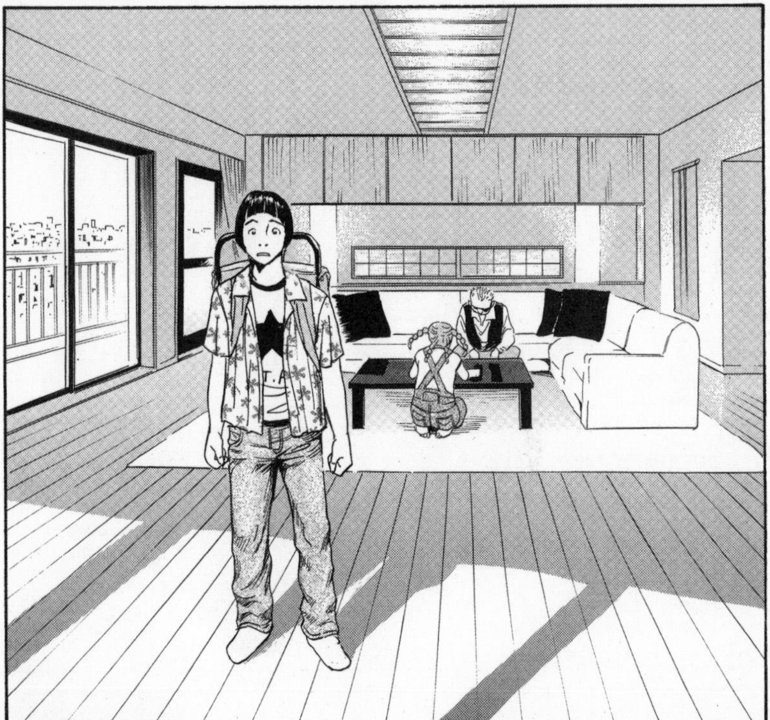

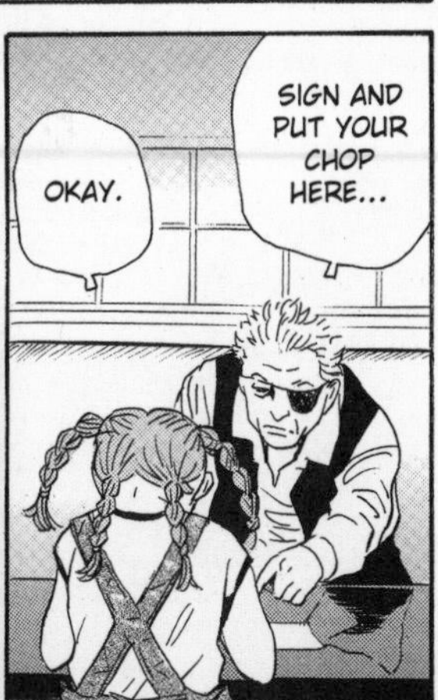
SIGN AND PUT YOUR CHOP HERE...
OKAY.

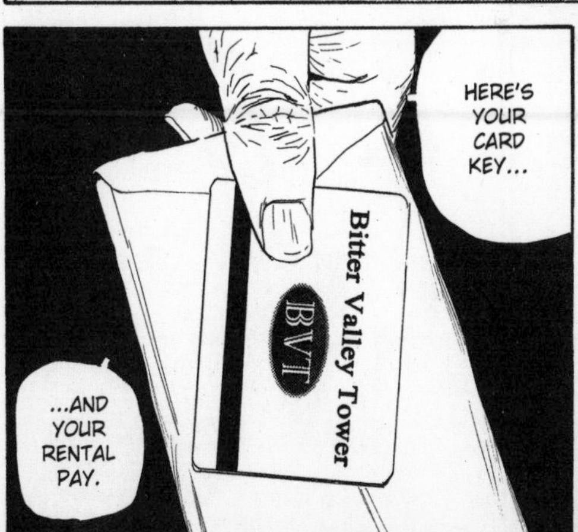
HERE'S YOUR CARD KEY...
Bitter Valley Tower
BVT
...AND YOUR RENTAL PAY.

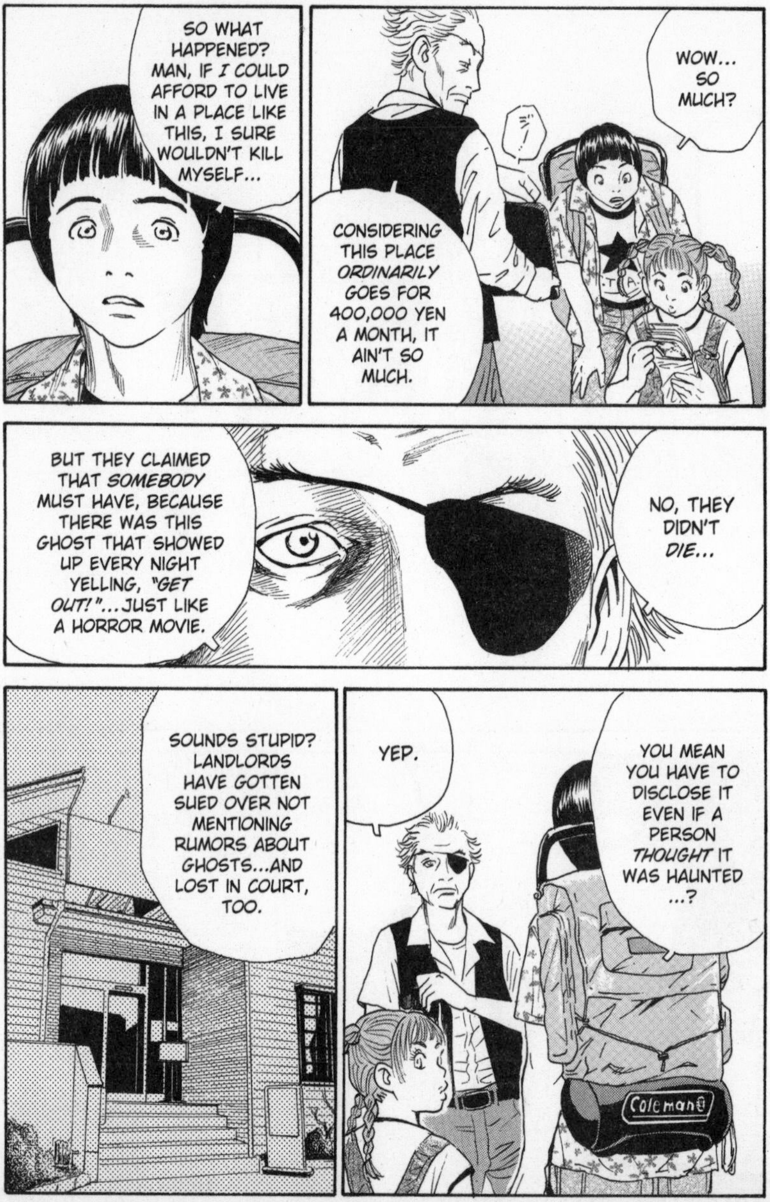
WOW... SO MUCH?
CONSIDERING THIS PLACE ORDINARILY GOES FOR 400,000 YEN A MONTH, IT AIN'T SO MUCH.
SO WHAT HAPPENED? MAN, IF I COULD AFFORD TO LIVE IN A PLACE LIKE THIS, I SURE WOULDN'T KILL MYSELF...
NO, THEY DIDN'T DIE...
BUT THEY CLAIMED THAT SOMEBODY MUST HAVE, BECAUSE THERE WAS THIS GHOST THAT SHOWED UP EVERY NIGHT YELLING, "GET OUT!"...JUST LIKE A HORROR MOVIE.
YOU MEAN YOU HAVE TO DISCLOSE IT EVEN IF A PERSON THOUGHT IT WAS HAUNTED ...?
YEP.
SOUNDS STUPID? LANDLORDS HAVE GOTTEN SUED OVER NOT MENTIONING RUMORS ABOUT GHOSTS...AND LOST IN COURT, TOO.
Coleman

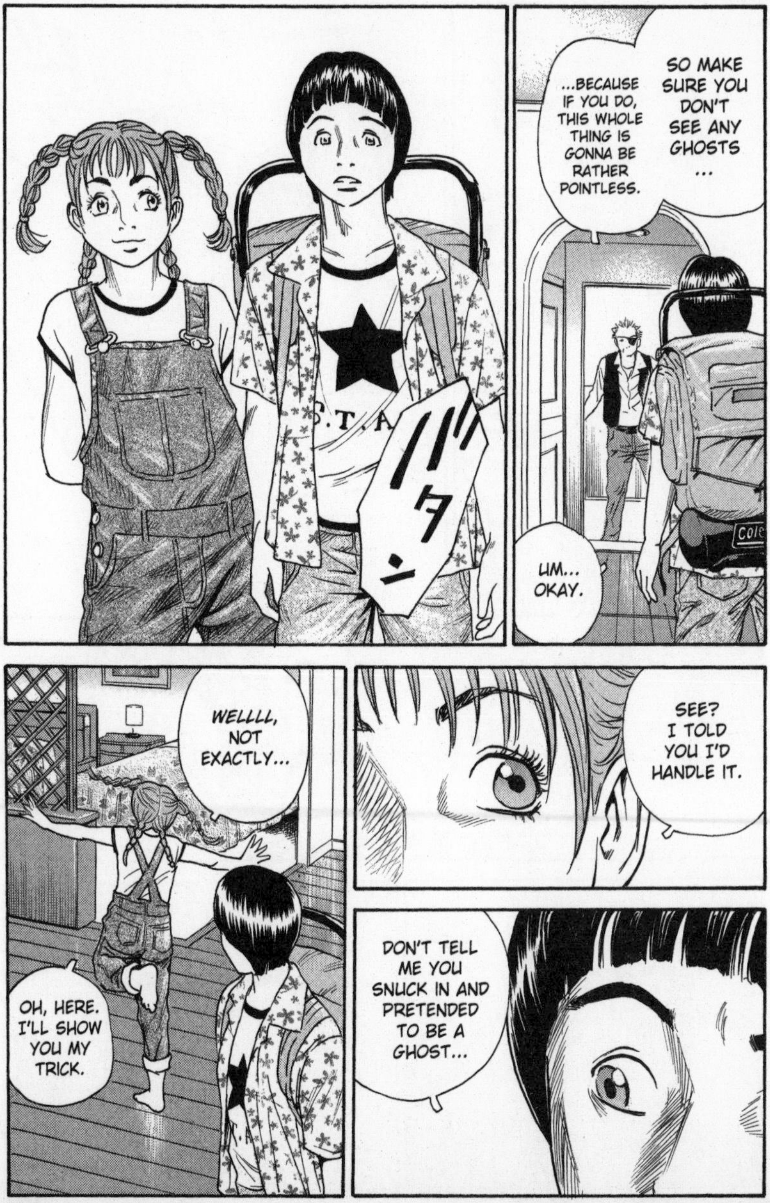
SO MAKE SURE YOU DON'T SEE ANY GHOSTS ...
...BECAUSE IF YOU DO, THIS WHOLE THING IS GONNA BE RATHER POINTLESS.
UM... OKAY.
バタン
SEE? I TOLD YOU I'D HANDLE IT.
DON'T TELL ME YOU SNUCK IN AND PRETENDED TO BE A GHOST...
WELLLL, NOT EXACTLY...
OH, HERE. I'LL SHOW YOU MY TRICK.

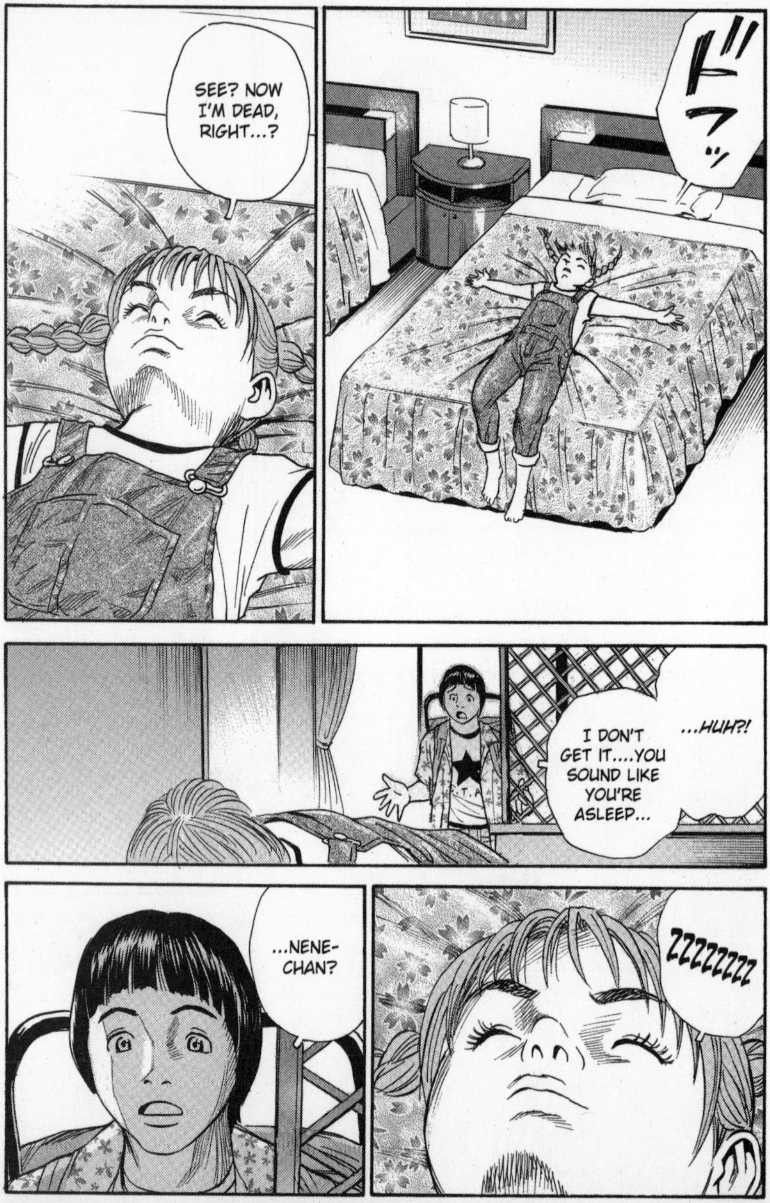
ドフッ
SEE? NOW I'M DEAD, RIGHT...?
...HUH?!
I DON'T GET IT....YOU SOUND LIKE YOU'RE ASLEEP...
ZZZZZZZZ
...NENE-CHAN?

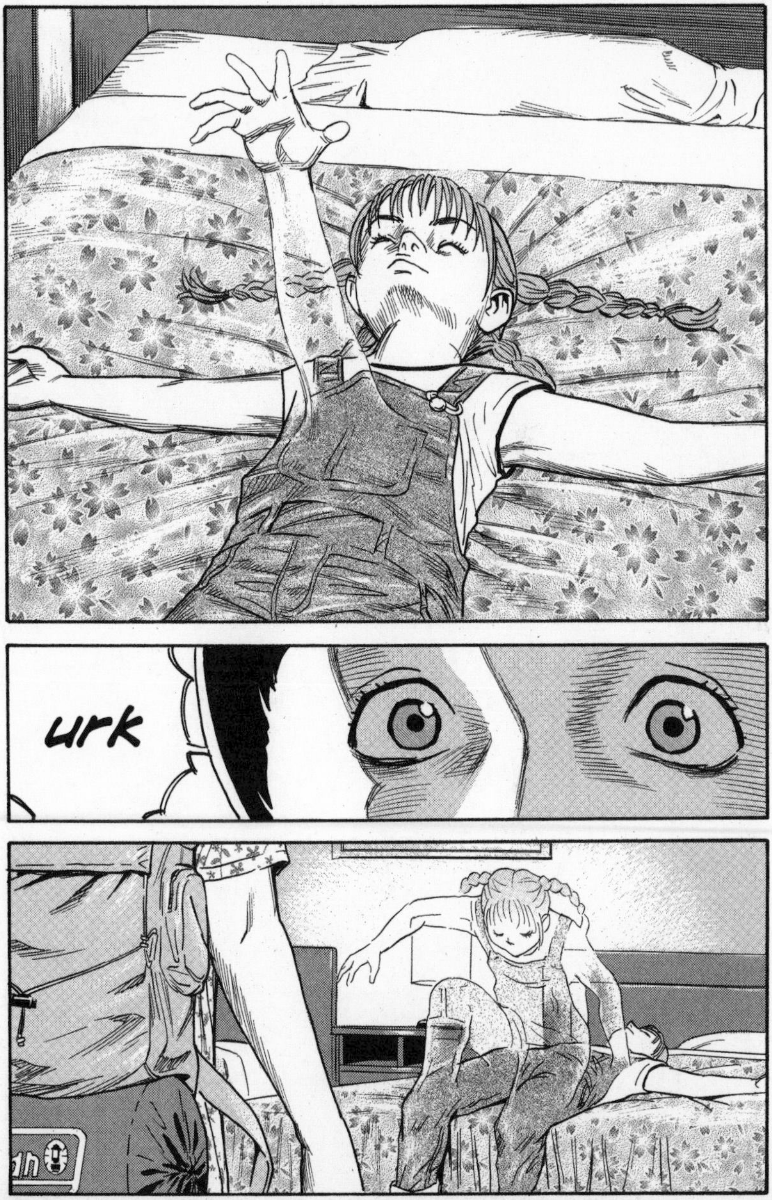
urk

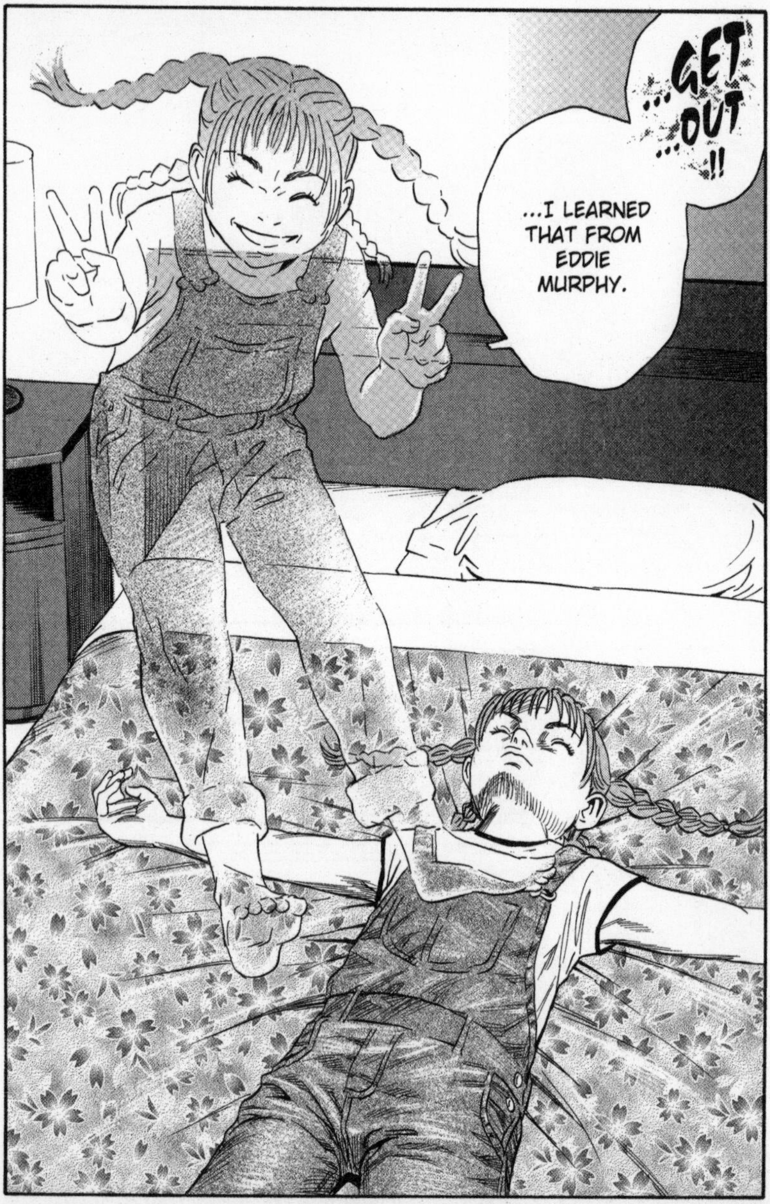
...GET ...OUT !!
...I LEARNED THAT FROM EDDIE MURPHY.

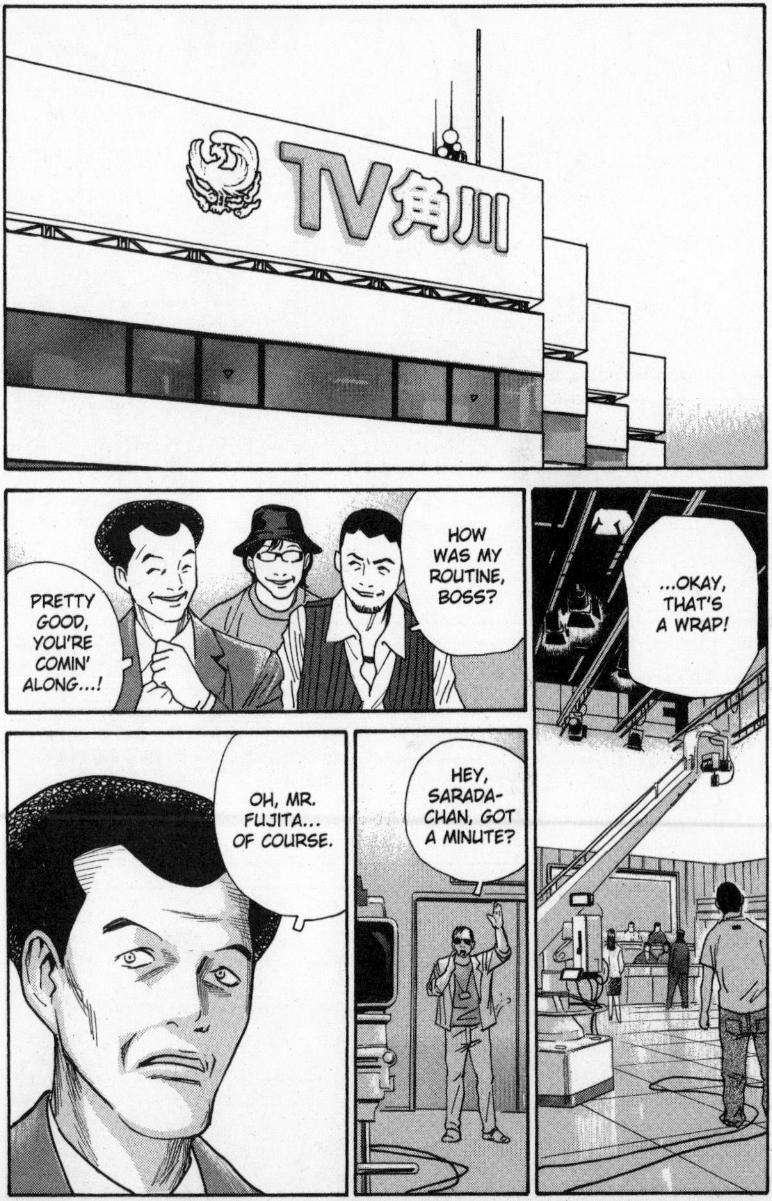
TV角川
...OKAY, THAT'S A WRAP!
HOW WAS MY ROUTINE, BOSS?
PRETTY GOOD, YOU'RE COMIN' ALONG...!
HEY, SARADA-CHAN, GOT A MINUTE?
OH, MR. FUJITA... OF COURSE.

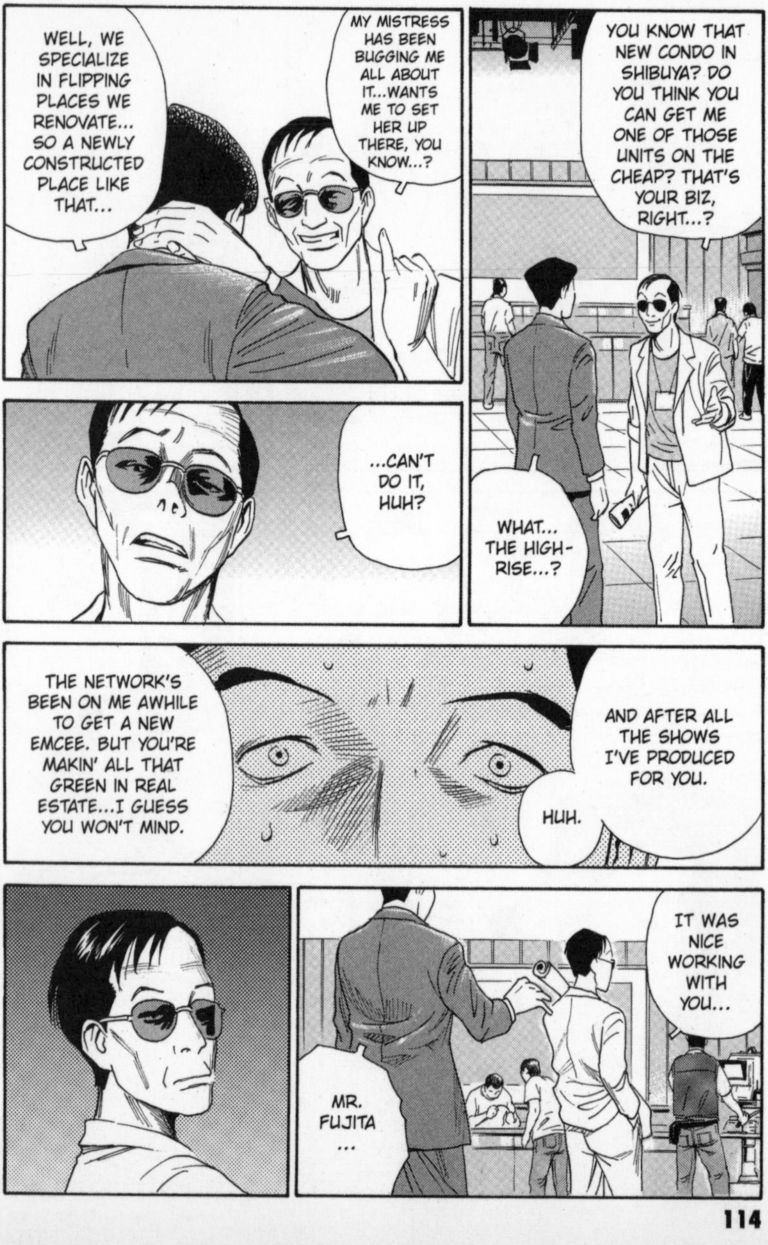
YOU KNOW THAT NEW CONDO IN SHIBUYA? DO YOU THINK YOU CAN GET ME ONE OF THOSE UNITS ON THE CHEAP? THAT'S YOUR BIZ, RIGHT...?
WHAT... THE HIGH-RISE...?
MY MISTRESS HAS BEEN BUGGING ME ALL ABOUT IT...WANTS ME TO SET HER UP THERE, YOU KNOW...?
WELL, WE SPECIALIZE IN FLIPPING PLACES WE RENOVATE... SO A NEWLY CONSTRUCTED PLACE LIKE THAT...
...CAN'T DO IT, HUH?
AND AFTER ALL THE SHOWS I'VE PRODUCED FOR YOU.
HUH.
THE NETWORK'S BEEN ON ME AWHILE TO GET A NEW EMCEE. BUT YOU'RE MAKIN' ALL THAT GREEN IN REAL ESTATE...I GUESS YOU WON'T MIND.
IT WAS NICE WORKING WITH YOU...
MR. FUJITA ...

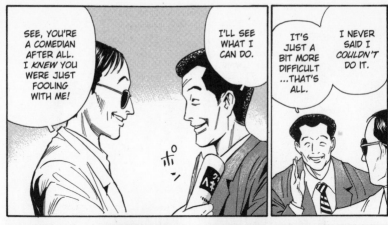

I NEVER SAID I COULDN'T DO IT.
IT'S JUST A BIT MORE DIFFICULT ...THAT'S ALL.
I'LL SEE WHAT I CAN DO.
ポン
SEE, YOU'RE A COMEDIAN AFTER ALL. I KNEW YOU WERE JUST FOOLING WITH ME!
ARRANGE IT SO SHE CAN MOVE IN BY NEXT MONTH. THANKS.
YOU CAN COUNT ON ME, MR. FUJITA! HELL, IT'LL BE FUN! THIS IS GONNA BE A LAUGH!
KOBAYASHI! QUIT READIN' THAT CRAP!
WH- WHAT IS IT, SIR...?

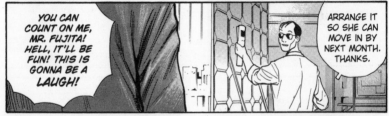

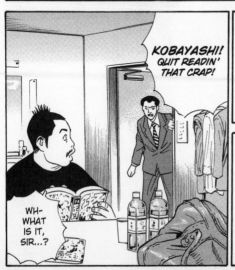

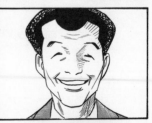

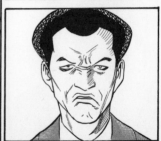

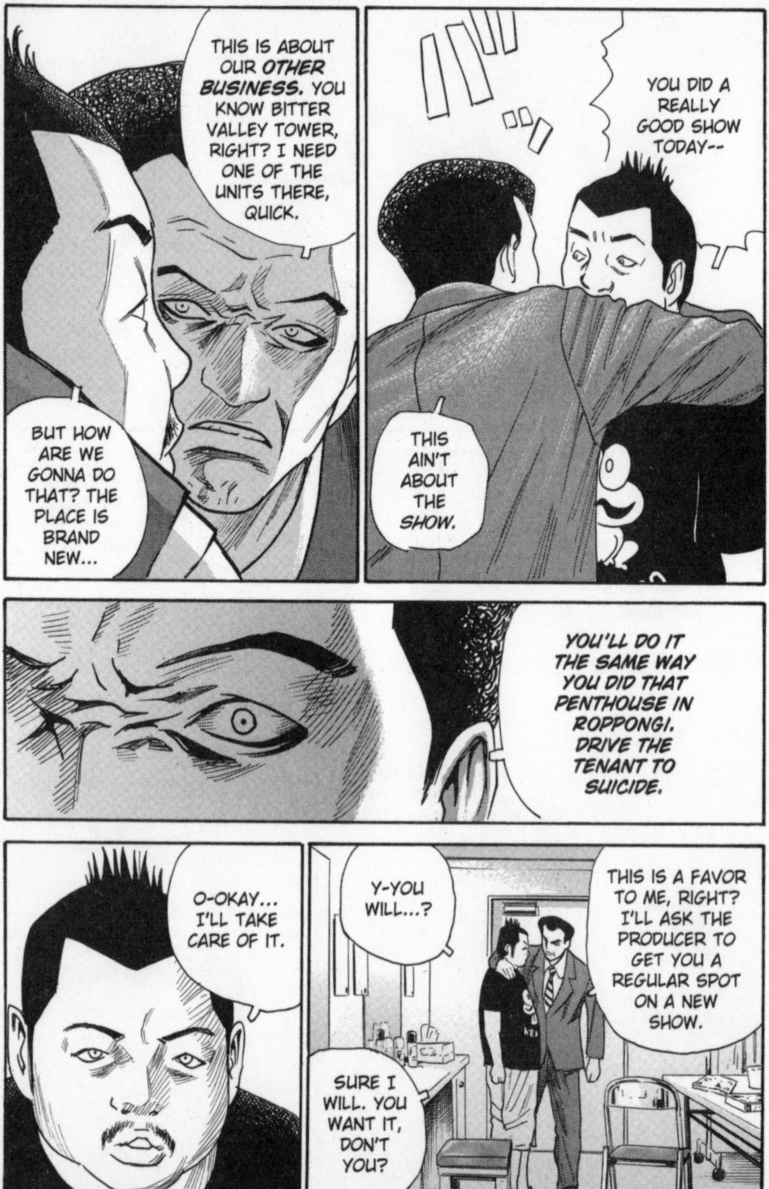
YOU DID A REALLY GOOD SHOW TODAY--
THIS AIN'T ABOUT THE *SHOW.*
THIS IS ABOUT OUR ***OTHER BUSINESS.*** YOU KNOW BITTER VALLEY TOWER, RIGHT? I NEED ONE OF THE UNITS THERE, QUICK.
BUT HOW ARE WE GONNA DO THAT? THE PLACE IS BRAND NEW...
YOU'LL DO IT THE SAME WAY YOU DID THAT PENTHOUSE IN ROPPONGI. DRIVE THE TENANT TO SUICIDE.
THIS IS A FAVOR TO ME, RIGHT? I'LL ASK THE PRODUCER TO GET YOU A REGULAR SPOT ON A NEW SHOW.
Y-YOU WILL...?
SURE I WILL. YOU WANT IT, DON'T YOU?
O-OKAY... I'LL TAKE CARE OF IT.

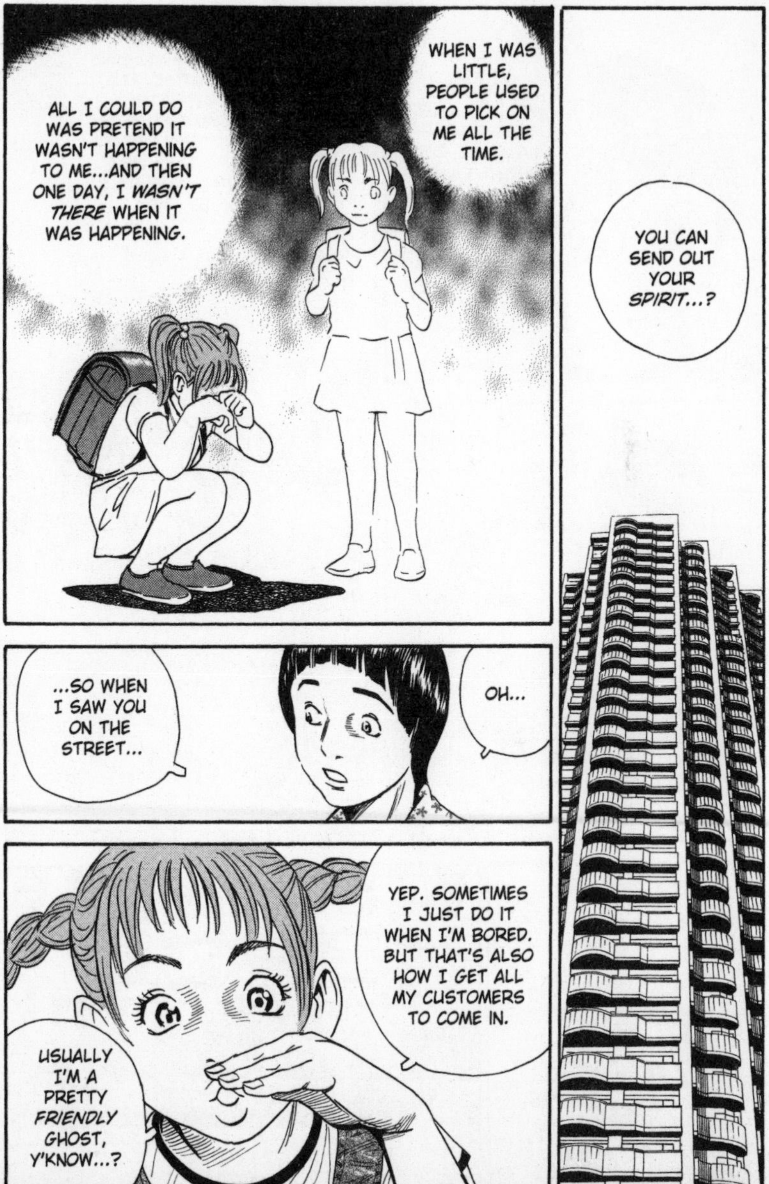
YOU CAN SEND OUT YOUR *SPIRIT*...?
WHEN I WAS LITTLE, PEOPLE USED TO PICK ON ME ALL THE TIME.
ALL I COULD DO WAS PRETEND IT WASN'T HAPPENING TO ME...AND THEN ONE DAY, I *WASN'T THERE* WHEN IT WAS HAPPENING.
OH...
...SO WHEN I SAW YOU ON THE STREET...
YEP. SOMETIMES I JUST DO IT WHEN I'M BORED. BUT THAT'S ALSO HOW I GET ALL MY CUSTOMERS TO COME IN.
USUALLY I'M A PRETTY *FRIENDLY* GHOST, Y'KNOW...?

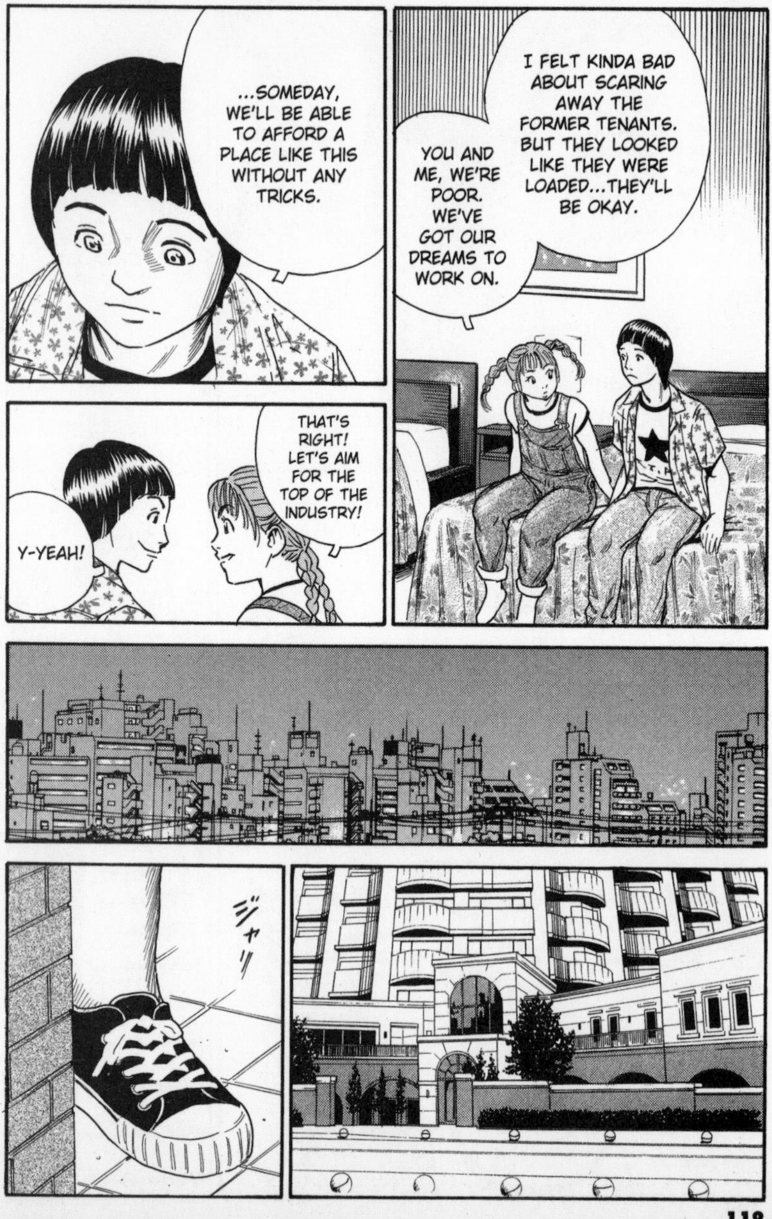
I FELT KINDA BAD ABOUT SCARING AWAY THE FORMER TENANTS. BUT THEY LOOKED LIKE THEY WERE LOADED...THEY'LL BE OKAY.
YOU AND ME, WE'RE POOR. WE'VE GOT OUR DREAMS TO WORK ON.
...SOMEDAY, WE'LL BE ABLE TO AFFORD A PLACE LIKE THIS WITHOUT ANY TRICKS.
THAT'S RIGHT! LET'S AIM FOR THE TOP OF THE INDUSTRY!
Y-YEAH!
ジャリ

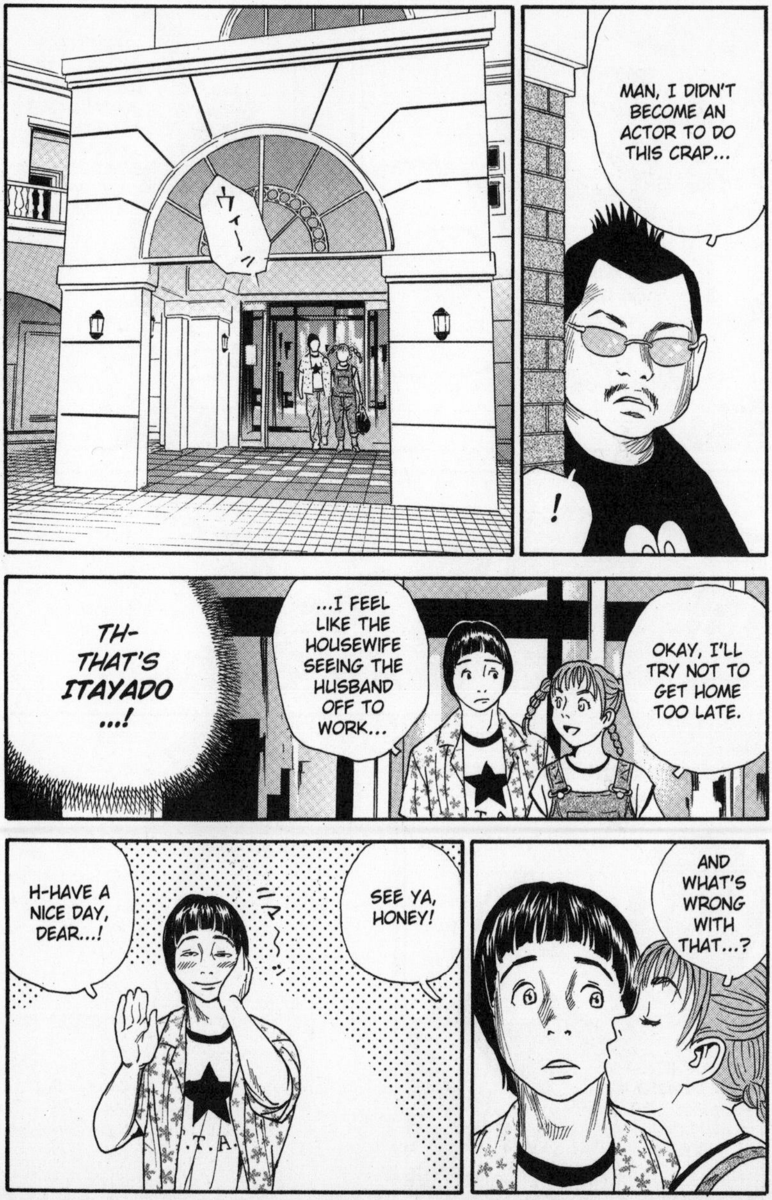
MAN, I DIDN'T BECOME AN ACTOR TO DO THIS CRAP...
!
ウィーン
OKAY, I'LL TRY NOT TO GET HOME TOO LATE.
...I FEEL LIKE THE HOUSEWIFE SEEING THE HUSBAND OFF TO WORK...
TH-THAT'S ITAYADO...!
AND WHAT'S WRONG WITH THAT...?
SEE YA, HONEY!
ニマ~~ッ
H-HAVE A NICE DAY, DEAR...!

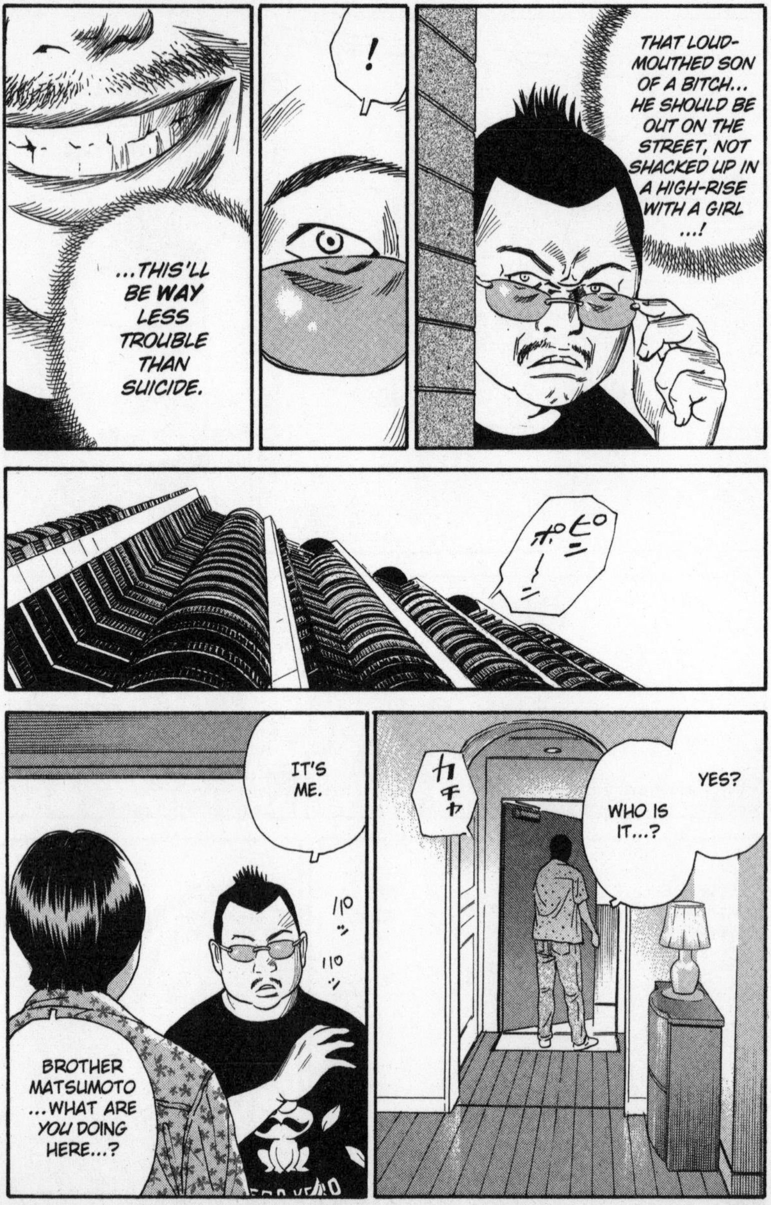
THAT LOUD-MOUTHED SON OF A BITCH... HE SHOULD BE OUT ON THE STREET, NOT SHACKED UP IN A HIGH-RISE WITH A GIRL ...!
!
...THIS'LL BE **WAY** LESS TROUBLE THAN SUICIDE.
ピンポーン
カチャ
YES?
WHO IS IT...?
IT'S ME.
パッ パッ
BROTHER MATSUMOTO ...WHAT ARE YOU DOING HERE...?

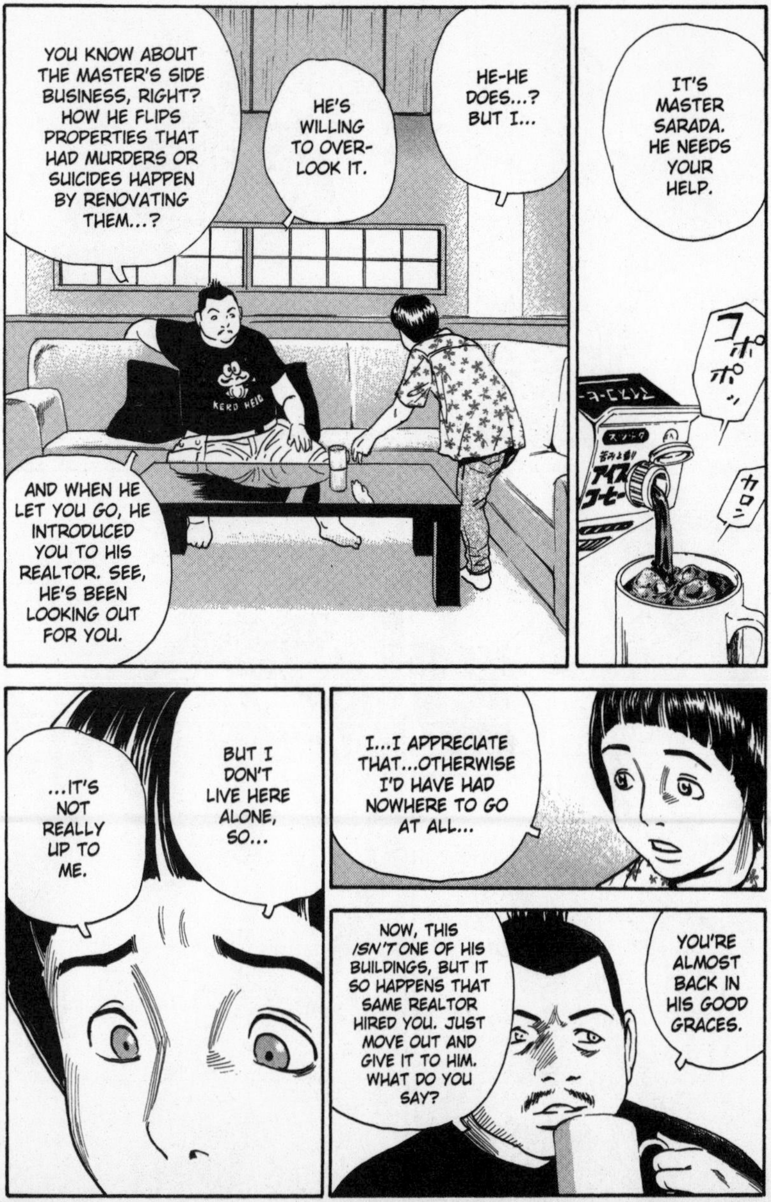
IT'S MASTER SARADA. HE NEEDS YOUR HELP.
コポポッ
カロン
HE-HE DOES...? BUT I...
HE'S WILLING TO OVER-LOOK IT.
YOU KNOW ABOUT THE MASTER'S SIDE BUSINESS, RIGHT? HOW HE FLIPS PROPERTIES THAT HAD MURDERS OR SUICIDES HAPPEN BY RENOVATING THEM...?
AND WHEN HE LET YOU GO, HE INTRODUCED YOU TO HIS REALTOR. SEE, HE'S BEEN LOOKING OUT FOR YOU.
I...I APPRECIATE THAT...OTHERWISE I'D HAVE HAD NOWHERE TO GO AT ALL...
YOU'RE ALMOST BACK IN HIS GOOD GRACES.
NOW, THIS *ISN'T* ONE OF HIS BUILDINGS, BUT IT SO HAPPENS THAT SAME REALTOR HIRED YOU. JUST MOVE OUT AND GIVE IT TO HIM. WHAT DO YOU SAY?
BUT I DON'T LIVE HERE ALONE, SO...
...IT'S NOT REALLY UP TO ME.

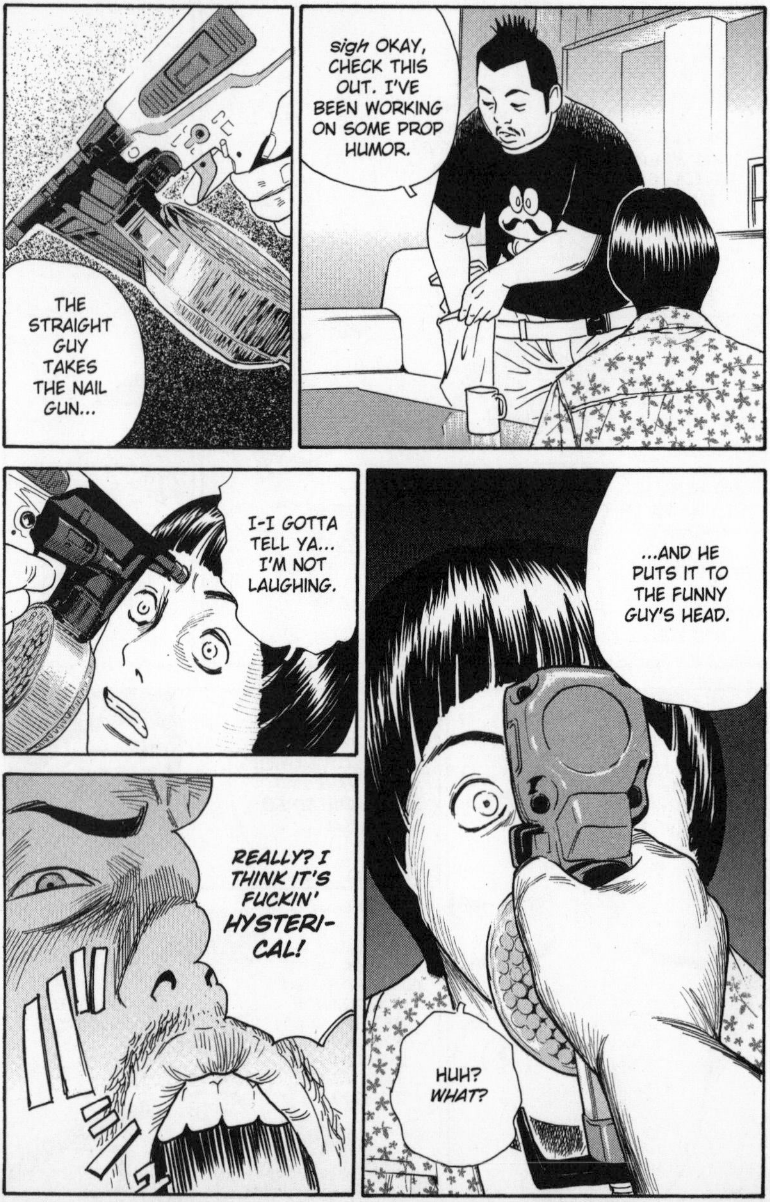
sigh OKAY, CHECK THIS OUT. I'VE BEEN WORKING ON SOME PROP HUMOR.
THE STRAIGHT GUY TAKES THE NAIL GUN...
...AND HE PUTS IT TO THE FUNNY GUY'S HEAD.
HUH? *WHAT?*
I-I GOTTA TELL YA... I'M NOT LAUGHING.
REALLY? I THINK IT'S FUCKIN' ***HYSTERICAL!***

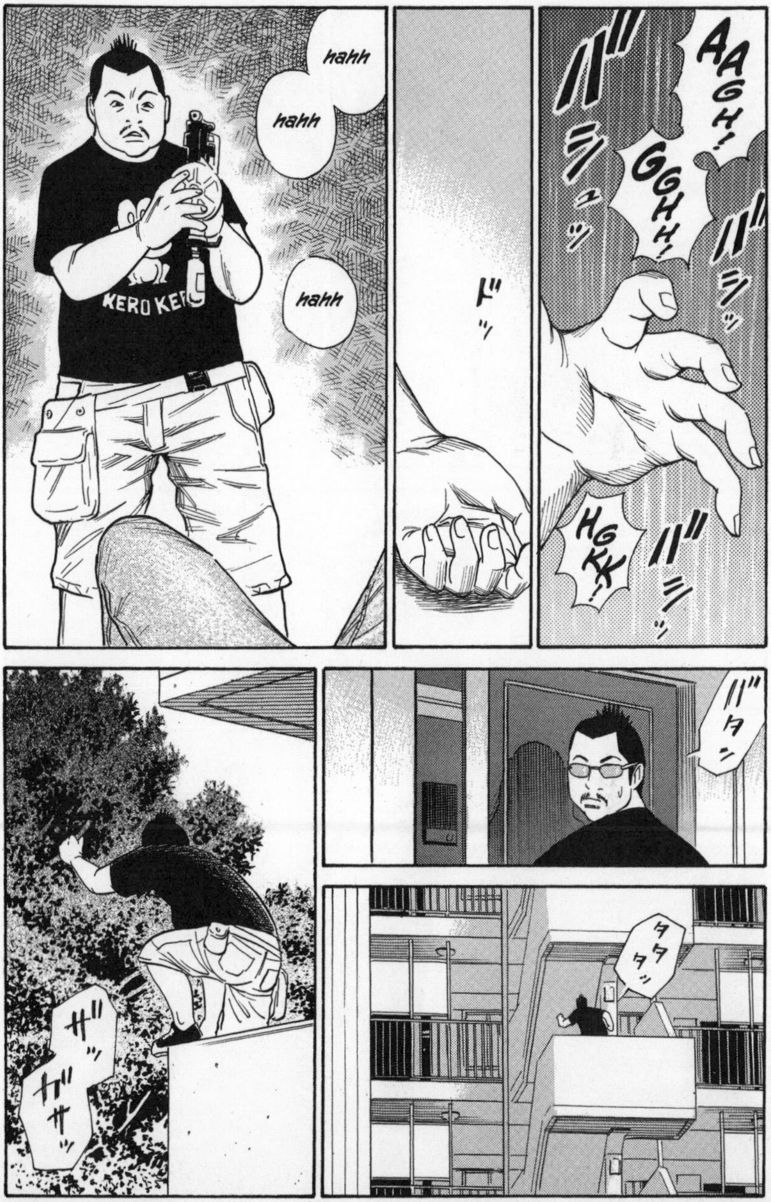

バシュッ
AAGH!
GGHH!
バシュッ
HGKK!
バシュッ
ドッ
hahh
hahh
hahh
バタン
タタタッ
ザッ
ザザッ

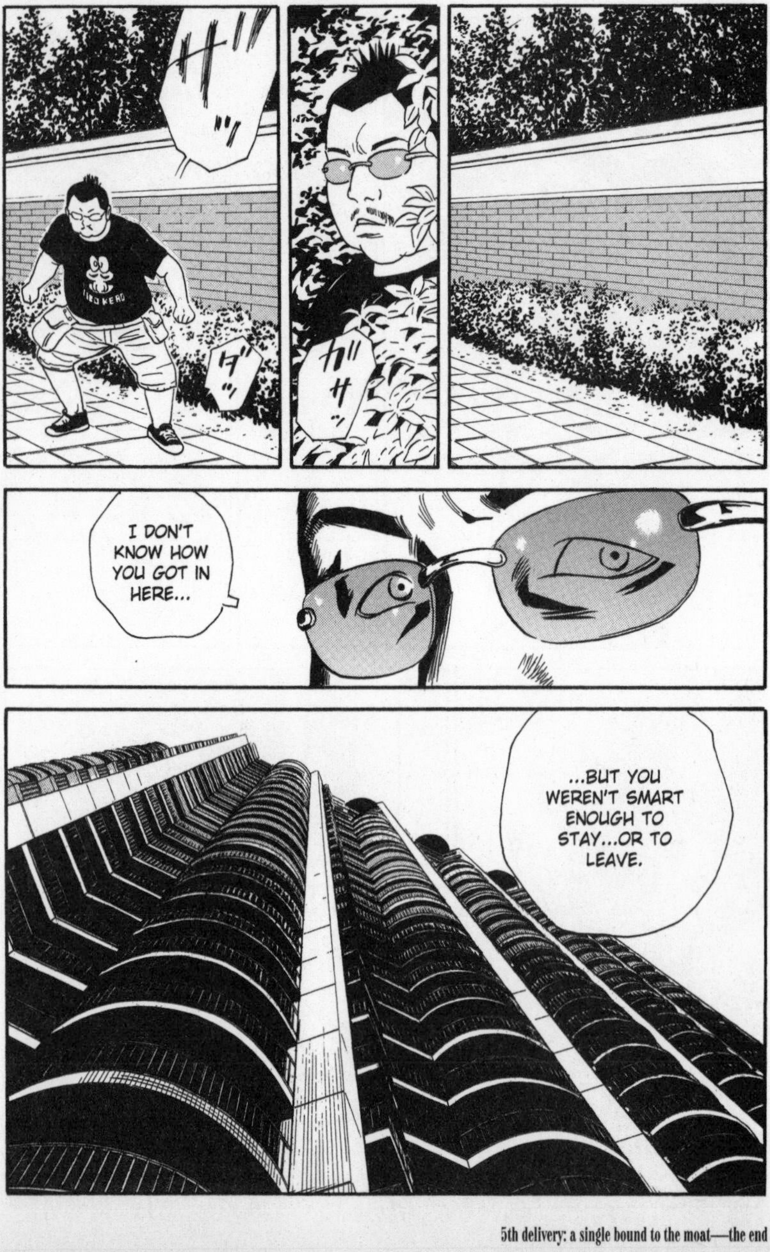
ガサッ
ダッ
I DON'T KNOW HOW YOU GOT IN HERE...
...BUT YOU WEREN'T SMART ENOUGH TO STAY...OR TO LEAVE.

5th delivery: a single bound to the moat—the end

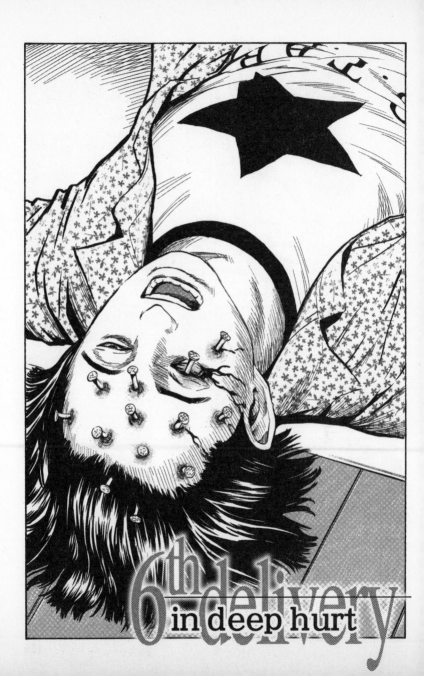

6th delivery
in deep hurt

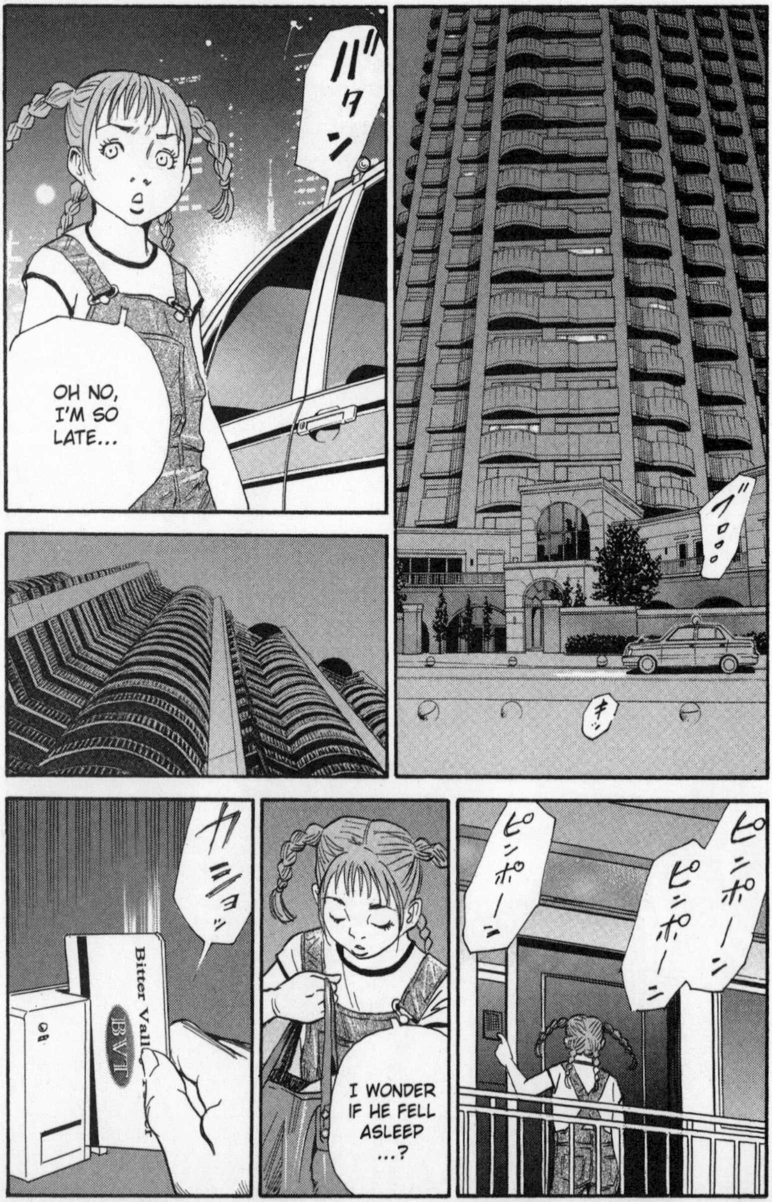
ブロロ
キッ
バタン
OH NO, I'M SO LATE...
ピンポーン
ピンポーン
ピンポーン
I WONDER IF HE FELL ASLEEP ...?

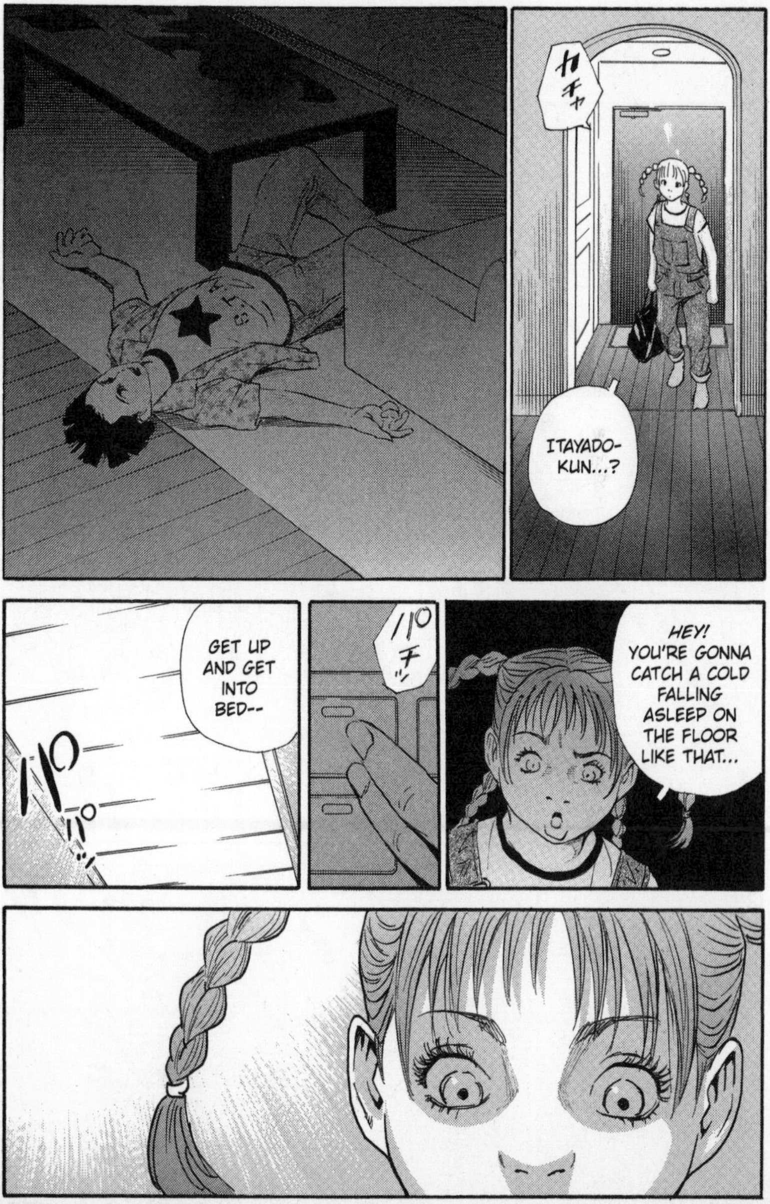

カチャ
ITAYADO-KUN...?
HEY! YOU'RE GONNA CATCH A COLD FALLING ASLEEP ON THE FLOOR LIKE THAT...
パチッ
GET UP AND GET INTO BED--
パッ
パッ

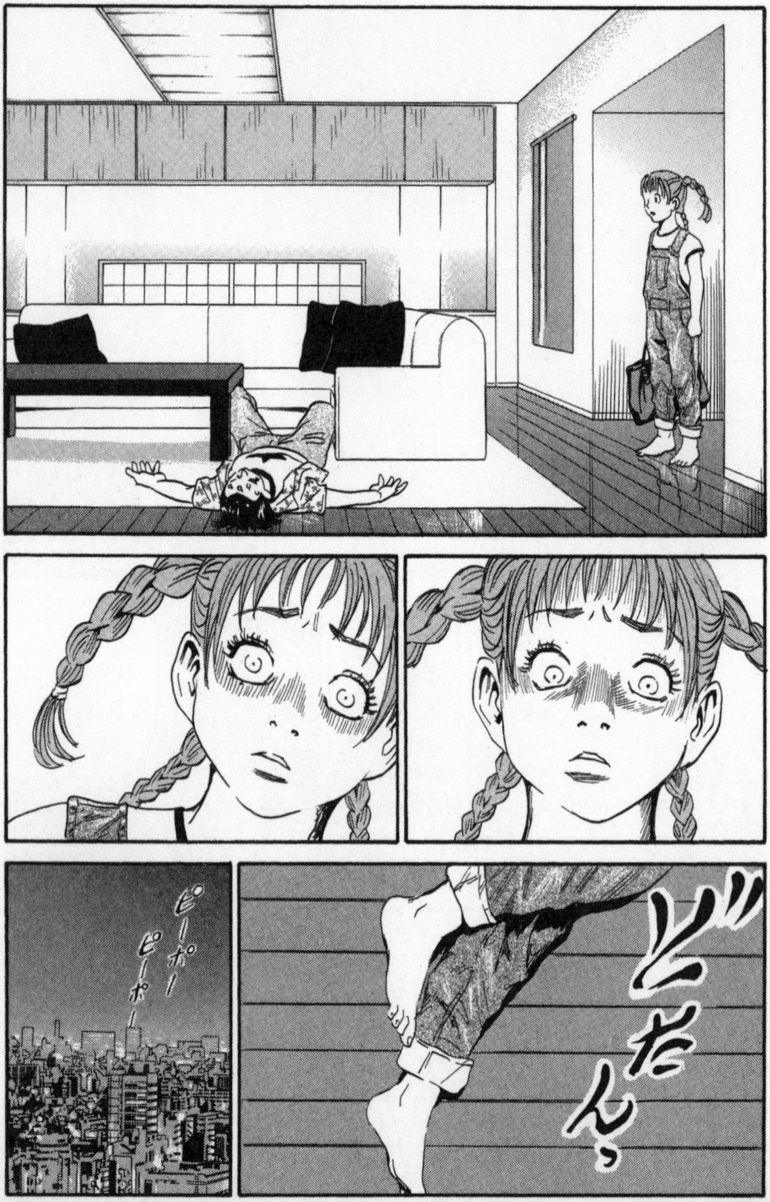
どだんっ
ピーポー
ピーポー

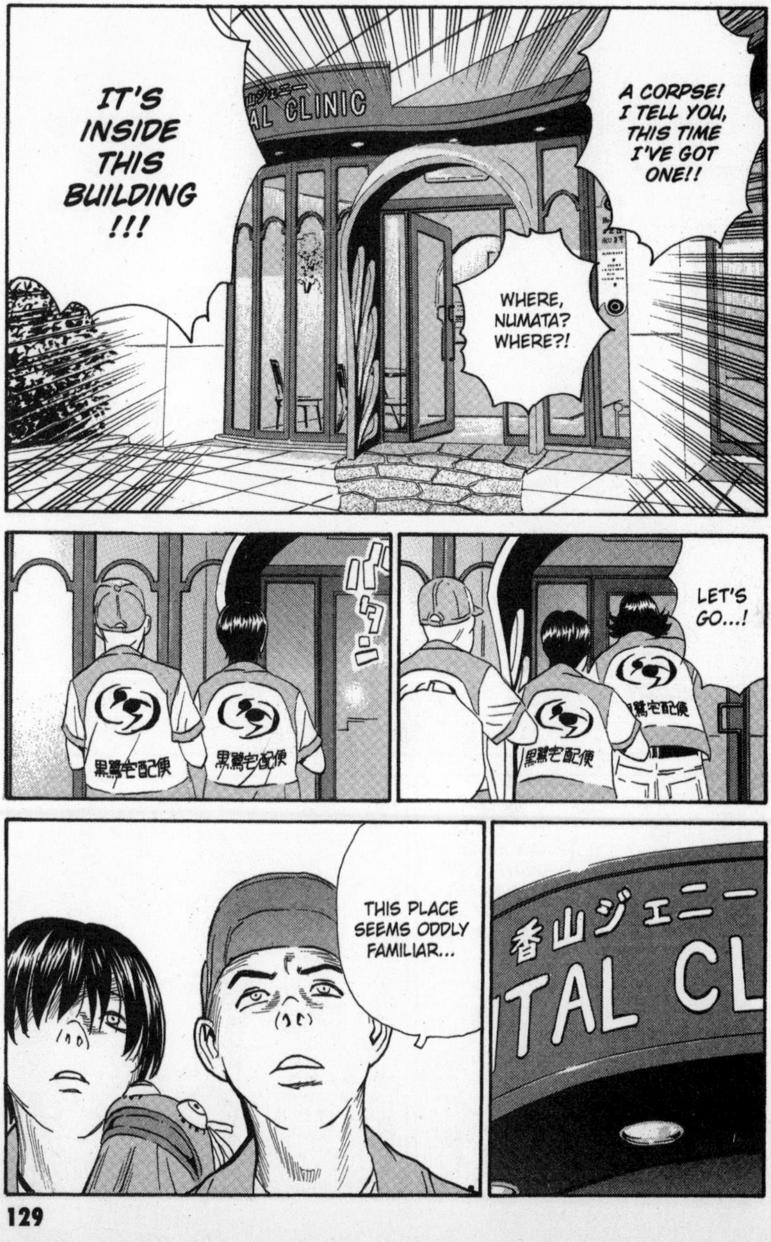
A CORPSE! I TELL YOU, THIS TIME I'VE GOT ONE!!
WHERE, NUMATA? WHERE?!
IT'S INSIDE THIS BUILDING!!!
AL CLINIC
LET'S GO...!
黒鷺宅配便
黒鷺宅配便
バタン
黒鷺宅配便
黒鷺宅配便
香山ジェニー
TAL CL
THIS PLACE SEEMS ODDLY FAMILIAR...

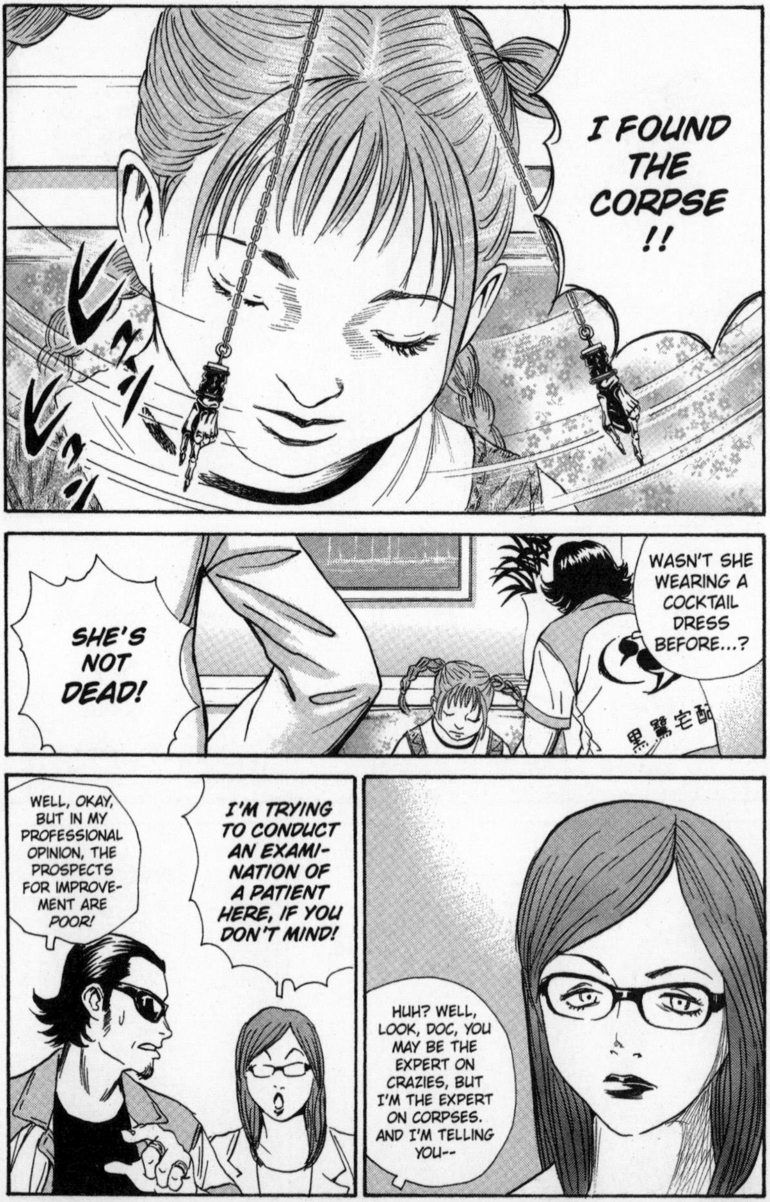
I FOUND THE CORPSE !!
WASN'T SHE WEARING A COCKTAIL DRESS BEFORE...?
黒鷺宅配
SHE'S NOT DEAD!
HUH? WELL, LOOK, DOC, YOU MAY BE THE EXPERT ON CRAZIES, BUT I'M THE EXPERT ON CORPSES. AND I'M TELLING YOU--
I'M TRYING TO CONDUCT AN EXAMINATION OF A PATIENT HERE, IF YOU DON'T MIND!
WELL, OKAY, BUT IN MY PROFESSIONAL OPINION, THE PROSPECTS FOR IMPROVEMENT ARE POOR!

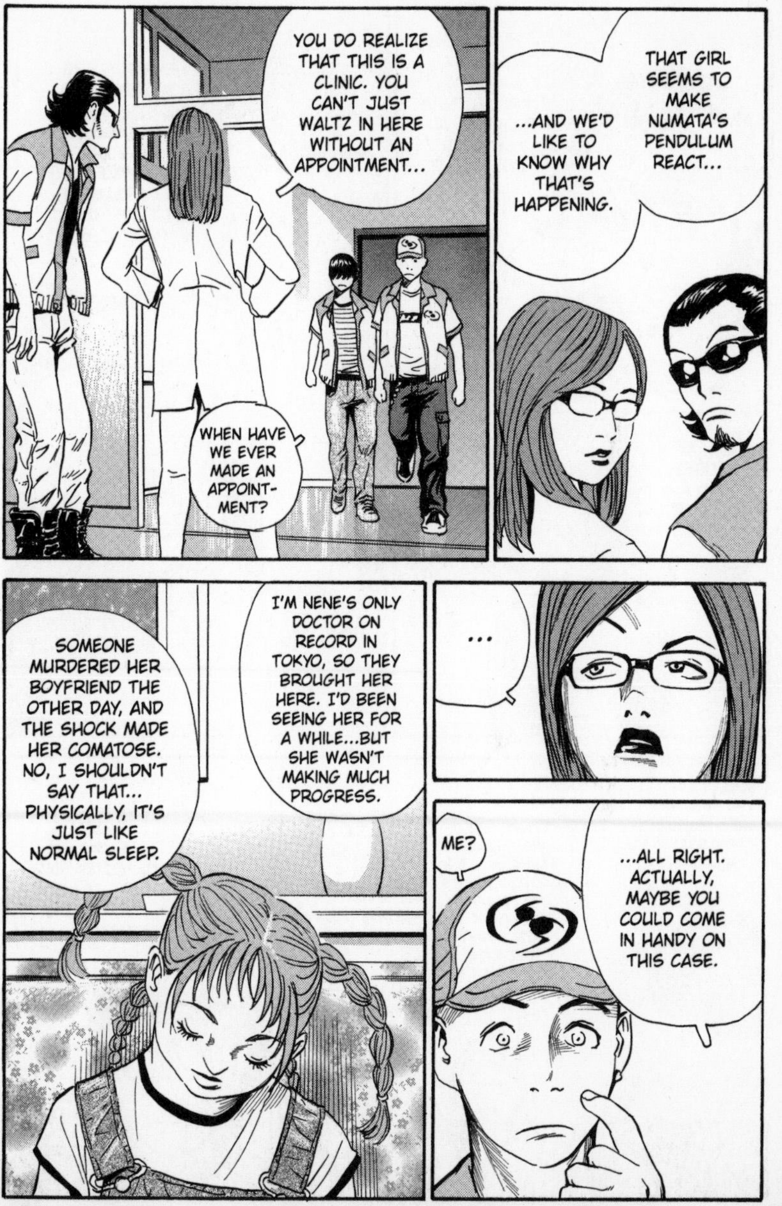
THAT GIRL SEEMS TO MAKE NUMATA'S PENDULUM REACT...
...AND WE'D LIKE TO KNOW WHY THAT'S HAPPENING.
YOU DO REALIZE THAT THIS IS A CLINIC. YOU CAN'T JUST WALTZ IN HERE WITHOUT AN APPOINTMENT...
WHEN HAVE WE EVER MADE AN APPOINT-MENT?
...
...ALL RIGHT. ACTUALLY, MAYBE YOU COULD COME IN HANDY ON THIS CASE.
ME?
I'M NENE'S ONLY DOCTOR ON RECORD IN TOKYO, SO THEY BROUGHT HER HERE. I'D BEEN SEEING HER FOR A WHILE...BUT SHE WASN'T MAKING MUCH PROGRESS.
SOMEONE MURDERED HER BOYFRIEND THE OTHER DAY, AND THE SHOCK MADE HER COMATOSE. NO, I SHOULDN'T SAY THAT... PHYSICALLY, IT'S JUST LIKE NORMAL SLEEP.

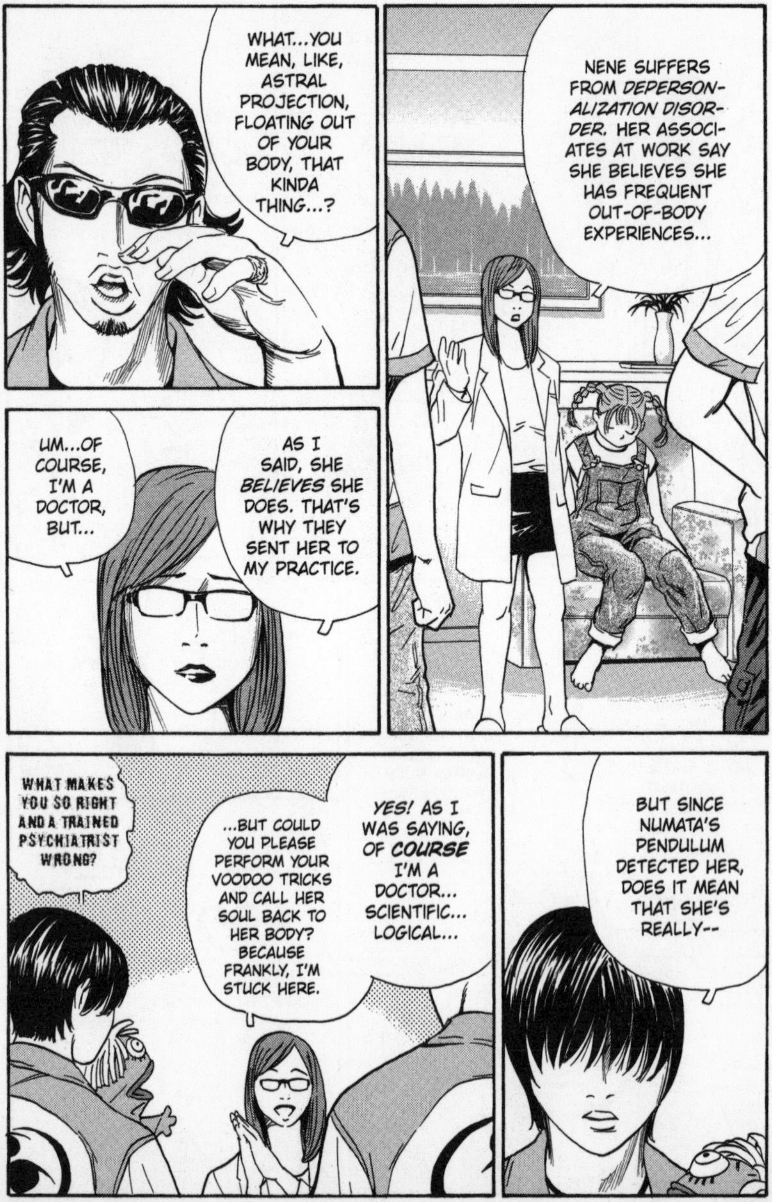
NENE SUFFERS FROM *DEPERSONALIZATION DISORDER.* HER ASSOCIATES AT WORK SAY SHE BELIEVES SHE HAS FREQUENT OUT-OF-BODY EXPERIENCES...
WHAT...YOU MEAN, LIKE, ASTRAL PROJECTION, FLOATING OUT OF YOUR BODY, THAT KINDA THING...?
AS I SAID, SHE *BELIEVES* SHE DOES. THAT'S WHY THEY SENT HER TO MY PRACTICE.
UM...OF COURSE, I'M A DOCTOR, BUT...
BUT SINCE NUMATA'S PENDULUM DETECTED HER, DOES IT MEAN THAT SHE'S REALLY--
YES! AS I WAS SAYING, OF ***COURSE*** I'M A DOCTOR... SCIENTIFIC... LOGICAL...
...BUT COULD YOU PLEASE PERFORM YOUR VOODOO TRICKS AND CALL HER SOUL BACK TO HER BODY? BECAUSE FRANKLY, I'M STUCK HERE.
WHAT MAKES YOU SO RIGHT AND A TRAINED PSYCHIATRIST WRONG?

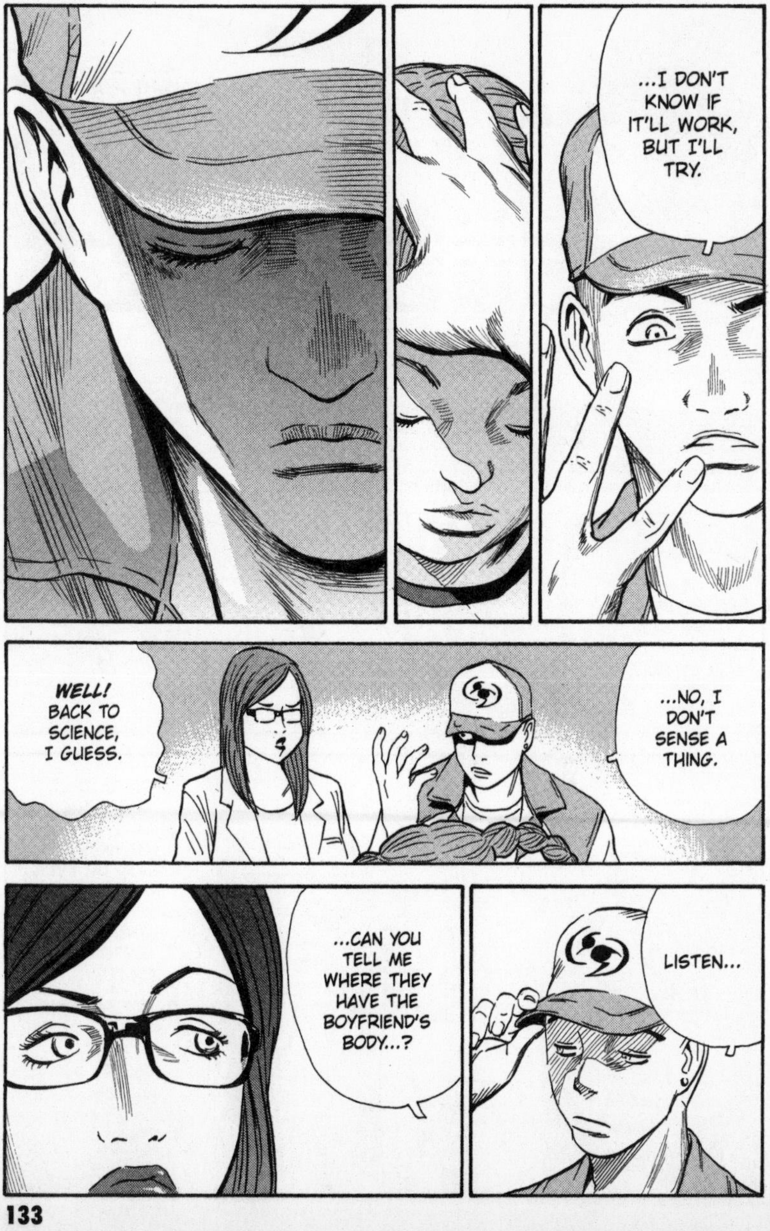
...I DON'T KNOW IF IT'LL WORK, BUT I'LL TRY.
...NO, I DON'T SENSE A THING.
WELL! BACK TO SCIENCE, I GUESS.
LISTEN...
...CAN YOU TELL ME WHERE THEY HAVE THE BOYFRIEND'S BODY...?

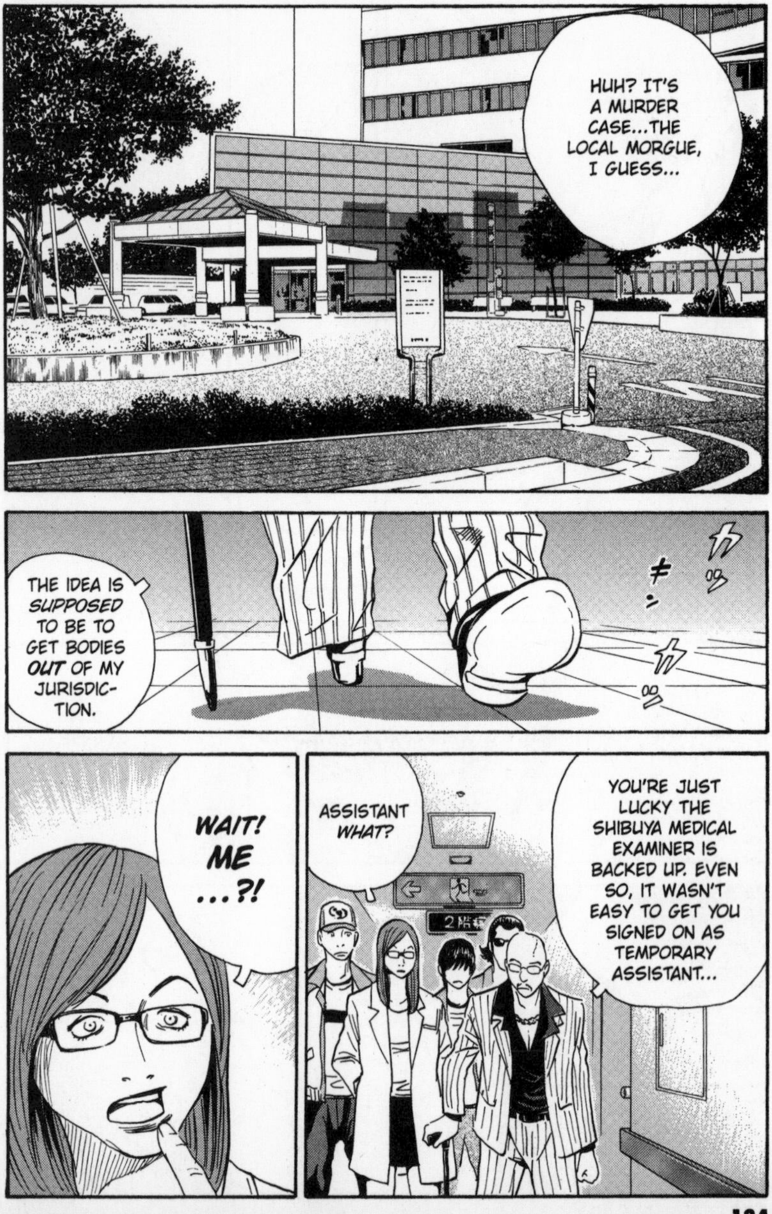
HUH? IT'S A MURDER CASE...THE LOCAL MORGUE, I GUESS...
THE IDEA IS SUPPOSED TO BE TO GET BODIES OUT OF MY JURISDICTION.
YOU'RE JUST LUCKY THE SHIBUYA MEDICAL EXAMINER IS BACKED UP. EVEN SO, IT WASN'T EASY TO GET YOU SIGNED ON AS TEMPORARY ASSISTANT...
ASSISTANT WHAT?
WAIT! ME ...?!

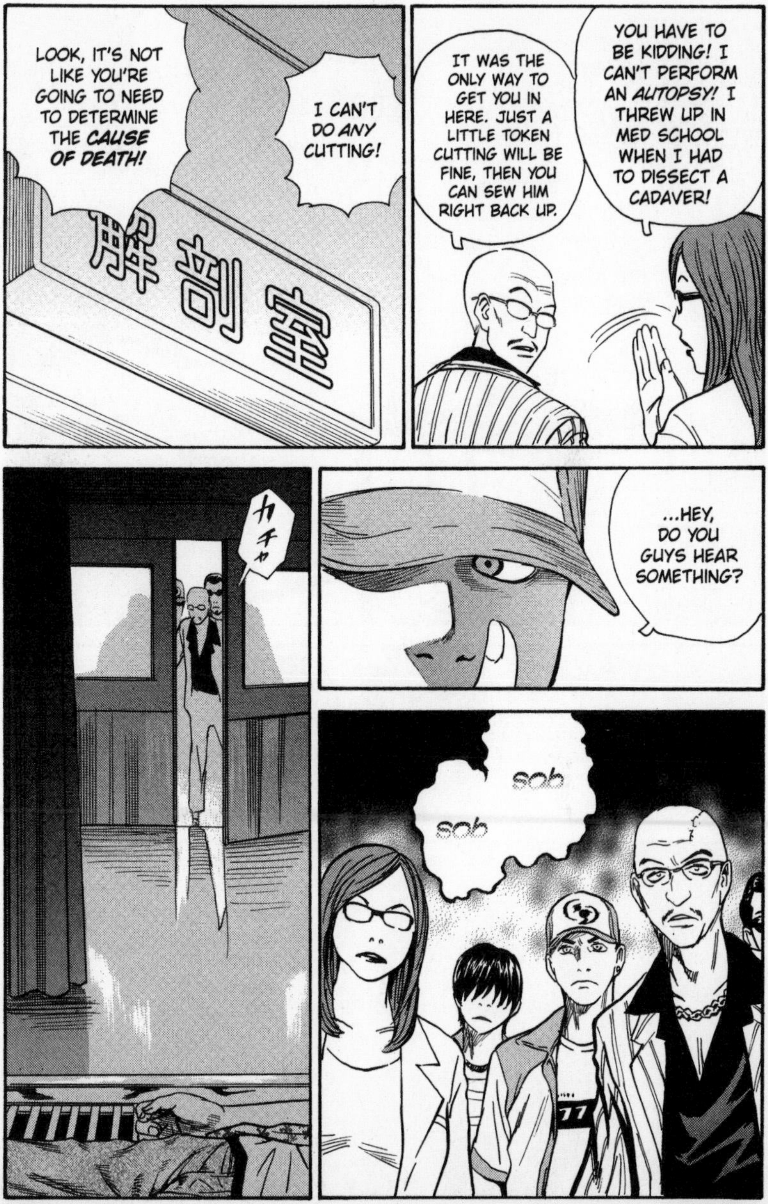
YOU HAVE TO BE KIDDING! I CAN'T PERFORM AN *AUTOPSY!* I THREW UP IN MED SCHOOL WHEN I HAD TO DISSECT A CADAVER!
IT WAS THE ONLY WAY TO GET YOU IN HERE. JUST A LITTLE TOKEN CUTTING WILL BE FINE, THEN YOU CAN SEW HIM RIGHT BACK UP.
I CAN'T DO *ANY* CUTTING!
LOOK, IT'S NOT LIKE YOU'RE GOING TO NEED TO DETERMINE THE ***CAUSE OF DEATH!***
解剖室
...HEY, DO YOU GUYS HEAR SOMETHING?
sob
sob
カチャ

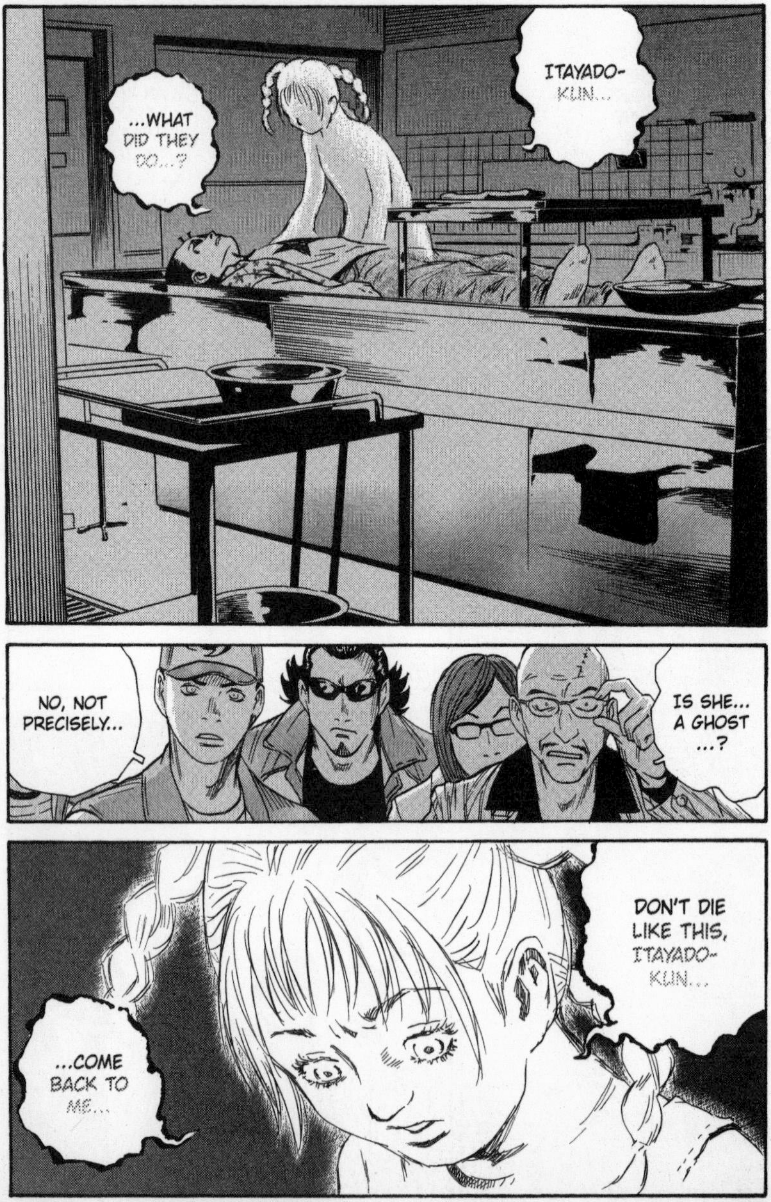
ITAYADO-KUN...
...WHAT DID THEY DO...?
IS SHE... A GHOST ...?
NO, NOT PRECISELY...
DON'T DIE LIKE THIS, ITAYADO-KUN...
...COME BACK TO ME...

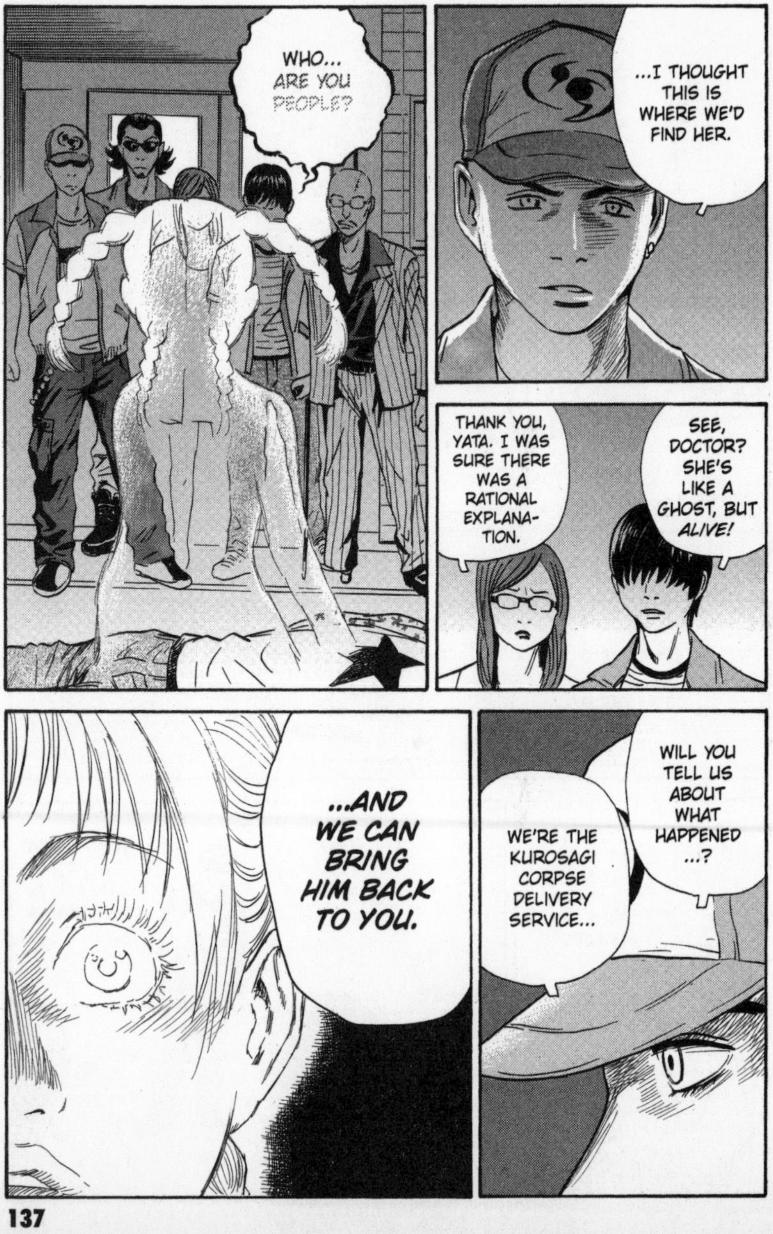
...I THOUGHT THIS IS WHERE WE'D FIND HER.
SEE, DOCTOR? SHE'S LIKE A GHOST, BUT ALIVE!
THANK YOU, YATA. I WAS SURE THERE WAS A RATIONAL EXPLANATION.
WHO... ARE YOU PEOPLE?
WILL YOU TELL US ABOUT WHAT HAPPENED ...?
WE'RE THE KUROSAGI CORPSE DELIVERY SERVICE...
...AND WE CAN BRING HIM BACK TO YOU.

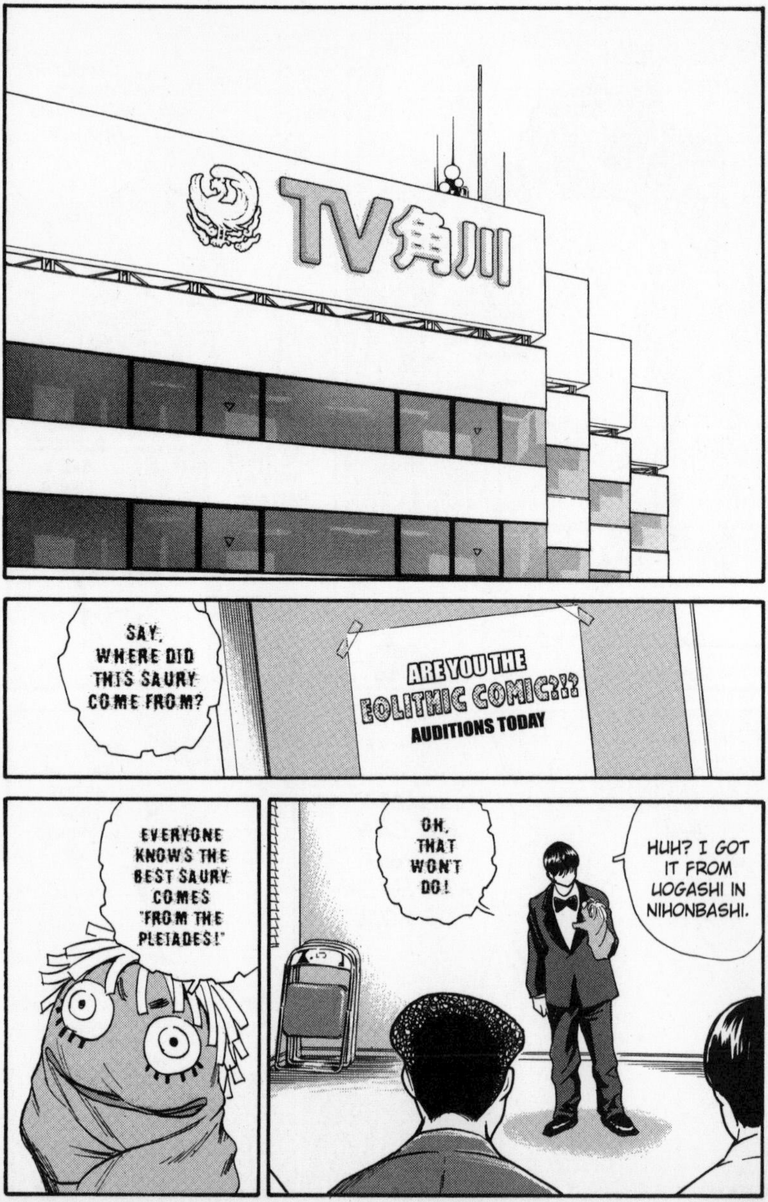
TV角川
ARE YOU THE EOLITHIC COMIC?!? AUDITIONS TODAY
SAY, WHERE DID THIS SAURY COME FROM?
HUH? I GOT IT FROM UOGASHI IN NIHONBASHI.
OH, THAT WON'T DO!
EVERYONE KNOWS THE BEST SAURY COMES "FROM THE PLEIADES!"

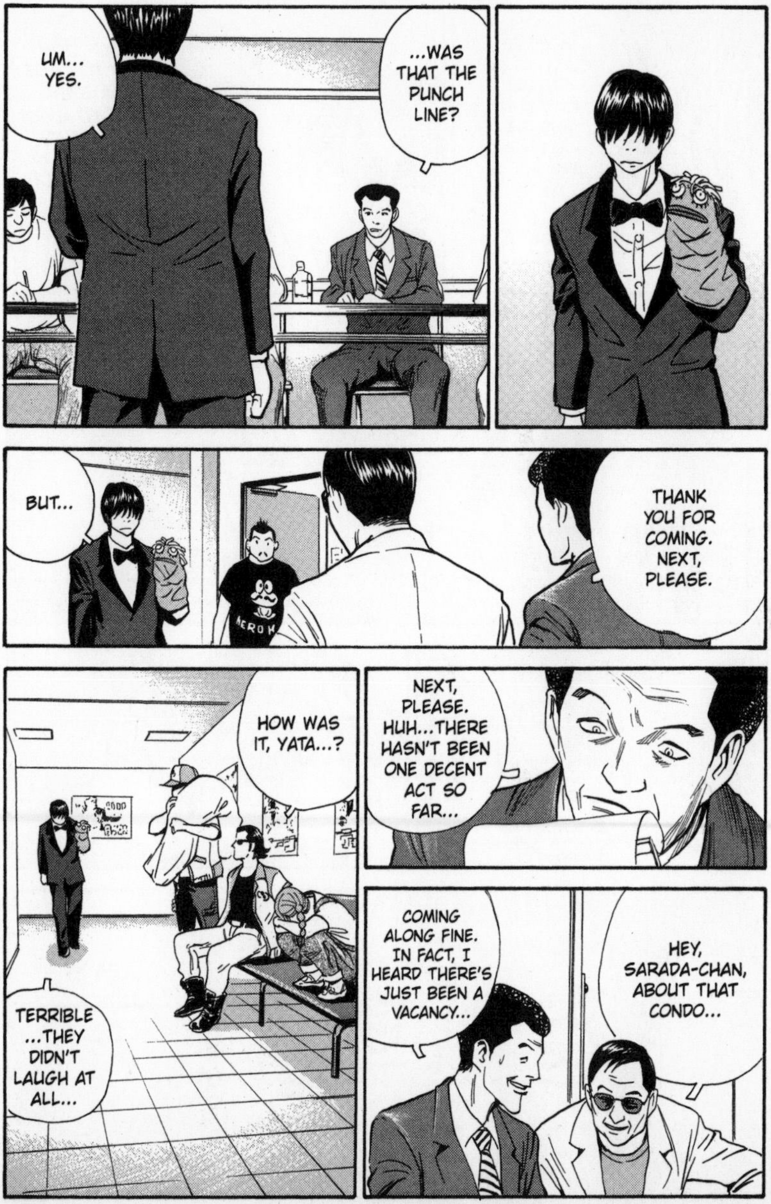
...WAS THAT THE PUNCH LINE?
UM... YES.
THANK YOU FOR COMING. NEXT, PLEASE.
BUT...
NEXT, PLEASE. HUH...THERE HASN'T BEEN ONE DECENT ACT SO FAR...
HEY, SARADA-CHAN, ABOUT THAT CONDO...
COMING ALONG FINE. IN FACT, I HEARD THERE'S JUST BEEN A VACANCY...
HOW WAS IT, YATA...?
TERRIBLE ...THEY DIDN'T LAUGH AT ALL...

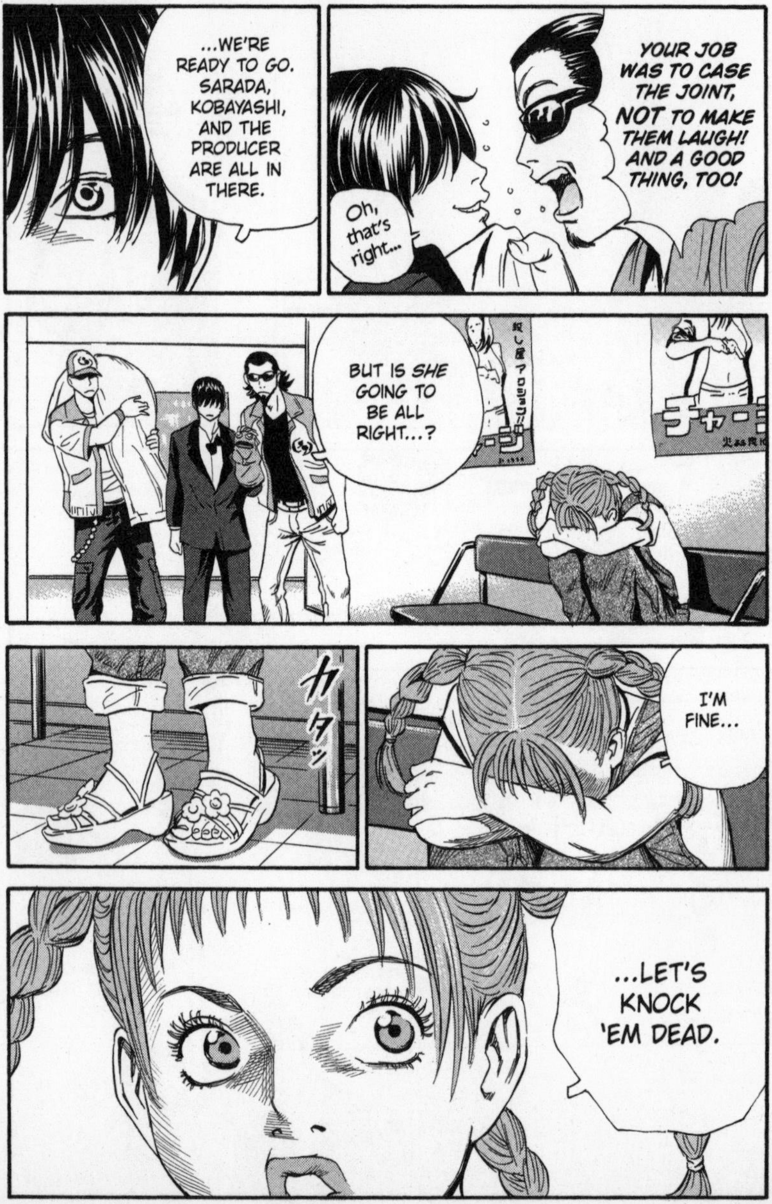
YOUR JOB WAS TO CASE THE JOINT, NOT TO MAKE THEM LAUGH! AND A GOOD THING, TOO!
Oh, that's right...
...WE'RE READY TO GO. SARADA, KOBAYASHI, AND THE PRODUCER ARE ALL IN THERE.
BUT IS *SHE* GOING TO BE ALL RIGHT...?
I'M FINE...
カタッ
...LET'S KNOCK 'EM DEAD.

KARATSU, PLEASE...

O-OKAY.

COM...ING...

HEY, NEXT ONE! WHERE'S THE NEXT...

I-I-I...IT... ITA...

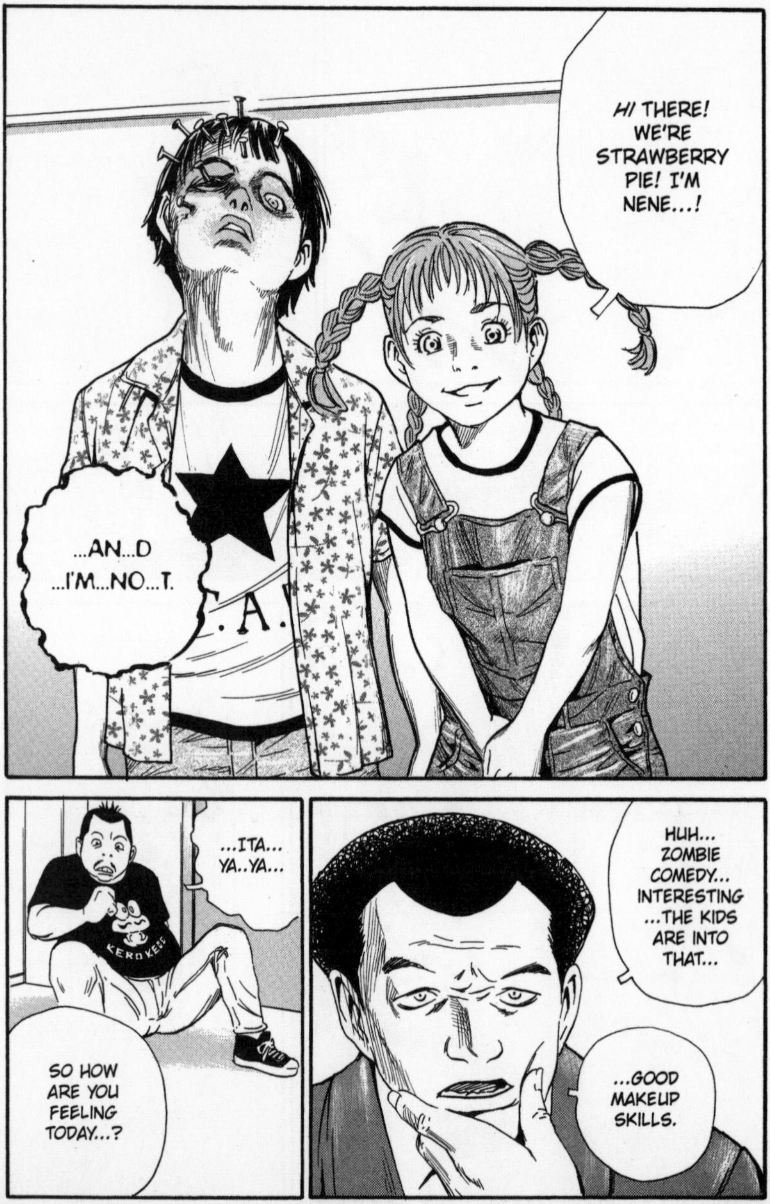
HI THERE! WE'RE STRAWBERRY PIE! I'M NENE...!
...AN...D ...I'M...NO...T.
HUH... ZOMBIE COMEDY... INTERESTING ...THE KIDS ARE INTO THAT...
...GOOD MAKEUP SKILLS.
...ITA... YA..YA...
SO HOW ARE YOU FEELING TODAY...?

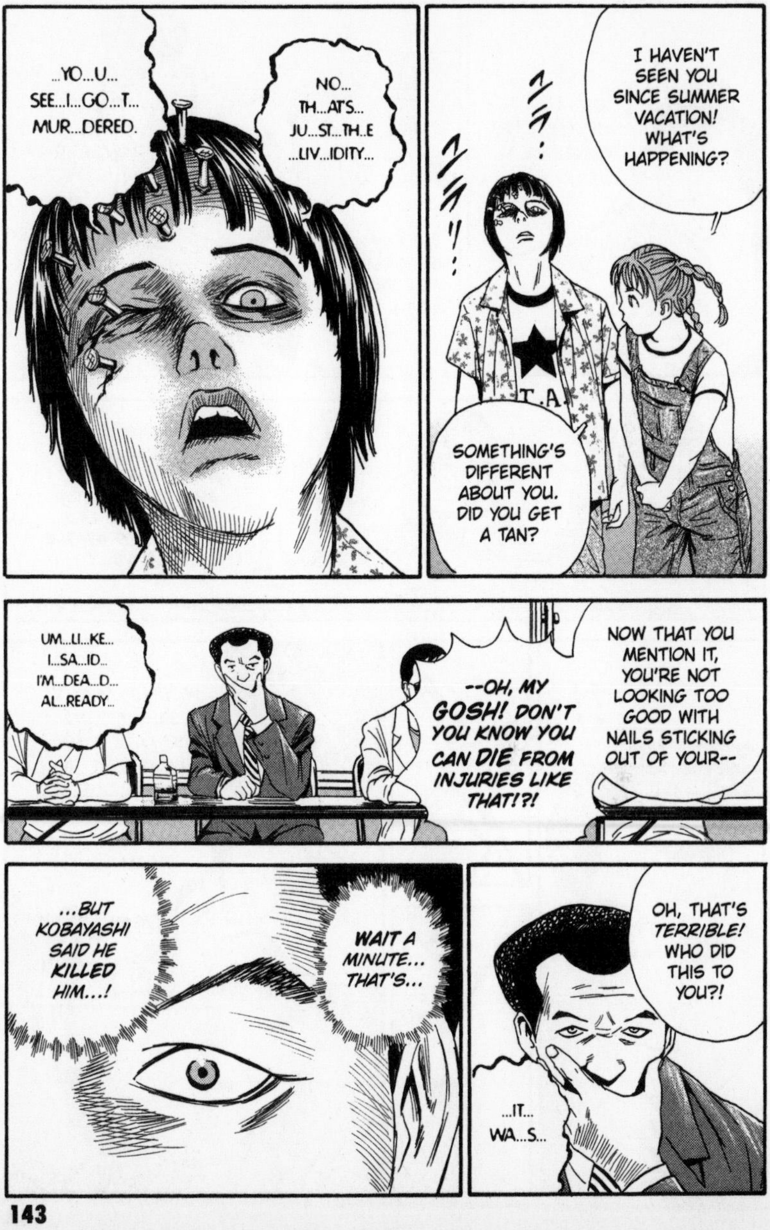
I HAVEN'T SEEN YOU SINCE SUMMER VACATION! WHAT'S HAPPENING?
SOMETHING'S DIFFERENT ABOUT YOU. DID YOU GET A TAN?
NO... TH...AT'S... JU...ST...TH..E ...LIV...IDITY...
...YO...U... SEE...I...GO...T... MUR...DERED.
NOW THAT YOU MENTION IT, YOU'RE NOT LOOKING TOO GOOD WITH NAILS STICKING OUT OF YOUR--
--OH, MY GOSH! DON'T YOU KNOW YOU CAN DIE FROM INJURIES LIKE THAT!?!
UM...LI...KE... I...SA...ID... I'M...DEA...D... AL...READY...
OH, THAT'S TERRIBLE! WHO DID THIS TO YOU?!
...IT... WA...S...
WAIT A MINUTE... THAT'S...
...BUT KOBAYASHI SAID HE KILLED HIM...!

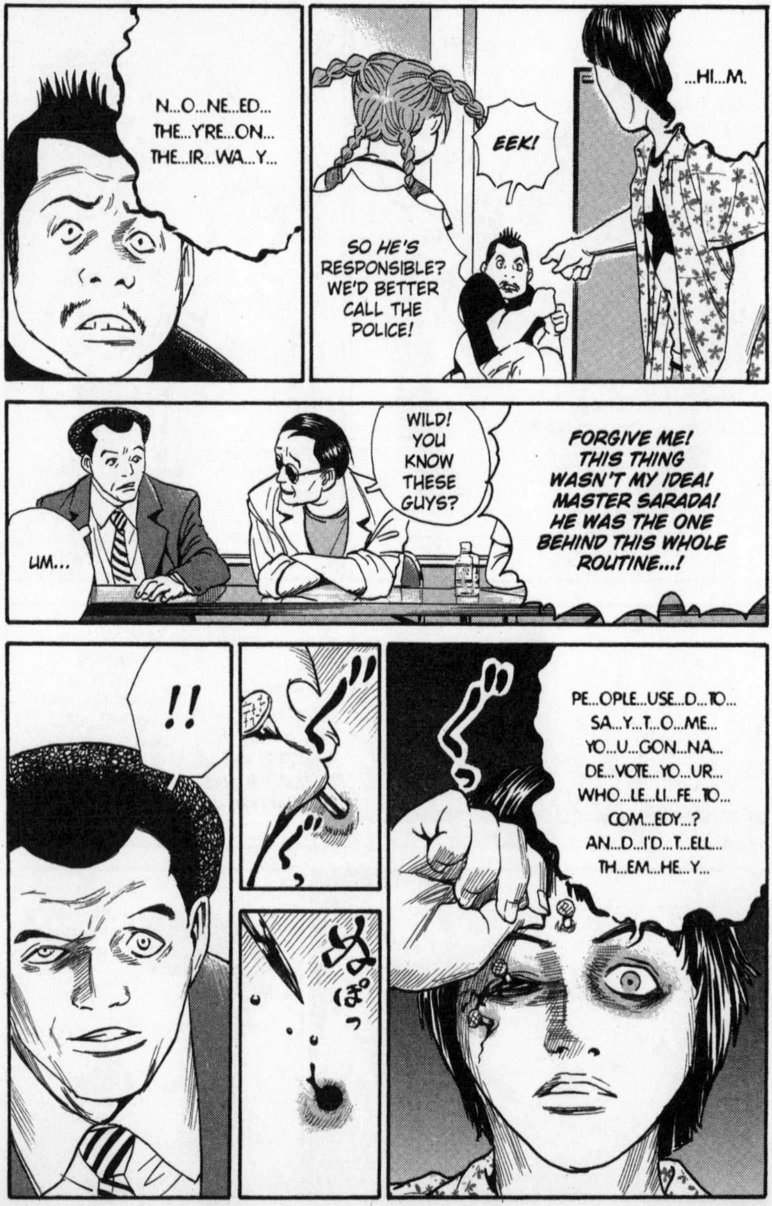
...HI...M.
EEK!
SO HE'S RESPONSIBLE? WE'D BETTER CALL THE POLICE!
N...O...NE...ED... THE...Y'RE...ON... THE...IR...WA...Y...
FORGIVE ME! THIS THING WASN'T MY IDEA! MASTER SARADA! HE WAS THE ONE BEHIND THIS WHOLE ROUTINE...!
WILD! YOU KNOW THESE GUYS?
UM...
PE...OPLE...USE...D...TO... SA...Y...T...O...ME... YO...U...GON...NA... DE...VOTE...YO...UR... WHO...LE...LI...FE...TO... COM...EDY...? AN...D...I'D...T...ELL... TH...EM...HE...Y...
ぬぽっ
!!

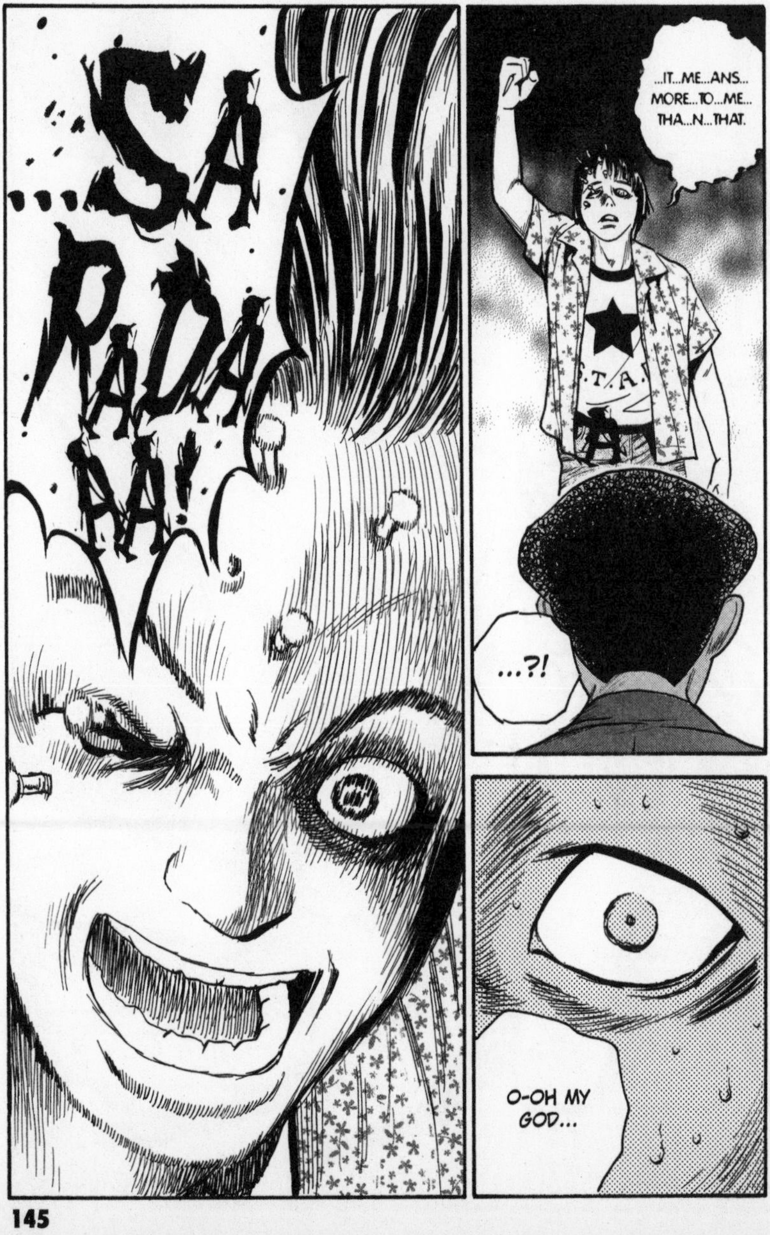
...IT...ME...ANS... MORE...TO...ME... THA...N...THAT.
...?!
O-OH MY GOD...
...SA RADA AA!

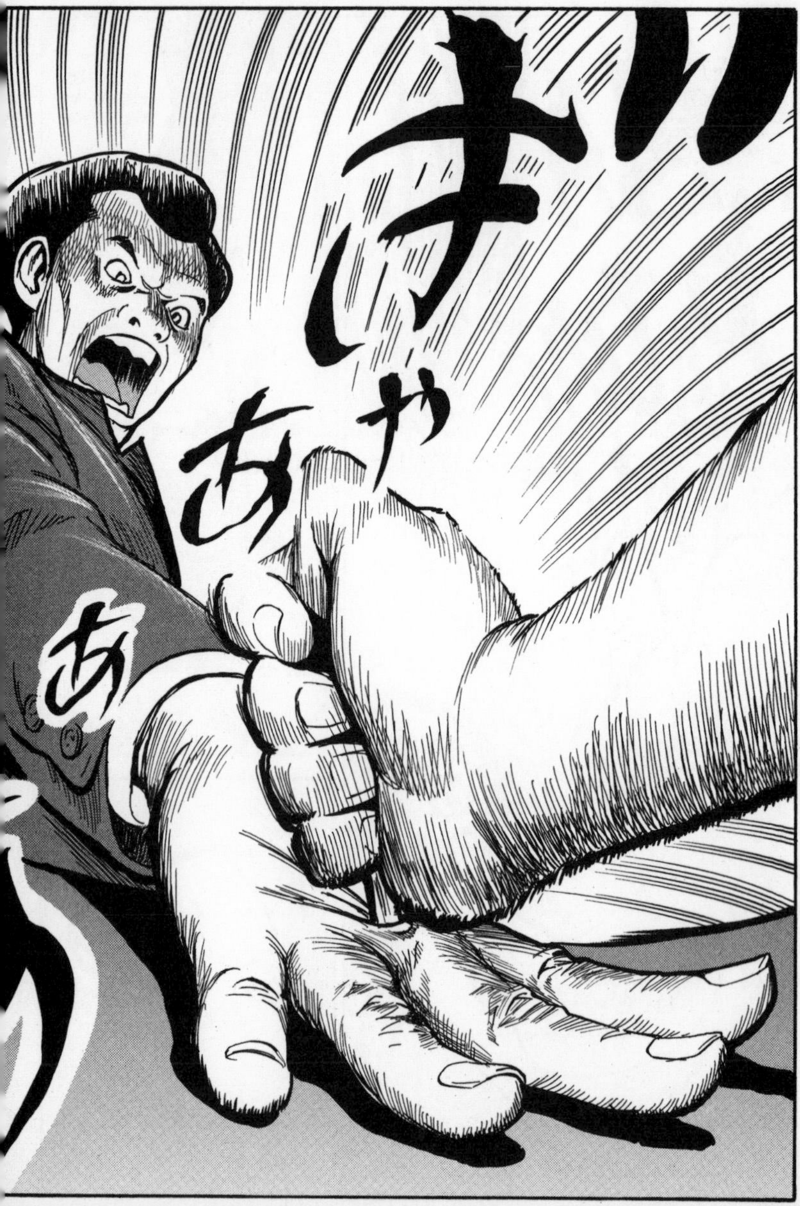
ぎゃああ

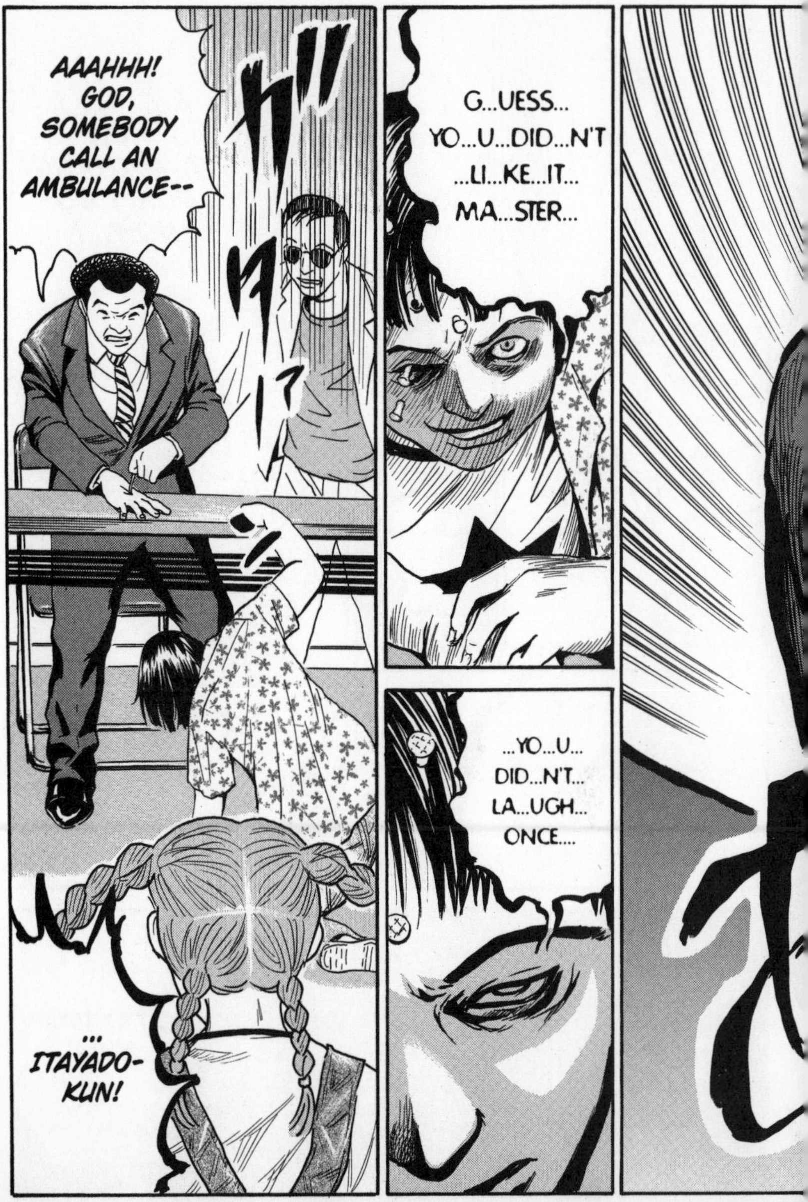
G...UESS... YO...U...DID...N'T ...LI...KE...IT... MA...STER...
...YO...U... DID...N'T... LA...UGH... ONCE....
AAAHHH! GOD, SOMEBODY CALL AN AMBULANCE--
... ITAYADO-KUN!

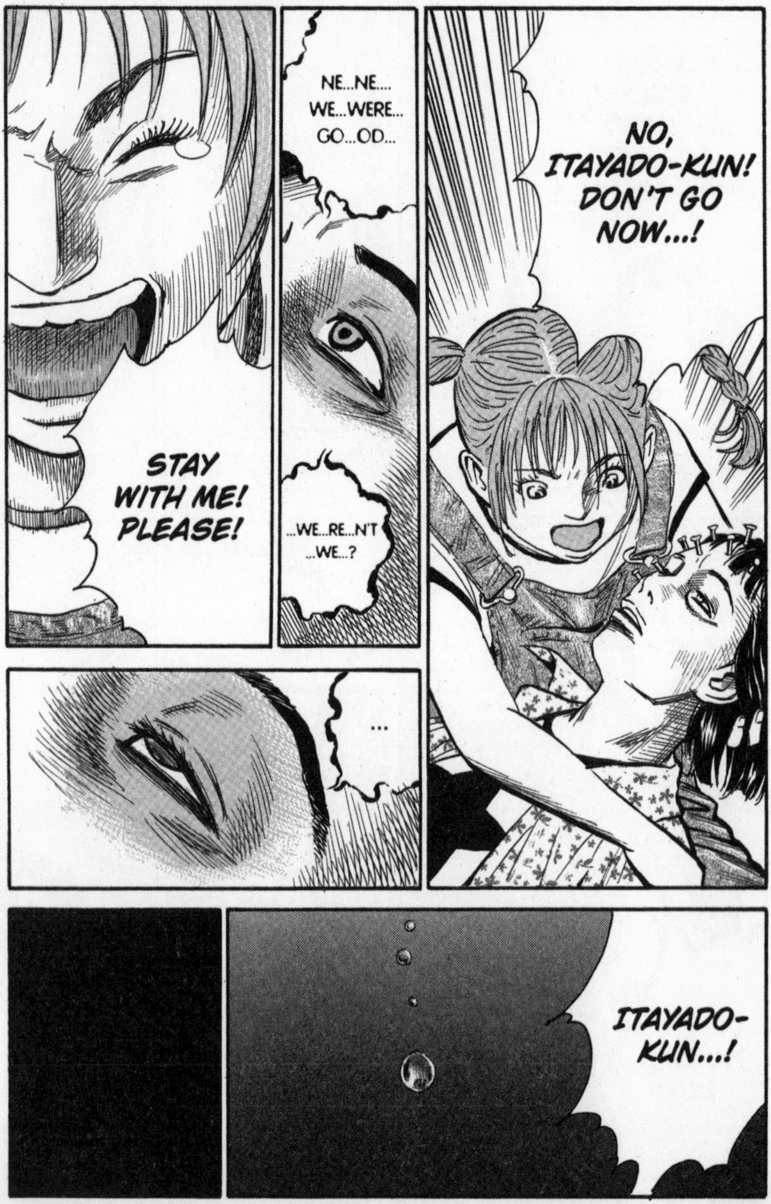

NO, ITAYADO-KUN! DON'T GO NOW...!
NE...NE... WE...WERE... GO...OD...
...WE...RE...N'T ...WE...?
STAY WITH ME! PLEASE!
...
ITAYADO-KUN...!

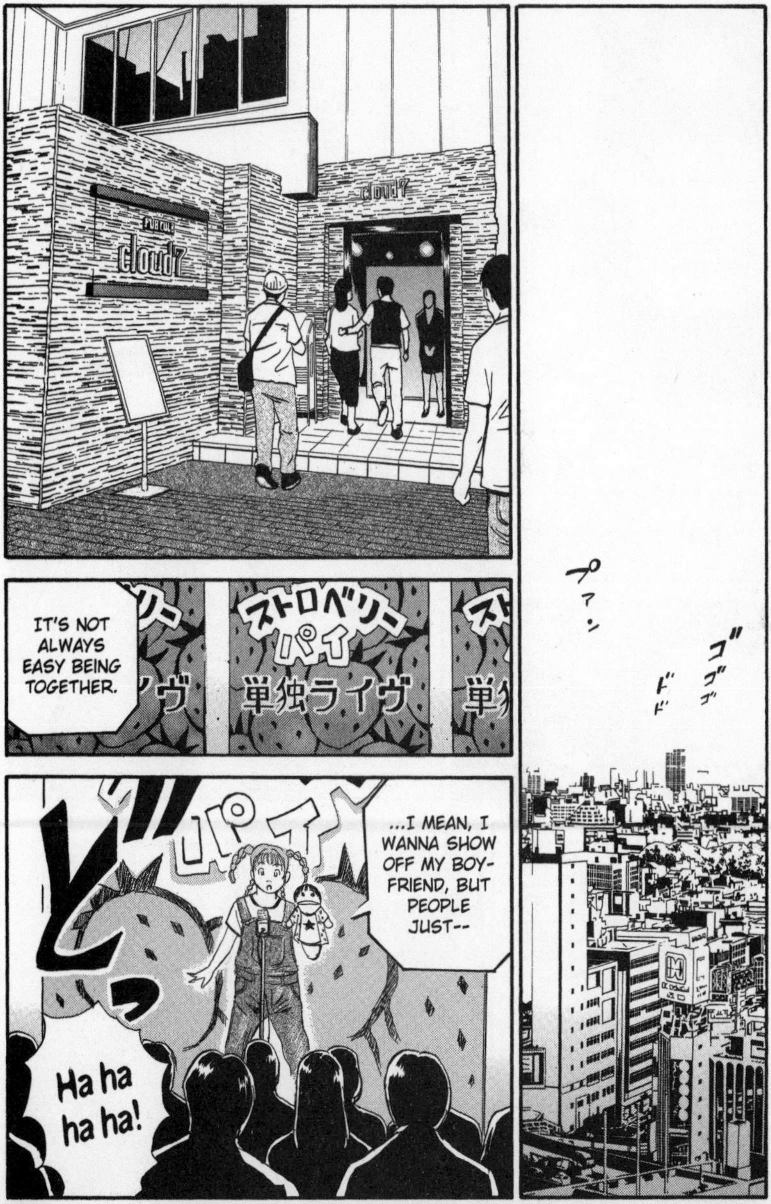
プァン
ゴゴゴ
ドドド
cloud7
cloud7
ストロベリーパイ
単独ライヴ
IT'S NOT ALWAYS EASY BEING TOGETHER.
...I MEAN, I WANNA SHOW OFF MY BOY-FRIEND, BUT PEOPLE JUST--
パイ
どっ
Ha ha ha ha!

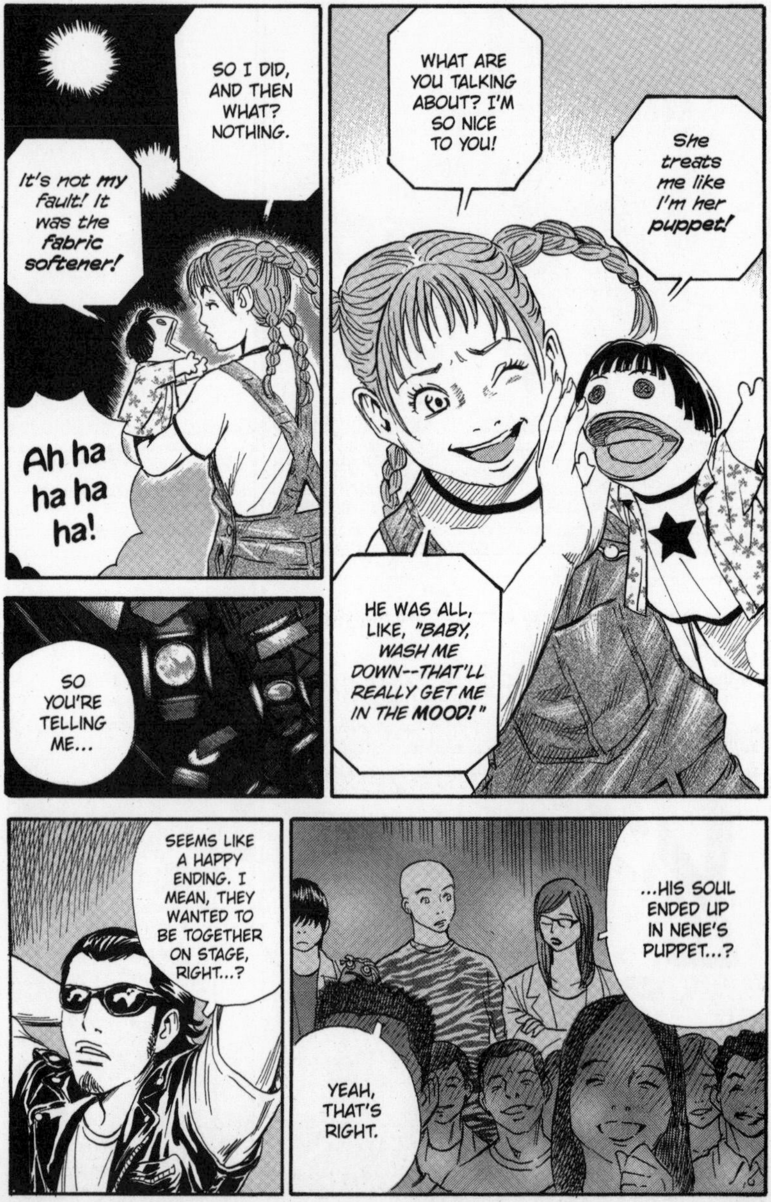
WHAT ARE YOU TALKING ABOUT? I'M SO NICE TO YOU!
She treats me like I'm her puppet!
HE WAS ALL, LIKE, "BABY, WASH ME DOWN--THAT'LL REALLY GET ME IN THE MOOD!"
SO I DID, AND THEN WHAT? NOTHING.
It's not my fault! It was the fabric softener!
Ah ha ha ha ha!
SO YOU'RE TELLING ME...
...HIS SOUL ENDED UP IN NENE'S PUPPET...?
YEAH, THAT'S RIGHT.
SEEMS LIKE A HAPPY ENDING. I MEAN, THEY WANTED TO BE TOGETHER ON STAGE, RIGHT...?

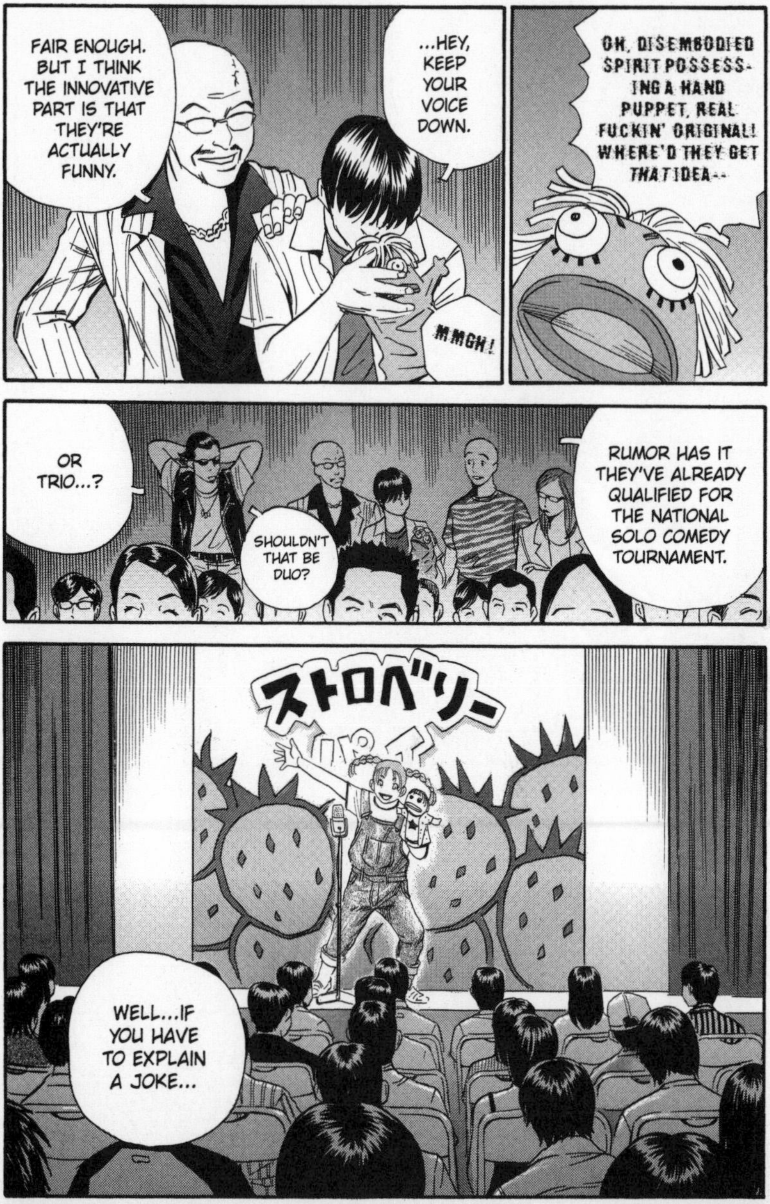
OH, DISEMBODIED SPIRIT POSSESSING A HAND PUPPET, REAL FUCKIN' ORIGINAL! WHERE'D THEY GET *THAT* IDEA--
MMGH!
...HEY, KEEP YOUR VOICE DOWN.
FAIR ENOUGH. BUT I THINK THE INNOVATIVE PART IS THAT THEY'RE ACTUALLY FUNNY.
RUMOR HAS IT THEY'VE ALREADY QUALIFIED FOR THE NATIONAL SOLO COMEDY TOURNAMENT.
SHOULDN'T THAT BE DUO?
OR TRIO...?
ストロベリー
WELL...IF YOU HAVE TO EXPLAIN A JOKE...

6th delivery: in deep hurt—the end

7th delivery

墨絵の国へ

to the land of ink paintings

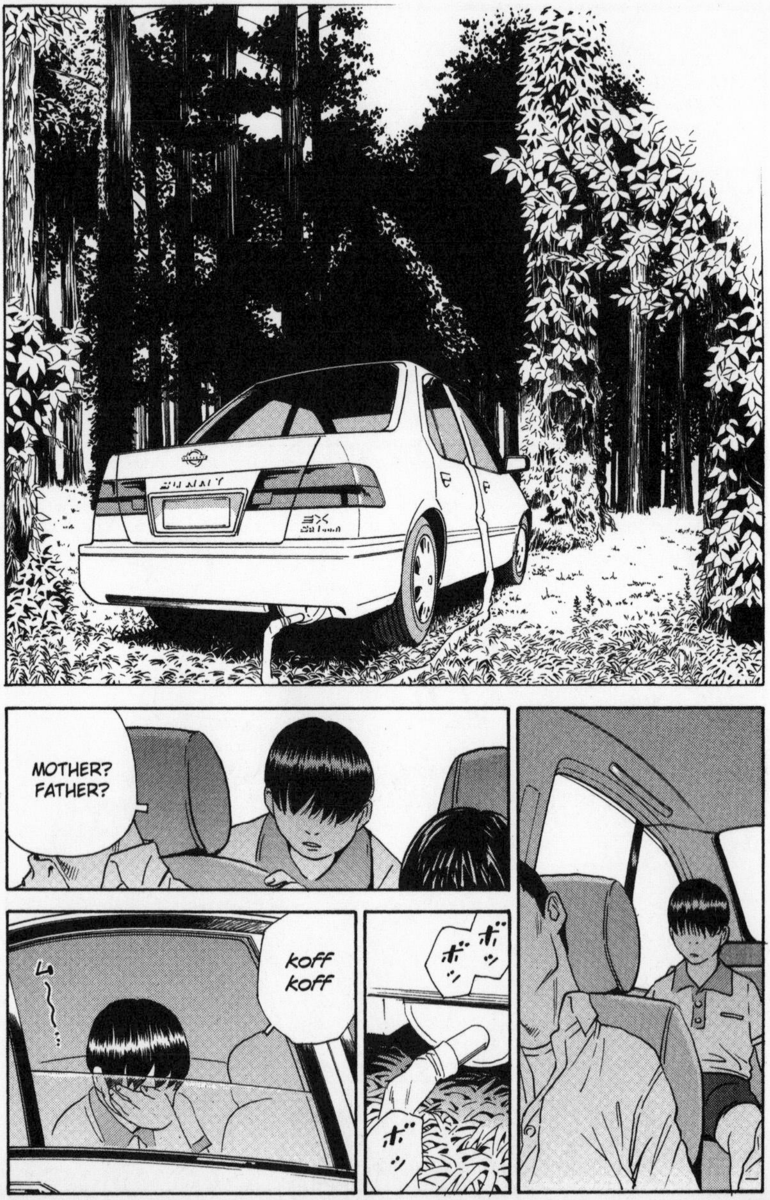
MOTHER? FATHER?
ボッ
ボッ
ボッ
koff koff
ム〜〜…

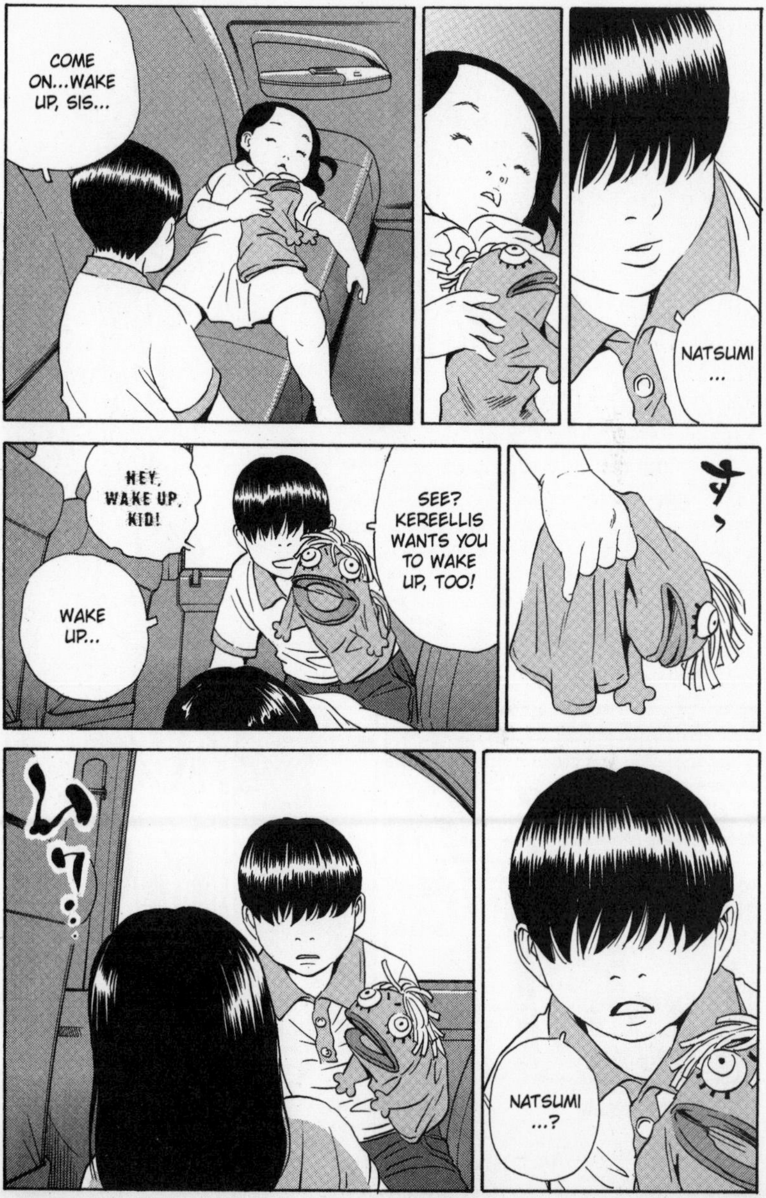
NATSUMI ...
COME ON...WAKE UP, SIS...
SEE? KEREELLIS WANTS YOU TO WAKE UP, TOO!
HEY, WAKE UP, KID!
WAKE UP...
NATSUMI ...?

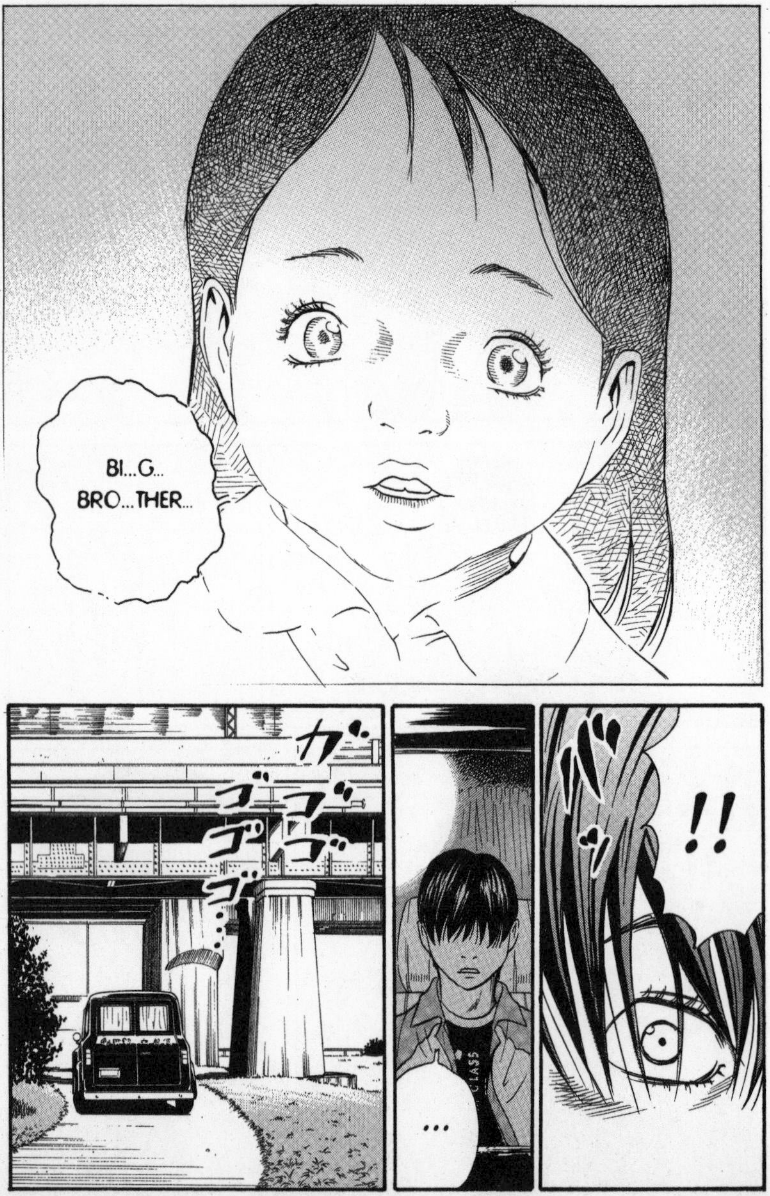
BI...G...
BRO...THER...
バッ
!!
...
ガゴゴ
ゴゴゴ...

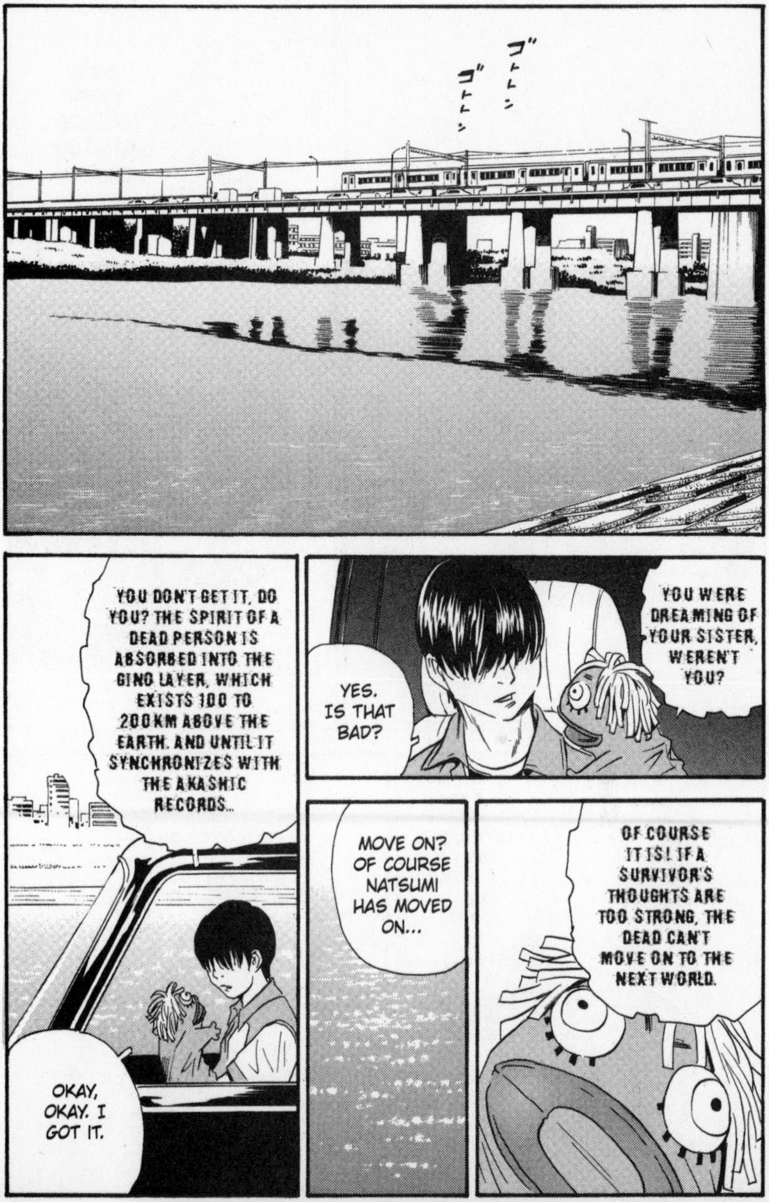

ゴトトン
ゴトトン
YOU WERE DREAMING OF YOUR SISTER, WEREN'T YOU?
YES. IS THAT BAD?
OF COURSE IT IS! IF A SURVIVOR'S THOUGHTS ARE TOO STRONG, THE DEAD CAN'T MOVE ON TO THE NEXT WORLD.
MOVE ON? OF COURSE NATSUMI HAS MOVED ON...
YOU DON'T GET IT, DO YOU? THE SPIRIT OF A DEAD PERSON IS ABSORBED INTO THE GINO LAYER, WHICH EXISTS 100 TO 200KM ABOVE THE EARTH. AND UNTIL IT SYNCHRONIZES WITH THE AKASHIC RECORDS...
OKAY, OKAY. I GOT IT.

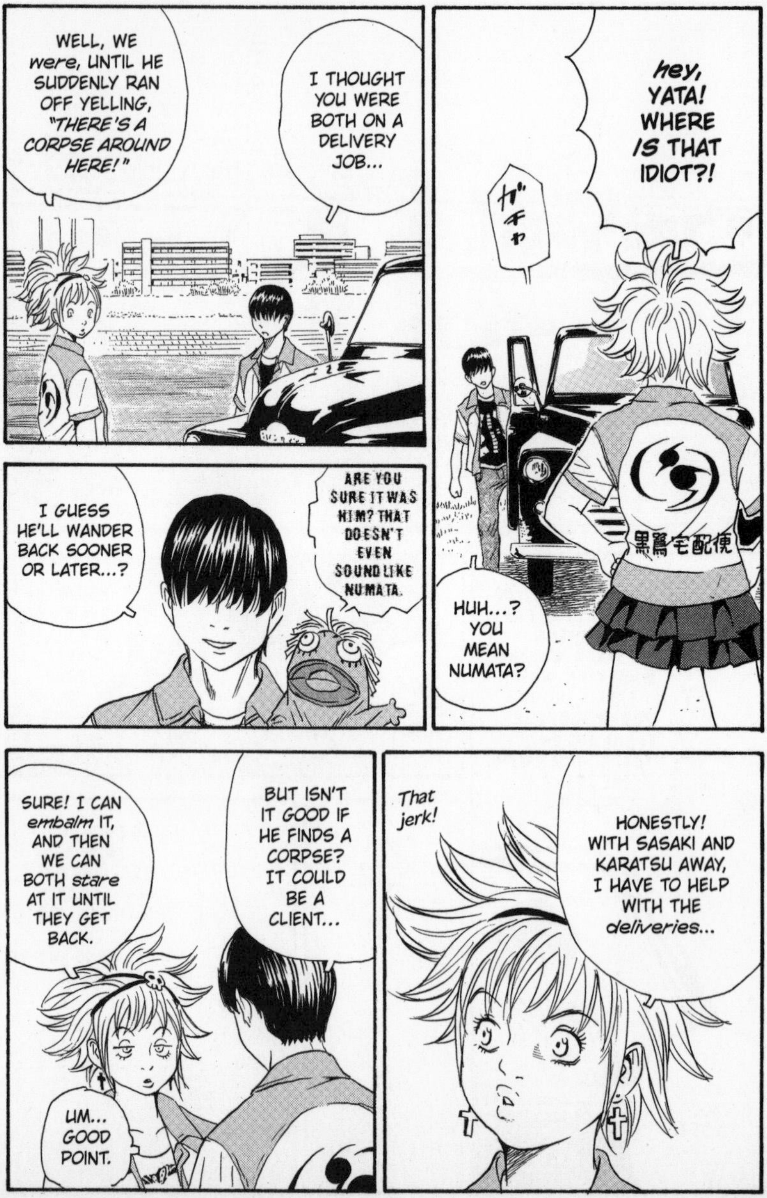
hey, YATA! WHERE IS THAT IDIOT?!
ガチャ
HUH...? YOU MEAN NUMATA?
I THOUGHT YOU WERE BOTH ON A DELIVERY JOB...
WELL, WE were, UNTIL HE SUDDENLY RAN OFF YELLING, "THERE'S A CORPSE AROUND HERE!"
ARE YOU SURE IT WAS HIM? THAT DOESN'T EVEN SOUND LIKE NUMATA.
I GUESS HE'LL WANDER BACK SOONER OR LATER...?
黒鷺宅配便
HONESTLY! WITH SASAKI AND KARATSU AWAY, I HAVE TO HELP WITH THE deliveries...
That jerk!
BUT ISN'T IT GOOD IF HE FINDS A CORPSE? IT COULD BE A CLIENT...
SURE! I CAN embalm IT, AND THEN WE CAN BOTH stare AT IT UNTIL THEY GET BACK.
UM... GOOD POINT.

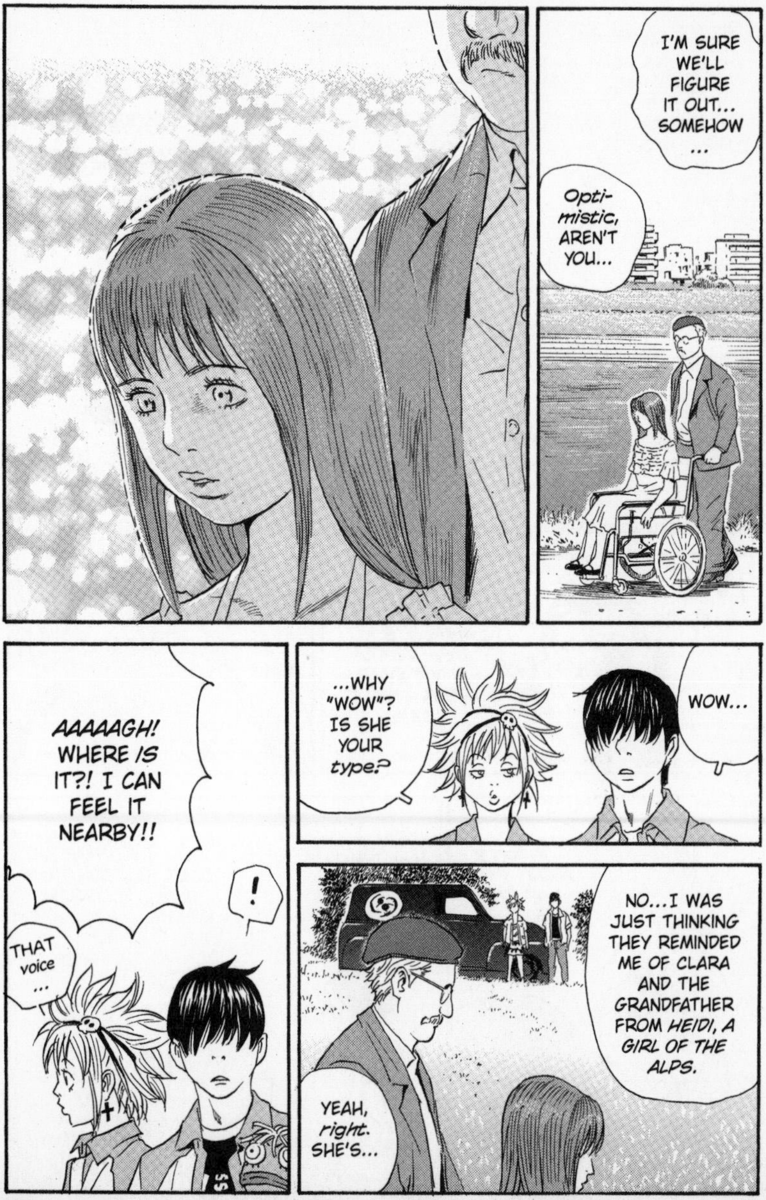

I'M SURE WE'LL FIGURE IT OUT... SOMEHOW ...
Opti-mistic, AREN'T YOU...
WOW...
...WHY "WOW"? IS SHE YOUR type?
NO...I WAS JUST THINKING THEY REMINDED ME OF CLARA AND THE GRANDFATHER FROM HEIDI, A GIRL OF THE ALPS.
YEAH, right. SHE'S...
AAAAAGH! WHERE IS IT?! I CAN FEEL IT NEARBY!!
!
THAT voice ...

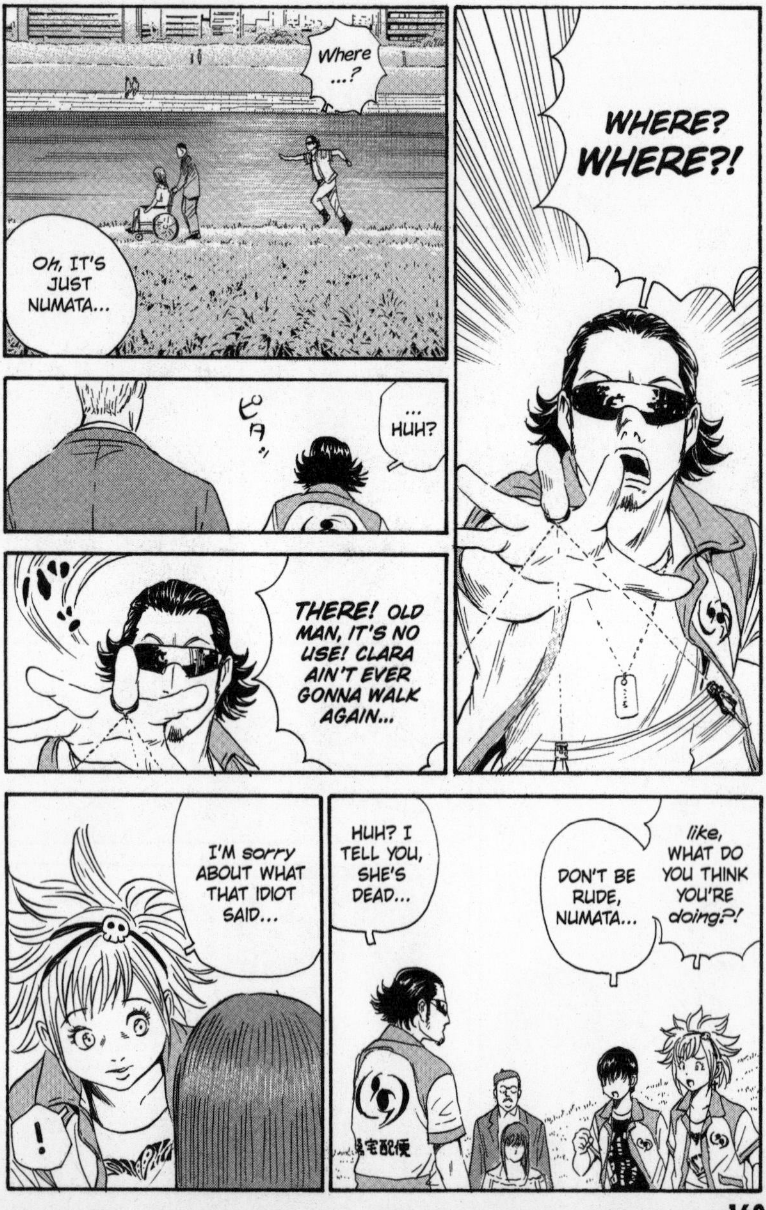
WHERE? WHERE?!
Where ...?
Oh, IT'S JUST NUMATA...
... HUH?
ピタッ
THERE! OLD MAN, IT'S NO USE! CLARA AIN'T EVER GONNA WALK AGAIN...
like, WHAT DO YOU THINK YOU'RE doing?!
DON'T BE RUDE, NUMATA...
HUH? I TELL YOU, SHE'S DEAD...
I'M sorry ABOUT WHAT THAT IDIOT SAID...
!

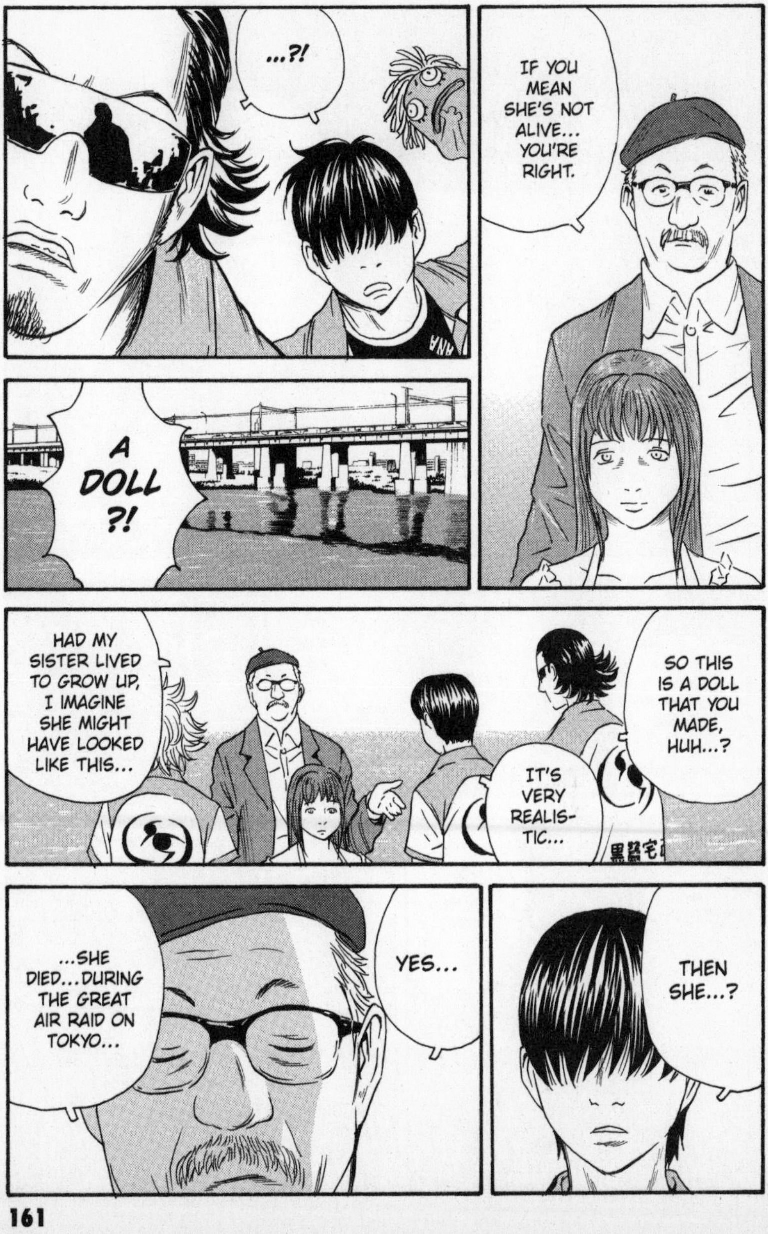
IF YOU MEAN SHE'S NOT ALIVE... YOU'RE RIGHT.
...?!
A DOLL ?!
SO THIS IS A DOLL THAT YOU MADE, HUH...?
IT'S VERY REALIS-TIC...
HAD MY SISTER LIVED TO GROW UP, I IMAGINE SHE MIGHT HAVE LOOKED LIKE THIS...
THEN SHE...?
YES...
...SHE DIED...DURING THE GREAT AIR RAID ON TOKYO...

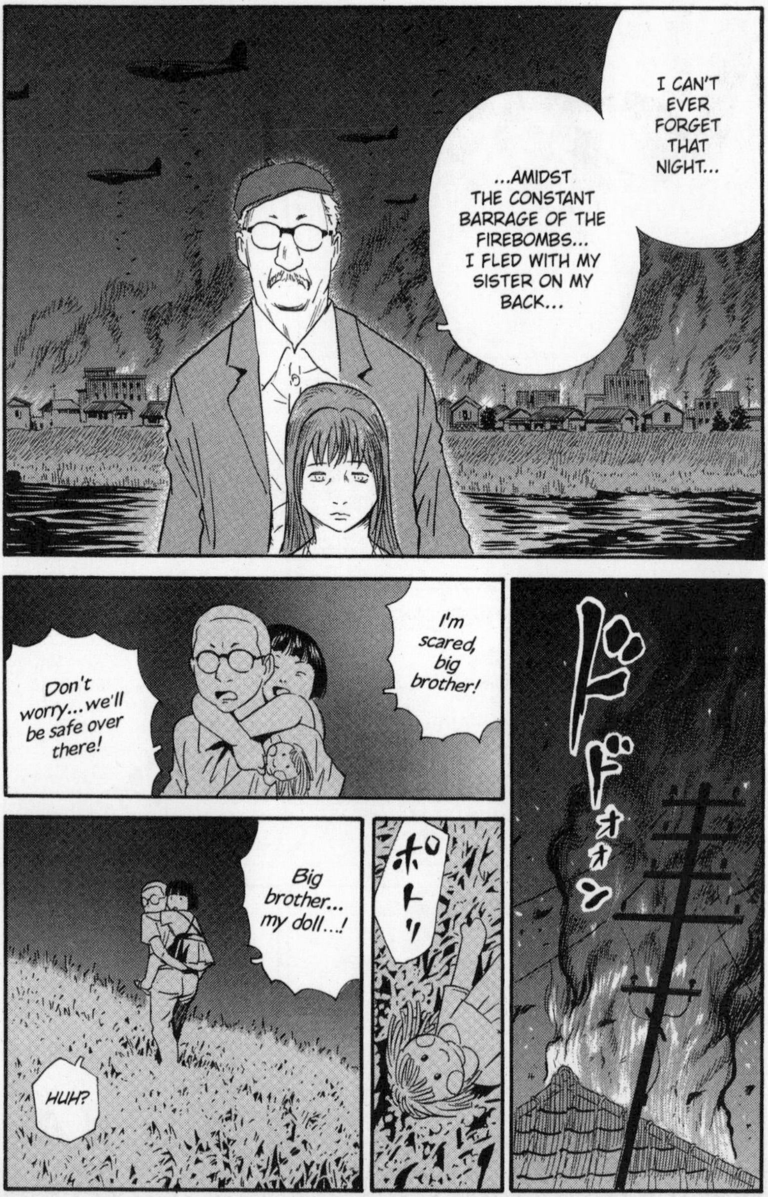
I CAN'T EVER FORGET THAT NIGHT...
...AMIDST THE CONSTANT BARRAGE OF THE FIREBOMBS... I FLED WITH MY SISTER ON MY BACK...
ドドォォン
I'm scared, big brother!
Don't worry...we'll be safe over there!
ポトッ
Big brother... my doll...!
HUH?

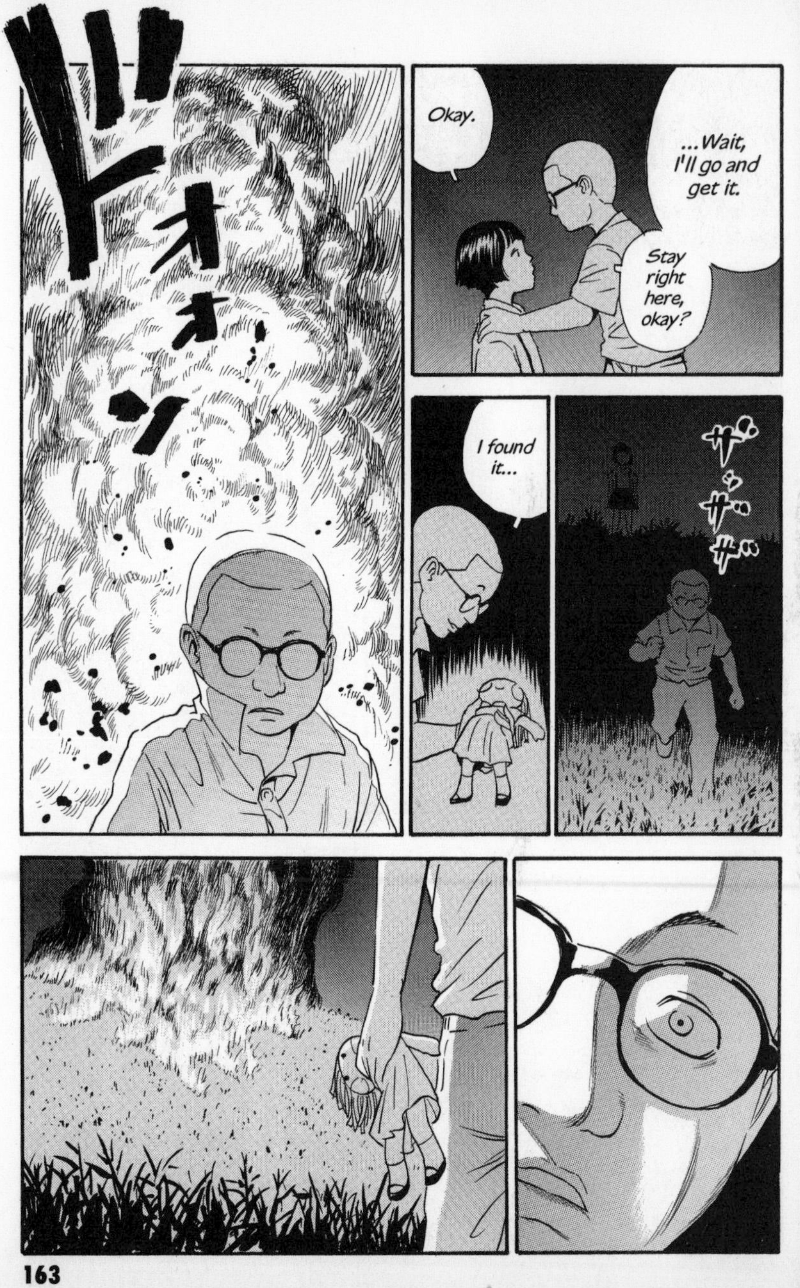
...Wait, I'll go and get it.
Stay right here, okay?
Okay.
ザッ ザッ ザッ
I found it...
ドオォン

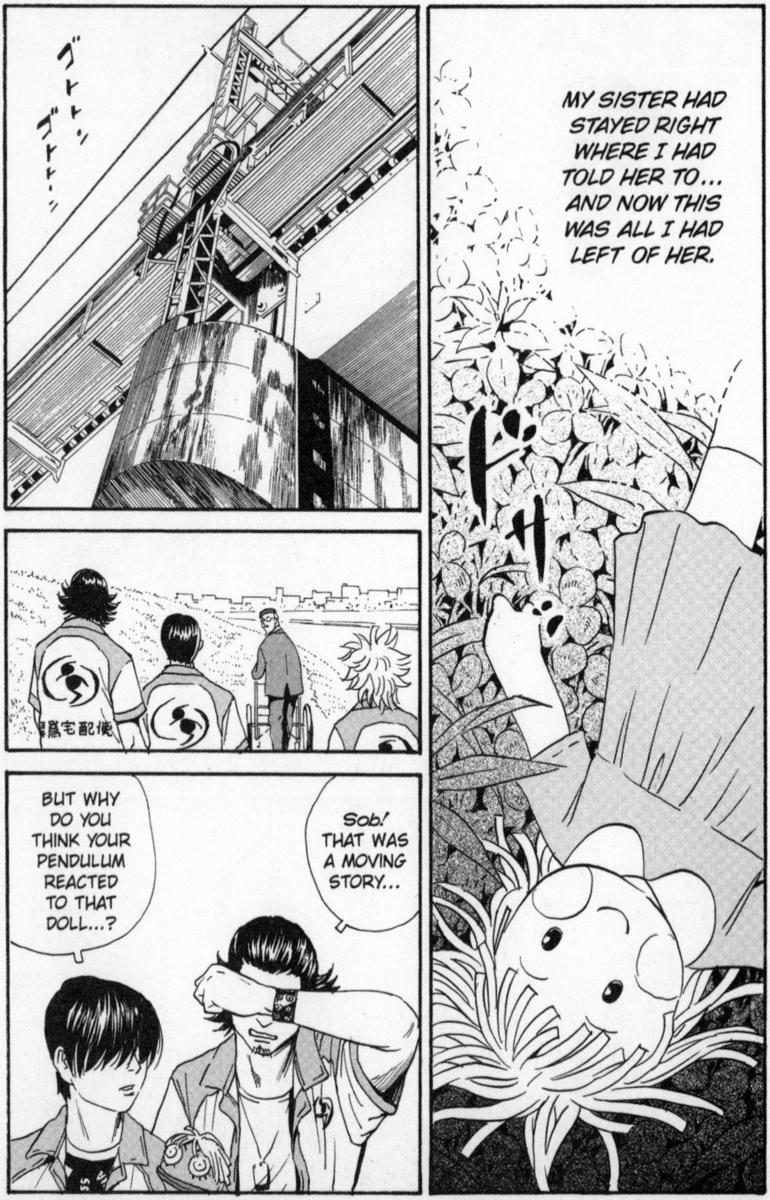
MY SISTER HAD STAYED RIGHT WHERE I HAD TOLD HER TO... AND NOW THIS WAS ALL I HAD LEFT OF HER.
ゴトトン
ゴトトン
ゴトトン
Sob! THAT WAS A MOVING STORY...
BUT WHY DO YOU THINK YOUR PENDULUM REACTED TO THAT DOLL...?

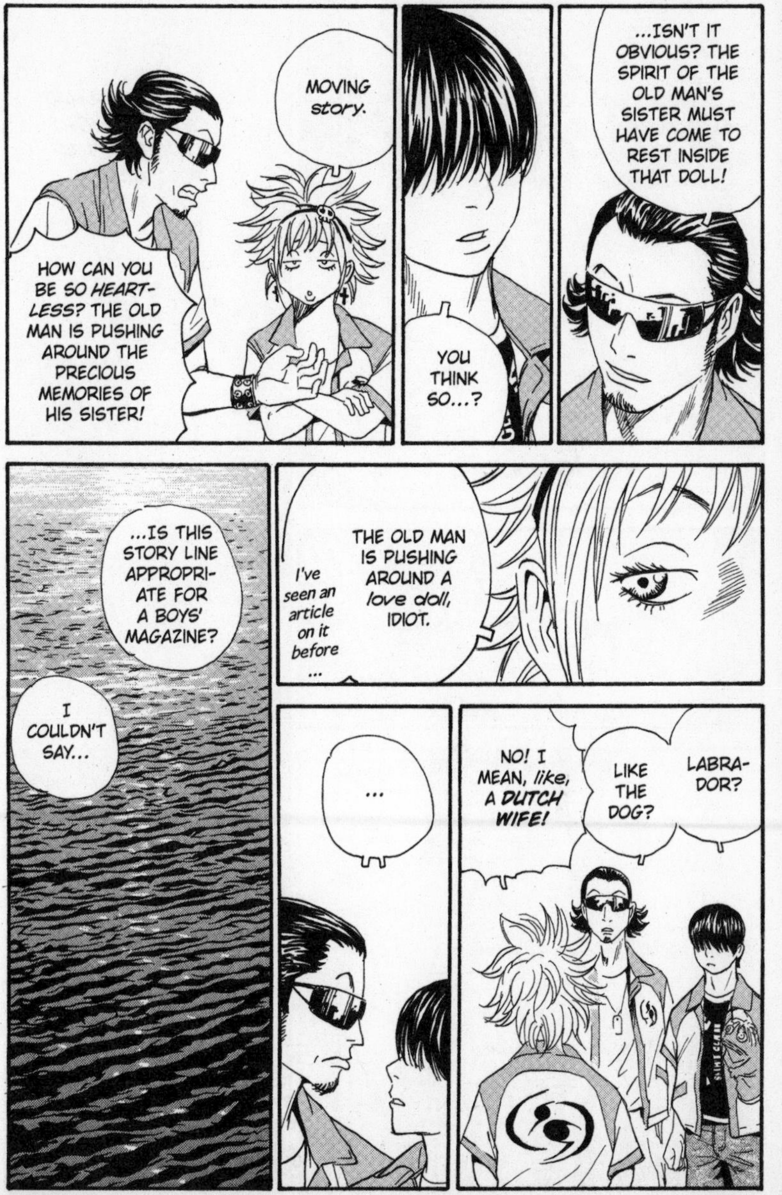
...ISN'T IT OBVIOUS? THE SPIRIT OF THE OLD MAN'S SISTER MUST HAVE COME TO REST INSIDE THAT DOLL!
YOU THINK SO...?
MOVING *story.*
HOW CAN YOU BE SO *HEART-LESS?* THE OLD MAN IS PUSHING AROUND THE PRECIOUS MEMORIES OF HIS SISTER!
THE OLD MAN IS PUSHING AROUND A *love doll,* IDIOT.
I've seen an article on it before ...
LABRA-DOR?
LIKE THE DOG?
NO! I MEAN, *like,* A **DUTCH WIFE!**
...
...IS THIS STORY LINE APPROPRI-ATE FOR A BOYS' MAGAZINE?
I COULDN'T SAY...

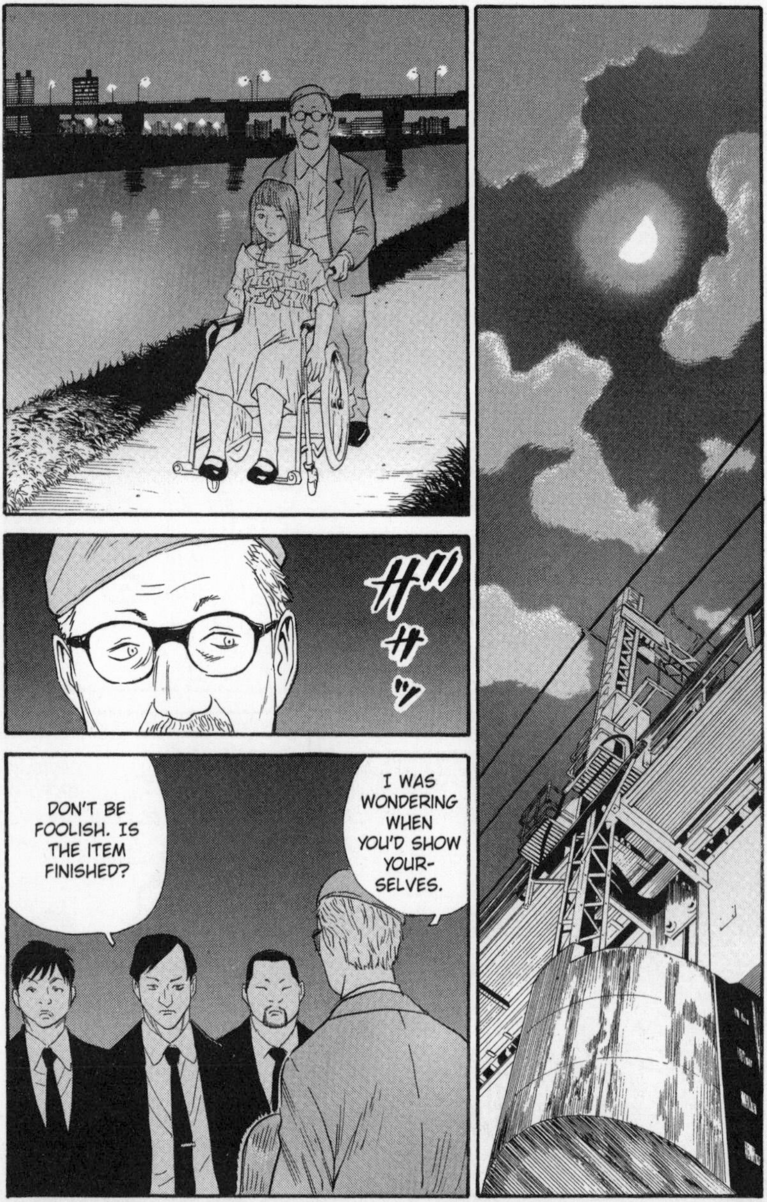
ザッ
ザッ
I WAS WONDERING WHEN YOU'D SHOW YOUR-SELVES.
DON'T BE FOOLISH. IS THE ITEM FINISHED?

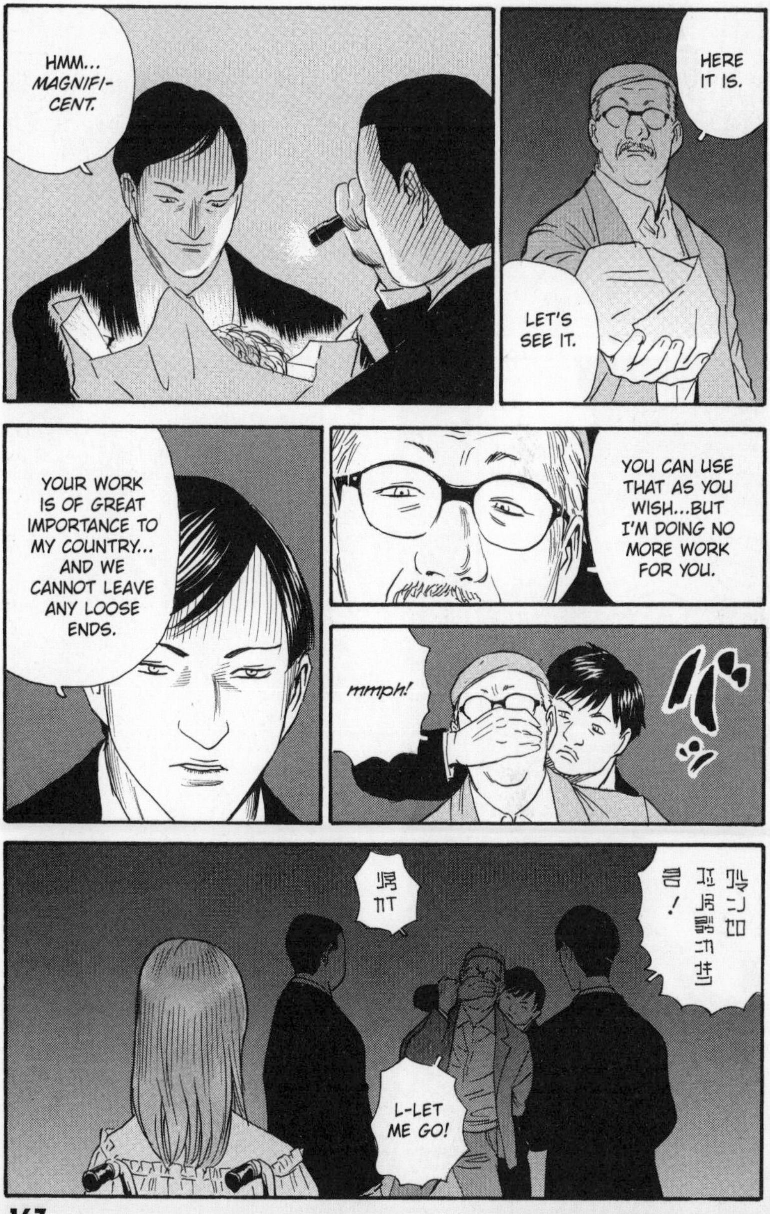
HERE IT IS.
LET'S SEE IT.
HMM... MAGNIFI-CENT.
YOU CAN USE THAT AS YOU WISH...BUT I'M DOING NO MORE WORK FOR YOU.
mmph!
YOUR WORK IS OF GREAT IMPORTANCE TO MY COUNTRY... AND WE CANNOT LEAVE ANY LOOSE ENDS.
L-LET ME GO!

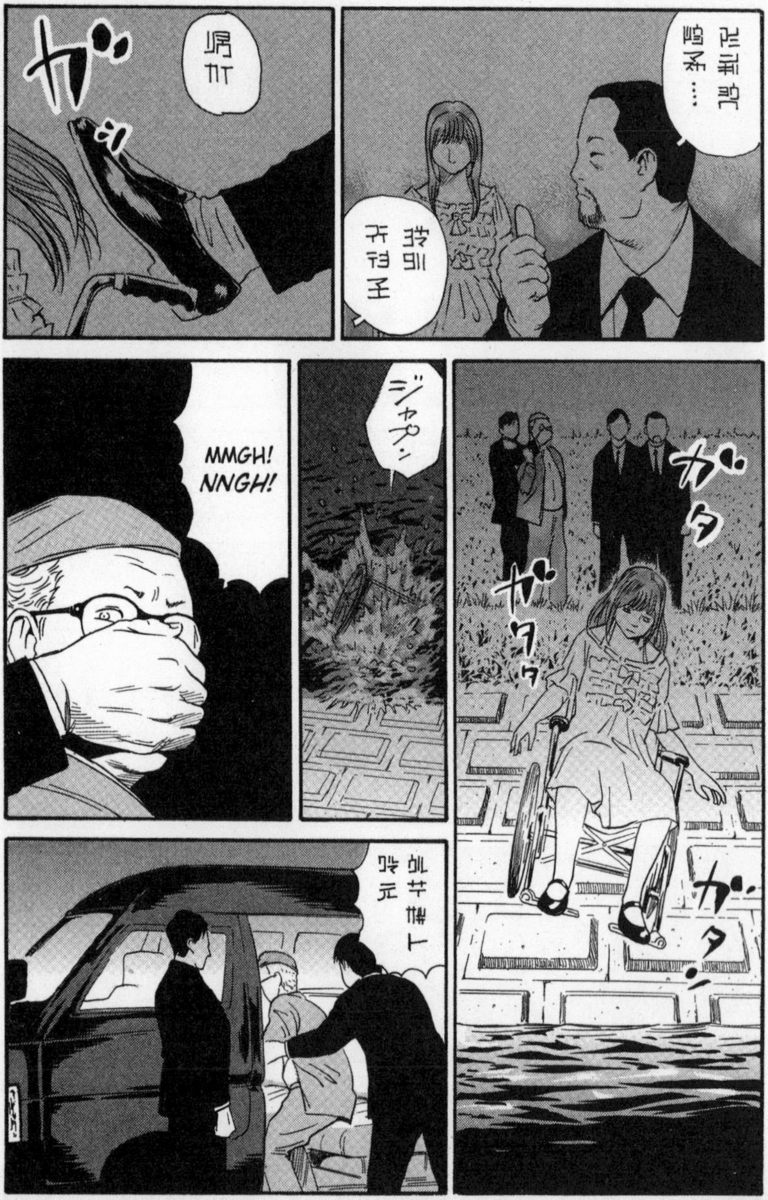
ガッ
ガタ
ガタタ
ガタン
ジャプン
MMGH!
NNGH!

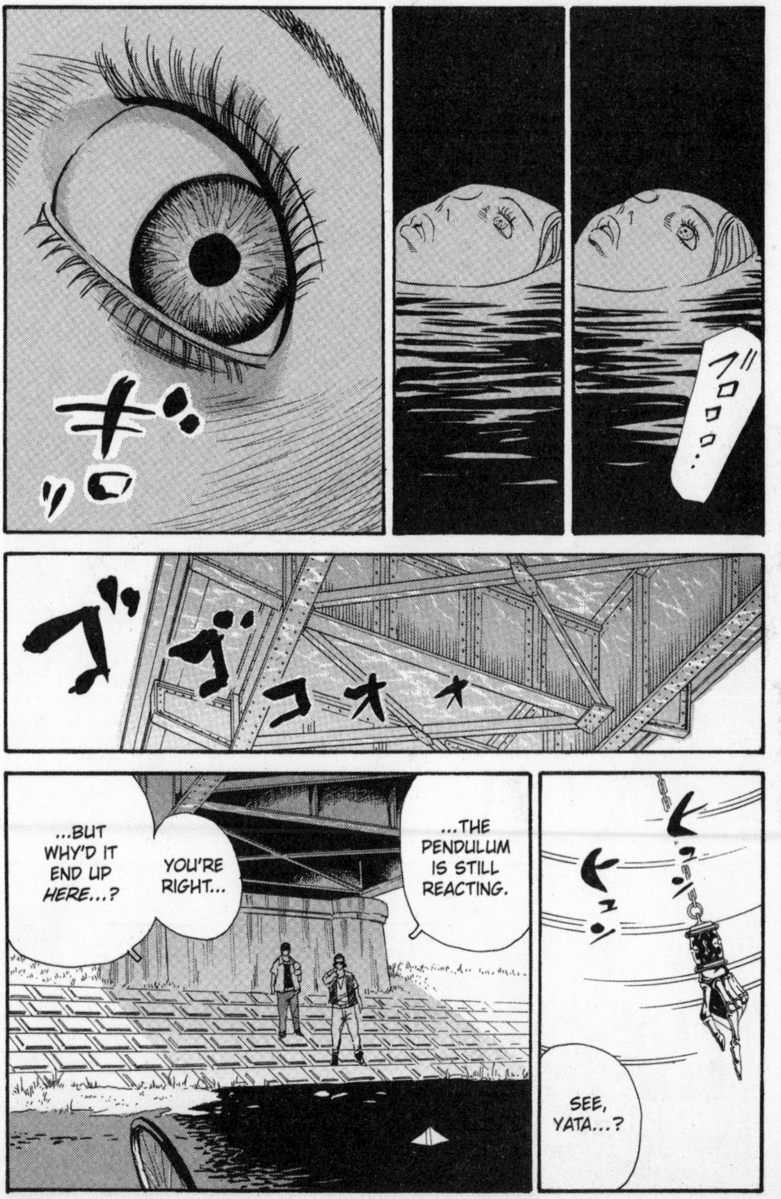
ブロロロ...
ギョロッ
ゴゴコオオ
ヒュンヒュン
SEE, YATA...?
...THE PENDULUM IS STILL REACTING.
YOU'RE RIGHT...
...BUT WHY'D IT END UP *HERE*...?

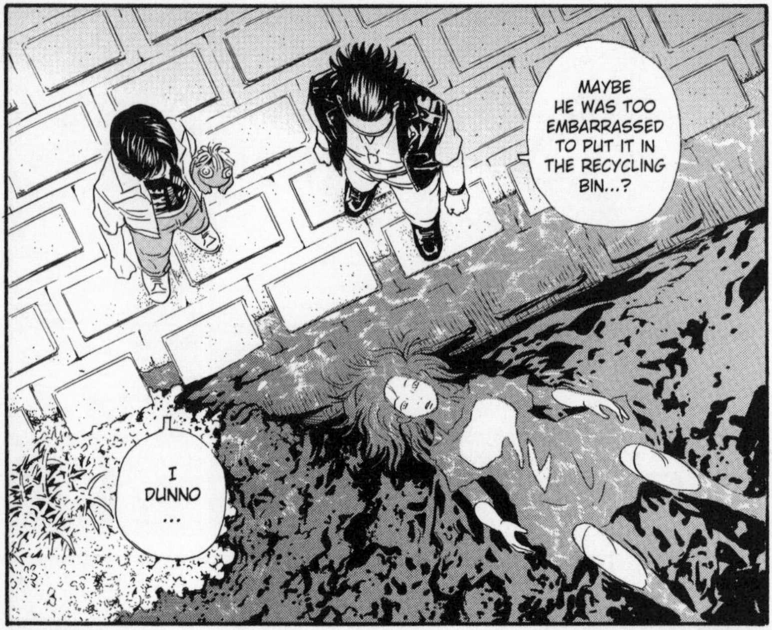
MAYBE HE WAS TOO EMBARRASSED TO PUT IT IN THE RECYCLING BIN...?
I DUNNO ...

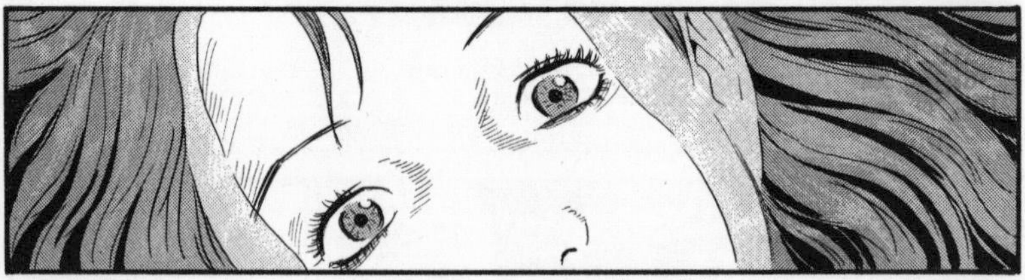

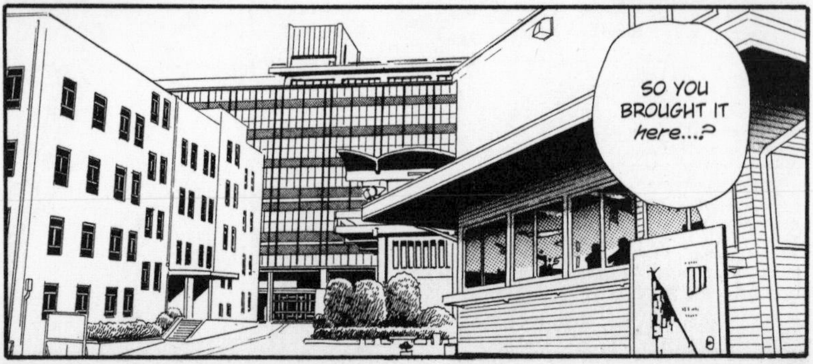
SO YOU BROUGHT IT *here*...?

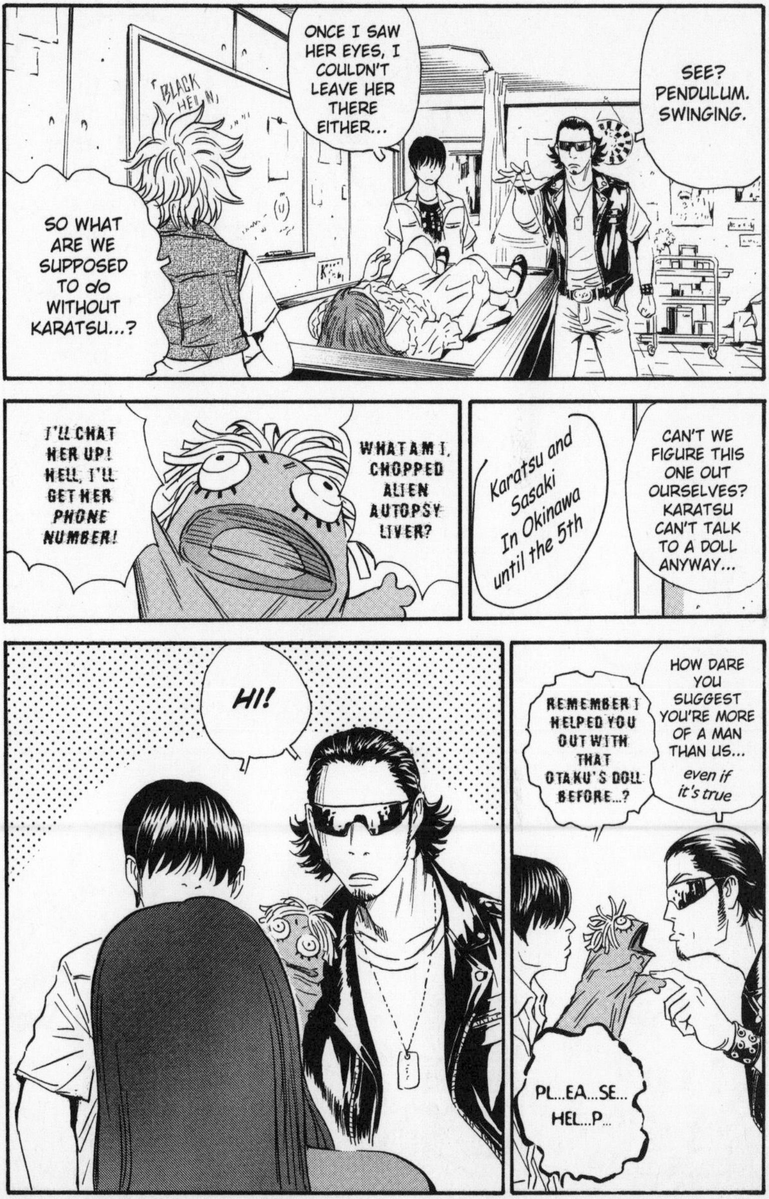
SEE? PENDULUM. SWINGING.
ONCE I SAW HER EYES, I COULDN'T LEAVE HER THERE EITHER...
SO WHAT ARE WE SUPPOSED TO do WITHOUT KARATSU...?
CAN'T WE FIGURE THIS ONE OUT OURSELVES? KARATSU CAN'T TALK TO A DOLL ANYWAY...
Karatsu and Sasaki In Okinawa until the 5th
WHAT AM I, CHOPPED ALIEN AUTOPSY LIVER?
I'LL CHAT HER UP! HELL, I'LL GET HER PHONE NUMBER!
HOW DARE YOU SUGGEST YOU'RE MORE OF A MAN THAN US... even if it's true
REMEMBER I HELPED YOU OUT WITH THAT OTAKU'S DOLL BEFORE...?
PL...EA...SE... HEL...P...
HI!

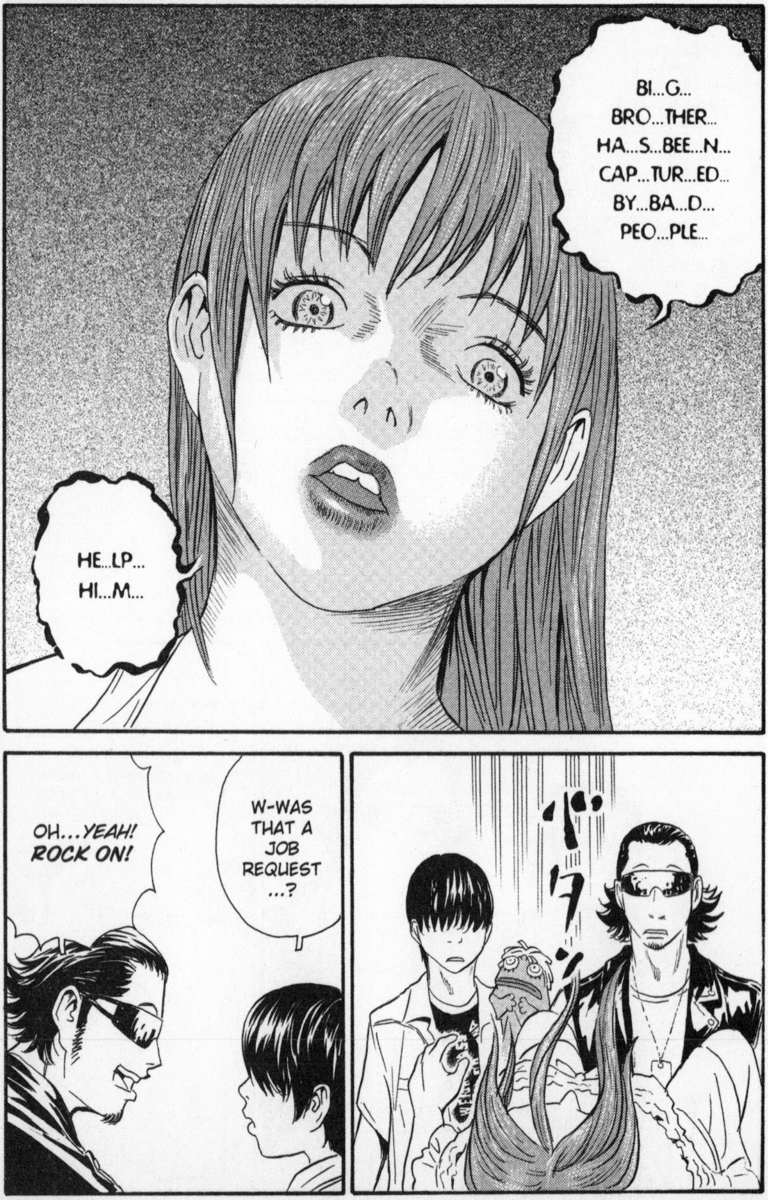
BI...G... BRO...THER... HA...S...BEE...N... CAP...TUR...ED... BY...BA...D... PEO...PLE...
HE...LP... HI...M...
W-WAS THAT A JOB REQUEST ...?
OH... YEAH! ROCK ON!

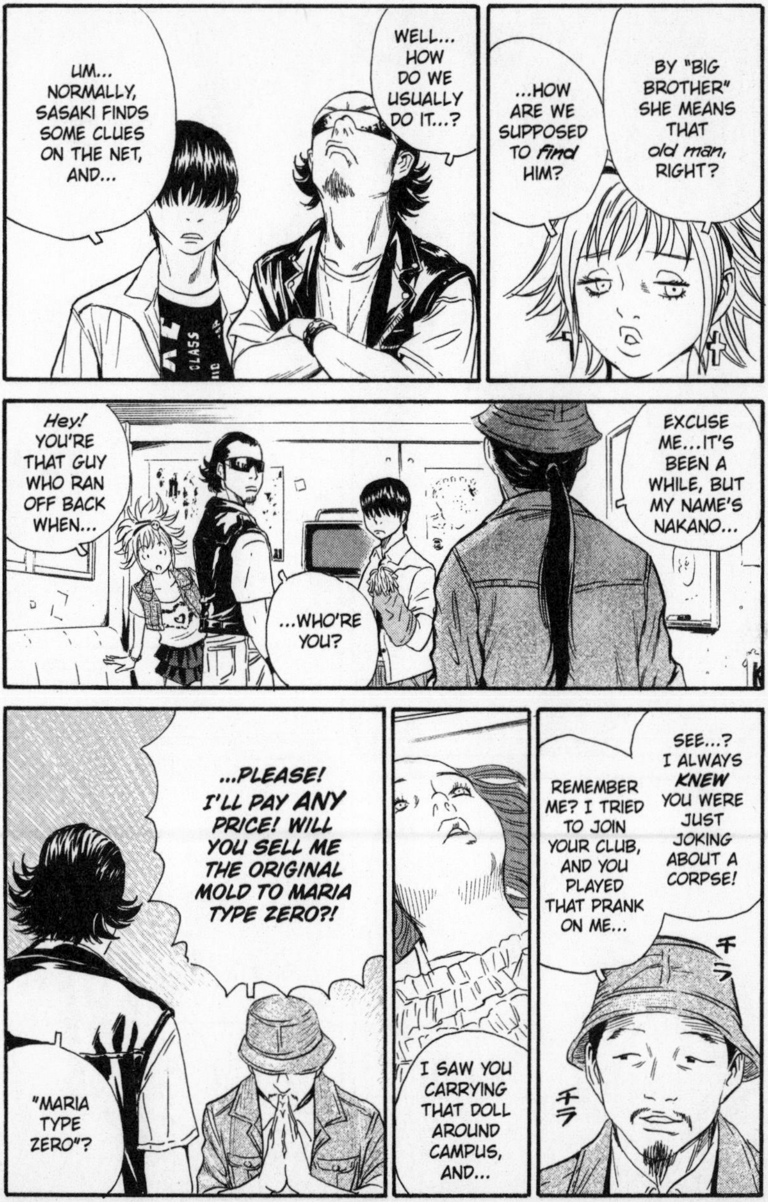
BY "BIG BROTHER" SHE MEANS THAT *old man*, RIGHT?
...HOW ARE WE SUPPOSED TO *find* HIM?
WELL... HOW DO WE USUALLY DO IT...?
UM... NORMALLY, SASAKI FINDS SOME CLUES ON THE NET, AND...
EXCUSE ME...IT'S BEEN A WHILE, BUT MY NAME'S NAKANO...
...WHO'RE YOU?
Hey! YOU'RE THAT GUY WHO RAN OFF BACK WHEN...
SEE...? I ALWAYS **KNEW** YOU WERE JUST JOKING ABOUT A CORPSE!
REMEMBER ME? I TRIED TO JOIN YOUR CLUB, AND YOU PLAYED THAT PRANK ON ME...
チラ
チラ
I SAW YOU CARRYING THAT DOLL AROUND CAMPUS, AND...
...PLEASE! I'LL PAY **ANY** PRICE! WILL YOU SELL ME THE ORIGINAL MOLD TO MARIA TYPE ZERO?!
"MARIA TYPE ZERO"?

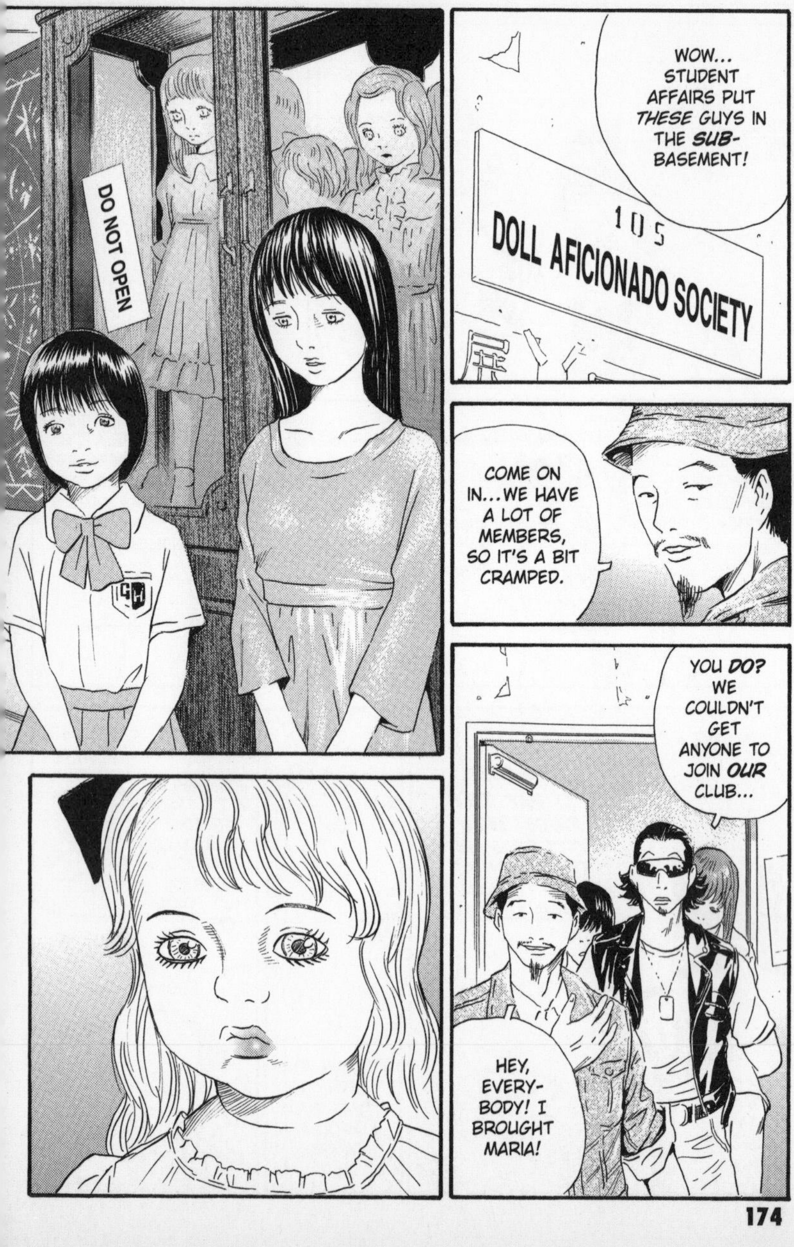
WOW... STUDENT AFFAIRS PUT *THESE* GUYS IN THE ***SUB-*** BASEMENT!
105
DOLL AFICIONADO SOCIETY
COME ON IN...WE HAVE A LOT OF MEMBERS, SO IT'S A BIT CRAMPED.
YOU ***DO?*** WE COULDN'T GET ANYONE TO JOIN ***OUR*** CLUB...
HEY, EVERY-BODY! I BROUGHT MARIA!
DO NOT OPEN

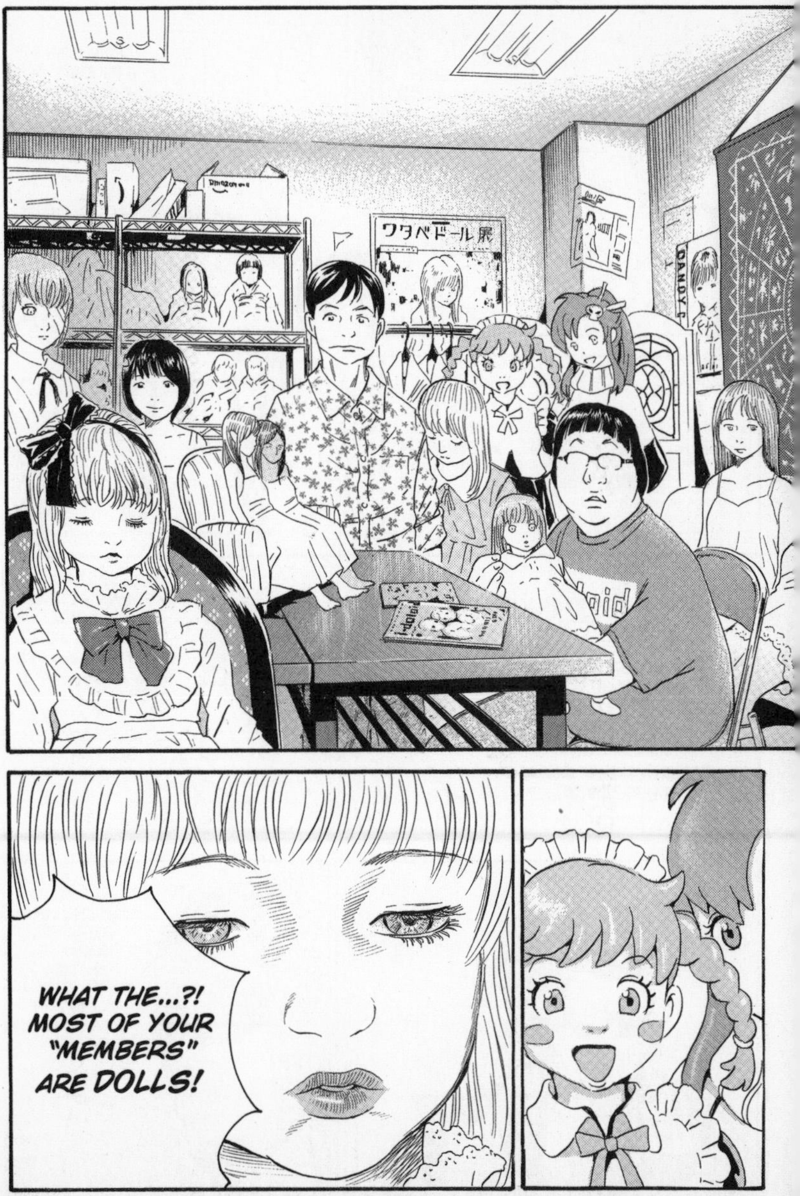
ワタベドール展
WHAT THE...?! MOST OF YOUR "MEMBERS" ARE DOLLS!

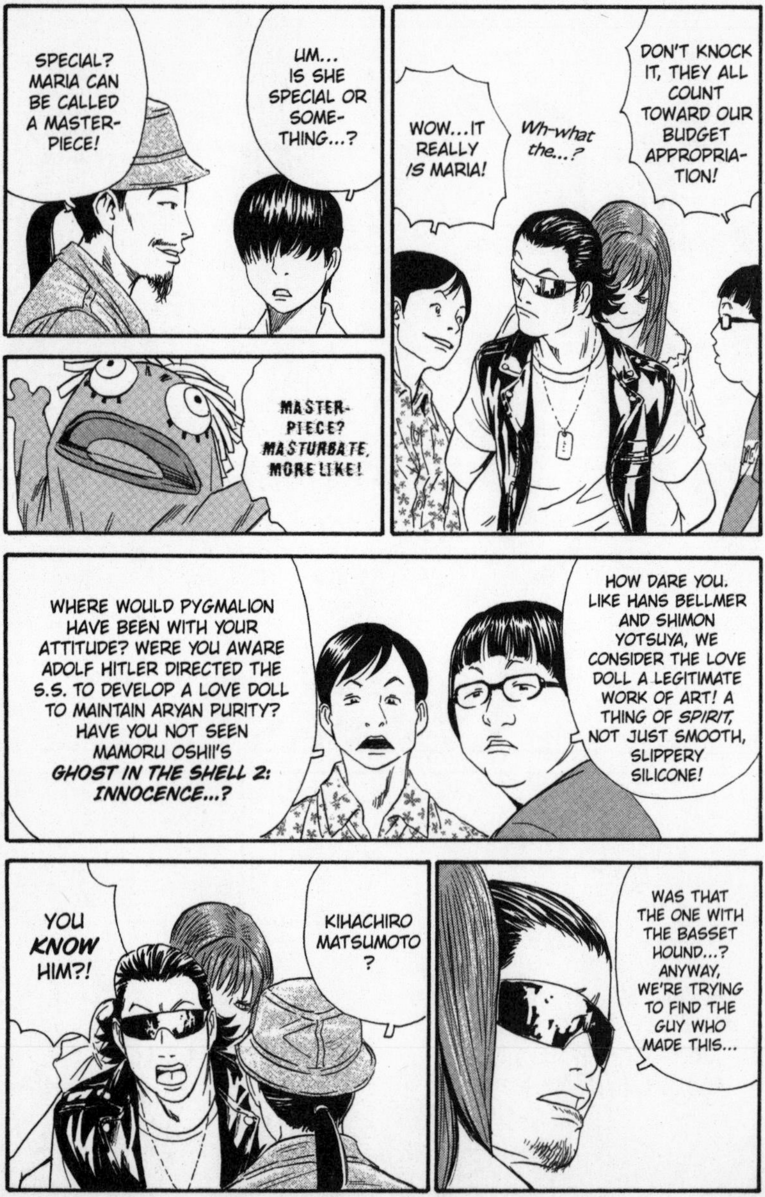
DON'T KNOCK IT, THEY ALL COUNT TOWARD OUR BUDGET APPROPRIATION!
Wh-what the...?
WOW...IT REALLY IS MARIA!
UM... IS SHE SPECIAL OR SOMETHING...?
SPECIAL? MARIA CAN BE CALLED A MASTERPIECE!
MASTERPIECE? MASTURBATE, MORE LIKE!
HOW DARE YOU. LIKE HANS BELLMER AND SHIMON YOTSUYA, WE CONSIDER THE LOVE DOLL A LEGITIMATE WORK OF ART! A THING OF SPIRIT, NOT JUST SMOOTH, SLIPPERY SILICONE!
WHERE WOULD PYGMALION HAVE BEEN WITH YOUR ATTITUDE? WERE YOU AWARE ADOLF HITLER DIRECTED THE S.S. TO DEVELOP A LOVE DOLL TO MAINTAIN ARYAN PURITY? HAVE YOU NOT SEEN MAMORU OSHII'S GHOST IN THE SHELL 2: INNOCENCE...?
WAS THAT THE ONE WITH THE BASSET HOUND...? ANYWAY, WE'RE TRYING TO FIND THE GUY WHO MADE THIS...
KIHACHIRO MATSUMOTO?
YOU KNOW HIM?!

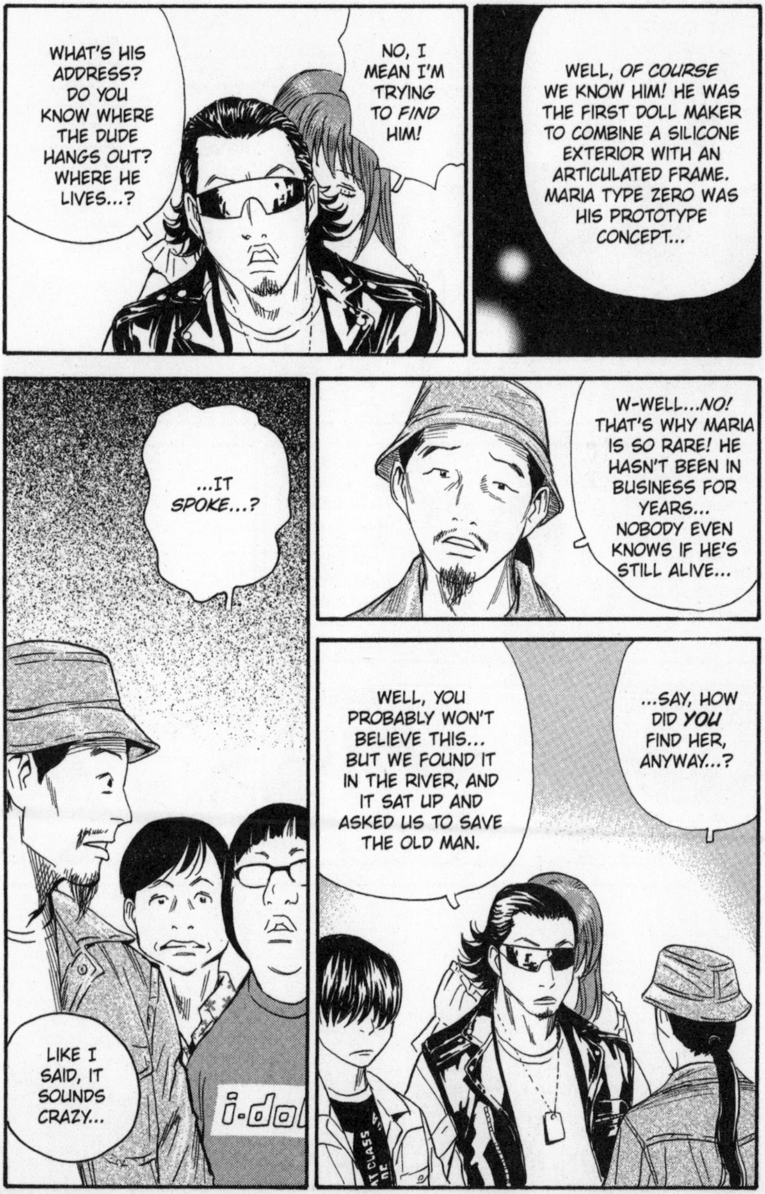
WELL, *OF COURSE* WE KNOW HIM! HE WAS THE FIRST DOLL MAKER TO COMBINE A SILICONE EXTERIOR WITH AN ARTICULATED FRAME. MARIA TYPE ZERO WAS HIS PROTOTYPE CONCEPT...
NO, I MEAN I'M TRYING TO *FIND* HIM!
WHAT'S HIS ADDRESS? DO YOU KNOW WHERE THE DUDE HANGS OUT? WHERE HE LIVES...?
W-WELL...*NO!* THAT'S WHY MARIA IS SO RARE! HE HASN'T BEEN IN BUSINESS FOR YEARS... NOBODY EVEN KNOWS IF HE'S STILL ALIVE...
...SAY, HOW DID ***YOU*** FIND HER, ANYWAY...?
WELL, YOU PROBABLY WON'T BELIEVE THIS... BUT WE FOUND IT IN THE RIVER, AND IT SAT UP AND ASKED US TO SAVE THE OLD MAN.
...IT *SPOKE*...?
LIKE I SAID, IT SOUNDS CRAZY...
i-dol

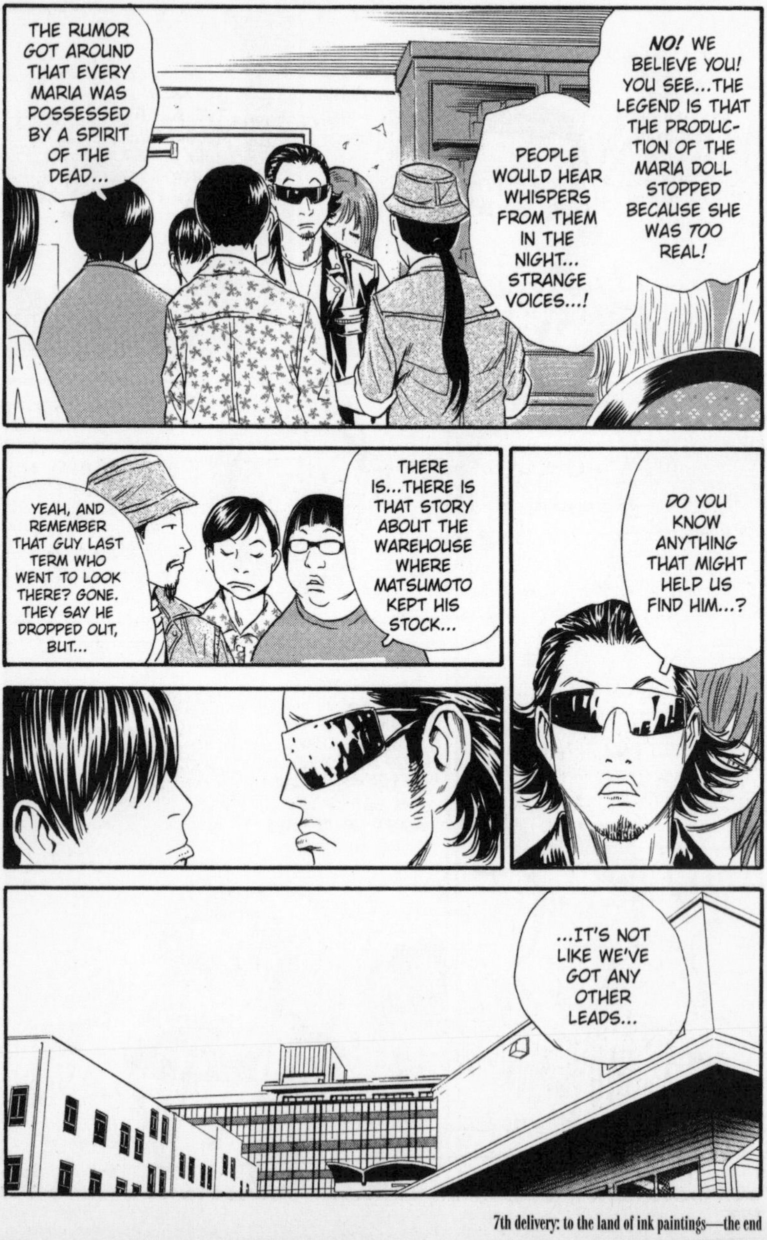
NO! WE BELIEVE YOU! YOU SEE...THE LEGEND IS THAT THE PRODUCTION OF THE MARIA DOLL STOPPED BECAUSE SHE WAS TOO REAL!
PEOPLE WOULD HEAR WHISPERS FROM THEM IN THE NIGHT... STRANGE VOICES...!
THE RUMOR GOT AROUND THAT EVERY MARIA WAS POSSESSED BY A SPIRIT OF THE DEAD...
DO YOU KNOW ANYTHING THAT MIGHT HELP US FIND HIM...?
THERE IS...THERE IS THAT STORY ABOUT THE WAREHOUSE WHERE MATSUMOTO KEPT HIS STOCK...
YEAH, AND REMEMBER THAT GUY LAST TERM WHO WENT TO LOOK THERE? GONE. THEY SAY HE DROPPED OUT, BUT...
...IT'S NOT LIKE WE'VE GOT ANY OTHER LEADS...

7th delivery: to the land of ink paintings—the end

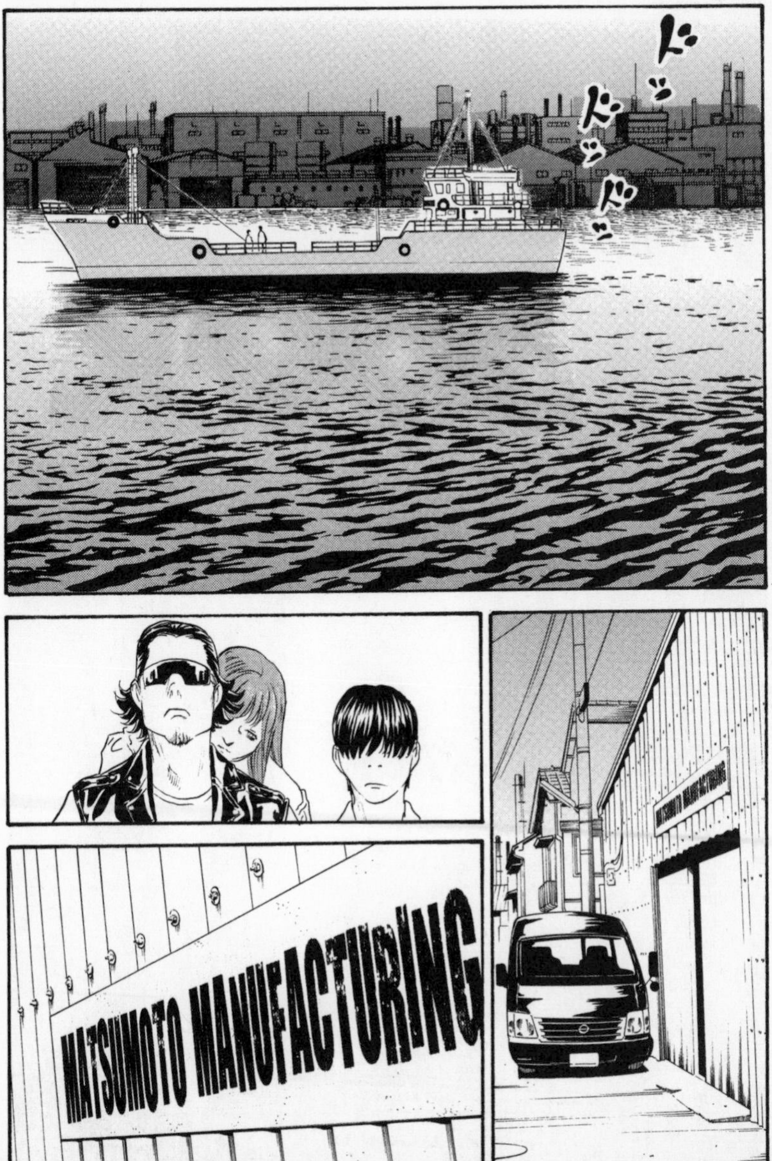
ドッ
ドッ
ドッ
MATSUMOTO MANUFACTURING
MATSUMOTO MANUFACTURING

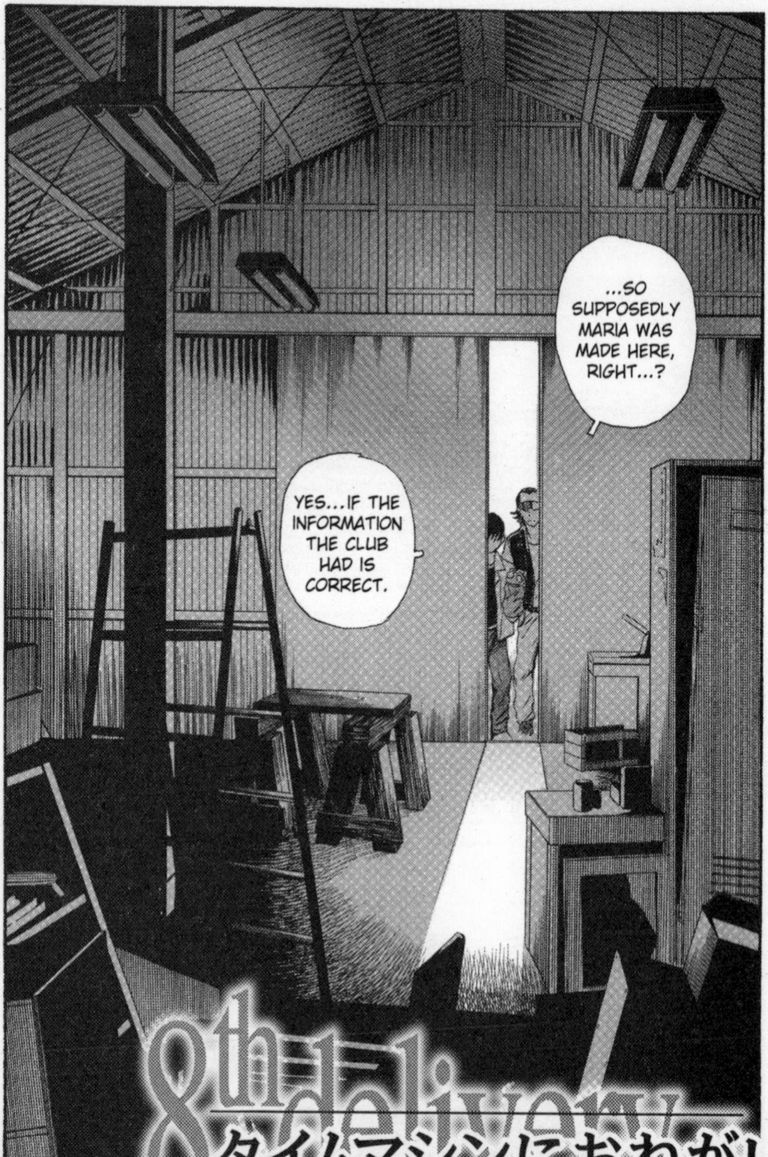
...SO SUPPOSEDLY MARIA WAS MADE HERE, RIGHT...?
YES...IF THE INFORMATION THE CLUB HAD IS CORRECT.

8th delivery
タイムマシンにおねがい
time machine

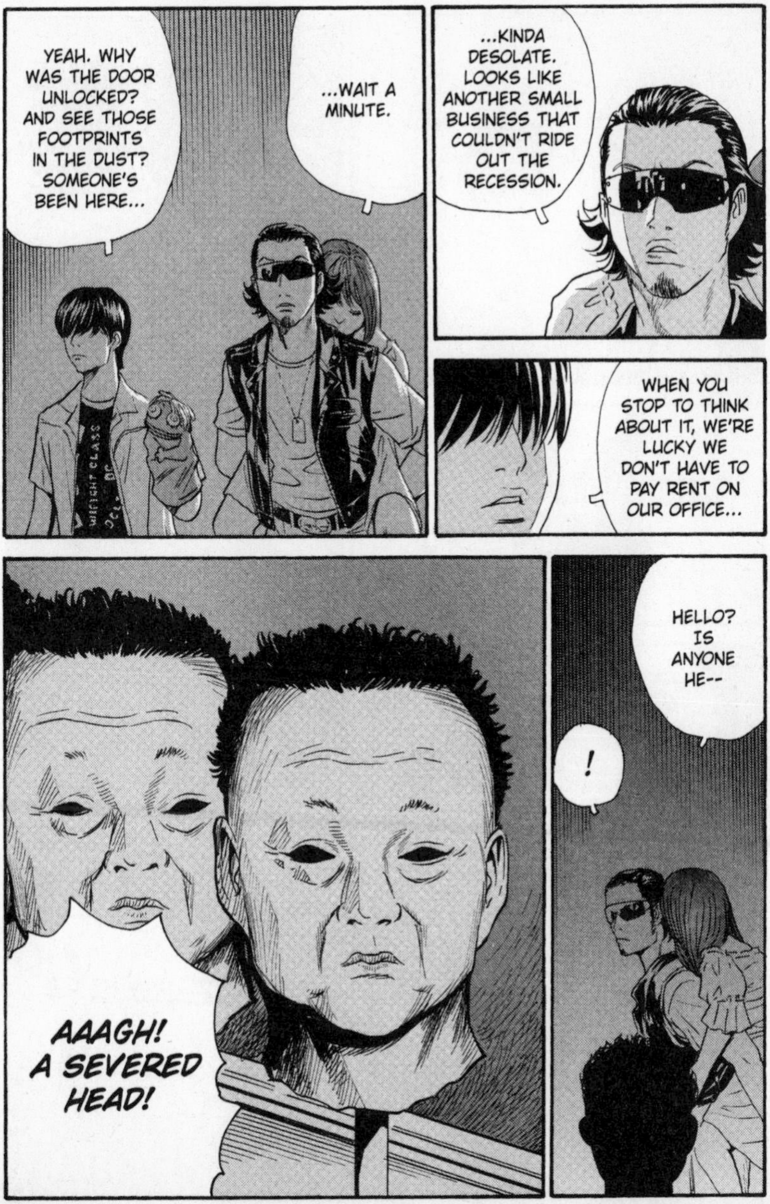
...KINDA DESOLATE. LOOKS LIKE ANOTHER SMALL BUSINESS THAT COULDN'T RIDE OUT THE RECESSION.
WHEN YOU STOP TO THINK ABOUT IT, WE'RE LUCKY WE DON'T HAVE TO PAY RENT ON OUR OFFICE...
...WAIT A MINUTE.
YEAH. WHY WAS THE DOOR UNLOCKED? AND SEE THOSE FOOTPRINTS IN THE DUST? SOMEONE'S BEEN HERE...
HELLO? IS ANYONE HE--
!
AAAGH! A SEVERED HEAD!

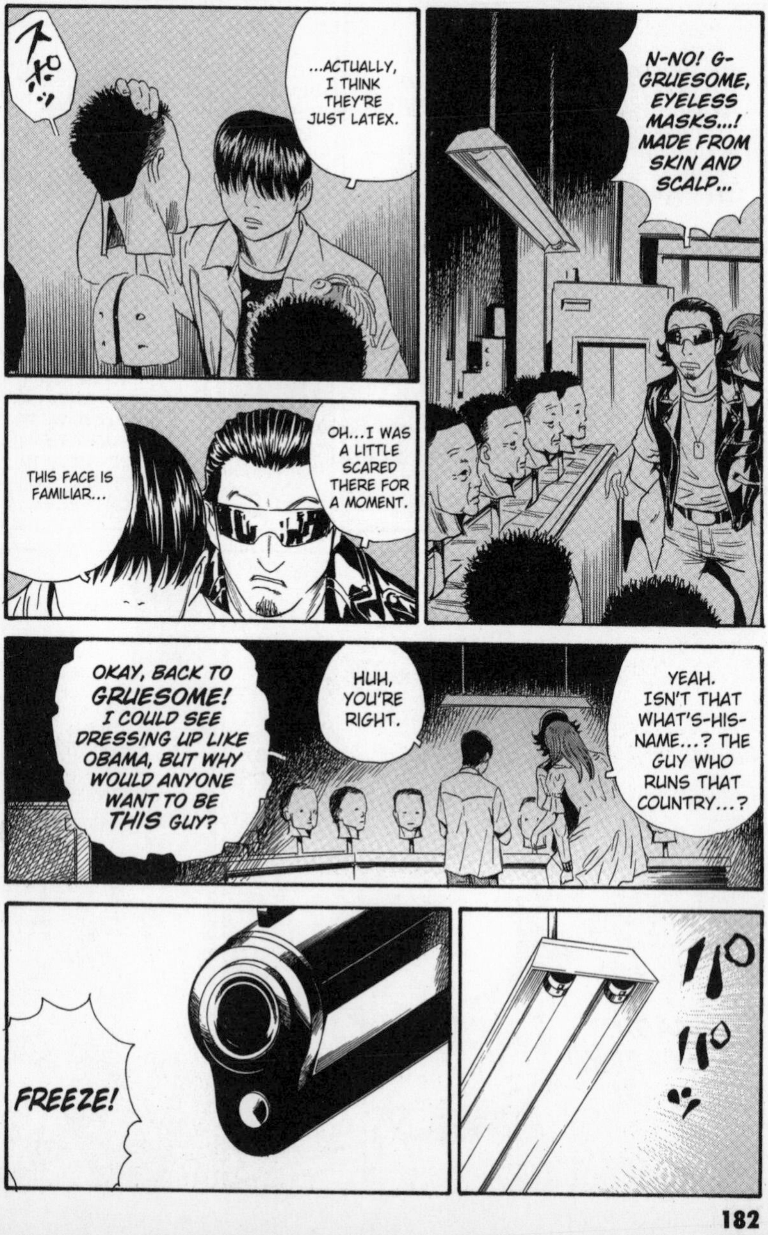

N-NO! G-GRUESOME, EYELESS MASKS...! MADE FROM SKIN AND SCALP...
スポッ
...ACTUALLY, I THINK THEY'RE JUST LATEX.
OH...I WAS A LITTLE SCARED THERE FOR A MOMENT.
THIS FACE IS FAMILIAR...
YEAH. ISN'T THAT WHAT'S-HIS-NAME...? THE GUY WHO RUNS THAT COUNTRY...?
HUH, YOU'RE RIGHT.
OKAY, BACK TO GRUESOME! I COULD SEE DRESSING UP LIKE OBAMA, BUT WHY WOULD ANYONE WANT TO BE THIS GUY?
パパッ
FREEZE!

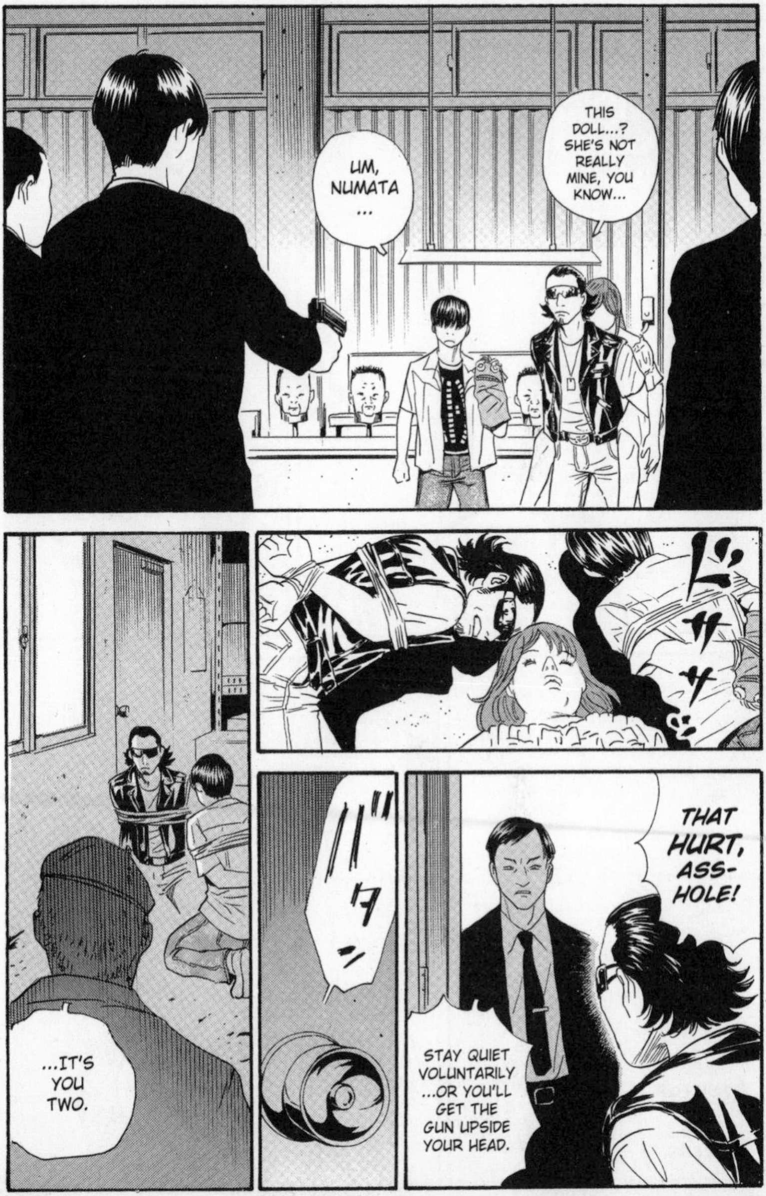
THIS DOLL...? SHE'S NOT REALLY MINE, YOU KNOW...
UM, NUMATA ...
THAT HURT, ASS-HOLE!
STAY QUIET VOLUNTARILY ...OR YOU'LL GET THE GUN UPSIDE YOUR HEAD.
バタン
...IT'S YOU TWO.

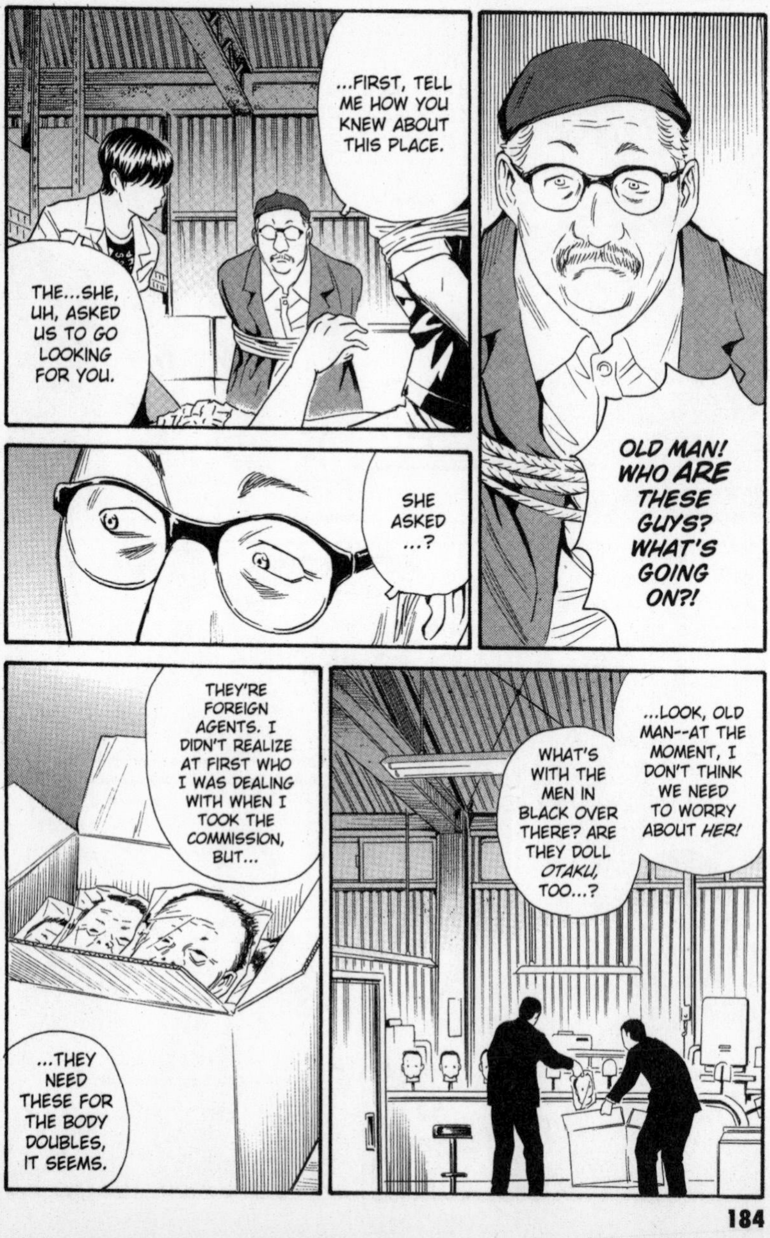
OLD MAN! WHO ARE THESE GUYS? WHAT'S GOING ON?!
...FIRST, TELL ME HOW YOU KNEW ABOUT THIS PLACE.
THE...SHE, UH, ASKED US TO GO LOOKING FOR YOU.
SHE ASKED ...?
...LOOK, OLD MAN--AT THE MOMENT, I DON'T THINK WE NEED TO WORRY ABOUT *HER!*
WHAT'S WITH THE MEN IN BLACK OVER THERE? ARE THEY DOLL *OTAKU,* TOO...?
THEY'RE FOREIGN AGENTS. I DIDN'T REALIZE AT FIRST WHO I WAS DEALING WITH WHEN I TOOK THE COMMISSION, BUT...
...THEY NEED THESE FOR THE BODY DOUBLES, IT SEEMS.

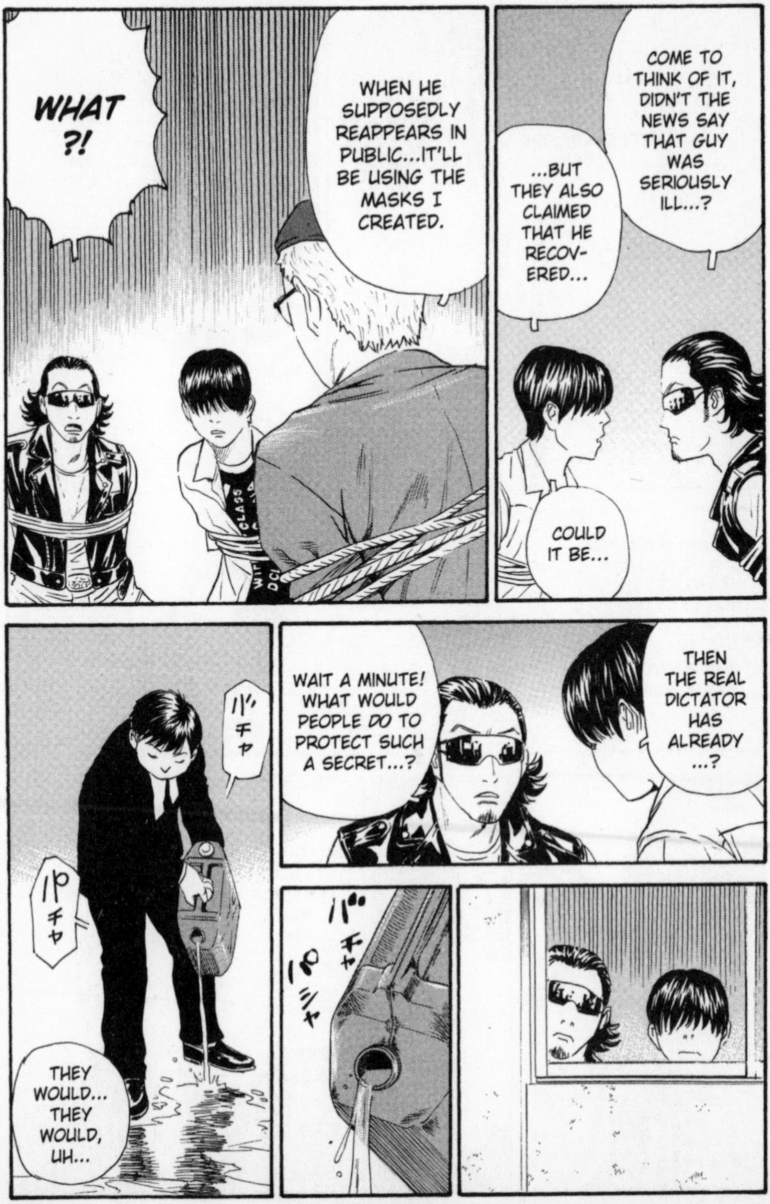
COME TO THINK OF IT, DIDN'T THE NEWS SAY THAT GUY WAS SERIOUSLY ILL...?
...BUT THEY ALSO CLAIMED THAT HE RECOV-ERED...
COULD IT BE...
WHEN HE SUPPOSEDLY REAPPEARS IN PUBLIC...IT'LL BE USING THE MASKS I CREATED.
WHAT ?!
THEN THE REAL DICTATOR HAS ALREADY ...?
WAIT A MINUTE! WHAT WOULD PEOPLE DO TO PROTECT SUCH A SECRET...?
バチャ
パシャ
バチャ
パチャ
THEY WOULD... THEY WOULD, UH...

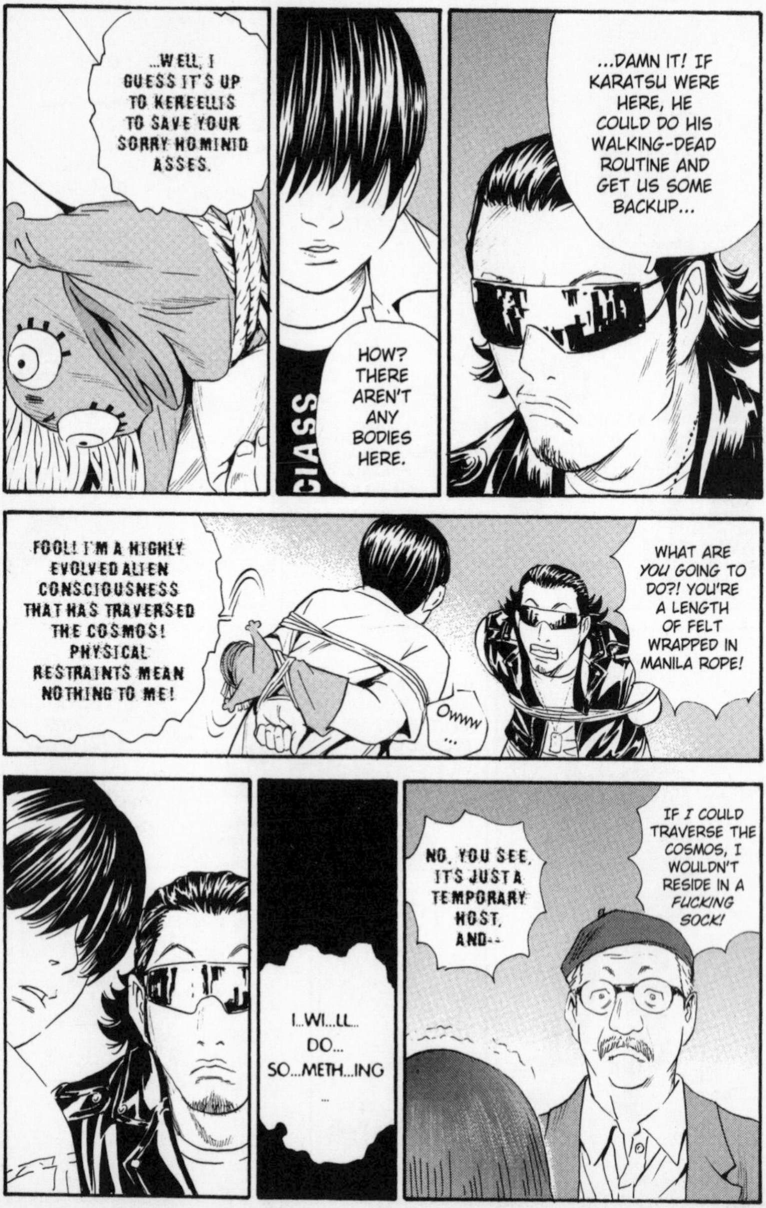
...DAMN IT! IF KARATSU WERE HERE, HE COULD DO HIS WALKING-DEAD ROUTINE AND GET US SOME BACKUP...
HOW? THERE AREN'T ANY BODIES HERE.
...WELL, I GUESS IT'S UP TO KEREELLIS TO SAVE YOUR SORRY HOMINID ASSES.
WHAT ARE *YOU* GOING TO DO?! YOU'RE A LENGTH OF FELT WRAPPED IN MANILA ROPE!
FOOL! I'M A HIGHLY EVOLVED ALIEN CONSCIOUSNESS THAT HAS TRAVERSED THE COSMOS! PHYSICAL RESTRAINTS MEAN NOTHING TO ME!
Owww ...
IF *I* COULD TRAVERSE THE COSMOS, I WOULDN'T RESIDE IN A *FUCKING SOCK!*
NO, YOU SEE, IT'S JUST A TEMPORARY HOST, AND--
I...WI...LL... DO... SO...METH...ING ...

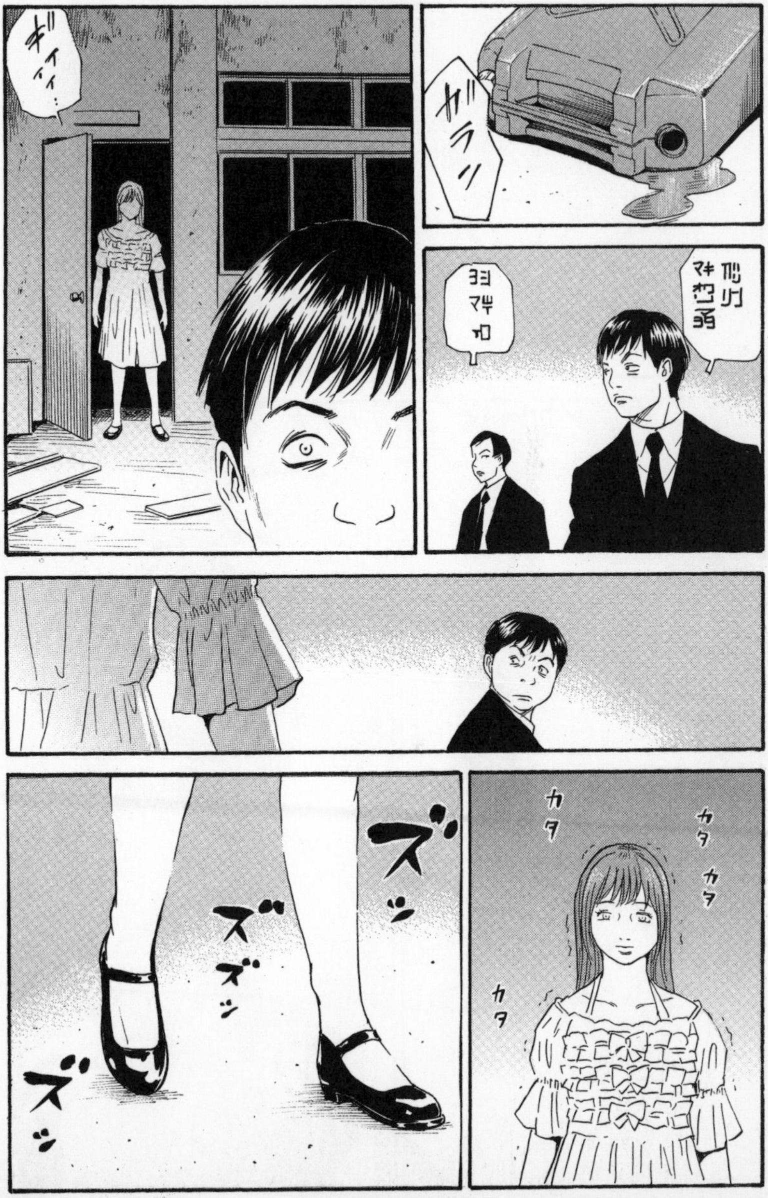
ガラン
ギィィ…
カタ
カタ
カタ
カタ
ズッ
ズズッ
ズッ

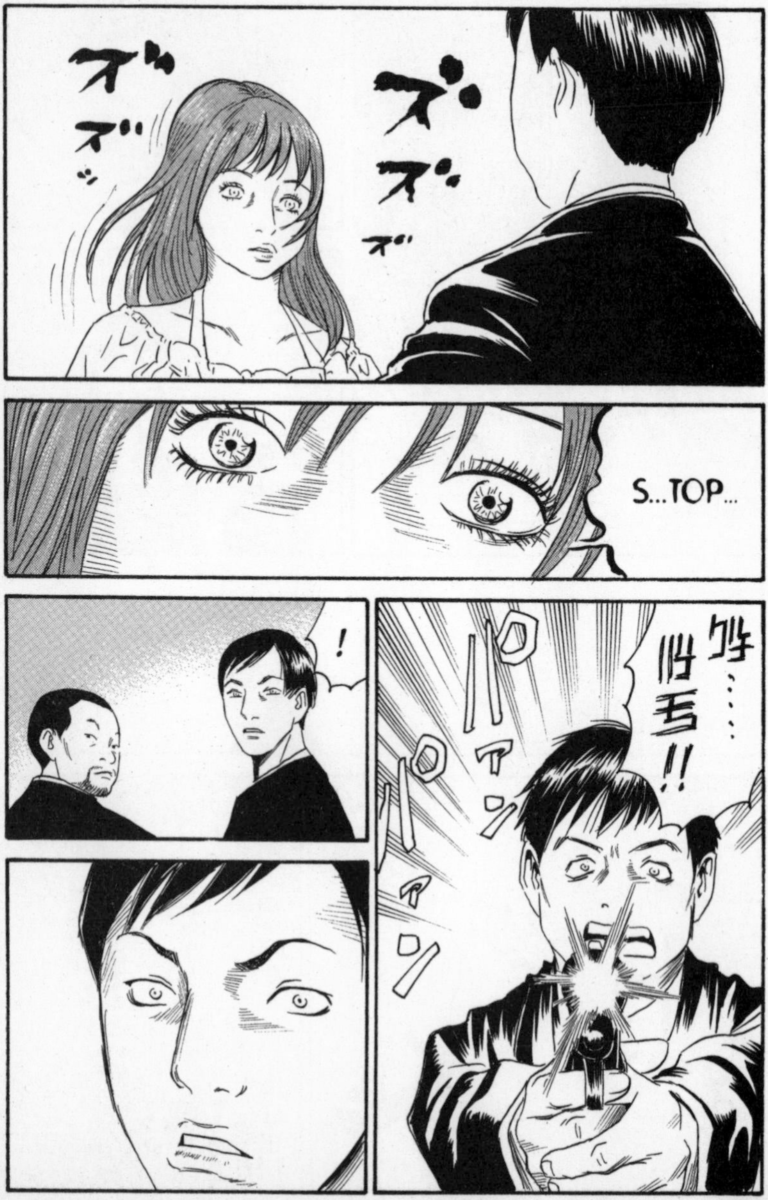
ズズズ
ズズズッ
S...TOP...
パァン
パァン
!

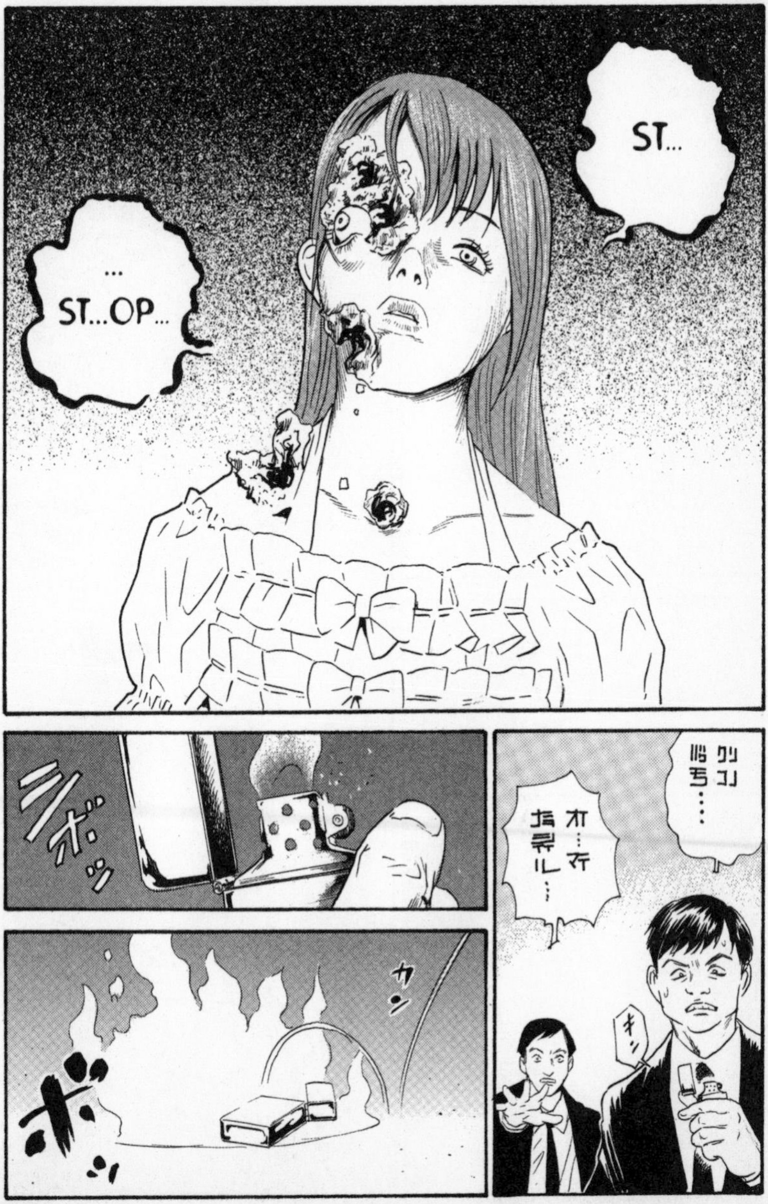
ST...
...
ST...OP...
キン
シボッ
カン
ボッ

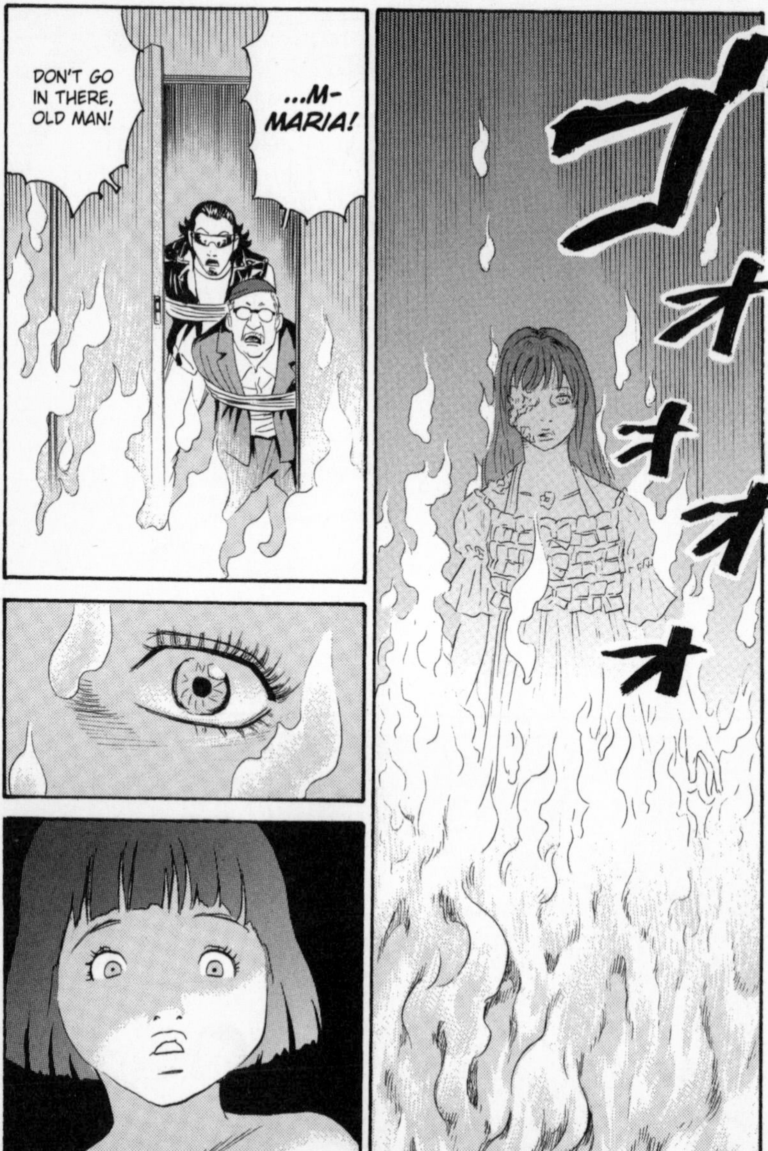
ゴオオオオ
...M-MARIA!
DON'T GO IN THERE, OLD MAN!

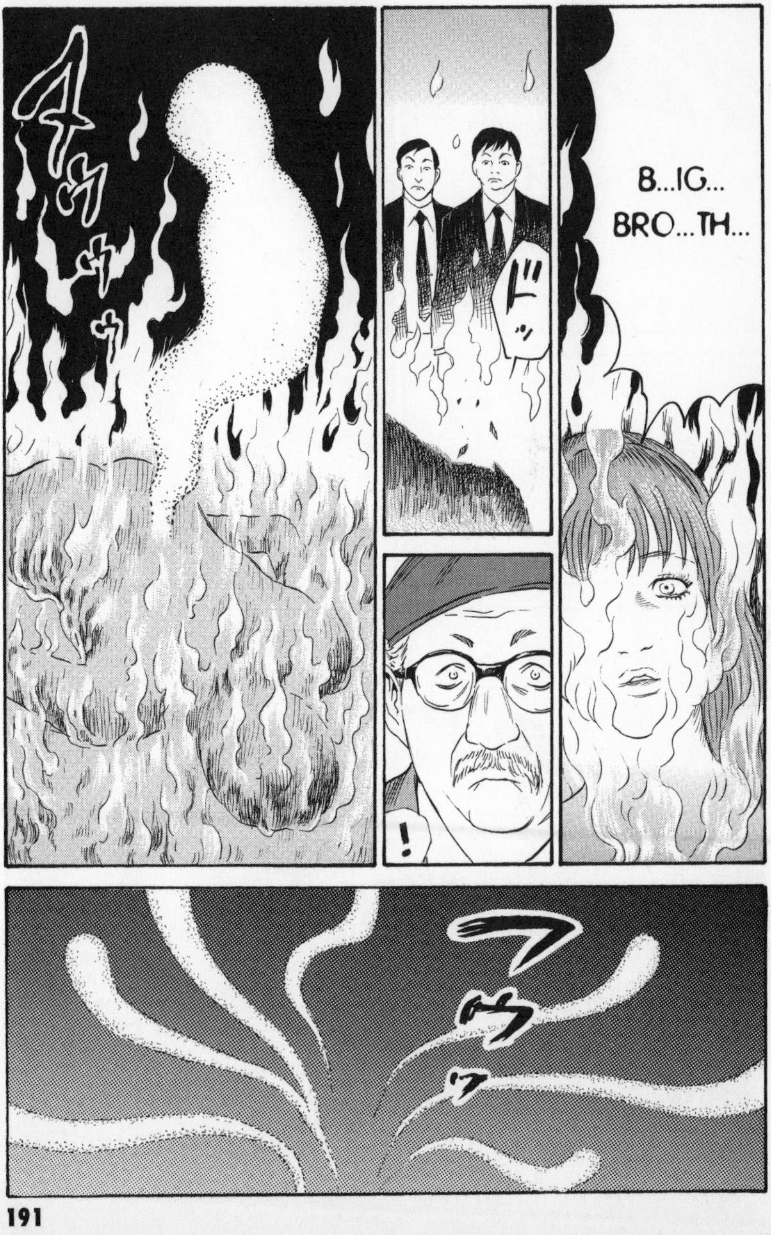
B...IG...
BRO...TH...
ドッ
!

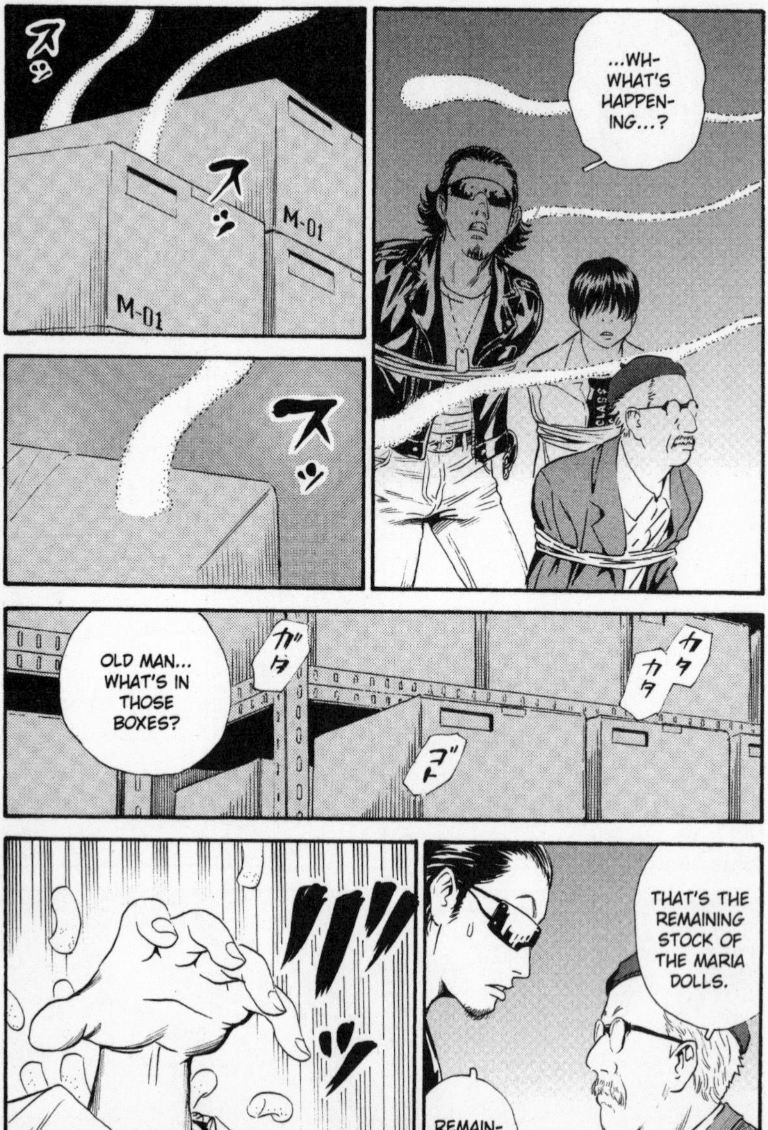

...WH- WHAT'S HAPPENING...?
スッ
スッ
M-01
M-01
カタ カタ
ガタ
OLD MAN... WHAT'S IN THOSE BOXES?
ゴト
THAT'S THE REMAINING STOCK OF THE MARIA DOLLS.
REMAINING...?

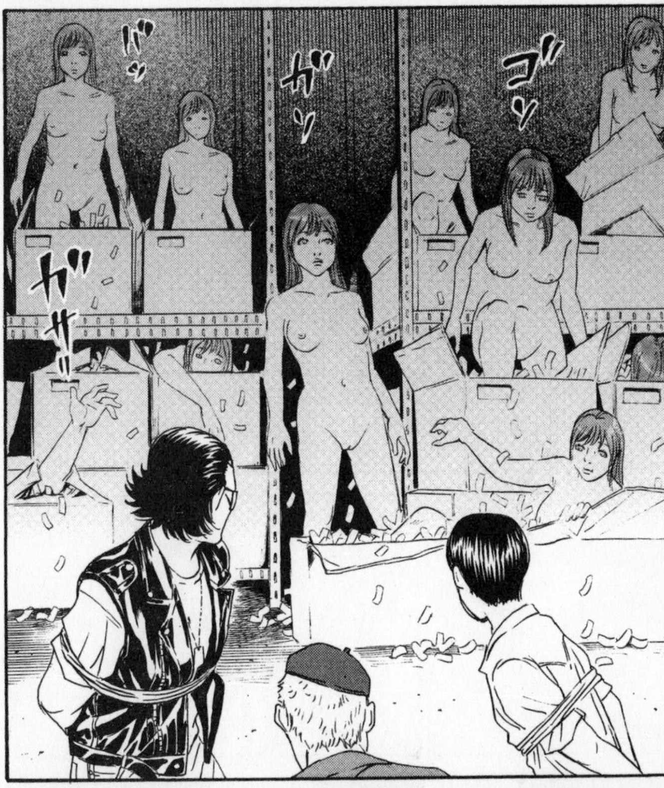
ゴッ
ガサ
ガッ
バッ
ガサ

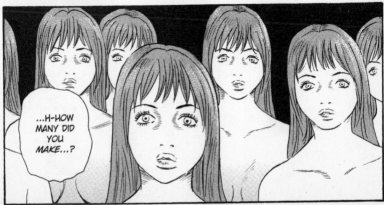

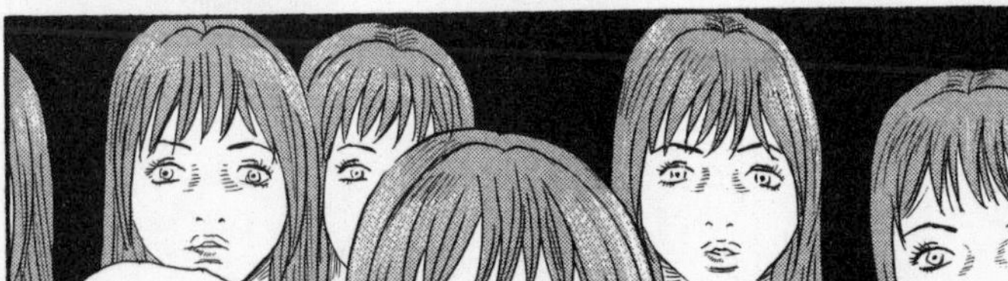
...H-HOW MANY DID YOU MAKE...?

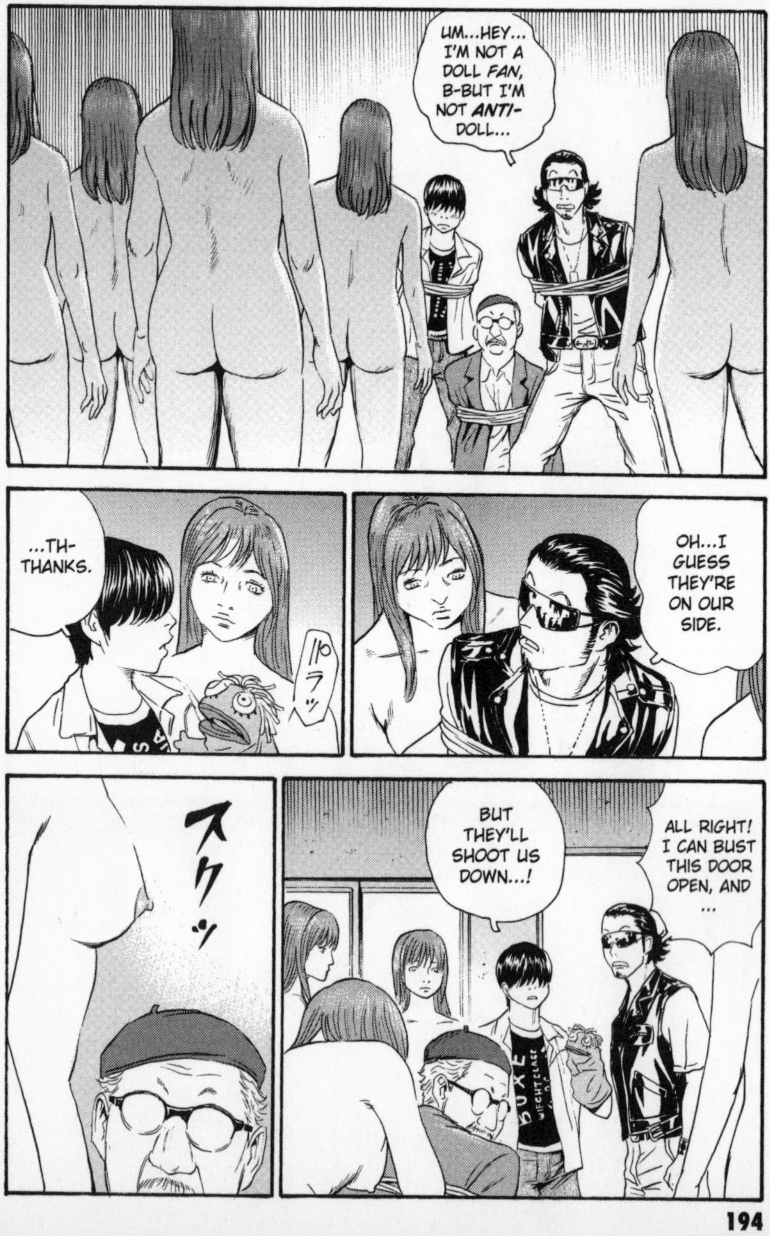
UM...HEY... I'M NOT A DOLL *FAN*, B-BUT I'M NOT ***ANTI***-DOLL...
OH...I GUESS THEY'RE ON OUR SIDE.
...TH-THANKS.
パラッ
ALL RIGHT! I CAN BUST THIS DOOR OPEN, AND ...
BUT THEY'LL SHOOT US DOWN...!
スクッ

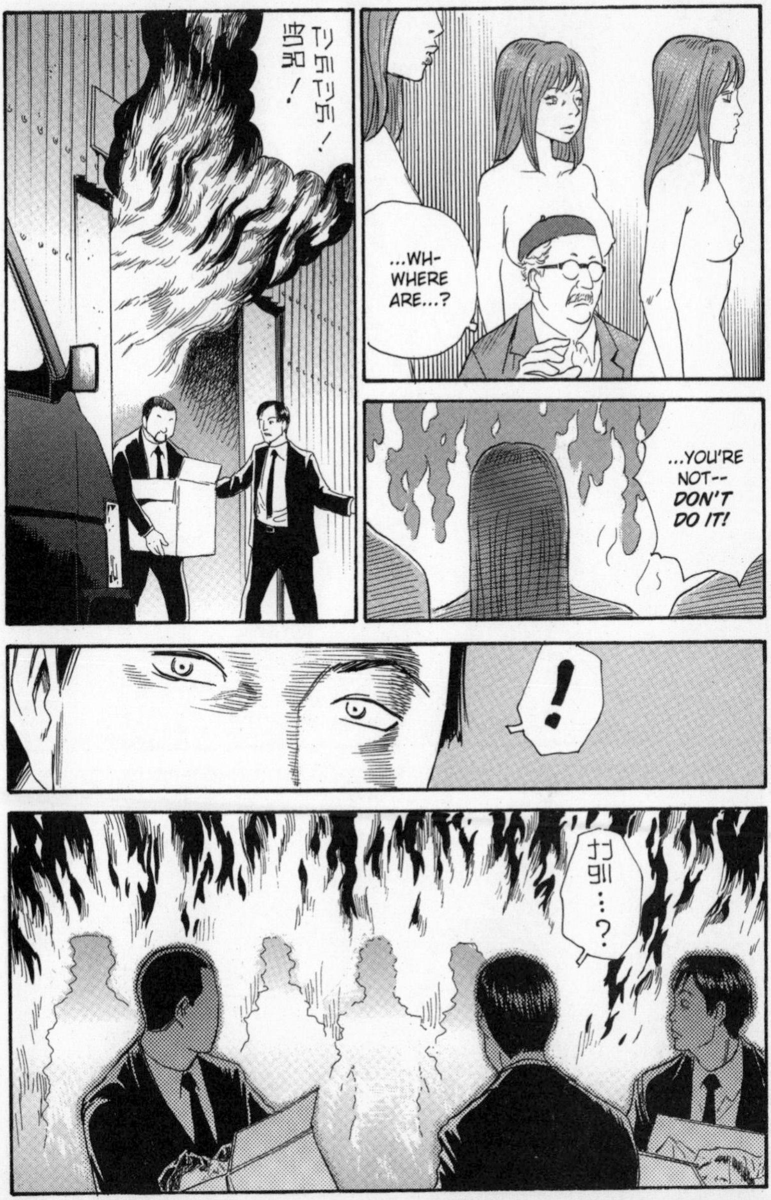
...WH- WHERE ARE...?
...YOU'RE NOT-- DON'T DO IT!
!

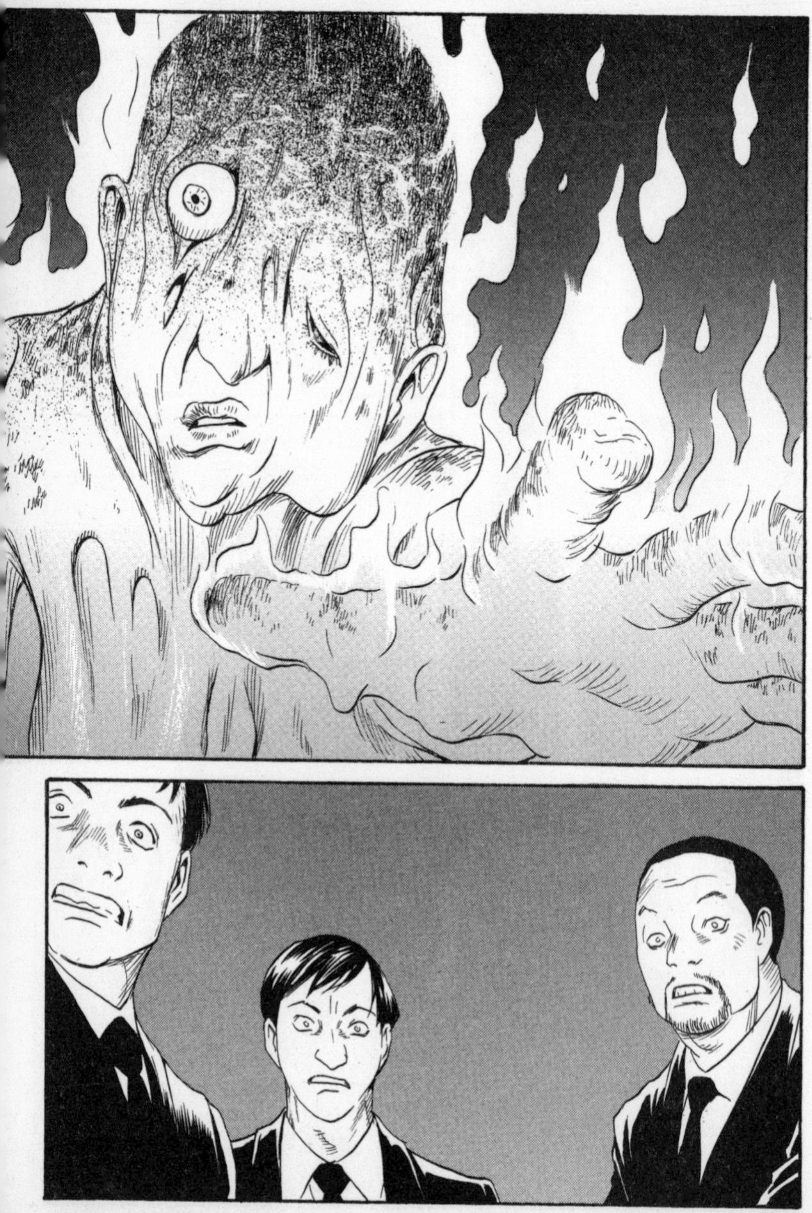

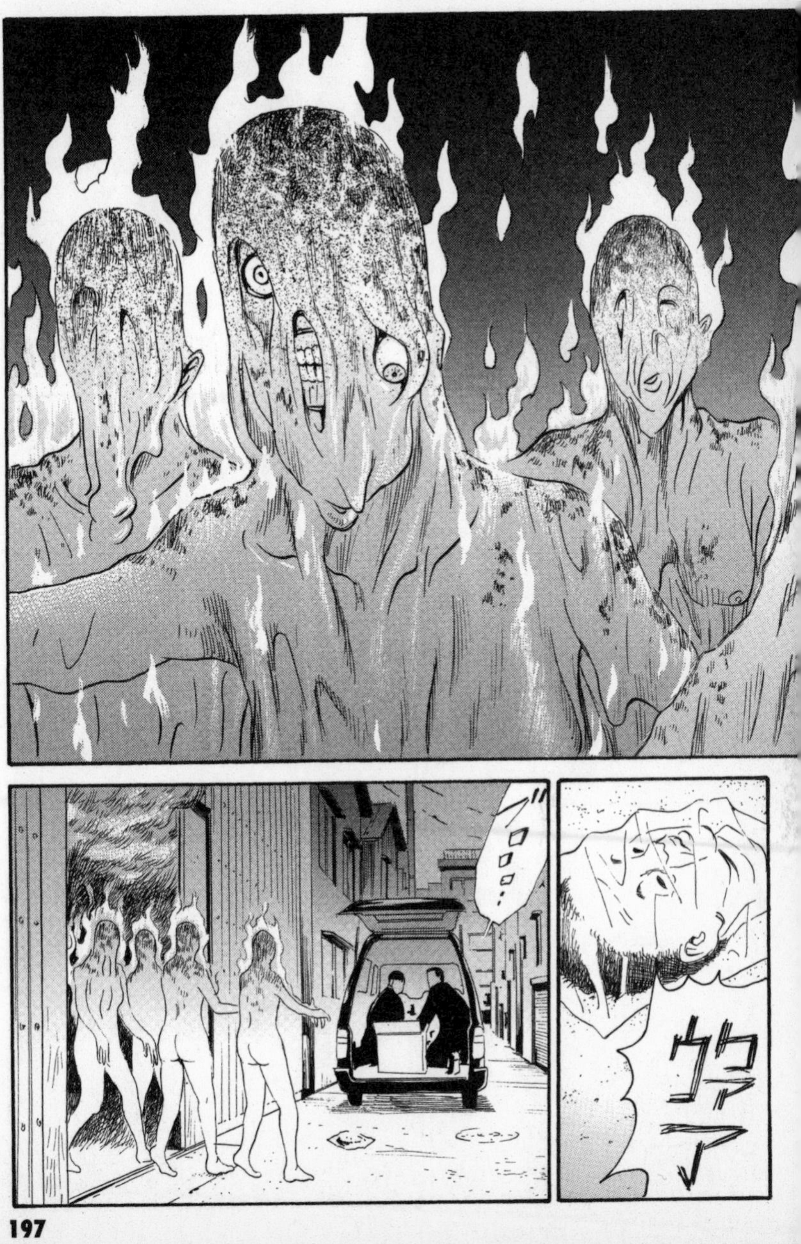
ウァ
ウア
ブロロロ…

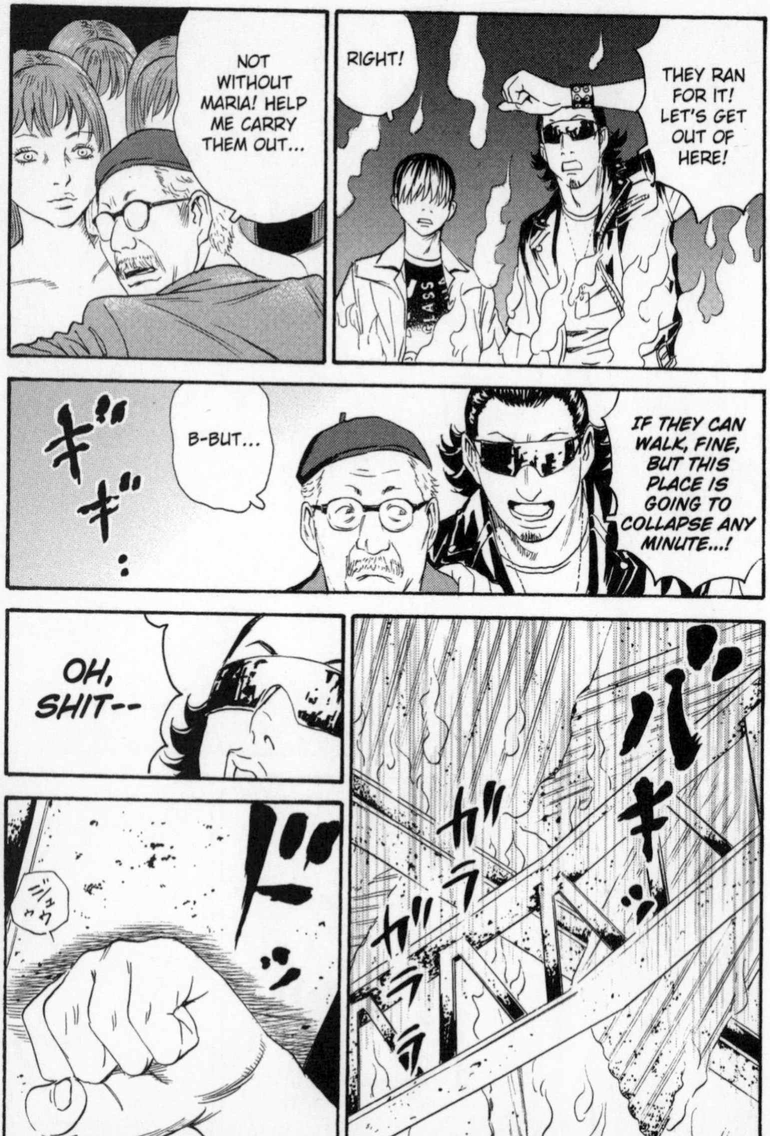
THEY RAN FOR IT! LET'S GET OUT OF HERE!
RIGHT!
NOT WITHOUT MARIA! HELP ME CARRY THEM OUT...
IF THEY CAN WALK, FINE, BUT THIS PLACE IS GOING TO COLLAPSE ANY MINUTE...!
B-BUT...
ギギ…
バキッ
ガラ
ガラ
OH, SHIT--
ドッ

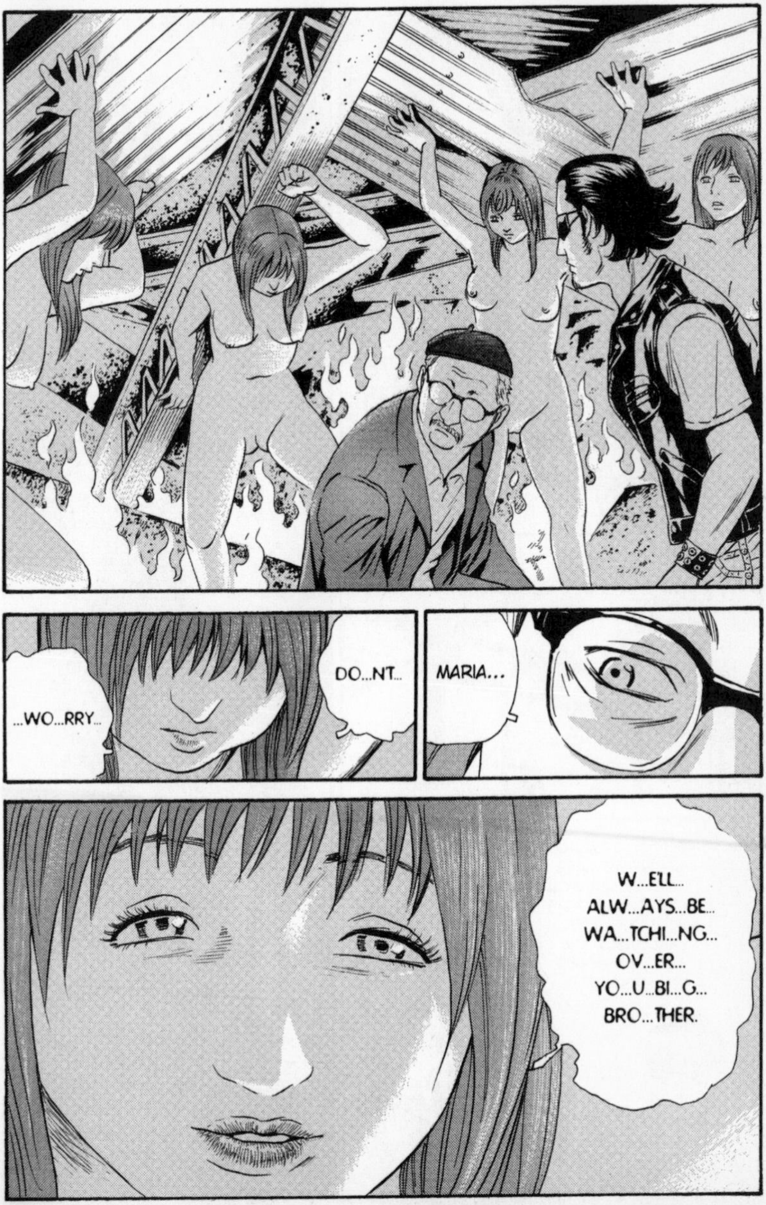
MARIA...
DO...NT...
...WO...RRY...
W...E'LL... ALW...AYS...BE... WA...TCHI...NG... OV...ER... YO...U...BI...G... BRO...THER.

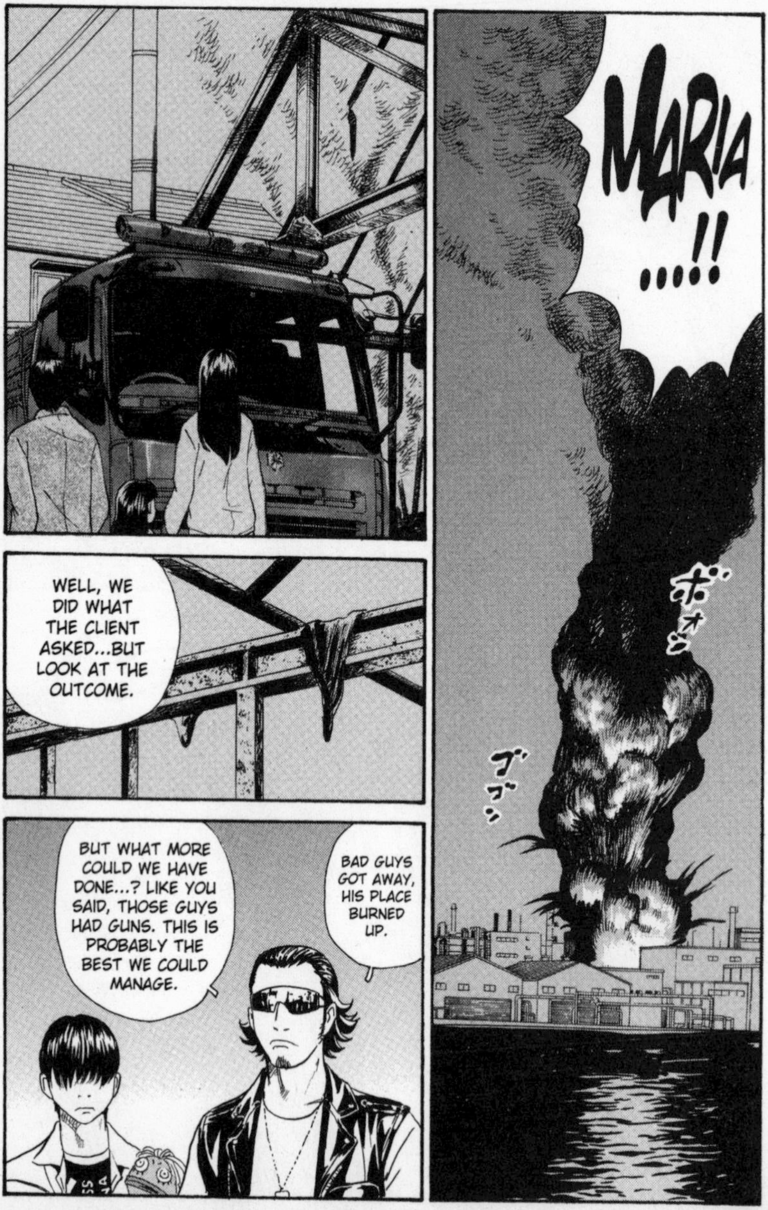
MARIA
....!!
BAD GUYS GOT AWAY, HIS PLACE BURNED UP.
WELL, WE DID WHAT THE CLIENT ASKED...BUT LOOK AT THE OUTCOME.
BUT WHAT MORE COULD WE HAVE DONE...? LIKE YOU SAID, THOSE GUYS HAD GUNS. THIS IS PROBABLY THE BEST WE COULD MANAGE.

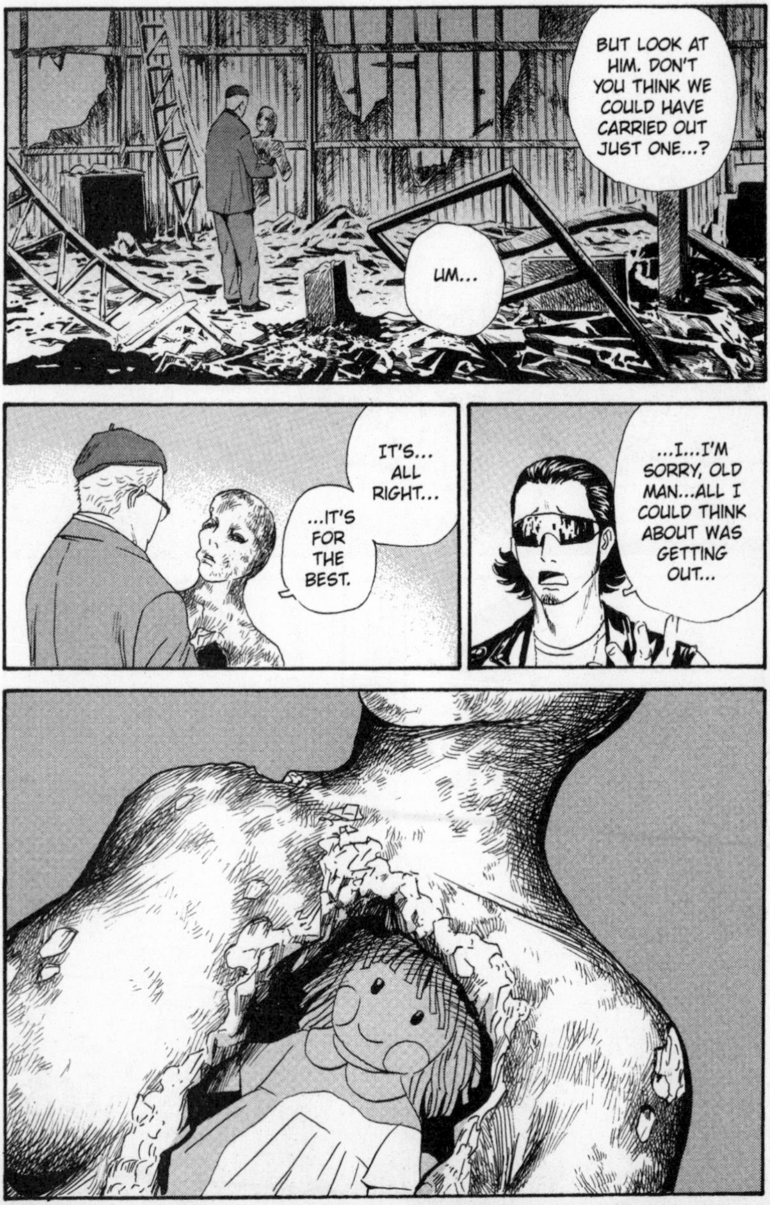
BUT LOOK AT HIM. DON'T YOU THINK WE COULD HAVE CARRIED OUT JUST ONE...?
UM...
...I...I'M SORRY, OLD MAN...ALL I COULD THINK ABOUT WAS GETTING OUT...
IT'S... ALL RIGHT...
...IT'S FOR THE BEST.

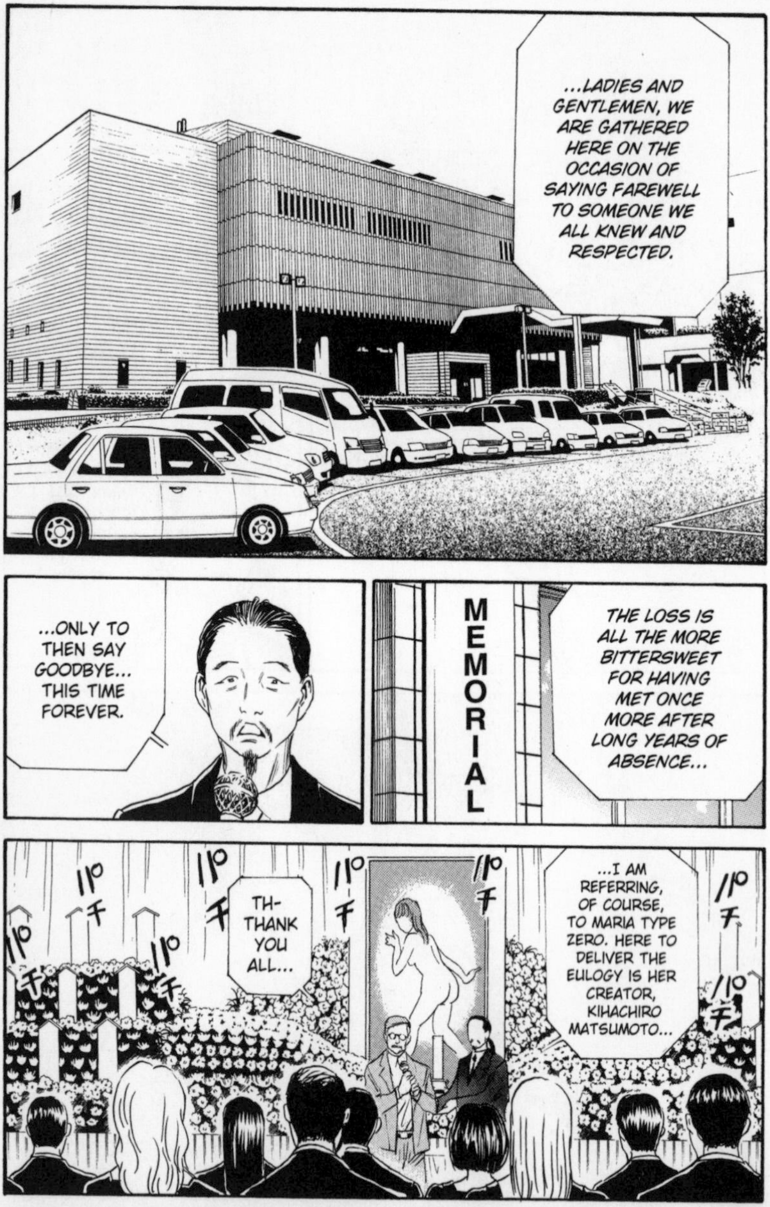

...LADIES AND GENTLEMEN, WE ARE GATHERED HERE ON THE OCCASION OF SAYING FAREWELL TO SOMEONE WE ALL KNEW AND RESPECTED.
MEMORIAL
THE LOSS IS ALL THE MORE BITTERSWEET FOR HAVING MET ONCE MORE AFTER LONG YEARS OF ABSENCE...
...ONLY TO THEN SAY GOODBYE... THIS TIME FOREVER.
パチ
パチ
...I AM REFERRING, OF COURSE, TO MARIA TYPE ZERO. HERE TO DELIVER THE EULOGY IS HER CREATOR, KIHACHIRO MATSUMOTO...
パチ
パチ
TH-THANK YOU ALL...
パチ
パチ
パチ
パチ

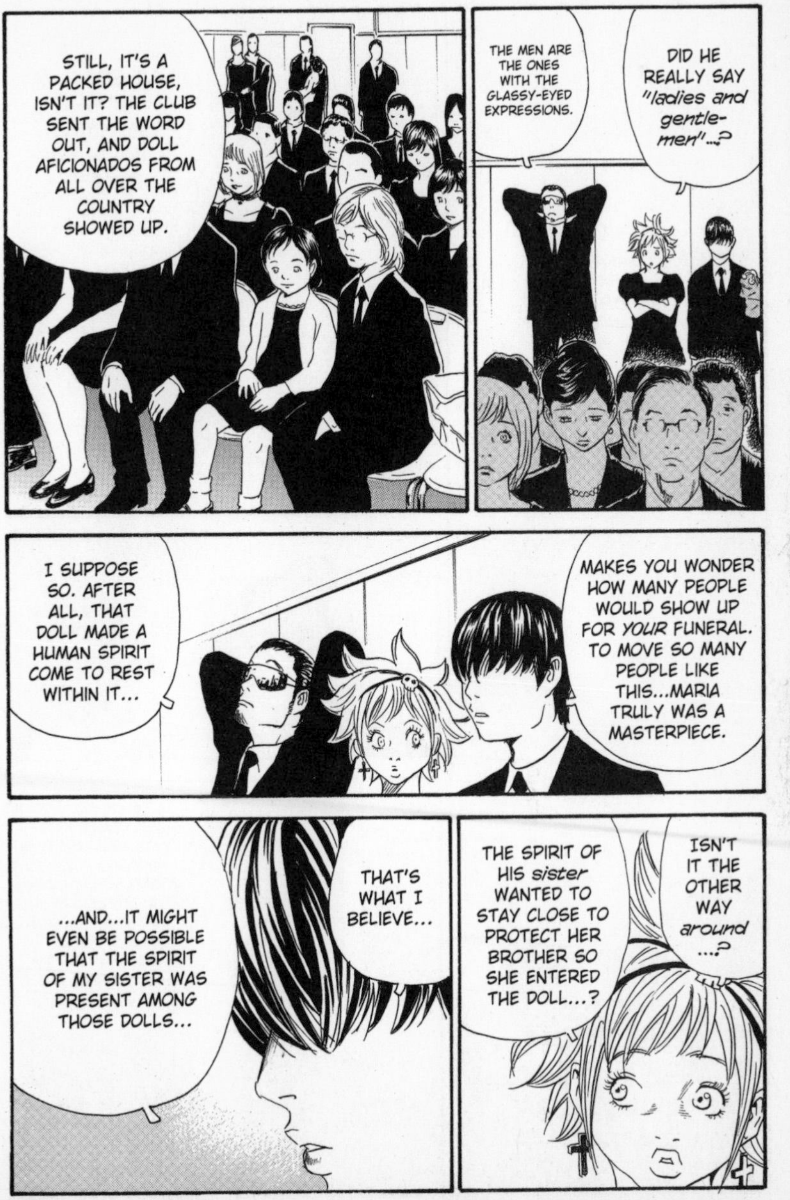
DID HE REALLY SAY "ladies and gentle-men"...?
THE MEN ARE THE ONES WITH THE GLASSY-EYED EXPRESSIONS.
STILL, IT'S A PACKED HOUSE, ISN'T IT? THE CLUB SENT THE WORD OUT, AND DOLL AFICIONADOS FROM ALL OVER THE COUNTRY SHOWED UP.
MAKES YOU WONDER HOW MANY PEOPLE WOULD SHOW UP FOR YOUR FUNERAL. TO MOVE SO MANY PEOPLE LIKE THIS...MARIA TRULY WAS A MASTERPIECE.
I SUPPOSE SO. AFTER ALL, THAT DOLL MADE A HUMAN SPIRIT COME TO REST WITHIN IT...
ISN'T IT THE OTHER WAY around...?
THE SPIRIT OF HIS sister WANTED TO STAY CLOSE TO PROTECT HER BROTHER SO SHE ENTERED THE DOLL...?
THAT'S WHAT I BELIEVE...
...AND...IT MIGHT EVEN BE POSSIBLE THAT THE SPIRIT OF MY SISTER WAS PRESENT AMONG THOSE DOLLS...

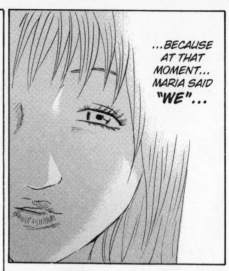

...BECAUSE AT THAT MOMENT... MARIA SAID "WE"...
YOU AND YOUR SISTER COMPLEX ...
IT'S NOT LIKE THAT...!
IT'S AN ANCIENT FOLK BELIEF OF JAPAN! KUNIO YANAGITA CALLED IT *IMO NO CHIKARA*, "THE LITTLE-SISTER FORCE," ALTHOUGH THE SPIRITUAL POWER COULD COME FROM ANY FEMALE RELATIVE...
ALL RIGHT, ALL RIGHT, *enough* ALREADY!
SASAKI-CHAN... KARATSU-KUN... *please* GET BACK HERE SOON...!

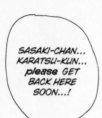

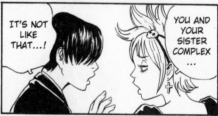

8th delivery: time machine—the end

continued in *the kurosagi corpse delivery service* vol. 13

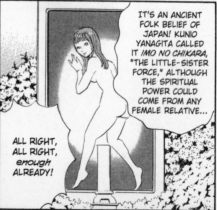

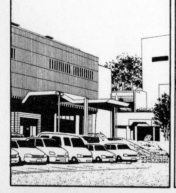

the KUROSAGI corpse delivery service

黒鷺死体宅配便

eiji otsuka 大塚英志 housui yamazaki 山崎峰水

designer **TINA ALESSI**
editor **CARL GUSTAV HORN**
editorial assistant **ANNIE GULLION**
publisher **MIKE RICHARDSON**

English-language version
produced by Dark Horse Comics

THE KUROSAGI CORPSE DELIVERY SERVICE VOL. 12
© OTSUKA Eiji Jimusyo 2009, © HOUSUI YAMAZAKI 2009. First published in Japan in 2009 by KADOKAWA SHOTEN Co., Ltd., Tokyo. English translation rights arranged with KADOKAWA SHOTEN Co., Ltd., Tokyo, through TOHAN CORPORATION, Tokyo. This English-language edition © 2012 by Dark Horse Comics, Inc. All other material © 2012 by Dark Horse Comics, Inc. Dark Horse Manga™ is a trademark of Dark Horse Comics, Inc. All rights reserved. No portion of this publication may be reproduced or transmitted, in any form or by any means, without the express written permission of the copyright holders. Names, characters, places, and incidents featured in this publication either are the product of the author's imagination or are used fictitiously. Any resemblance to actual persons (living or dead), events, institutions, or locales, without satiric intent, is coincidental.

Published by
Dark Horse Manga
A division of Dark Horse Comics, Inc.
10956 SE Main Street
Milwaukie, OR 97222
DarkHorse.com

To find a comics shop in your area,
call the Comic Shop Locator Service
toll-free at 1-888-266-4226

First edition: March 2012
ISBN 978-1-59582-686-2

1 3 5 7 9 10 8 6 4 2

PRINTED AT LAKE BOOK MANUFACTURING, INC., MELROSE PARK, IL, USA

Mike Richardson President and Publisher **Neil Hankerson** Executive Vice President **Tom Weddle** Chief Financial Officer **Randy Stradley** Vice President of Publishing **Michael Martens** Vice President of Book Trade Sales **Anita Nelson** Vice President of Business Affairs **Micha Hershman** Vice President of Marketing **David Scroggy** Vice President of Product Development **Dale LaFountain** Vice President of Information Technology **Darlene Vogel** Senior Director of Print, Design, and Production **Ken Lizzi** General Counsel **Davey Estrada** Editorial Director **Scott Allie** Senior Managing Editor **Chris Warner** Senior Books Editor **Diana Schutz** Executive Editor **Cary Grazzini** Director of Print and Development **Lia Ribacchi** Art Director **Cara Niece** Director of Scheduling

DISJECTA MEMBRA

SOUND FX GLOSSARY AND NOTES ON KUROSAGI VOL. 12 BY TOSHIFUMI YOSHIDA
introduction and additional comments by the editor

TO INCREASE YOUR ENJOYMENT of the distinctive Japanese visual style of this manga, we've included a guide to the sound effects (or "FX") used inside. It is suggested the reader *not* constantly consult this glossary as they read through, but regard it as supplemental information, in the manner of footnotes, or perhaps one of those nutritional supplements, the kind that's long and difficult to swallow. If you want to imagine it being read aloud by Osaka, after the manner of her lecture to Sakaki on hemorrhoids in episode five of *Azumanga Daioh*, please go right ahead. In either Yuki Matsuoka or Kira Vincent-Davis's voice—I like them both.

Japanese, like English, did not independently invent its own writing system, but instead borrowed and modified the system used by the then-dominant cultural power in its part of the world. We still call the letters we use to write English today the "Roman" alphabet, for the simple reason that about 1,600 years ago, the earliest English speakers, living on the frontier of the Roman Empire, began to use the same letters the Romans used for their Latin language to write out English.

Around that very same time, on the other side of the planet, Japan, like England, was another example of an island civilization lying across the sea from a great empire—in this case, that of China. Likewise, the Japanese borrowed from the Chinese writing system, which then, as now, consisted of thousands of complex symbols—today in China officially referred to in the Roman alphabet as *hanzi*, but which the Japanese pronounce as *kanji*. For example, all the Japanese characters you see on the front cover of *The Kurosagi Corpse Delivery Service*—the seven which make up the original title and the four each which make up the creators' names—are examples of kanji. Of course, all of them were hanzi first—although the Japanese did also invent some original kanji of their own, just as new hanzi have been created over the centuries as Chinese evolved.

Whereas the various dialects of Chinese are written entirely in hanzi, it is impractical to render the Japanese language entirely in them. To compare once more, English is a notoriously difficult language in which to spell properly, and this is in part because it uses an alphabet designed for another language, Latin, whose sounds are different (this is, of course, putting aside the fact the sounds of both languages experienced change over time). The challenges the Japanese faced in using the Chinese writing system for their own language were even greater, for whereas spoken English and Latin are at least from a common language family, spoken Japanese is unrelated to any of the various dialects of spoken Chinese. The complicated writing system the Japanese evolved represents an adjustment to these great differences.

When the Japanese borrowed hanzi to become kanji, what they were getting was a way to write out (remember, they already had ways to *say*) their vocabulary. Nouns, verbs, many adjectives, the names of places and people—that's what kanji are used for, the fundamental data of the written language. The practical use and processing of that "data"—its grammar and pronunciation—is another matter entirely. Because spoken Japanese neither sounds nor functions like Chinese, the first work-around tried was a system called *manyogana*, where individual kanji were picked to represent certain syllables in Japanese. A similar method is still used in Chinese today to spell out foreign names; companies and individuals often try to choose hanzi for this purpose that have an auspicious, or at least not insulting, meaning. As you will also observe in *Kurosagi* and elsewhere, the meaning behind the characters that make up a personal name are an important literary element of Japanese as well.

The commentary in *Katsuya Terada's The Monkey King* (also available from Dark Horse, and also translated by Toshifumi Yoshida) notes the importance that not only Chinese, but also Indian culture had on Japan at this time in history—particularly, through Buddhism. Just as in Western history at this time, religious communities in Asia were associated with learning, as priests and monks were more likely to be literate than other groups in society. It is believed the northeast Indian Siddham script studied by Kukai (died 835 AD), founder of the Shingon sect of Japanese Buddhism, inspired him to create the solution for writing Japanese still used today. Kukai is credited with the idea of taking the *manyogana* and making shorthand versions of them—which are now known simply as *kana*. The improvement in efficiency was dramatic: a kanji previously used to represent a sound, which might have taken a dozen strokes to draw, was now replaced by a kana that took three or four.

Unlike the original kanji they were based on, the new kana had *only* a sound meaning. And unlike the thousands of kanji, there are only forty-six kana, which can be used to spell out any word in the Japanese language, including the many ordinarily written with kanji (Japanese keyboards work on this principle). The same set of forty-six kana is written two different ways depending on its intended use: cursive style, *hiragana*, and block style, *katakana*. Naturally, sound FX in manga are almost always written out using kana.

Kana works somewhat differently than the Roman alphabet. For example, while there are separate kana for each of the five vowels (the Japanese order is not A-E-I-O-U as in English, but A-I-U-E-O), there are, except for *n*, no separate kana for consonants (the middle *n* in the word *ninja* illustrates this exception). Instead, kana work by grouping together consonants with vowels: for example, there are five kana for sounds starting with *k*, depending on which vowel follows it—in Japanese vowel order, they go KA, KI, KU, KE, KO. The next set of kana begins with *s* sounds, so SA, SHI, SU, SE, SO, and so on. You will observe this kind of consonant-vowel pattern in the FX listings for *Kurosagi* Vol. 12 below.

Katakana are generally used for manga sound FX, but on occasion hiragana are used instead. This is commonly done when the sound is one associated with a human body, but can be a subtler aesthetic choice by the artist as well. In *Kurosagi* Vol. 12 you can see an example on 54.1, with the ZUUN, as Yaichi manifests him(?)self; it is written ずうん. Note its more cursive appearance compared to other FX. If it had been written in katakana style, it would look like ズウン.

To see how to use this glossary, take an example from page 10: "10.2 FX: KIII—car coming to a stop." 10.2 means the FX is the one on page 10, in panel 2. KIII is the sound these kana—キイイツ—literally stand for; note that the small character "tsu" (ツ) at the end, commonly seen in manga FX, is not actually considered part of the sound itself, but serves to indicate that this is the kind of sound that stops suddenly. After the dash comes an explanation of what the sound represents (in some cases it will be less obvious than others). Note that in cases where there are two or more different sounds in a single panel, an extra number is used to differentiate them from right to left; or, in cases where right and left are less clear, in clockwise order.

The use of kana in these FX also illustrates another aspect of written Japanese—its flexible reading order. For example, the way you're reading the pages and panels of this book in general—going from right to left, and from top to bottom—is similar to the order in which Japanese is also written in most forms of print: books, magazines, and newspapers. However, some of the FX in *Kurosagi* (and manga in general) read left to right. This kind of flexibility is also to be found on Japanese web pages, which usually also read left to right. In other words, Japanese doesn't simply read "the other way" from English; the Japanese themselves are used to reading it in several different directions.

The explanation of what the sound represents may sometimes be surprising, but every culture "hears" sounds differently. Note that manga FX do not even necessarily represent literal sounds. Such "mimetic" words, which represent an imagined sound, or even a state of mind, are called *gitaigo* in Japanese. Like the onomatopoeic *giseigo* (the words used to represent literal sounds— i.e., most FX in this glossary are classed as *giseigo*), they are also used in colloquial speech and writing. A Japanese, for example, might say that something bounced by saying PURIN, or talk about eating by saying MUGU MUGU. It's something like describing chatter in English by saying "yadda yadda yadda" instead.

One important last note: all these spelled-out kana vowels should be pronounced as they are in Japanese: *A* as *ah*, *I* as *eee*, *U* as *ooh*, *E* as *eh*, and *O* as *oh*.

0.0   Thank you for waiting. I'm not sure where to start apologizing—so why not with the front cover? No sooner did you rip off the bestickered shrink wrap than your fingers sensed something was wrong. Something was different—namely, *Kurosagi* no longer has the rough cover stock it had for the first eleven volumes. This stock was originally introduced in an attempt to echo the brown wrapping-paper dust jacket used by designer Bunpei Yorifuji on the original editions of *Kurosagi*. Writer Eiji Otsuka is unusual among manga creators in using separate design studios (as opposed to the interior artist) to create the cover, and often the covers of his manga involve experimentation with the stock (fancy printer speak for the kind of paper) as well as the cover's graphic design; for example, other manga to come out of his studio had covers with the texture of rice paper or linen. As mentioned, the original Japanese covers of *Kurosagi* used stock with the look and feel of brown wrapping paper. This is workable as a slip-cover (the standard kind of cover on Japanese paperbacks) but far too light to serve as the cover of an American-style paperback, so we used the brown cardboard with which you've been familiar. The irony is that this "rough"-looking stock is actually rather expensive compared to the kind used in typical US editions of manga, and as *Kurosagi* regrettably doesn't sell very well, we decided this would be the least compromising place to cut costs. If you've run into some recent reprintings of earlier volumes of *Kurosagi*, you might have already seen that they use this new stock—perhaps we should have made the transition when the covers also switched to black with vol. 11, but here we are. And we are still here. As Joker said in *Full Metal Jacket*, germane to this series, "The dead know only one thing. It is better to be alive." The fact some volumes of *Kurosagi* have gone into multiple printings may seem to contradict the notion it has low sales, but it is much cheaper to reprint volumes that have already been produced, than it is to produce new ones. By the way, on the cover of the original Japanese vol. 12, right where "YOUR BODY IS THEIR BUSINESS!" is on the English edition, it says *Masaka no Hariuddo eizooka shinkoo naka!*—"Hard to believe, but a Hollywood movie is in the planning!" I would make a *1941* reference at this point, but we are professionals, after all.

2.1 This time around, all the chapter titles in the volume are songs by the seventies rock group Sadistic Mika Band, whose name was in part a play on John Lennon and Yoko Ono's (were the editor a boomer instead of Gen-X, he would have just said "John and Yoko's") Plastic Ono Band. The "Mika" in the name was their lead vocalist, Mika Fukui; various stories are given to explain the "Sadistic" part, but one is the manner in which she was said to wield her knife in the kitchen. Fukui was married to the band's rhythm guitarist and lead figure, Kazuhiko Kato, who had already achieved success in the late 1960s with the single "Kaettekita yopparai" ("I Only Live Twice"—a riff on the 1967 James Bond movie filmed in Japan, *You Only Live Twice*). Their first and second albums, the 1972 self-titled *Sadistic Mika Band* and 1974's critically acclaimed concept album *Black Ship* (the concept was the arrival to a largely isolated Japan in 1853 of Commodore Matthew Perry from the US in his fleet of "black ships," and the new ideas the visit helped spread) can be found together on one CD as a 1998 rerelease from the British label See For Miles. The fact it was issued on a UK label reflects Sadistic Mika Band's connections there; *Black Ship* was produced in London by Chris Thomas, at the time associated with Roxy Music, for whom Sadistic Mika Band would open on their 1975 tour. The band broke up after Mika and Kazuhiko divorced (she then married Thomas) but its members continued successful careers, including percussionist Yukihiro Takahashi, who became drummer and vocalist of electropop pioneers Yellow Magic Orchestra. Kazuhiko Kato would later make a famous contribution to anime as the composer of the eponymous "Ai Oboeteimasuka" ("Do You Remember Love?"), sung by Lynn Minmay during the climactic battle in the 1984 *Macross* movie of the same name. On October 17, 2009, Kato's body was found hanging in a hotel bathroom in the resort city of Karuizawa, accompanied by two suicide notes; Kato, aged sixty-two, was said to have told friends, "I have nothing left that I want to do." The translator remarks that if the Kurosagi Corpse Delivery Service really existed, this would have been a prime setup for one of their adventures.

5.2　The sign says "Jukaiyama Entrance." Jukaiyama, meaning "tree sea mountain," is a popular nickname for the vast Aokigahara Forest, the infamous real-life locale for suicide that's figured in *Kurosagi* since the very first story.

7.2　In the original Japanese, she said *u fu fu*, a sound that (at least in manga) is considered to be a sexy chuckle.

10.2　**FX: KIII**—car coming to a stop

10.3　**FX: GACHA**—door opening

15.1　**FX: GOGOGO PUWAAAN DODO**— traffic/construction noises

16.4　The last time we ran into Dr. Kayama (in vol. 6), Karatsu noted that she got to call Sasaki (her patient) by her first name, Ao, first-name intimacy being more rare in Japan than in the United States. Even men who have known each other for years and consider themselves friends might use last names; their familiarity will be shown by the fact they don't use -*san* at the end of it. Yata has apparently gotten to the point where he calls Makino by her first name (Keiko), but none of the other characters address each other this way.

18.4　**FX: DOSA**—dropping garbage

19.3　Whereas you have to register with the government in the US to, for example, vote or get a driver's license, there is no general requirement to register your residence, as there is in certain countries, including Japan. The registration in Japan is often done at the ward level (for example, Shinjuku, whose municipal government Sasayama works for, is a ward).

20.6　**FX/balloon: GASA**—taking magazine out of bag

21.1　Note the square "QR code" ("quick response") in the center right of the cover. Despite the near-ubiquity of cell phones in America, it is estimated that only a third of American cell users have used a QR code yet, although numbers are increasing rapidly as US retailers such as Ralph Lauren and Starbucks use them in their own advertising campaigns. But the codes date back to 1994 in Japan, where they were invented by Denso Wave to track vehicle parts. By 1999, Kadokawa was using them on the spines of the original Japanese *tankobon* of the manga *The Ring* to help coordinate promotion with the movie. In Japan, where these are much more common, a person would be more likely to access them through their mobile phone than a webcam. The editor doesn't have a cell phone, reflecting that while it might be important to be able to get in touch with, say, a doctor or James Bond in a hurry, I can't really ever picture a dramatic shot of the president at his desk, the Cabinet gathered around him in silence . . . his head in his hands as he grapples with the weight of some terrible decision . . . then underlit as he slowly picks up the hotline to say . . . *"Get me . . . the **manga editor**."*

21.3 The phrase with *ero* ("erotic") suggests "otaku" is not confined to those lacking depth perception. During a recent appearance on the always-recommended Anime World Order podcast, Patrick Macias suggested that whatever scariness the word *otaku* might retain in Japan in 2012, it's among the older generation and not the young. Unfortunately, just as in America, in Japan, it is the older generation that votes, and not the young . . .

22.2 FX/balloon: PAN—flesh slapping together. "The slapping's getting louder/You don't want them to clown you/In this situation/What do you do?"—Digital Underground, "Freaks of the Industry."

23.3 FX/balloon: GACHA—door opening

24.2 FX: BASA—sound of newspapers hitting table

26.4 FX/balloon: JAKKA JAN JARARA-RAN—ringtone

27.1 Dr. Kayama called her "Suzuki-*san*," but Karatsu uses "Yuka-*san*." Very smooth, that Karatsu.

29.1 In Japanese, *arienu* is a phrase that means "doesn't exist" or "not possible." Even though the entire name of the song is in Japanese, "Arienu kyoowa-koku," the *arienu* part is written in katakana, as if it were trying to spell out the name of a foreign country. For example, the official name of France, *République française*, is written in Japanese in a similar way to this chapter title, as フランス共和国 (*Furansu kyoowa-koku*). Because Japanese uses four different scripts, having their origins in three different cultures (the Western Roman alphabet, the Chinese-derived

kanji, and the Japanese-developed katakana and hiragana), the possibilities of shading, tone, and double meaning in the language go beyond just wordplay to incorporate what might be called "script play" as well. I'm not sure there actually is a proper term for this idea in English writing, since we only use one script in our language.

30.2 FX: GASASA—spreading map open

31.5 FX/balloon: ZA—footstep

33.5 FX/balloon: GACHA—door opening

34.1.1 FX/balloon: GISHI—sound of squeaking bed springs

34.1.2 FX/balloon: GISHI—sound of squeaking bed springs

34.1.3 FX/balloon: GISHI—sound of squeaking bed springs

34.3 FX/balloon: PEKO—bowing sound

34.4 FX/balloon: GII—door creaking closed

35.6 FX/balloon: NUPO—popping-out sound of Momoka getting up

37.3 FX/balloon: SHUBA—clothes appearing

38.1 FX/balloons: PINPOON PINPOON PINPOON—doorbell sounds

38.4 FX: KACHARI—unlatching sound

40.1 FX: GATA—picking up laptop

40.2 FX: PARA—piece of paper fluttering out

42.4 FX: GOTO—putting down laptop

42.5 FX: GACHA—door opening

44.1.1 FX/balloon: CHIKO—hitting Enter key

44.1.2 FX/balloon: KAKO—hitting Enter key

44.1.3 FX/balloon: KACHI—hitting Enter key

44.2 FX: GYRURURU—sound of spinning

44.3 FX: GURUN—login sound for Second Life?

46.5 FX/balloon: SHUPAA—teleporting sound

47.1.1 **FX/balloon: SHUPAPA**—teleporting sound

47.1.2 **FX/balloon: SHUPAA**—teleporting sound

47.1.3 **FX/balloon: SHUPAPAPA**—teleporting sound

47.4 **FX/balloon: SHUPA**—teleporting sound

48.1 **FX/balloon: CHARAN**—sound of pendulum dangling

48.5.1 **FX/balloon: HYUN**—sound of pendulum swinging

48.5.2 **FX/balloon: HYUN**—sound of pendulum swinging

49.1 **FX/balloon: DADADADADA**—running sound

50.1 **FX: CHARA**—sound of handcuffs rattling

51.1.1 **FX/balloon: HYUN**—sound of pendulum swinging

51.1.2 **FX/balloon: HYUN**—sound of pendulum swinging

53.6 **FX: SU**—placing hand on body

54.1 **FX: ZUUN**—Yaichi manifesting

54.2 **FX: SU**—Yaichi touching Kuro's hand

54.3 **FX/balloon: PIKUN**—dead body twitching

54.4.1 **FX/balloon: BIKU**—dead body twitching

54.4.2 **FX/balloon: BIKUN**—dead body twitching

54.5.1 **FX/balloon: KAKO**—sound of keys being typed

54.5.2 **FX/balloon: KO**—sound of keys being typed

54.5.3 **FX/balloon: KAKO**—sound of keys being typed

54.5.4 **FX/balloon: KO**—sound of keys being typed

56.3 On the sign, you can read "Internet café" in English, but above the English word "CHARGE" is the word "MANGA" in katakana (written here in all caps because another effect of using katakana to write Japanese words is to suggest emphasis). This is, of course a reference to the magazine *Kurosagi* was running in at the time, the now-defunct *Comic Charge* (see note for 34.3 in vol. 10's Disjecta Membra). This is not the first time *Kurosagi* has referenced *Charge*, just as it has referenced its publisher Kadokawa on multiple occasions—I love how Eiji Otsuka has no compunctions about suggesting the very magazine his readers are holding is complicit in the terrible crimes depicted within. You can see this establishment does in fact have bookshelves full of manga against the far walls, and it seems not too dissimilar a place to the manga café that was the abode of the hapless part-timer in vol. 8's 2nd Delivery. It may also seem not too dissimilar to how their habitués feel about their prospects of employment.

60.4 The virtual farm the residents of Second Stage were laboring on might seem inspired by such online games as *Happy Farm*, *FarmVille*, or *Farm Town*, but this story, having begun in the spring of 2008 in *Comic Charge*, predates them all by several months.

60.5 Miss Momoka's business model is somewhat reminiscent of a lesser-known (and even creepier) work by the director of *The Manchurian Candidate*, John Frankenheimer's 1966 film *Seconds*, which starred Rock Hudson as a successful businessman who (semi)willingly goes along with a sinister company's offer to fake his death and create a new identity through plastic surgery and reeducation. Rock Hudson, known as a handsome leading man in romantic comedies of the 1950s and sixties, kept his homosexuality secret for the sake of his career, and it remained unknown to the general public until his death from AIDS in 1985—perhaps understandably, some critics have re-viewed Hudson's performance in *Seconds* in this light.

61.1 FX: GORORO—sound of office chair casters rolling

61.3 Dr. Evil, of course, does the smile with the little finger to show how pleased he is with an evil plan, but long before that, sinister and haughty women in manga did it to accompany an open-mouthed laugh (usually an *oh ho ho ho!* although in the original, Momoka did an *ah ha ha ha!*). This is to show one's refinement, a variation of the gesture traditionally associated with "proper" feminine manners in Japan (and elsewhere) of covering one's mouth to screen sudden changes of expression, such as laughing, shock, or yawning. The editor, by the way, would like to see a gender-neutral revival of the practice for yawning.

61.4 A soapland, in its various incarnations, has for decades been the Japanese equivalent of a "massage parlor," only rather than receive a therapeutic massage, you receive a therapeutic washing. So if there is a place in your town offering "Oriental massage," but it turns out they only use a thin folding mat and oil, complain that you have received a mere *Orientalist* massage.

62.2 FX/balloon:SHA—taking out knife

62.4 FX/balloon:BUTSU—piercing skin

62.5.1 FX/balloon:ZAKU—cutting sound

62.5.2 FX/balloon:ZAKU—cutting sound

63.1.1 FX/balloon: JI—cutting sound

63.1.2 FX/balloon: JI—cutting sound

63.1.3 FX/balloon: BARI—ripping skin off

63.1.4 FX/balloon: BI—ripping skin off

63.1.5 FX/balloon: BI—ripping skin off

64.1 FX: PECHA—wet slapping sound

65.3 FX/balloon: KON KON—knock knock

66.1 FX: BAAAN—sound of the door slamming open

67.4 FX: SU—placing hand on floor

68.2 FX/balloon: PIKU—twitch

68.3.1 FX/balloon: KATA—rattling in chair

68.3.2 FX/balloon: KATA—rattling in chair

68.3.3 FX/balloon: GATAN—rattling in chair

68.5.1 FX/balloon: GATA—thrashing in chair

68.5.2 FX/balloon: GATAN—thrashing in chair

68.5.3 FX/balloon: GATAN—thrashing in chair

69.1 FX: GATAAAN—chair falling over

69.2 FX: PETA PETARI—slow footsteps

69.3 FX: TATATA DADADA—faster and faster running sounds

75.1 Just as Western artists might, it's not uncommon for manga artists to go back and make changes when their work is collected as a graphic novel (*tankobon*). Sometimes this is for reasons of controversy, but many times it's simply because, on second thought (and away from deadline pressure to turn it in) they wanted to do a scene differently, or perhaps add a bit, since in the *tankobon* they don't have to worry about taking page count needed for the other stories in the magazine. As you can see, in the *tankobon*, there are three pages prior to page 78. But when this story originally ran in *Comic Charge*, there was only one page prior to it. The double-page spread on pages 76–77 didn't appear at all, and Nene's monologue from pages 75 and 77 of the *tankobon* appeared in just that one single page. Moreover, that single page wasn't the same as the one you see on page 75; it was three panels instead of two, starting with a close-up on Nene's eye, then an overhead shot of the city streets, then a shot of Nene perched on the rooftop—all done with different drawings.

78.1 The iconic 109 is a ten-story (eight above ground, two below) shopping mall in Tokyo's Shibuya ward; it has long been a signature destination for young women's fashion in Japan (but by no means the only place; there are, of course, also street and club fashion boutiques that couldn't afford the rents at 109, or wouldn't fit in there in the first place). According to the *Japan Times*, in 2008 its 120 stores racked up a staggering 28 billion yen in combined sales. 109 is credited by the *Times* with constant adjustment to changing styles, with almost a third of the stores either being remodeled or changing tenants each year; beginning in the 1990s, fashion magazines began to make stars of the store staff themselves, as so-called "charisma clerks" (a notion which brings to mind the bizarre fact that Moyoco Anno did a partial manga adaptation of *Chasing Amy*) and fashion leaders in their own right. You can find their English page at 109guide.com/top_f.html, although Shibuya 109 would like to remind foreigners that there is no bargaining, and you are not allowed to try on tops. My guess is that the first restriction is aimed at Chinese tourists, and the second at Americans.

80–81: Note that this is the same model TV set the KCDS has in their clubroom; its rotary dial and carrying handle bear mute witness to their poverty.

82.2 The sign says "Dorotabo Realtors," a play on *dorobo*, "thief." If this were *Dropsie Avenue*, someone would be telling Izzy Cash, "Ganef!" In Bob Andelman's biography of Will Eisner, *A Spirited Life*, a story is told about Eisner's visit to Japan in 1960 for research—not on Japan, per se, but on the needs of the US military forces in Asia; this was during Eisner's long tenure producing a comics feature on contract to the army for *PS: The Preventive Maintenance Monthly.* Not in Andelman's book (but what biography can cover everything? Well, maybe S. T. Joshi's *I Am Providence*) is a trip Eisner took to Japan decades later, in 1994, to attend a forum that brought Japanese and American comics creators together; he was accompanied in the US contingent by Wendy Pini and Brian Stelfreeze. *Ghost in the Shell*'s translator, Frederik L. Schodt, who interpreted for Eisner on that occasion, relates the encounter in his classic survey of the manga industry at its high tide, *Dreamland Japan* (much of the detail omitted there for space was included in Schodt's article in the January 1995 issue of *Animerica*). Richard Pini has remarked that among the *mangaka* they met were Buichi Terasawa, Tetsuya Chiba, Yumiko Igarashi, Shotaro Ishinomori, and Monkey Punch and Fujiko Fujio (A). Looking at these names in retrospect, there is the impression of this 1994 meeting as having been with the "elders" of the industry, those who made their reputation in the 1960s and seventies, rather than those who had become famous in the 1980s or the up-and-comers of the early nineteen; imagine, for example, them meeting an alternate group that would have been composed of people like Rumiko Takahashi, Katsuhiro Otomo, Akira Toriyama, Tatsuya Egawa, Tsukasa Hojo, and Kaiji Kawaguchi. I bring it up out of a curiosity as to what extent the Japanese hosts were interested in contacts between the *contemporary* industry and American creators. I wonder if there wasn't a generation gap that worked in two respects: one, the long-established creators were those who had the actual time and leisure to take an interest in foreign comics; two, those creators came of age in an era when the "success gap" between manga and American comics had not been nearly so wide, and thus may have had more respect for the latter. For example, in 1974, *Mad* magazine (which had such an influence on Monkey Punch) had a higher circulation in the US than *Shonen Jump* did in Japan, but by the time of the 1994 visit, *Shonen Jump*'s circulation in Japan was *twelve times* that of *Mad* in the US.

82.3 For more on the chop, or *jitsuin*, please see the note for 71.3 in vol. 2's Disjecta Membra.

82.5 **FX: SHA SHA**—writing sound. The male protagonist in this story's name, Shakuya Itayado, is another joke; *shakuya*, when written with different kanji, means "a rented house"; *itayado* could mean "a shingle-roofed dwelling."

84.1.1 **FX/balloon: GACHA**—backpack rattling

84.1.2 **FX/balloon: KACHA**—backpack rattling

85.4 **FX: GOSHI GOSHI**—rubbing eyes

87.2 **FX: FUNYA MUNYA**—sleepy sounds

88.2 The first of the two kanji, *sara*, used to spell *Sarada*, means "plate" or "dish," and *sarada*, when spelled in katakana, also means "salad." Furthermore, the kanji *sara* and katakana *sarada* are both used in the phrase *sarada hitosara*, "one plate of salad." Plate . . . shrimp . . . plate of shrimp.

89.1 Itayado's sweeping pose with raised palm is a classic "Enough already!" gesture in double-act Japanese comedy.

90.1 See the note for 122.3 in vol. 5's Disjecta Membra for a quick refresher on the hostess club. That note mentioned that it's at the discretion of the client to try to convince the host or hostess (or vice versa) to hook up later on. Nene uses the standard phrase for this, literally asking if he wanted to go on an *afutaa*, an "after."

96.1 **FX: GWOOOO DODO PU-WAAAAN**—traffic and construction sounds

98.5 **FX: GWOOOO**—car sound

99.6.1 **FX: KIIIII**—brakes squealing

99.6.2 **FX/black: DOKA**—face hitting dash

100.1 **FX: CHIKA CHIKA**—hazard lights flashing

100.3 **FX: HYUN HYUN HYUN**—pendulum swinging

103.1 **FX: CHARARA CHARAAN**—ringtone

107.3 "Bitter Valley" is the literal meaning of Shibuya, from the ward's original status as a clump of villages in a valley formed by the merger of two small rivers, located about four km east-southeast of the walls of Edo Castle (today the site of the Imperial Palace) during the Tokugawa era of 1603–1868. It's a reminder that districts that are today known for being parts of great cities often began outside of them; for example, during much the same period in history, Greenwich Village was not a neighborhood of New York, but, as its name implies, an independent town about as far from New York City proper (which in the eighteenth century occupied only lower Manhattan) as Shibuya was from Edo Castle. Edo is in fact the traditional name of Tokyo, and some hint of the city's riparian roots is seen in the fact *Edo* means "estuary." The name is still in use in such expressions as *Edokko*, "child of Edo," said of one whose family has resided in Tokyo for some time—at a minimum, back to one's grandparents. The idea that a large number of the residents in Tokyo are actually from somewhere else well predates the modern era—under Tokugawa rule, the famous *sankin kotai* ("alternating attendance") system required the vassal lords of the shogun, no matter from what distant part of Japan they hailed, to spend every other year (and being noblemen, accompanied by a retinue) in Edo. The system, which was designed in part to drain resources provincial lords might have otherwise used to build up a power base, also filled the city with an ever-fresh supply of country-ass hicks who may have carried two swords, but still left with their pockets emptied by the crafty commoner *Edokko*.

108.1 FX/balloon: JI—zipping up bag

108.5 This is, of course, not the first time the idea has come up in *Kurosagi* that realtors might have trouble renting a place where the previous occupant had met a tragic end; this was how Numata negotiated his price down in vol. 6's story that introduced the Shirosagi Corpse Cleaning Service (who will return in the next volume, by the way). This motif has occurred in other manga as well; in *Excel Saga* Vol. 20, a realtor attempts to get around the disclosure laws via strained euphemisms, saying that previous suicidal tenants "failed to achieve takeoff from the railing," or "arranged a self-suspension of questionable safety."

109.2 FX: BATAN—door closing

110.1 FX: DOFU—falling onto the bed

113.1 We return to the TV Kadokawa building seen in vol. 9's 2nd Delivery—once again, *Kurosagi*'s original publisher is mixed up in this business. Note that in 115.6, Sarada's henchman/understudy Kobayashi, AKA Duke Kerekero (named, of course, for the sound a frog makes in Japanese, as emblazoned on his T-shirt) is reading *Shonen Ace* (see note for 153.1, below).

113.4 Sarada does not have the kind of appearance that typically has a -*chan* appended to it in manga, but Fujita's use of it here reflects what might be called showbiz talk, as in "Sarada, baby!"

114.2 Fujita's gesture is the one used by Japanese men to indicate they're talking about a woman in their life.

115.2 FX: PON—tapping with a rolled-up script

116.1 FX: BA—pulling close

116.4 Although Japanese has its own native words for "regular" when used as an adjective, when used as a noun, as in "make you a regular," they are more likely to use the English loanword *regyuraa*, as is used here. This was apparently first used in Japan to describe sports players in a starting lineup.

118.7 FX: JYARI—footstep in gravel

119.2 FX: WEEEN—automatic doors opening

119.5 FX: NIMAA—smirk

120.4 FX: PINPOON—doorbell

120.5 FX: KACHA—door opening

120.6 FX: PA PA—brushing off leaves. Just as Itayado and Matsumoto refer to Sarada as "Sarada-*shishoo*" ("Master Sarada"—the same "master" as Numata used to address Master Azuma in vol. 10), this use of "brother" (Itayado greets Matsumoto as "Matsumoto-*niisan*," as his elder brother) is traditional for two apprentices under the same master. If you go back to the note for 165.4, it suggests that *shishoo* implies a venerable craft. The example given there was calligraphy, but there are comedy traditions in Japan that are centuries old, such as *rakugo*; see note for 151.3 below.

121.1.1 FX/top: KOPOPO—iced coffee burping out of carton

121.1.2 FX/bottom: KARON—sound of clinking ice

122.5 FX: BASHU—sound of nail gun firing

123.1 FX: BASHU BASHU BASHU—getting nailed

123.2 FX: DO—thump

123.4 FX: BATAN—closing door

123.5 FX: TATATA—running sound

123.6 FX: ZA GASA—climbing into tree through the leaves. The translator noticed (as the editor did not) that Matsumoto was brushing off leaves in 120.6, suggesting that he's leaving the scene of the crime the way he entered . . . climbing a tree to gain access to the emergency-exit stairwell, presumably to avoid being placed by witnesses or security

cameras as having ever entered the building. Judging by 128.1, it looks like he took the mug he touched, as well.

124.2 FX: GASA—pushing through leaves

124.3.1 FX/top: ZA—jumping out of leaves

124.3.2 FX/bottom: DA—landing sound

125.1 This sort of murder is what happens in a culture where you're not allowed to kill people with firearms, the way Jesus intended. It's like the bizarreries that come of not being able to show genitalia.

126.1.1 FX/top: BURORORO—car idling

126.1.2 FX/bottom: KI—braking sound

126.2 FX: BATAN—car door closing

126.3.1 FX: PINPOON PINPOON—doorbell

126.3.2 FX: PINPOON—doorbell

126.5 FX: KASHO—sound of card key being slid

127.1 FX: KACHA—sound of door latching closed

127.4 FX: PACHI—click

127.5 FX: PA PA—fluorescent lights coming on

128.4 FX: DOTAN—thud

128.5 FX: PEEPOO PEEPOO—ambulance sound

129.3 FX: BATAN—door closing

130.1 FX: HYUN HYUN—pendulum swinging

132.1 The idea that the regular experience of depersonalization is a mental disorder has serious implications for those who believe in a nonmaterial dimension to individual consciousness. Is this enlightenment diagnosed as a disease, or is it a disease that gives a false sense of enlightenment? The late Suzanne Segal attempted to grapple with these questions in her 1996 book *Collision with the Infinite*, which reflected on depersonalization disorder from both a psychiatric and a Buddhist perspective.

132.5 Ironically, Kereellis is deadpanning via a Kirk quote rather than Spock. Kereellis usually never misses the chance to suggest aliens' superiority to *Homo sapiens*, although his penchant for doing so with fictional aliens keeps the glimmer of suspicion alive that Yata is nothing more than an insane fanboy ventriloquist. Or perhaps it's just that since his host is such a big sci-fi fan, it influences the way Kereellis expresses itself? Or perhaps I'm overthinking it? No. Never in Disjecta Membra.

134.2.1 FX/white: KA KA—footsteps

134.2.2 FX/black: KIN—metal tip of cane striking floor

135.5 FX: KACHA—door opening

138.2 *Eolithic*, although not an actual scientific term, refers to a postulated earliest period of human culture preceding the Lower Paleolithic. This would be somewhat meaningless in archaeology, where the Paleolithic is held to have begun with the advent of the genus *Homo*; i.e., humans—hence there would be no period of human culture before that. It seems to be used here in the sense of auditioning new comedians at the earliest stage of their careers.

140.5 FX: KATA—rattling chair

141.2 FX: DOSA—thud

141.3 FX: JIJIJIII—zipper opening

141.6 FX: GATAN—falling down and knocking something over

143.1 FX: YURA YURA—unsteadily rocking back and forth

144.4 FX: GU—gripping nail

144.5 FX: GUGU—pulling on nail

144.6 FX: NUPO—nail coming out of flesh

146–147.1 FX: GYAAAAAAA—scream

146–147.4 FX: GATAAAAN—body crumpling to floor

149.1 FX: GOGO DODO PUWAAN—construction and traffic noises

149.3 The signs say "Strawberry Pie—One-Man Show"; Nene, of course, named her act after her old club.

149.4 FX: DO—crowd bursting out in laughter

150.1 I guess we were each waiting for the other to say the name "Yotsuba." Well, I'm not saying she'll turn out this way, but on the other hand I wouldn't rule it out entirely.

151.3 In the original Japanese, they talked about Strawberry Pie's prospects of winning the M-1 Grand Prix, an annual *manzai* (see vol. 7's Disjecta Membra, note for 68.2) contest sponsored by car-parts retailer Autobacs with a ten-million-yen first prize. Since *manzai* is a double act, Numata and Karatsu debated on whether the R-1 Grand Prix, which features *rakugo* (solo comedy where one person plays multiple characters) might not be more appropriate.

153.1 It was with this chapter that *The Kurosagi Corpse Delivery Service*, after much bouncing around between different Kadokawa magazines, returned to its original (and current) home, *Shonen Ace*—home also of Dark Horse's *Neon Genesis Evangelion: The Shinji Ikari Raising Project*, although in the words of the late John Leslie, "they're not very much alike."

154.4.1 FX/balloon: BO BO—sound of exhaust coming out

154.4.2 FX/balloon: BO—sound of exhaust coming out

154.5 FX: MMMM—sound of power window coming down

155.4 FX: SU—picking up puppet

155.7 FX: MUKU—sitting up

156.2 FX: BA—eyes snapping open

156.4 FX: GAGOGO GOGOGO—sound of train passing overhead

157.1 FX: GOTOTON GOTOTON—sound of train passing

157.5 This is not the first time Kereellis has gone on about the Akashic Records; please see the note for 191.5 in vol. 9's Disjecta Membra.

158.1 FX: GACHA—door opening

159.4 Not long ago, a foreign licensing company brought some samples of merchandise into Dark Horse from *Heidi, a Girl of the Alps,* wishing to know if we would be interested in releasing goods based on this classic anime, directed by Studio Ghibli's Isao Takahata (perhaps anime's greatest director, when he feels like it; his longtime friend and collaborator Hayao Miyazaki described him in his must-read *Starting Point* as a "descendant of a giant sloth"). Unfortunately, the charming, yodeling theme emitted by the *Heidi* notebook upon opening suggests the answer: ***"A-bue-li-to-di-ME-tú . . . que sonidos son los que-oi-go-yo . . ."*** It wouldn't really find a market in North America, for *Heidi* was one of the many anime series of the past that Spanish-speaking anime fans got to enjoy, but never showed on English-language television. ("Never" is perhaps a dangerous word among anime fans; I'm always learning things about where and when anime showed back in the day from con panels like Dave Merrill's "Dave's Old School Classroom" or Mike Toole's "Dubs That Time Forgot.")

160.1 If you're wondering why Numata has suddenly switched sunglass styles, it's probably because a little time—we don't know how much—has passed between 6th and 7th Delivery. There was also a hiatus for the *Kurosagi* manga itself in Japan during this time (see note for 153.1); 6th Delivery ran in the September 2, 2008, issue of *Comic Charge,* whereas 7th Delivery ran in the July 2009 issue of *Shonen Ace.* If these glasses don't do it for you, relax—he goes back to his classic shades midway through vol. 13.

160.3 FX: PITA—coming to a stop

160.4 FX: BA—dramatic pointing

162.1 The old man is likely referring to the great American firebombing raid on Tokyo the night of March 9–10, 1945, which killed 100,000 people. Mincing no words, commanding general Curtis LeMay said the dead were "scorched, boiled, and baked to death," and once remarked he believed that had Japan won the war, he would have been tried as a war criminal. John Dower, the great scholar of the propaganda aspects of the Pacific War whose *Embracing Defeat* won the Pulitzer Prize, discusses this in his recent, controversial comparison of WWII and the War on Terror, *Cultures of War.* Dower's aim is not so much to condemn LeMay as to point out that he, unlike many political and military leaders today, was willing to face up to the terrible reality of what he was doing, even as he believed it was the correct thing to do from a war-winning perspective. Dower also points out that, although Hiroshima made mass killing possible with a single bomb, the moral line to commit such killing had already been crossed with such acts as the Tokyo firebombing, which actually took more lives than the atom bomb at Nagasaki.

162.2 FX: DOOOOON—boom

162.4 FX/balloon:POTO—plop

163.2 FX: ZA ZA ZA—running in grass

163.4 FX: DWOOOOM—boom

164.1 FX: DOSA—dropping doll

164.2 FX: GOTOTON GOTOTON—train passing overhead

165.5 "Love doll" is pronounced *rabu-dooru* in Japanese; hence Numata and Yata's confusion.

165.7 His comment is of course in reference to *Shonen Ace* magazine, which theoretically should have content suitable for boys, i.e., *shonen*. This is something of a gag by now, as *Shonen Ace* is also the magazine that serialized Otsuka's *MPD-Psycho*. I've been editing the omnibus of CLAMP's *Angelic Layer* recently, which itself ran in *Shonen Ace* at the same time as *MPD-Psycho*, and reflected on the fact the two titles were considered to have the same readership. The irony is also that *Angelic Layer* really *is* an old-fashioned *shonen* manga in mood—a story based around fighting tournaments where the protagonist is a scrappy, pure-hearted kid who fights hard but fair, and wants to make friends with rivals. "Dutch wife" (in Japanese, *Dacchi waifu*) is a term said to have its origins in the period of exclusion between 1641 and 1853 when the only foreigners allowed to legally trade (or even set foot near) the Japanese home islands were a small group of Dutch merchants, who even so weren't allowed to live on the mainland proper, but on a small (9,000 square feet, or about 836 square meters for those of you with guaranteed health care) artificial island in Nagasaki Bay called Deshima. Because the Dutch merchants there also weren't allowed to bring their wives to the trading post, it was assumed that together with the clocks, astrolabes, and telescopes they were bringing to Japan, they were relying on gadgets to fulfill less celestial needs as well. *Samurai Champloo*, of course, advanced another theory.

166.2 FX: ZASA—rustling bushes

167.4 FX: BA—grabbing arm

168.3 FX: GATA GATA GATA—wheelchair rattling down slope

168.4 FX/balloon:JAPUN—splash

169.3 FX: GIRORI—glaring eye sound

160.4 FX: GOGOKWOOO—sound of traffic up above

160.5 FX: HYUN HYUN—sound of pendulum swinging

171.2 You read that right; Sasaki and Karatsu have gone off to Okinawa together (in American terms, like taking a trip to Hawaii). More on this in vol. 13.

172.2 FX: BATAN—thump

173.4 FX: CHIRA CHIRA—glancing

175.1 *Otaku* not yet gone entirely blind will note besides Rei Ayanami on the far left, a doll of Yoko Littner from *Gurren Lagann* on the right (and to the right of Mumume-tan in panel 2). Yoko's presence is intriguing, as she doesn't really seem to fit in with the otherwise wan, waifish, and *moé* dolls the club possesses. And it can't be the Dollfie Dream version of Yoko, because she's only 58 cm tall. I didn't actually just write that, did I?

176.4 It has been suggested that this story about the S.S. has its origins in a prank research paper that was picked up as a real news article by several international papers in 2005. Part of Otsuka's joke here is that the old man's account of his dead sister also recalls *Grave of the Fireflies* (which, like *Heidi*, Isao Takahata directed) and that the records of the Nazi love doll project were supposedly themselves destroyed during the notorious firebombing of Dresden. For more information, see the Slovenian arts site RE:akt!'s article "SS-XXX: Die Frau Helga" at www.reakt.org/ssxxx.

179.1   **FX: DO DO DO**—sound of tugboat putting along

182.2   **FX: SUPO**—sliding mask off of post

182.4   The joke here is that Numata can't remember Kim Jong-Il's name (he died just as this chapter was being lettered), despite the fact he's even more notorious a figure in Japan than in the US. On the other hand, this may also be related to the strangely coy practice in *Kurosagi* of not using actual Korean script (see note for 187.2 below) even when other cues strongly suggest— and by suggest, I mean proclaim it in a banshee screech—the characters are Korean. By contrast, when Chinese characters appeared in vol. 4, they spoke in actual Chinese. It doesn't seem to come from any anti-Korean bias on the part of the manga; in vol. 10 the North Korean refugees were portrayed sympathetically, whereas the murderous drug smuggler preying upon them was Japanese. My guess is that the practice reflects more a desire not to offend Koreans in Japan through not literally using their language. This might be seen as simply offensive in another way (think of the long history in Western comics of Chinese or Japanese being portrayed as a random bunch of scratches), but a symbolic fig leaf goes further in Japan than it does in the West— like the thin bar of white-out in a porno manga, it serves not so much to conceal as to satisfy propriety. Japan is still coming to terms with its Korean minority (and the larger idea that you can be Japanese and yet not of Japanese descent), a process that involves the legacy not only of racism and politics but the unresolved issues of the Korean War, including a sizeable faction of Korean residents (the *Chongryon*) who swear explicit allegiance to North Korea. Despite casual online racism expressed in Japan and by nationalist groups (but don't we have those things too in America?), things *have* changed somewhat in Japan; the much-reported 2005 manga *Hating the Korean Wave*, after all, was only an attempted backlash against the fact that Korean TV stars and singers have found popularity in Japan. The richest man in Japan is ethnically Korean: Masayoshi Son, the founder of the venture capital firm SoftBank (he went to UC Berkeley, by the way). The sublime pointlessness of worrying about Korean influence "impurifying" Japan is suggested by Emperor Akihito's remark during a 2001 visit to Korea that Japan's own ancient chronicle, the *Shoku Nihongi*, states that the mother of the eighth-century Emperor Kammu was of Korean descent, and thus, so also is the Japanese imperial line.

182.5   **FX: PAPAA**—lights coming on

183.2   **FX: DOSASA**—th-thud

183.4   **FX: BATAN**—door slamming

185.5   **FX: BACHA BACHA**—splashing gasoline

185.6.1 **FX/balloon:BACHA**—splash

185.6.2 **FX/balloon:BACHA**—splash

187.1 **FX/balloon:GARAN**—empty gas can hitting floor

187.2 The thugs' speech is portrayed using the same kind of pseudo-*Hangul* script (i.e., Korean) that was used in vol. 10's story about illegal immigrants.

187.3 **FX/balloon:GIIIII**—door creaking open

187.4 **FX: KATA KATA KATA KATA**—doll body rattling slightly

187.5 **FX: ZU ZUZU ZU**—feet dragging across floor

188.1 **FX: ZUZUZU ZUZU**—doll approaching slowly

188.3 **FX: PAAN PAAN**—blam blam

189.2 **FX/balloon: KIN**—opening Zippo lighter

189.3 **FX: SHIBO**—sound of Zippo getting lit

189.4.1 **FX: KAN**—lighter hitting floor

189.4.2 **FX: BO**—gas igniting

190.1 **FX: GWOOOO**—blazing flames

191.2 **FX/balloon: DO**—body hitting floor

191.4 **FX: NUUUU**—sound of the spirit coming out

191.5 **FX: FUWA**—the spirit floating/splitting up

192.2 **FX: SU SU**—sound of spirits passing into boxes

192.3 **FX: SU**—sound of the spirit entering box

192.4.1 **FX/balloon: KATA KATA**—boxes rattling

192.4.2 **FX/balloon: GO**—something moving inside box

192.4.3 **FX/balloon:GATA**—box moving

192.6 **FX: BA**—arm coming out

193.1 **FX: GASA GOSO GASA BA GASA**—dolls coming out of boxes

194.3 **FX/balloon:PARA**—sound of ropes falling away

194.5 **FX: SUKU**—standing up

196.2 I think our British readers would agree that this story might have easily been a "Jack Black and His Dog Silver" mystery. "So what happened to the evil foreigners, Jack?" "They fell into the grasp of the flaming sex dolls, Aunt Meg. The melting latex burned their features beyond recognition, and I helped PC Brown bury them in a lonely field."

196–197.4 **FX/balloon: BURORORO**—sound of car driving away

198.3 **FX: GI GI**—sound of roof straining

198.4 **FX: BAKI GARA GARA**—roof giving away and falling

198.6.1 **FX: DO**—stopping falling roof

198.6.2 **FX/balloon: JYU**—sound of silicone sizzling

200.1 **FX: BWOOON GOGON**—burning/crumbling sound

202.4 **FX: PACHI PACHI PACHI PACHI PACHI**—clapping

204.2 In Japanese, *shisukon*. You may sometimes get the impression this motif was cooked up by otaku in the cemetery of Prague, but bear in mind the Shinto creation myth that the islands of Japan themselves were the children of the sibling goddesses Izanagi and Izanami (to be fair, their relationship was more Shintaro Kago than Bow Ditama). No doubt the concept would have a larger place in Western culture, too, had Genesis commenced with the line *"In the beginning, God and his little sister . . ."* By the way, the editor recently had the chance at last to read an issue of the venerable British war comic series *Commando Comics*. I always knew from books like *Sgt. Fury* what WWII German soldiers said during moments of crisis—"Ach du lieber!" "Himmel!"—but what did Japanese soldiers say? Thanks to *Commando*, I now know it was "By Shinto!"

204.3 The tales of old Japan collected by folklorist Kunio Yanagita (1875–1962) have of course figured as an inspiration to *Kurosagi* since vol. 1; if you'll recall, in vol. 6, Eiji Otsuka even made him into a sort of Edwardian detective character (that is, in the equivalent Japanese period—the last years of the Meiji era).

221 We leave you with our first-ever piece of *Kurosagi* fan art, by my co-worker Philip Simon, who edits Eiji Otsuka's *MPD-Psycho* as well as *Eden*, *Blade of the Immortal*, and many, many other manga. I told Philip that I was jealous of the beautiful pieces of fan art he was always getting for *Blade*, so he said he would help me out, and managed to produce this in only sixty seconds. I pointed out to him that Sasaki looks like the little chick that Foghorn Leghorn tried to babysit to win the heart of the Widow Prissy: "But you said you needed my love to keep you warm!" "Madam, I don't need your love. I've got, I say, I've got my *bandages* to keep me warm." But Philip pointed out that no one under the age of thirty-five is likely to understand what I just said, so that settled the matter. See you in vol. 13—or maybe someday even vol. 83, as Philip suggests . . . ?

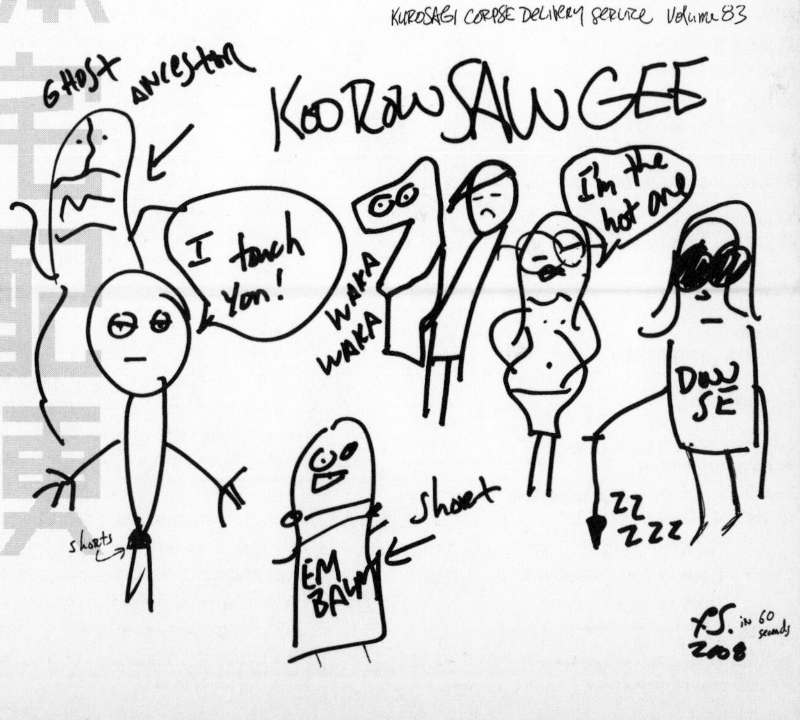
KUROSAGI CORPSE DELIVERY SERVICE Volume 83
GHOST ANCESTOR
KOOROWSAWGEE
I touch you!
WAKA WAKA
I'm the hot one
DOWSE
short
shorts
EM BALM
ZZ ZZZ
P.S. in 60 seconds 2008

EDEN

Be sure to check out Tanpenshu, Hiroki Endo's incredible slice-of-life short-story collections! Volumes 1 and 2 available now from Dark Horse Manga!

It's an Endless World!

Volume 1
ISBN 978-1-59307-406-7

Volume 2
ISBN 978-1-59307-454-8

Volume 3
ISBN 978-1-59307-529-3

Volume 4
ISBN 978-1-59307-544-6

Volume 5
ISBN 978-1-59307-634-4

Volume 6
ISBN 978-1-59307-702-0

Volume 7
ISBN 978-1-59307-765-5

Volume 8
ISBN 978-1-59307-787-7

Volume 9
ISBN 978-1-59307-851-5

Volume 10
ISBN 978-1-59307-957-4

Volume 11
ISBN 978-1-59582-244-4

Volume 12
ISBN 978-1-59582-296-3

Volume 13
ISBN 978-1-59582-763-0

$12.99 each

AVAILABLE AT YOUR LOCAL COMICS SHOP OR BOOKSTORE!

To find a comics shop in your area, call 1-888-266-4226.
For more information or to order direct visit DarkHorse.com or call 1-800-862-0052, Mon.–Fri. 9 A.M. to 5 P.M. Pacific Time. *Prices and availability subject to change without notice.

Eden © Hiroki Endo. First published in Japan by Kodansha Ltd., Tokyo. Publication rights for these English editions arranged through Kodansha Ltd. (BL 7041)